Education, Technology and Industrial Performance in Europe explores the development of advanced scientific and technical education in seven European countries and the USA between the mid nineteenth century and the 1930s. The essays seek to replace the conventional notion of a simple interaction between education and industry with a far broader perspective in which not only educational institutions and industrial employers but also national and local governments, professional bodies, and private patrons can be seen to have made distinctive and often conflicting contributions. Although most of the essays are concerned with individual countries, the thrust of the volume is comparative. As the authors show, in nations as diverse as Belgium, Britain, France, Germany, Italy, Spain, and Sweden there were similarities in the conditions from which the spectacular innovations in higher technical education emerged in the later nineteenth century. But the results that were achieved were by no means uniform. A provision for education that was highly effective in one industrialized or industrializing economy could well be ineffectual in another. And everywhere the balance between the supply of educated manpower and the capacity of industry to exploit knowledge and skills was a delicate one. As educational innovators throughout Western Europe (as well as the USA) came to realize, there was no universally applicable ideal of education for industry.

Education, technology and industrial performance in Europe, 1850–1939

This book is published as part of the joint publishing agreement established in 1977 between the Fondation de la Maison des Sciences de l'Homme and the Press Syndicate of the University of Cambridge. Titles published under this arrangement may appear in any European language or, in the case of volumes of collected essays, in several languages.

New books will appear either as individual titles or in one of the series which the Maison des Sciences de l'Homme and the Cambridge University Press have jointly agreed to publish. All books published jointly by the Maison des Sciences de l'Homme and the Cambridge University Press will be distributed by the Press throughout the world.

Cet ouvrage est publié dans le cadre de l'accord de co-édition passé en 1977 entre la Fondation de la Maison des Sciences de l'Homme et le Press Syndicate of the University of Cambridge. Toutes les langues européennes sont admises pour les titres couverts par cet accord, et les ouvrages collectifs peuvent paraître en plusieurs langues.

Les ouvrages paraissent soit isolément, soit dans l'une des séries que la Maison des Sciences de l'Homme et Cambridge University Press ont convenu de publier ensemble. La distribution dans le monde entier des titres ainsi publiés conjointement par les deux établissments est assurée par Cambridge University Press.

Education, technology and industrial performance in Europe, 1850–1939

Edited by
Robert Fox and Anna Guagnini

EDITIONS DE
LA MAISON DES SCIENCES DE L'HOMME

Published by the Press Syndicate of the University of Cambridge
The Pitt Building, Trumpington Street, Cambridge CB2 1RP
40 West 20th Street New York, NY 10011–4211, USA
10 Stamford Road, Oakleigh, Victoria 3166, Australia
and Editions de la Maison des Sciences de l'Homme
54 Boulevard Raspail, 75270 Paris Cedex 06

First published 1993

Printed in Great Britain at the University Press, Cambridge

A catalogue record for this book is available from the British Library

Library of Congress cataloguing in publication data

Education, technology and industrial performance in Europe, 1850–1939
/ edited by Robert Fox and Anna Guagnini.
p. cm.
Includes bibliographical references and index.
1. Technical education – Europe – History.
2. Efficiency, Industrial – Europe – History.
3. Technology – Europe – History.
I. Fox, Robert, 1938– . II. Guagnini, Anna.
T105.E33 1993
607.1'14–dc20 92–23171 CIP

ISBN 0 521 38153 3 hardback
ISBN 2 7351 0481 8 hardback (France only)

RP

Contents

Notes on contributors

GÖRAN AHLSTRÖM is associate professor and senior lecturer in the Department of Economic History at Lund University. His doctoral thesis of 1974 dealt with Swedish economic policy and price development in the late eighteenth century. Since then, he has published on Swedish economic thought and the Swedish national debt in the eighteenth and nineteenth centuries, and is currently working on the role of international industrial exhibitions in the diffusion of technology. This study is a sequel to his comparative study of technical education and industrial development, *Engineers and Industrial Growth* (1982).

JEAN BAUDET is a *docteur ès sciences* of the University of Paris. He is the author of *Les ingénieurs belges* (1986) and editor-in-chief of the Belgian periodical *Ingénieur et industrie*. After early work in phytochemistry, he has been engaged, since 1978, in an epistemological reflection on the relations between science and industry, with special reference to the place of the engineer as the intermediary between science and industry. He lectures on the history of the engineering profession in the Belgian National Programme for the History of Science and Technology at the University of Liège.

ARTHUR DONOVAN is a member of the Humanities Department at the US Merchant Marine Academy. Although primarily an historian of science, he has published several essays on engineering education and the profession of engineering in the United States. His books include *Philosophical Chemistry in the Scottish Enlightenment. The Doctrines and Discoveries of William Cullen and Joseph Black* (1975) and (as editor with Larry and Rachel Laudan) *Scrutinizing Science. Empirical Studies of Scientific Change* (1988). He has also edited *The Chemical Revolution. Essays in Reinterpretation*, published as volume 4 of the second series of *Osiris* (1988), and written a biography of Antoine Lavoisier (to be published by Blackwell, Oxford).

ROBERT FOX became professor of the history of science at the University of Oxford in 1988. He had previously taught at the University of Lancaster and had been Assistant Director of the Science Museum, London, and (as a *directeur de recherche associé* in the CNRS) Director of the Centre de Recherche en Histoire des Sciences et des Techniques at the Cité des Sciences et de l'Industrie in Paris. His main publications have been concerned with early theories of heat and thermodynamics, the social and institutional history of science and technology in France, and the history of technical education and applied research in modern Europe.

ANDRE GRELON is *maître de conférences* in the Ecole des Hautes Etudes en Sciences Sociales in Paris and *chercheur associé* in the LASMAS/CNRS (Institut de Recherche sur les Sociétés Contemporaines). His publications have been chiefly concerned with the history and sociology of French engineers in the nineteenth and twentieth centuries, with special reference to their education and training. He is the editor of *Les ingénieurs de la crise. Titre et profession entre les deux guerres* (1986), and recently contributed two substantial chapters to the first volume of the *Histoire générale de l'électricité en France* (1991).

ANNA GUAGNINI studied the philosophy of science at the University of Milan. She worked at the University of Manchester Institute of Science and Technology and the University of Lancaster and was a *chercheur associé* in the CNRS, in the Centre de Recherche en Histoire des Sciences et des Techniques at the Cité des Sciences et de l'Industrie in Paris before holding a Senior Research Fellowship at Linacre College, Oxford, from 1989 to 1992. She is the author of *Scienza e filosofia nella Cina contemporanea. Il dibattito teorico negli anni 1960–1966* (1981) and of several articles on the history of technical education and research in Britain and Italy. She is currently working at the University of Bologna on a comparative study of the relations between applied research and industrial practice in modern Europe.

WOLFGANG KÖNIG studied history, geography, sociology, and political science, and was subsequently secretary for the history of technology and technology assessment in the Verein Deutscher Ingenieure before becoming professor of the history of technology at the Technical University of Berlin in 1985. His interests include the history of education, the engineering profession, and mechanical and electrical engineering, the historiography of technology, technology assessment, and the philosophy of technology. He is currently working on technology in consumer society, the early history of electrical engineering as an academic discipline, and the history of machine design.

SANTIAGO RIERA I TUEBOLS holds doctorates in engineering and in contemporary history and is now professor of the history of science and technology at the University of Barcelona and the current president of the Societat Catalana d'Estudis Històrics. His published works include *Ciència i tècnica a la Il.lustració* (1985) and *L'Associació i el Col.legi d'Enginyers Industrials de Catalunya* (1988), as well as numerous articles on the history of engineers and the engineering profession in modern Spain. His present research is chiefly concerned with industrialization and the institutions for technical training in Spain during the nineteenth century.

MARI WILLIAMS took her doctorate at Imperial College of Science and Technology, London, after studying at the University of Cambridge. In addition to working in the corporate history unit of BP, she has held research positions at the Business History Unit of the London School of Economics and, as a *chercheur associé* in the CNRS, at the Centre de Recherche en Histoire des Sciences et des Techniques at the Cité des Sciences et de l'Industrie in Paris. She now works in the Policy Division of the Agricultural and Food Research Council, where she specializes in the evaluation of research and development. Her publications have been concerned with the history of technology, of astronomy, and of the oil industry.

Preface

This volume is the result of a long collaboration fashioned in the context of two international workshops, the first held at the University of Lancaster in July 1985, the second at the Cité des Sciences et de l'Industrie and the Maison des Sciences de l'Homme in Paris in July 1987. Comparative and interdisciplinary research of the kind which those workshops tried to promote is always difficult and, as editors, we are grateful not only for the patience and commitment of the authors of *Education, Technology and Industrial Performance in Europe* but also for the support we have received from a number of colleagues who have made important contributions as critics and through independent work of their own. These include Albert Broder, Ronald Ferrier, Thomas Hughes, Jonathan Liebenau, Peter Lundgreen, Joe Marsh, Gottfried Plumpe, Geoffrey Price, Robert Rosenberg, and Terry Shinn.

We also express our thanks for the funding that made the workshops and the many subsequent informal exchanges of views possible. In Lancaster in 1985, we were generously supported by the Economic and Social Research Council and the University of Lancaster; and the meeting in Paris was made possible by grants from the Fondation pour la Promotion des Entreprises à la Cité des Sciences et de l'Industrie and the Maison des Sciences de l'Homme and by the help we received in the Centre de Recherche en Histoire des Sciences et des Techniques of the Cité des Sciences et de l'Industrie, in particular from Anna Pusztai.

Robert Fox
Anna Guagnini

Introduction

Robert Fox and Anna Guagnini

This volume treats the development of higher technological education and its relations with industry in some of the main industrialized and industrializing countries of Europe between the mid nineteenth century and the Second World War. Already, by the beginning of this period, virtually all countries made some provision, often of an elaborate kind, for the preparation of engineers, chiefly for service in the Army and both the private and public sectors of mining and construction. But what was new about the second half of the nineteenth century was the emergence of institutions and courses that aimed specifically to prepare technical employees for posts in manufacturing. In this period, as several of the following chapters show, it is impossible, and it would be misleading, to separate completely the burgeoning world of the new breed of engineers from the older traditions of military and civil engineering: the threads of continuity are simply too strong. Nevertheless, here, it is the former that receives more attention.

Essentially, the contributions to *Education, Technology and Industrial Performance in Europe* were written with two main objectives. The first was to show how the common task of providing for advanced technical instruction in universities and other institutions was broached in a number of very diverse economic, political, and social contexts. In doing this, all the contributors were wary of the trap of analyzing the interaction between education and industry in terms of simple causal relationships. They sought instead – and this was their second objective – to insist on the complexity of the circumstances in which education and industry have related to each other since the mid nineteenth century and to stress the often conflicting roles of professional bodies, governmental authorities, and other mediating agencies.

Although most of the contributions are concerned with individual countries, the organization of the volume emphasizes its comparative character. There can be no suggestion that this is a novel approach. But the collective thrust of the essays is somewhat different from that of most earlier studies. For well over a century, the comparative method has been used predominantly to bring out the distinctiveness of different national patterns in education, often for the purpose of identifying the causes of economic success or failure. We believe that there is a dangerous one-sidedness in this way of handling the evidence. To counter it, we have all given serious consideration to the similarities in the conditions in which advanced technical education developed in our various countries from the later nineteenth century. As we would insist, the existence of these points of similarity is not at all incompatible with the palpable diversity of the results that were achieved, but it does serve as a reminder that this diversity can only be explained by reference to the complex interweaving of multiple circumstances, rather than to a single root-cause.

The similarities to which we refer were nowhere more evident than in the near-simultaneity of attempts to reform technical instruction in the forty years or so before the First World War. All the contributions touch on this period, in which the quest for modernization and the advancement of technical education were seen, throughout Europe, as two sides of a single coin. Everywhere – and Arthur Donovan's 'transatlantic perspective' shows that this was true of the USA as well – the late nineteenth and early twentieth centuries were a period in which the welfare of industry was routinely stated, and widely believed, to depend on the availability of courses and institutions capable of preparing large numbers of potential employees for careers in industry and commerce.

The case for technical and commercial education was put most vociferously by educationists, for reasons (by no means all of them economic) that are easily identified. In all the cases discussed here, concern with the state of education at every level grew to an unprecedented pitch during the second half of the nineteenth century. In contexts as diverse as the German states, Italy both before and in the early stages of unification, and France under the Second Empire and then the Third Republic, education assumed a central role in movements for political unity and economic and cultural renewal, and there was no country in which educational reform did not have its vociferous champions. One consequence of this was a marked expansion of the teaching profession at just the time when industry entered its own phase of dramatic change. As the growth of the profession gathered momentum, a new generation of teachers in the universities and other sectors of higher education was only too ready to consolidate its position and future prospects by seizing the opportunity of serving what they eagerly advanced as the needs of industry. In a complementary vein, the spokesmen for the institutions that employed these teachers honed a scarcely distinguishable rhetoric justifying the proliferation of industrially relevant courses, schools, and institutes for teaching and research.

It is not hard to understand why the rhetoric of the educational lobby struck a responsive chord in the main industrial nations, those we characterize in part I as the pace-makers: Britain, France, and Germany. But it is one of the most important conclusions to emerge from this book that the needs of industry were invoked just as confidently and with no less a response in the four smaller nations discussed in part II. The cases of two of these nations, Belgium and Sweden, which industrialized intensively from an early stage though on a necessarily lesser scale than the 'giants', make the point clearly enough. But even more striking instances were the manufacturing regions of Spain and northern Italy. In both of these regions, despite some moves towards modernization in the mid-century, industrialization was in no sense advanced, and the demand for technical manpower remained modest, even in 1900. Nevertheless, educational initiatives were made there as promptly as anywhere.

The similarities between the different countries were as apparent in the impediments to industrially related education as they were in the factors leading to growth. Among the constraints that were felt everywhere, the most pervasive was cultural prejudice, expressed in values inimical to manufacturing and trade and hence also to vocational instruction. In a considerable secondary literature on this theme, Fritz Ringer's analysis of the influence of the purist academic culture in European education is particularly notable.[1] It treats the failure of the new departures in technical and commercial instruction to win the status associated with curricula founded in the classical languages or abstract mathematics. In Ringer's view, the situation only began to change about 1930, when what he calls the 'late industrial phase' in the relations between education and the economy began to emerge. Even in the 1980s, however, the argument about the retarding weight of high literary culture has recurred, being used with special force in discussions of Britain. Here, Martin Wiener and Correlli Barnett have both founded their explanations of Britain's industrial decline since the later nineteenth century on the power of an anti-utilitarian bias in British culture which, as they argue, has persistently condemned new industrially oriented courses and institutions to an inferior place in public esteem.[2]

The evidence emerging from this volume leaves no doubt that Britain, in this respect, was far from unique. Similar considerations are relevant not only to most other European countries but also, as Donovan's account of American trends to 'academization' shows, the USA. Cultural prejudices, it seems, were ubiquitous and they necessitated some reaction from those who resented their influence. In Italy, the prevailing cultural style, promoted in the higher secondary schools through the emphasis on the study of the ancient languages, was seen by many critics as at least partially responsible for the poor state of the country's scientific and technical education.[3] The same was true in France, where the influence of a high academic culture founded on Latin and philosophy was challenged only by the variant favoured in some of the most advanced classes of the *lycées*. In these classes, the emphasis was placed on the equally 'pure' pursuit of mathematics, studied mainly as a means of entry to the most prestigious technical *grandes écoles* but also as a training for the mind and a foundation for careers which, if successful, would be administrative rather than technological in character.[4] Even in Germany, the advocates of modern forms of technical and commercial (or 'realistic') education had to struggle against the other-worldly values of the 'mandarins' of the late nineteenth and early twentieth centuries, who wielded their high neo-humanist culture in defence of the dominant position they had come to occupy in the German universities and the learned professions.[5]

Another circumstance that affected the new departures in technical education lay in the need to incorporate, or at least take account of, the older traditions in the training of civil engineers and others destined for the public services, the Army, or private consultancy. In some cases, as in Belgium, Sweden, and the Italian states before unification, adjustment was achieved through the piecemeal modernization of existing institutional structures; in France and Spain, on the other hand, completely separate structures had to be created. But whatever route the advocates of change chose to follow, they normally had to face indifference or even (where vested interests appeared to be threatened) hostility. Their adversaries included governments, institutions, or interest-groups that saw the training of engineers for civil and military appointments as a more important or nobler activity – certainly one that should remain unsullied by the confusingly different requirements of the industrial sector.

It must be said that, on this score, Sweden emerges as something of an exception. Göran Ahlström's account of the fruitful integration of academically qualified engineers in Swedish industry, especially in 'big' industry, points to the high social standing enjoyed both by technical education and by the engineering profession. A more common picture is that presented by André Grelon, whose chapter demonstrates the enduring and damaging consequences of the defensive demarcations between different types of engineering education in France: as Grelon shows, the established privileges of the various technical *corps d'état* bred a profound suspicion of the new industrial engineer. Where, as in Britain, there was no tradition of a powerful state corps of engineers, the friction took a different form. In this case, it was a strong 'aristocracy' of mechanical engineers that remained most stubbornly loyal to the traditions of apprenticeship. They were conspicuously slow to accept the methods of training favoured by academic engineers, and it was only just before the First World War that degrees became accepted currency in Britain in the *cursus* leading to membership of their institutions.[6]

Despite the powerful and essentially similar impediments to change that had to be faced everywhere, the seeds for a major readjustment were too widely sown to allow the reform movement to fail. Yet, as a growing body of case-histories confirms, the ways in which reform proceded were extraordinarily diverse. It was consequently an obvious task for the contributors to *Education, Technology and Industrial Performance in Europe* to determine how the seeds of change came to fruition in such different ways and with such different degrees of success in the various contexts they chose to consider. In tackling that question, they turned to an examination of economic, political, and cultural contexts which they saw as crucial in fashioning not just the course of educational development but also that of industry. As they did so, it became increasingly difficult to conceive of education as having in any significant sense a direct causal effect on industrial performance. Likewise, the notion that industry had been a single or even a dominant driving force in the progress of technical education lost much of its plausibility. Instead, both education and industry appeared as the products of the same multi-faceted social and economic background that easy generalizations about the relations between education and industry all too frequently gloss over.

A clear illustration of the complexity that general conclusions in this area must accommodate emerges from the contrast between the results obtained in three national contexts that were characterized by persistent and deep-rooted political fragmentation: Germany, the USA, and Italy. As König argues, competition between the individual *Länder* of the German Empire fostered a constructive spirit of emulation. This helped to endow the *Reich* with the stimulatingly diverse network of *Technische Hochschulen*, *Mittelschulen*, and other lower-level technical schools that provided German industry with large numbers of technical staff at all levels. The pattern was not unlike that in the USA, as described by Donovan, where competition between the states was a powerful stimulus to the multiplication of opportunities for technical instruction. In the Italian peninsula, too, a long tradition of fragmentation created the conditions for the existence of as many as seven university-based engineering schools. As Anna Guagnini shows, these institutions were the fruits of the universities' determination to consolidate their engagement in the training of engineers. Here, however, unification did little to foster the modernization of the existing structures. Consequently, the growth of the schools about the turn of the century was seen not as a matter for congratulation (as it was in the USA) but rather as an object of criticism: the schools were attacked for producing too many highly qualified engineers at a time when the opportunities for employment were severely limited. To explain this contrast between Germany and the USA on the one hand and Italy on the other, the detailed analysis of the ways in which the products of higher education were absorbed by the industries of the three countries is essential. As such an analysis would surely show, despite apparently comparable political conditions, Italian industry had not yet developed sufficiently to allow the exploitation of a relative abundance of educational provision that was, for Germany or the USA, a source of strength.

The two contributions to part III broach another aspect of the interaction between education and industry. Both of them are concerned with the exploitation of knowledge in important science-based sectors of manufacturing, and both of them illustrate the inability of education, in isolation, to stimulate industry. Robert Fox's study of the training and careers of French electrical engineers between 1880 and 1914 shows how little a plentiful supply of qualified manpower could do to advance an industry hamstrung by economic depression, excessive fragmentation, and cripplingly unfavourable legislation on tariffs and patents. In the electrical construction industry as in organic chemicals, France was so 'invaded' by foreign, in particular German, interests that the stimulus to independent innovation, which might have created a demand for scientific expertise, was simply not there. Mari Williams's essay also brings out the difficulty of harnessing the fruits of educational initiatives in the advancement of industry. As she shows, the lack of suitable education for recruits to the precision instruments industry in Britain and France was commonly cited, in the first decade of the twentieth century, as a cause of the failure of those countries to keep pace with Germany. But when eventually formal educational structures were established, the industry derived little benefit from them. The small size of British and French companies made it tempting for the owners to continue to rely on their own scientific know-how or on that of occasional external consultants and, even after the First World War, to staff their small design offices with men trained by the traditional route of a trade apprenticeship.

In drawing attention to the inevitable corollary that education and industry cannot be interpreted as two poles in an isolated relationship with each other, it is not our intention to depreciate the stimulus which, in certain circumstances, manufacturing was capable of exerting on the process of educational reform. It must be said, however, that even in Britain, France, and other countries that had long-established industrial traditions, such support for technical education as was voiced in entrepreneurial circles did not emanate from a coherent or united philosophy. What we see in these countries and *a fortiori* in those that were industrially less developed, is something far from straightforward. Superimposed on general national characteristics in the development of technical education, there were, in all nations (in the USA as in Europe), recognizable regional patterns.

Naturally, these patterns were more noticeable in some countries than in others. In Sweden, for example, where they do not appear to have been particularly marked, the institutional structure of technical education had an uncommonly unified character, with the Royal Technical University (KTH) in Stockholm, Chalmers in Gothenburg, and other technical colleges forming part of a 'total system', as Ahlström describes it. But where regional patterns in education were strong, these can be traced back to political and economic circumstances of a highly localized nature, which were often suffused with tensions, in culture as well as politics, between the national centres of administrative power and the rising seats of economic activity. In most countries, as a result, there were examples of educational initiatives that owed little, if anything, to support from central government and a great deal to carefully constructed pressure-groups of industrialists, municipal and regional councils, and teachers.

The strength of local initiatives and pressures is brought out well in the contrast between the vision of a national educational need emanating from Madrid and the very different objectives fostered in the manufacturing regions of Catalonia and the Basque region, which Santiago Riera i Tuèbols sees as so debilitating in Spain's struggles to enter the modern industrial world between 1850 and 1914. In France too, the pattern was remarkably similar. As both Grelon and Fox observe, the Ecole Supérieure d'Electricité was founded in 1894 by the independent Société Internationale des Electriciens in the face of governmental attitudes that never went beyond the most grudging and parsimonious support. It was part and parcel of this gulf between local enterprise and central lethargy that the Institut Electrotechnique at the University of Grenoble achieved its relative prosperity and high reputation after 1904 through the intervention of a local manufacturer and engineer, Casimir Brenier. It was Brenier who supplemented the modest core funding provided by the Ministry of Public Instruction with a huge personal donation and the support he was able to secure from the local Chamber of Commerce and the municipal and departmental councils of Grenoble and the Isère.[7]

Guagnini's studies of Italy and England provide ample evidence of a similar degree of dependence on local enterprise. The kind of alliance between entrepreneurial, academic, and administrative interests that allowed the Istituto Tecnico Superiore in Milan to expand its teaching in industrial subjects in 1862 is a particularly good illustration, but it had its counterparts virtually everywhere. In different countries and different regions, however, the nature of the alliance was always slightly different. Jean Baudet's contribution shows how in Belgium, for example, the founding of certain institutions of technical education was stimulated by the growing assertiveness of the Flemish minority in support of its own language and distinctive culture. Here, the decisive alliance, of a peculiarly Belgian character, was one between the Flemish working-class community and the Catholic Church.

In placing such a consistent emphasis on the influence of specific local conditions, albeit with due reference to more general patterns in the economy, culture, or politics, the authors of this volume have been conscious of the danger inherent in the type of finely focused contextualization they have attempted. Contextualization can lead all too easily to the formless accumulation of disconnected studies. However, we believe that such an approach offers the only way of achieving a main purpose of our collaboration, which has been to offer both specific explanations and a more generalized warning against easy universal prescriptions – for example, about the necessarily damaging effects of traditional culture, the dependence of education on a buoyant industrial demand, or the capacity of education to stimulate economic growth.

Finally, all the contributors to *Education, Technology and Industrial Performance in Europe* recognize the loose ends that remain. We have placed the emphasis on the *higher* levels of technical education and only to a lesser extent on the middle and lower levels. And rather little has been said about the *content* of the various engineering disciplines. On this latter point, there can be no doubt that in the period we have covered, from the mid nineteenth century to the 1930s, the various specialities within engineering underwent profound internal developments. They all became more dependent on sophisticated and expensive experimental techniques. The impact of such changes on curricula and, through them, on the academic character of schools and departments of engineering has yet to be determined. But it is clearly an essential task for historians to integrate these 'internalist' disciplinary considerations with the currently more familiar sociological approaches. No one would doubt the importance of the quest for status as one cause of the widespread process of 'academization' in technical education. But equally we cannot pretend that this motive alone provides a complete explanation of the drive to raise academic standards and the emergence of what König sees, in the German context, as an 'overtheorization' of courses in the *Technische Hochschulen* and a consequent mismatch between those schools and the industrial sectors they purported to serve.

We appreciate that, quite apart from the loose ends, readers who are looking for uncomplicated explanations of success or failure in the development of higher technical education and its relations with industry may find this a disquieting book. For while we accept that education (not necessarily of a specifically technical nature) has been an essential condition for economic prosperity for the last hundred years, we have stressed that educational provision should not be conceived as anything but part of a much broader mosaic of inter-related factors. Each factor can be expected to have only a limited explanatory power when viewed in isolation, and it is only by trying to embrace all of them together that historians and the policy-makers and analysts who use their work will achieve any real conviction. It is emphatically on the condition of the mosaic, rather than on that of its individual parts, that economic prosperity has always depended and continues to depend in our own day.

Notes

1 Fritz K. Ringer, *Education and Society in Modern Europe* (Bloomington, Ind., and London, 1979).

2 Martin J. Wiener, *English Culture and the Decline of the Industrial Spirit, 1850–1980* (Cambridge, 1981), and Correlli Barnett, *The Audit of War. The Illusion and Reality of Britain as a Great Nation* (London, 1986), pp. 201–33.

3 Luigi Besana, 'Il concetto e l'ufficio della scienza nella scuola', in Gianni Micheli (ed.), *Scienza e tecnica nella cultura e nella società dal Rinascimento ad oggi* [*Storia d'Italia. Annali*, vol. 3] (Turin, 1980), pp. 1165–284.

4 On the high levels of mathematical skill required for entry to the Ecole Polytechnique and the abstract quality of the syllabus, see Terry Shinn, *Savoir scientifique & pouvoir social. L'Ecole Polytechnique, 1794–1914* (Paris, 1980), especially chapters 2 and 4.

5 Fritz K. Ringer, *The Decline of the German Mandarins. The German Academic Community, 1890–1933* (Cambridge, Mass., 1968), especially pp. 25–61.

6 Robert H. Parson, *A History of the Institution of Mechanical Engineers 1847–1947* (London, 1947), pp. 47–8, and Anna Guagnini's comment in this volume, pp. 36–7.

7 On the early history of the Institut Electrotechnique at Grenoble, see 'L'Institut – son histoire', in *Institut Polytechnique de l'Université de Grenoble 1900–1950* (Grenoble, 1950), pp. 11–116.

Part I

Setting the pace

Introduction

The chapters in this section treat the three countries that are usually regarded as the pacemakers of modern industrial Europe. As would be expected in nations that industrialized in such different ways and at such different times, each of them fostered a distinctive structure for technical education that reflected the circumstances in which it emerged. In England, the structure was coloured, as late as the early twentieth century, by a suspicion of new forms of academic instruction dispensed in university-level institutions and, more specifically, of any claim that theoretical knowledge dispensed in this way should be accepted as a qualification for appointments in industry. In France, the new industrially oriented schools and university institutes of the 1880s and 1890s had to adjust to the entrenched privileges of the Ecole Polytechnique and the other 'grandes écoles', most of which fashioned engineers for coveted careers in the Army and the public services. Even in Germany, the *Technische Hochschulen*, which British and French observers about the turn of the century so admired, had to struggle for status in the context of a dominant neo-humanist culture rooted in the universities and the *Humanistische Gymnasien*. In all three countries, therefore, the new departures in advanced academic education for industry had to establish themselves in contexts which, for different reasons, were far from favourable. Yet the fact remains that the new institutions *did* establish themselves, in substantial numbers, from the last decades of the nineteenth century.

The years of this educational expansion were precisely those in which industry in Germany is usually believed to have pulled ahead of that in Britain and France. But, as Wolfgang König observes, the debt that Germany's industrial take-off owed to her technical schools is not easily determined. All that can be said, in fact, is that the German system of technical education allowed the growth in the quarter of a century before the First World War to take place. In others words, for König, educational provision in the German Empire was a facilitating and not a causal factor.

König's account is unusual in that it stresses the often disorderly character of German provision for technical education and casts what he describes as 'heterogeneity' as a source of strength rather than of weakness. A more familiar distinguishing feature was the sheer size of the German system, especially impressive when account is taken not only of the well-studied and determinedly academic *Technische Hochschulen* but also of the middle-level schools, the *Technische Mittelschulen*. It was these schools, as König argues, that provided German industry with the majority of its practising engineers in the years of most rapid expansion between the 1890s and 1914.

In its diversity and administrative untidiness, the German system resembled the systems of England and France. It could hardly have been otherwise, since in all three countries, technical education depended heavily on local support from private, municipal, or regional sources. Even when local funding was plentiful, however, the matching of educational provision with industrial demand was not easy. In France, for example, former pupils of the *écoles d'arts et métiers* and of the technical institutes that were attached to most faculties of science from the 1890s found the monetary rewards and immediate career-prospects that awaited them in industry disappointing. As André Grelon shows, they had to recognize that their formal education was only one element in a career which had to be built equally on performance on the job. Even more blatantly, in England, graduates in engineering tended to find that their formal qualifications were of little value. It was in response to that problem that many of them chose to follow individual courses which they or their employers judged to be more relevant than the full curriculum leading to a degree or diploma. The result was what Anna Guagnini portrays as a sense of frustration in academic institutions struggling to secure a role as sources of manpower for the industrial world.

So while the three chapters that follow help us to see why the patterns of growth in higher technical education in England, France, and Germany were so diverse, they also bring out an important unifying theme. In all three countries, academic communities were ready to make the running by providing instruction for what they saw as the needs of industry. But however cogently they proffered their services, the success or failure of their courses was largely determined by the contemporary state of industry and by the assessment that industrialists made of the instruction on offer. It is significant, for example, that the *Mittelschulen* were only founded from the 1890s, by which time their expansion was ensured by a boom in manufacturing that was already under way, creating employment opportunities for young men with the kind of practical skills that they instilled. By the same token, in England and France, the reluctance of employers to recognize the value of academic qualifications was unquestionably an inhibiting factor. There, the new engineering departments and technical schools and institutes had succeeded in winning a significant lobby of support within the manufacturing community by 1914. Nevertheless, they suffered from their essentially subordinate position as suppliers of knowledge and manpower to two industrial economies in which the drive to technological change was conspicuously modest. As their champions learned to their cost, education could do little to stimulate the renewal of a nation's industry if the economic context was not favourable.

1 Worlds apart: academic instruction and professional qualifications in the training of mechanical engineers in England, 1850–1914

Anna Guagnini

By the end of the 1880s, the relentless campaign of the advocates of scientific and technological education in England had begun to bear fruit. The results were impressive. Complete university-level courses in engineering were offered by nine colleges, four of them in London, the remainder in the provinces. By 1892, Cambridge too had launched its Mechanical Sciences Tripos. It must be said that most of these courses did not have an easy passage in the first twenty years or so of their existence: dependence on students' fees and private patronage was a source of constant uncertainty, while the reception within the academic environment was at best cool, and often hostile. But in 1889 the new Technical Instruction Act enabled local authorities to raise a penny rate in support of education, and a year later the Local Taxation (Customs and Excise) Act released further funds for technical education. These grants allowed existing institutions to improve their facilities, and helped those that had originally been established as lower technical schools to begin a process of upgrading that culminated, by the time of the First World War, in their becoming part of the university system.

Enrolments too began to increase. Yet the growth was of a kind that disappointed the champions of expansion. Most disturbingly, the full-time courses leading to degrees in engineering had failed to attract students. High fees, a consequence of insufficient governmental support, were blamed by contemporaries, and they have been cited by historians ever since as one of the greatest inhibiting factors. The slackness of the demand for the products of higher technological education has also been advanced as an explanation. Undoubtedly, there is truth in both of these arguments.[1] It is also the case that the prevailing anti-utilitarian bias that emanated from the most prestigious educational institutions played a part in reducing the appeal of engineering degrees. Even when these obstacles are taken into account, however, the attendance at complete courses of instruction in engineering in English (or, for that matter, British) universities at the turn of the century was strikingly lower than in the other industrialized countries of Europe – not only Germany but even Italy.

To explain this phenomenon in terms of factors that were present in these continental countries but missing in Britain is one way of approaching the problem. But another way is to look at what Britain had that was absent elsewhere. One of the most obvious elements is a deeply rooted industrial tradition, reinforced not only by its long-standing success but also by its well-tried organizational structure. In this chapter, I shall take this alternative approach, examining, with special reference to mechanical engineering, the relations between the slow growth in the enrolments of full-time students and the difficulty which the various schools offering engineering courses experienced in the quest for full recognition as centres for professional training.

One of the peculiar features of this process as it occurred in England was that higher technological education had to make its way in the face of uncommonly well-established procedures for the training of engineers on the job, through premium pupillage and apprenticeship. It should not be forgotten that while the supporters of the liberal ideal of education found it hard to admit technical subjects into their curricula, it was no less difficult for education to win acceptance as a requirement for entry to the engineering profession. In fact, the profession's intensely practical self-image, and the *cursus* of professional qualifications that confronted its recruits, were as resistant to change as the curricula of the ancient universities. The fact is that it was quite as difficult to establish courses of higher technical instruction that had the confidence of prospective engineers and industrial employers as it was for those courses to achieve academic recognition. Innovations in this area, in other words, had to be made with an eye as much on acceptance by the community of practitioners as on assimilation to the traditional education values of the kind that emanated from Oxford and Cambridge. Both constituencies had to be satisfied if full-time engineering courses were to become established and to attract significant numbers of students.

Early ventures in higher technical education

In London, the opening of the Royal College of Chemistry in 1845 and of the Royal School of Mines in 1851 marked the first appearance of institutions devoted specifically to higher education in scientific and technical subjects.[2] However, engineering courses had entered the syllabuses of institutions of higher education at an earlier stage. Two other institutions in London, both of which were to become cornerstones of the metropolitan university system had already set the pace. At University College, a chair of engineering was founded in 1828, although it was not filled until 1840; and a course of instruction for engineers was inaugurated at King's College in 1838.[3] Even in Durham, where the educational ideals of the University were modelled on those of the ancient universities, a chair of engineering was instituted by 1837.[4] It was soon after this, in 1840, that a regius professorship of engineering (in the giving of the crown) was created in Scotland at the University of Glasgow.[5]

Needless to say, this provision was not intended to cater for the lower ranks of the engineering profession; its aim was to provide for men who were destined for positions of responsibility, mainly in civil engineering. In the early decades of the nineteenth century, it was the continuing expansion of roads and canals that most favoured the growth of the community of engineers. The foundation of the Institution of Civil Engineers in 1818 gave official expression to the professional ideals of the most senior representatives of the community, and membership of the Institution, and of other, locally based engineering associations, grew significantly as the expansion of the railways in the 1840s and 1850s created a new demand for surveyors and draughtsmen.[6] Public interest in the achievements of civil engineers and the fame and wealth earned by a few of them had undoubtedly contributed to making their profession more visible, or at least visible enough to be regarded by universities as a potential outlet for their graduates. As the calendar of Durham University declared in the announcement of the opening of its course in 1837,

> The extensive public works of this country, and the vast national interests involved in them, seemed to require that the civil engineer should have an education expressly adapted to his profession. The course is intended for the higher departments of civil engineering, and it is meant to benefit them from the close association with the learned profession.[7]

The students whom the university sought to attract were an élite, and the conditions for entry were set accordingly. Candidates were examined, for example, not only in arithmetic and the elements of mathematics but also in Latin. The full course of study, as described in the university calendars, lasted three years, with students who passed the final examination being admitted to the academic rank of Civil Engineer, a title devised by the University of Durham. For less committed candidates, an examination at the end of the second year gave access to a lower qualification, the certificate of proficiency.[8]

In London, King's College used similar terminology in justifying its decision to offer a complete course of instruction. But whereas Durham referred only to the instruction of civil engineers, King's College extended its provision to the teaching of mechanical and mining engineering. Here, a 'Department of civil engineering and science, as applied to arts and manufactures' was instituted in 1838. By 1840, the complete course in the department extended over three years and comprised (in addition to mathematics, mechanics, and chemistry) teaching in the theory and practice of machine construction (including steam engines), descriptive geometry, and the theory of railway construction. The qualifications offered on completion of the full programme were similar to those offered by Durham: at the end of the second year, students who gave satisfactory evidence of their attainments were awarded a certificate of proficiency, while an examination on completion of the third year gave access to the diploma of associateship of King's College.[9] When, in the late 1840s, University College relaunched its engineering course, the pattern was the same, with courses in civil as well as mechanical engineering, and with a complete curriculum leading to a certificate.

But the recipe of relevant knowledge purveyed in a gentlemanly environment was not sufficient to convince either the parents of would-be-engineers or industrial employers of the value of formal education as a complement to practical training. One important way of winning confidence was to show that although the purpose of the courses was to offer theoretical instruction, the teaching was entrusted to men who had had solid experience of manufacturing or, at least, close connections with it. Thus at King's College the chair of manufacturing arts and machinery was held, in the 1840s, by Edward Cowper, whose main qualification was a long and successful career in the design and construction of printing machinery. Similarly, William Hosking, an experienced hydraulic and railway engineer, taught the arts of construction.[10]

University College was as intent as King's on the recruitment of teachers with a suitably practical pedigree. In 1841 the College succeeded in hiring Charles B. Vignoles, a noted railway engineer, as professor of civil engineering.[11] For the chair of mechanical engineering, founded in 1846, the choice fell on Eaton Hodgkinson, already well known for his work on the strength of materials. Hodgkinson himself was not a thoroughbred shop-floor engineer, but what made him attractive was his association with leading manufacturers, such as Robert Stephenson and William Fairbairn, with whom he carried out some of his research from a base in Fairbairn's large Manchester works.[12] In the same year, Bennet Woodcroft was appointed to the chair of descriptive machinery. The son of a Manchester textile merchant and manufacturer, a pupil of John Dalton (like Hodgkinson), and a friend of Fairbairn, Woodcroft took out a number of important patents for improvements in the design of textile and other machinery, and, at the time of his appointment, was working in London as a consulting engineer.[13]

To induce people with sound practical experience to abandon lucrative positions and become professors was by no means easy. Vignoles, for example, was persuaded to accept the appointment at University College only as a solution to a temporary set-back in his career, and after a brief spell in the chair, he returned to his main occupation. Moreover, the additional requirement that professors should be good teachers made them extremely rare. In fact, even the most gifted teachers would have found it hard to communicate their patrimony of experience in the uncongenial environment of the lecture room. In addition, the limitations of their own formal education made it difficult for most practising engineers to keep pace with the theoretical developments in mechanical engineering that were now to be found in the most up-to-date text-books.[14] The case of University College, London, is a clear example of the difficulty of choosing suitable teachers. For neither Hodgkinson nor Woodcroft, for all their experience, proved successful as professors. The result was so disappointing that when Woodcroft left and Hodgkinson died, the two chairs were merged into one, devoted primarily to civil engineering.

However, by the mid-1860s, a new generation of teachers with a sounder theoretical formation and, increasingly often, a university degree, began to emerge. This was the generation inaugurated by William Rankine at the University of Glasgow and Osborne Reynolds at Owens College, Manchester.[15] The formal background of such teachers as Rankine and Reynolds made it easier for them to fit into the academic setting, and to fight the entrenched resistance to the appointment of 'engineers' to university chairs. However, the change did not signal any flagging of the emphasis on the desirability of engaging instructors with practical experience. On the contrary, a direct familiarity with manufacturing practices remained, until well after the First World War, one of the most prized requisites for appointment to a chair of engineering.

Other ways of enhancing the vocational relevance of higher technological education were constantly being sought. It would obviously have been pointless simply to present education as an alternative to training on the shop-floor. However, since much of any curriculum in mechanical engineering was necessarily devoted to the description of working machinery, a complete separation of the academic and practical realms was thought to be detrimental to an understanding of the subject and, even more importantly, to the image of the courses.

The organization of workshops was the solution to both of these problems, although it did little to advance the integration of technical instruction in the liberal environment of institutions of higher education. Of course, the introduction of machines was not a novelty; they were already used as models in the teaching of natural philosophy. In the case of engineering, however, the reason for their presence in the workshop was not just to explain the principles of their construction, but also to instruct students in the actual practice of constructing and using them. By 1866, George Carey Foster, professor of experimental physics at University College, London, was described in the calendar of the college as responsible for running both the physical laboratory and the mechanical workshop, in which an assistant taught 'joinery, turning, wood working, and metal working'.[16] Even more markedly than at University College, workshop instruction became one of the distinctive features of the course at King's College. In the later 1850s, engines and machine-tools began to be purchased, and students were instructed in their design as well as in their use under the supervision of an assistant, and were expected, at the end of the course, to be able to construct models of any machine and engine. In subsequent decades, efforts were made to update and extend the range of the workshop's equipment, which was favourably reviewed in 1884 by the Samuelson Commission as the mark of the strong practical orientation characteristic of the College's engineering department.[17]

It is difficult to assess the benefit that students derived from the school-based practical exercises. A sceptical reading of the calendars, and of other fragmentary evidence, suggests that the descriptions were, in some measure, window-dressing. Nevertheless, the fact remains that the availability of workshop facilities had a significant place in the public face of the institutions: the quantity and quality of such facilities were presented as an indicator of the schools', or more often the teachers', commitment to relevant, as opposed to purely theoretical, instruction. At the same time as the syllabuses were becoming theoretically more demanding, therefore, the workshops had the important function of countering the accusation of excessive abstraction.

Enrolments

Even in the relatively modern-minded climate of the London colleges, the establishment of chairs of engineering did not reflect any clear consensus on the place of technical instruction in higher education. Indeed, it was internal hostility that delayed the filling of the chair at University College, London, for twenty years. Everywhere, resistance ran deep, and it would have died hard even if the courses had been unequivocally successful. But they were not. In Durham, the engineering course soon sank into oblivion,[18] and it was only in 1871 that higher technological education was restored in the area, with the creation of the College of Physical Science at Newcastle-upon-Tyne. The College was supported by the University of Durham and had a strong applied bias. The courses in London were more successful. Here, King's College reached a peak of seventy-one matriculated students of engineering in 1847, but enrolments fell in the following decade and although they returned to the same level in 1860, they remained stable, at between seventy and eighty, until the late 1870s.[19] Moreover, only a small minority of the students were committed to the systematic programme that was offered by the engineering department.

In Durham as well as in London, the entrants' lack of preparation was commonly regarded as a main obstacle to recruitment, not only in the sciences but in the humanities as well. The standard of the candidates for admission was so poor that some colleges set up internal preparatory

Table 1.1. *Dates of the opening of institutions offering engineering courses and of the establishment of engineering chairs in England*

	Opening of institution	Establishment of engineering chair
King's College, London	1831	1839
University College, London	1828	1841
University of Durham	1835	1838[a]
Owens College, Manchester	1851	1868
Royal Indian Engineering College, London	1871	1871
University of Cambridge	medieval	1875[b]
Yorkshire College, Leeds	1874	1876
University College, Bristol	1876	1878
Mason College, Birmingham	1880	1882
Firth College, Sheffield	1884	1884
Finsbury College, London	1884	1884
Nottingham University College	1881	1885
University College, Liverpool	1881	1885
Central Institution, London	1885	1885
University College, Bristol	1876	1886
Newcastle College of Physical Science	1871	1891

[a] Although there was no chair, a course leading to a degree in engineering was created in this year. Engineering became fully established in Durham in 1890, when a chair was founded at the Durham College of Science.

[b] Cambridge had a professorship of mechanism, first held by James Stuart, from 1875. The department of engineering was created in 1891, and in the following year the new Tripos in Engineering was instituted.

schools.[20] However, a more important obstacle continued to rest in the fact that, when it came to professional advancement, a degree was often of no significant benefit. In this respect, the expansion that was experienced, at least relatively, by King's College in the second half of the 1860s and in the 1870s is worthy of comment. One cause of the growth at King's was the very specific demand for technical men that resulted from British involvement in the Crimean war and, in the 1860s, from the acceleration of railway building in the Empire. The introduction of scientific and technical subjects in the examinations for admission to the Royal Military Academy at Woolwich and to the Indian Department of Public Works provided another opportunity that King's, like colleges everywhere, sought to exploit.[21] In 1862, the University College calendar had been proud to announce (in the earliest statement of its kind) that 'the College is recognized by the Secretary of State for India in Council as possessing an efficient class of Civil Engineering'. Other schools followed suit, and by the 1870s comparable notices were regularly put about by every institution that offered engineering courses.[22]

The message did not go unheeded. Between 1866 and 1890, 169 students of engineering at King's College passed the examination for admission to the various branches of the Indian Department of Public Works. Although this figure may seem unremarkable in absolute terms, it indicates that, where scientific and technical instruction was recognized as a qualification for a professional career, students, and their parents, did not shun it.

In the light of this evidence, the lack of motivation that underlay the poor enrolments deserves closer scrutiny. It is generally supposed that engineering, in particular mechanical engineering, was not recognized as a respectable occupation, certainly not as respectable as the liberal professions.[23] Since some degree of formal education was regarded as one way of endorsing the superior status of these professions, the fact that engineering required no such preparation might appear, in retrospect, as further evidence that its status was low. The difficulties experienced in establishing higher technological education might also be seen to buttress this conclusion. But does this square with the realities of contemporary judgements?

In answering this question, it is essential to bear in mind that the engineering profession was not a socially homogeneous group. It is perhaps too easy to dismiss as freaks the instances of sons of respectable professional families, well-off middle-class merchants and manufacturers, and even wealthy gentry, who chose mechanical engineering as a career. But even a cursory look at the biographical notices of deceased members of the Institution of Mechanical Engineers suggests that such a dismissal would be false.[24] The fact is that young men had to be financially secure in order to enter the profession, at least if they did so via the royal road of premium pupillage. This was the fastest and most direct means of attaining the top level of the engineering profession and of preparing for managerial responsibilities as well as for independent careers as consulting engineers. It consisted of three years of training, in which experience would be gained in a variety of offices, from the workshops to the drawing and commercial offices. At the end of this period, a young man would usually be employed as a draughtsman, although for the most ambitious this was only a temporary step before moving on to commercial and, eventually, managerial positions.

This form of initiation, however, was a costly one. In the 1860s and 1870s, the fees required for pupillage in reputable firms varied between £100 and £300 a year, to which it was necessary to add the cost of accommodation and living expenses[25] (only partially offset in certain works, where a modest wage was offered). But high premiums were not the only obstacle. Admission to the most sought-after establishments was so competitive that young men often had to wait a considerable time before being accepted. Hence, such a move had to be prepared well in advance or, as often happened, secured through a personal introduction.

A comparison with the cost of formal education is revealing. Fees for teaching and boarding in a public school were, on average £120 per year, and in Oxford and Cambridge the total expenditure on college, university, and degree fees, plus the bills for tutoring and boarding over three years, was reckoned to amount to £350–400.[26] These figures make it hard to maintain that a premium pupillage in engineering was realistically open to any but the wealthier strata of society. Of course, the right to practise the profession of mechanical engineer was acquired through institutional structures somewhat different from those that fed the traditional professions. But the structures were hardly less exclusive than those of the ancient universities or the bar.

For those who could afford the solution of premium pupillage, some kind of previous formal education was normal. In fact, the positions to which pupillage gave access were ones that exploited the worldliness and grooming that might have been acquired, more often than historians seem to have recognized, in a good grammar or, in some cases, public school. Clearly the aim of this previous schooling was to provide what was regarded as an appropriate general education, rather than to prepare for the technical aspects of the future engineer's career.

Despite the various impediments I have described, the spokesmen for higher technical education were right to insist that a significant pool of potential candidates for their wares existed. However, having identified the target, they underestimated how difficult it was for the newly established engineering courses to achieve the elusive objective of combining the status bestowed by higher education with the provision of relevant instruction, and, more importantly, to serve as a qualification for a professional career. In reality, practical experience was stubbornly regarded as the proper way of rising to the most senior position in engineering.

Fleeming Jenkin, who held the chair of mechanical engineering at University College for two years before moving to the newly established chair at Edinburgh University in 1868, clearly acknowledged the problem in his evidence to the Devonshire Commission.

> If an engineering college were really supposed to be a good thing [he declared] it would be instituted by private enterprise, and it would be a very highly paying institution: 100 young men paying £100 a year, and they pay more than that, would keep an institution of that kind going.[27]

As he pointed out, the fact was that pupillage was regarded in England as the best system for preparing for an engineering career, and while he blamed industrialists for not supporting technical education, he was even more embittered by parents who 'think that they have done enough when they have made a man a pupil'.

It is true, of course, that premium pupillage was a minority route reserved for young men who were intent from the start on rising to the highest levels of the engineering profession, and on moving on as soon as possible to non-technical responsibilities. For those who could not afford pupillage, apprenticeships in mechanical engineering establishments provided the normal route.[28] Small fees, or no fees at all, were paid for this kind of training, although admission was, if anything, even more competitive than in the case of premium apprenticeships. The route, however, was a far longer one, taking from five to seven years, followed by a further period as an 'improver'. Moreover, the positions to which it led were generally more modest than those available to premium pupils and, at least initially, were largely confined to the workshops. Even so, apprenticeship provided the route for very many engineers who rose from the shop-floor to senior positions of a technical or even managerial nature.

For most of those who embarked on an apprenticeship, formal education was just not an option. First, enrolment fees were high: at King's College, London, the composition fee for a three-year course of engineering, inclusive of workshop exercises, was £129 in the 1870s, and £153 in the 1890s. Elsewhere, and especially in the provincial colleges, costs were lower, but still substantial. Another major obstacle was that the lower age limit for admission to most colleges was sixteen, the age at which apprentices were normally taken on. In this way, enrolment in a course in engineering would inevitably have delayed the start of an already long professional training, without offering any advantage in terms of career prospects. As a result, higher technical education failed to reach many potential students who, as a group, might have been even more important than premium pupils in helping to create a new generation of technical experts. It was, in fact, the sons of clerks, teachers, and clergymen, interested in engineering careers but unwilling to start them at the very bottom as apprentices, who would have benefited most from higher technical education as part of an alternative to the costly option of pupillage.

It is one of the paradoxical consequences of the rapid growth of science teaching in the 1880s and 1890s, favoured as it was by the campaign for the improvement in the provision for technical education, that it tended to lure away even those students who entered higher education with a special interest in technology. For a post in science teaching, which offered a higher salary immediately after graduation, was a more obviously attractive alternative for those who might otherwise have wished to pursue a career in engineering. This was certainly the case with Ambrose Fleming, later professor of electrical engineering at University College, London. Recalling the beginning of his career in the mid-1860s, he wrote:

> With my love of machinery I had hoped to be an engineer . . . But there were no engineering colleges in those days, and the only way in which a boy could become a mechanical engineer was by being articled to an engineering firm. But this involved the payment of a premium, often very large. This my father, with his young family, could not afford.[29]

So it was that the young Fleming abandoned his original plan and became a science teacher.

It is plain that experience was seen as constituting the only worthwhile qualification for engineering. And it was training, whether 'purchased' with high premiums or acquired through the lengthier process of apprenticeship, that made experience available. The situation was one with which the Institution of Mechanical Engineers found no fault. Founded in 1846, the Institution embodied the essence of the engineering aristocracy.[30] Its criteria for membership at once reflected the public face and the self-image of the profession and contributed to parading them far beyond the limited circle of its members. As late as 1894, in sharp contrast with corporate associations on the Continent, admission to the rank of full Associate Member was granted solely on the basis of experience and practical achievements. Significantly, a quite separate and relatively marginal category of Honorary Member was reserved for other candidates whose qualifications were purely academic. Hence, while the Institution actively supported the diffusion and advancement of technical knowledge, it remained loyal to the old emphasis on experience where corporate qualifications were concerned.

The hesitancy of manufacturers

Because of its regulations for admission, the Institution of Mechanical Engineers counted among its members a substantial number of managers and technical directors of major companies. Clearly, these men were an important channel for the transmission of the attitudes towards education that prevailed in the Institution. But while there is no doubt that their role has to be taken into account in any study of the slow development of higher technological education, the direction of their influence was characterized less by consistency than by contradictions and a confusing lack of common purpose. Many manufacturers and practising engineers, in fact, remained indifferent or even hostile to bookish instruction in technical matters.

But this was by no means the only obstacle. For even the support that was offered by a vociferous, if limited, section of the industrial community created its own problems. The supporters included some of the leading manufacturers, who at a very early stage joined the academic lobbies in campaigning for better educational provision and in pointing towards scientific and technical instruction as one of the factors that favoured the recent industrial progress of other European countries. In his report as chairman of the jury for one of the mechanical engineering sections at the Paris Exhibition of 1855, William Fairbairn clearly conveyed his surprise, as well as his concern, at the achievements of Germany, France, and the United States. One of the features that most impressed him in his survey of foreign machinery was the ingenuity of its design, and he made a point of warning his fellow countrymen that, in his view, the availability of good educational facilities was one reason for the remarkable performance of the countries he was reviewing.[31] It was a warning which, over the next two decades, was to reappear time and again as growing numbers of manufacturers expressed their anxiety about the progress made by Britain's industrial competitors.

The concern of Fairbairn and other manufacturers went beyond mere words. Indeed, the great majority of the initiatives for the improvement of higher technological education until the late 1880s were the fruits of private patronage, and private funding remained crucial in subsequent decades as well. In Manchester, for example, a meeting of local industrialists and entrepreneurs in 1867 denounced the lack of provision for engineering education in the area, and urged the creation of a chair of civil and mechanical engineering at Owens College. Passing from precepts to deeds, the participants, among them William Fairbairn, Joseph Whitworth (regarded as the doyen of British mechanical engineers), and Charles Beyer, of Beyer and Peacock, a prosperous locomotive manufacturer of German origins, offered £9,505 to endow the chair. When it transpired that the salary was insufficient to attract good candidates, Beyer topped it up with an additional annual grant of £250.[32] In 1868, Osborne Reynolds a Fellow of Queen's College, Cambridge, was appointed, and one year later a department of civil and mechanical engineering was inaugurated.

The names of local manufacturers were also associated with the creation of chairs of engineering and other moves to provide for technical education at most of the provincial university colleges in the 1880s. Andrew Fairbairn (William Fairbairn's nephew and a successful textile manufacturer on his own account) in Leeds, the steel manufacturer Frederick T. Mappin in Sheffield, and the Liverpool ship-owners and shipbuilders Alfred Holt, T. H. Isnay, and Thomas Harrison, were all generous in the patronage of chairs and, at the turn of the century, in helping to finance the expansion and fitting out of engineering departments.[33]

Further substantial support for higher technological education came in the form of grants and prizes for students. Although they were still rare in the 1860s, many donations of this kind were made from the 1870s.[34] The scheme that made the greatest impact was launched by Whitworth, respected but now ageing and no longer the innovative force he had once been. In 1867, Whitworth submitted a proposal to the Science and Art Department in London for the endowment of scholarships and prizes 'to be applied for the further instruction of young men . . . with a view to the promotion of engineering and mechanical industry in this country'. The regulations for the scholarships were considerably modified in the early years, but by 1873 they were well defined. Candidates, who had to be under twenty-two years of age, were selected by a competition that tested both theoretical and practical proficiency. One of the requirements for entry to the competition was evidence of two years of service in the workshop or drawing office of a mechanical engineering firm, and of good manual skills. But equally crucial were the high standard and breadth of the candidates' theoretical background.[35] As an unidentified former Whitworth scholar was later to warn younger candidates, preparation for the competition demanded either a three-year course of full-time instruction at a good college or a minimum of six years attendance at evening classes.[36] The use to which the scholarships were put was also subject to the scrutiny of the examiners, who had to approve the proposed programme of study as well as the institution in which it was to be pursued.

Quite apart from the financial support they offered to students, the Whitworth scholarships bestowed prestige on the institutions that prepared successful candidates and on those that were chosen by Whitworth Scholars for their studies. The scholarships were touted as a stamp of approval endorsed by one of the most distinguished industrial authorities in the country, and colleges boasted of the presence of Whitworth scholars and prizemen among their students as an indicator of the quality and industrial relevance of their courses. At the same time, the scheme gave new departments much-needed leverage in their efforts to introduce technical courses and to raise funds for equipment. In all this, it was highly effective. In order to attract candidates who held Whitworth scholarships, institutions had no choice but to provide adequate teaching facilities. The argument was used by Grylls Adams and Miller in 1868 to obtain £300 from the council of King's College for the improvement of the laboratories, and it was invoked with equal success in 1877, when it helped to elicit another £700 from the council, as well as £200 from Whitworth himself.[37]

Needless to say, a belief in the beneficial effects of higher technological education was not the only motive for these acts of generosity. Philanthropy and a desire to leave a mark on a town's cultural and social life induced manufacturers and businessmen to endow chairs in subjects ranging from physiology to ancient languages. A more telling gauge of their specific interest in technological education, though, was their readiness to make use of its products and, above all, to recognize in some tangible way the new kinds of technical qualification. In due course, this recognition began to be granted, to the extent that certain manufacturers showed an increasing willingness to take on young men who had attended engineering courses, and to regard a certificate as a substitute for at least part of the period of apprenticeship.

Such recognition was frequently coloured by the close links that existed between manufacturers and their local institutions: in these cases, the decision to employ students tended to be based on a sense of trust in the institution concerned, rather than on a more general recognition of the value of education for technical careers. Clear indicators of the alliances that were beginning to be struck were the notices that appeared in the calendars of the provincial colleges from the 1880s, suggesting that local manufacturers were prepared to accept students as apprentices on particularly favourable terms. In 1887 the Calendar of Owens College announced that 'some of the principal mechanical engineers in Manchester and the neighbourhood have signified their willingness to receive certificated engineering students of the college into their works, either as premium apprentices for a short time, or as ordinary apprentices without premiums'.[38] Yorkshire College published a similar notice in 1887, as University College, Liverpool, had done in the Calendar for 1886–7.

This slow but growing recognition of education as a desirable element in the preparation of men destined for technical appointments is an unequivocal sign of change. Yet reactions continued to be a reflection of individual or, at the most, geographically circumscribed policies. For it is clear that not even the benefactors of the engineering chairs were prepared to take anything approaching a united stance in formally recognizing the role of higher technological education. To this extent, and for all their generosity, they did little to sustain the most difficult battle in which old and new engineering departments alike were engaged in the last two decades of the century – to promote recruitment to systematic courses rather than to individual classes, and, more generally, to make attendance at those courses an integral part of an engineer's training.

The move towards systematic instruction and certification

As I have already observed, the attempt to promote systematic, day-time technological instruction, leading to certificates in engineering, had already guided the pioneering efforts of London and Durham. To achieve a similar arrangement in Glasgow, Rankine had to fight hard, but eventually, in 1862, he won the approval of the university senate, and a certificate of proficiency in engineering science was established. Certificates were also offered by Owens College, Manchester, the University of Edinburgh, and the Queen's Colleges in Ireland; and from the 1880s, following the establishment of new provincial colleges, similar schemes were launched in several of the country's main manufacturing towns. The characteristics of these degrees were broadly similar.[39] They were diplomas awarded by the institutions on the successful completion of a course lasting either two or three years. Regular attendance was required, and the proficiency of the candidates was assessed by a final examination.

It is clear that the introduction of certificates did not diminish the colleges' willingness to accept enrolments in individual classes; in fact, in a manner similar to what happened with evening classes, the majority of the day-students in technical subjects continued to attend no more than one or two classes. The reason is that since fees made up a substantial share of their income, colleges had no choice but to admit as many students as they could, regardless of the narrowness of their academic interests. The professors, too, had a vested interest in this policy, since they received a percentage of their students' fees as part of their salary. As a result, some of them engaged in a prodigious amount of supplementary teaching, ranging from specialized subjects to elementary technical lectures, so as to offer the widest possible variety of options.

Despite these impediments, the calendars of the 1880s make it clear that full-time day courses were slowly becoming more prominent, if not in terms of the numbers of students, at least in the place they were perceived to have within engineering departments. Not surprisingly, the emphasis on the benefit that could be gained from a thorough, broadly based education was particularly strong in prospectuses drafted by the staunch advocates of a scientific approach to engineering. Here, Osborne Reynolds at Owens College is typical. But soon a concern to demonstrate the value of following a systematic programme of instruction became apparent also in departments that had a far stronger commitment to the practical side of engineering. Yorkshire College, in Leeds, is a good example. In 1885 the college's annual report concluded a description of the new certificates in civil, mechanical, mining, and electrical engineering with the hope that 'these certificates will prove of such value to the holders that a large number of students will be induced to prosecute the complete and systematic course of study referred to'.[40]

The worries that professors felt about the proliferation and growing complexity of the disciplines relevant to mechanical engineering, allied to their determination to establish a role for higher technological education in the training of engineers, go a long way towards explaining this new emphasis. But there were other reasons too, linked to developments in the institutional position of the civic colleges. About the turn of the century, they were gradually upgraded to full university status and began to be allowed to award degrees. As a consequence, while certificates continued to be offered, new Bachelor of Science degrees in engineering were introduced at a level higher than that of the certificates, and with syllabuses that required a more thorough theoretical preparation. This meant that the curricula for the new degrees had to fulfil prescribed standards in the quality as well as in the variety of the disciplines they embraced. It also meant that, as the range of specialities expanded, departments of engineering organized themselves more tightly around the core activity of teaching for the full degree and certificate qualifications as opposed to individual courses.

Systematic full-time instruction at an advanced level was at the heart of the ambitious scheme which the City & Guilds of London Institute for the Advancement of Technical Education inaugurated in London in the early 1880s. Founded in 1878 by eleven Livery Companies and the Corporation of the City of London, the Institute immediately launched a system of examinations focused on technology, creating a successful alternative to the older Science and Art Department's scheme for industrially related subjects. In addition, however, the Institute aspired to a more immediate involvement in education. To this end, in 1881, Finsbury Technical College was created as a dependent institution, with two distinct sections devoted, respectively, to day classes and evening classes. The day classes, like the evening classes, were at an elementary level, their aim being to prepare boys of between fourteen and seventeen years for immediately useful employment.

When the Central Institution was opened, three years later, as part of the same scheme, its curriculum was far more advanced. It admitted pupils from sixteen years of age and offered full programmes leading to diplomas in mechanical, electrical, and chemical engineering.[41] By British standards at least, the endowment was exceptional: the building cost £92,000, and £21,630 was spent on permanent fittings, apparatus, and materials. Special care was also taken with the choice of the teachers. William E. Ayrton, with his solid experience in the telegraphic industry and a successful career as a teacher in Tokyo and London behind him, was appointed to the chair of electrical engineering, and William C. Unwin – Fairbairn's assistant in his research on the strength of materials – was appointed to the chair of mechanical engineering. They were joined by Henry E. Armstrong for chemistry and Olaus Henrici for mathematics and applied mechanics.

The fact that London already had other institutions offering higher technological instruction makes the Central Institution's success in attracting students, especially in the sections of mechanical and electrical engineering, even more remarkable. As tables 1.2 and 1.3 show, by British standards, the school was firmly among the leaders. But when the enrolments are compared with the corresponding ones for students in technical education abroad, the notion of the Central as a success story becomes hard to maintain.

A great deal of effort continued to be devoted to promulgating the importance of following a complete course of study. To encourage students, adjustments and compromises were readily made. In some institutions, notably Yorkshire College in Leeds and University College in Liverpool, formal instruction was spread over no more than two terms, so that students could enter local factories for the remaining six months of each of the three years of the course. However, interest in the certificates

Table 1.2. *Number of full-time day-students attending engineering classes in selected English colleges, 1850–1914*

	King's College London	Owens College Manchester	Yorkshire College Leeds	Central Institution London	
				mech. eng.	elect. eng.
1850	71	–	–		
1855	58	–	–		–
1860	86	–	–		–
1865	88	–	–		–
1870	80[a]	34	–		–
1875	70	48	–		–
1880	65	26	28		–
1885	119	32	24		
1890	75	48	43	14	13
1895	81	65		57	13
1900	85[a]	67	69	67	88
1905	102	53		117	99
1910	119[b]	107	100	140	147

[a] Approximate figures.
[b] Of these, 81 were internal students. The others were regular external students.
Sources: College calendars for the years concerned

was consistently disheartening: while attendances at individual classes was high, the number of students taking the final examinations remained insignificant.

So it was that, year after year, the sections of the university calendars dealing with the departments of engineering had to recount a sad story, although there were ways of making the low levels of full-time enrolments less obvious. One way was to give figures for individual classes only. But no amount of juggling could totally conceal the truth.

From workshop to laboratory

As these developments were occurring, in the 1880s, changes in industrial practices as well as in the theoretical side of mechanical engineering were leading to a redefinition of the role of higher education in the preparation of engineers. Until 1870, machine construction was no more than a practical speciality on the fringes of the broader realm of mechanical engineering. Its foundation was a variety of practical skills and experience that educational institutions were in no position to purvey. Even in the schools where attempts were made to engage students in workshop exercises, the exposure to real industrial practices was necessarily limited.

Table 1.3. *Degrees, diplomas, and certificates awarded in engineering*

King's College London		Owens College Manchester				Yorkshire College Leeds						Central Institution London	
Associates		Certificates		Honours degrees		Certificates		Diplomas		Honours degrees		Diplomas	
1870–9	57	1870–9	17			1891–1903	21	1904–12	28	1904–12	26	1885–93	150
1880–9	85	1880–9	26	1882–9	17							1894–1903	382
1890–9	64	1890–9	56	1890–9	54								
		1900–9	82	1900–10	130								

However, research on the strength of materials, prompted by governmental and private bodies, as well as by a growing concern with the efficiency of steam engines, conspired to encourage more rigorous attitudes in the day-to-day life of mechanical engineers. In due course, the more sophisticated techniques of testing and analysis that emerged from research began to be used in private industry.[42] Academic engineers were frequently involved in these activities as consultants, often collaborating closely with practising engineers in ways that drew on the facilities of both the manufacturing workshop and the teaching laboratory. The creation of this pool of shared expertise was important. In a decisive way, it promoted the moves leading to the establishment of teaching laboratories and to their integration in syllabuses of mechanical engineering from the late 1880s.

The moves to which I refer occurred virtually simultaneously in Europe and in the United States, and England was as quick to respond as any other nation. London, in fact, had two of the finest laboratories in the world, both of them regarded as models by visiting engineers. Alexander Kennedy's laboratory, opened at University College in 1879, was admired not only in Britain but also in Europe and in the United States.[43] It was here that a 100-ton testing machine, with a variety of subsidiary apparatus, was first introduced in a teaching laboratory. Another notable innovation was an experimental steam engine, constructed specially for thermodynamic investigations, in particular of the conditions for economy. Unwin's laboratory at the Central Institution, established in 1884, was likewise well equipped and greatly admired.

The repercussions of the creation of new laboratories were as complex as the interplay of the forces from which they grew. Most obviously, they did a great deal to enhance the academic prestige of the engineering departments that housed them: in England, as in Germany and the United States, the engagement in experimental work, performed in an academic context and with 'scientific' aims, served to make engineering departments more acceptable in university life. But, in addition to promoting the academic status of engineering, the new laboratories also presented a more convincing image both to industry and to potential entrants. This appeal to constituencies outside the immediate academic world was decisive in helping higher education to secure a role in the training of engineers, in the face of the engineering profession's traditionally high premium on experience. Pointing to the new laboratory exercises and instruction in the practice of sophisticated measurement, institutions for higher technological education could at last identify a special contribution that they were able to make to the fashioning of engineers – one that apprenticeship and experience alone could not provide. At University College, London, Alexander Kennedy observed in 1886, in a paper on 'The use and equipment of engineering laboratories', that the ordinary apprenticeship system did not leave young engineers time to study the physical properties of metals, the strength of materials, the efficiency of machines, and the economy of different types of engine; for this, access to a laboratory was essential. The Central Institution went even further, proclaiming that the laboratory, rather than the lecture room, was not just a part but the core of its teaching.

The laboratory, in fact, became the symbol of the emancipation of mechanical engineering from the enduring primacy of apprenticeship, and laboratories sprang up everywhere. Following Kennedy's pioneering experience at University College in 1878, there were comparable developments at Finsbury Technical College in 1881, at Mason's Science College, Birmingham in 1882, and University College, Bristol in 1883. Firth College, Yorkshire College, Owens College, and the University Colleges of Liverpool and Dundee all followed suit in the later 1880s.

Conclusion

On a far less ambitious scale, attempts to establish alternatives to the new provision for engineering education in university-level institutions were taking shape in other centres, all of which were trying to adjust their courses so as to fill a variety of niches at different levels. In Manchester, the Mechanics' Institute was reorganized in 1885, and became the Manchester Technical School. Its aim was to provide advanced technical instruction, though – in contrast with the engineering department at Owens College – instruction of a strictly practical nature. This attempt to create courses more relevant to practice was at the root of the proliferation of new schools that occurred in the 1880s, and it proceeded even more rapidly in the following decade. From 1890, with the introduction of the Local Taxation Act, governmental grants began to flow more copiously into higher technical education. Funds were administered by municipal authorities, which clearly favoured technical schools rather than the engineering departments in the university colleges. By 1895, as a result, a number of municipal institutions throughout the country were able to offer full-time as well as very successful part-time courses in engineering for students from sixteen years of age. And it was precisely this kind of course, combined with practical training, that continued to produce the bulk of English engineers until well after the First World War.

Despite this expansion, however, the number of students who prepared for certificates or degrees, whether at a university college or at a technical school, remained modest. A main reason for this was the unabated reluctance of the Institution of Mechanical Engineers to recognize higher technical education as a necessary part of an engineer's training. Until the eve of the First World War, in fact, no clear procedure was fixed for evaluating the standard of the theoretical preparation of the candidates for associate membership.[44] This lack of regulation had the important effect of allowing the old guard to maintain the traditional virtues of practical achievement and expertise as a bulwark against the emergence of academically trained engineers. But a concern to exercise a stricter control over the academic background of candidates became apparent in the early years of the century. It emanated from the highest reaches of the Institution, most notably when Edward B. Ellington used his presidential address in 1911 to deliver a plea for the introduction of some elements of formal education as a pre-requisite for admission.[45] One year later, despite resistance from the Institution's older members, a proposal to adopt entrance examinations and to grant exemptions to candidates holding a university degree or a diploma from a technical school was approved.

At last, the struggle for the recognition of qualifications from institutions of higher education, as at least one means of entry to the senior ranks of professional industrial engineers, was won. The success owed a great deal to the fact that, in the first decade of the twentieth century, departments of engineering had strengthened their position in many universities: even in Oxford, the stronghold of liberal education, a chair of engineering science had been created in 1908. Whether the universities liked it or not, engineering was there to stay. Yet, one fundamental battle had still to be won – for the confidence of the students. By international standards, the number of the students entering for certificate or degree courses in engineering remained low. As was all too apparent, the proliferation of educational opportunities in the decade before the First World War did little to stimulate the interest of young people in gaining university-level technological qualifications. That interest remained sluggish, and, when war came, it was still growing painfully slowly, in the face of a scarcely diminished confidence in the value of experience.

Notes

1 A good general survey of the development of higher technical education in England is: Michael Argles, *South Kensington to Robbins. An Account of*

English Technical and Scientific Education since 1851 (London, 1964). On the failure to produce graduates in scientific and technical subjects, see Donald S. L. Cardwell, *The Organisation of Science in England* (London, 1957). In a similar vein, the delay in providing adequate funding for scientific and technological education is discussed in Peter Alter, *The Reluctant Patron. Science and the State in Britain, 1850–1920* (Oxford, Hamburg, and New York, 1987). The reluctance of industry to take advantage of the products of higher education is highlighted in Stephen F. Cotgrove, *Technical Education and Social Change* (London, 1958), and Michael Sanderson, *The Universities and British Industry, 1850–1970* (London, 1972).

2 Initially, neither of these institutions provided specialized instruction in mechanical engineering. It was only in 1853, with the appointment of Robert Willis to a lectureship in applied mechanics, that the Royal School of Mines filled the gap in its syllabus. See Margaret Reeks, *Register of the Associates and Old Students of the Royal School of Mines, and the History of the Royal School of Mines* (London, 1920).

3 On the early history of these institutions, see H. Hale Bellot, *University College London, 1826–1906* (London, 1929), and Francis J. C. Hearnshaw, *The Centenary History of King's College, 1828–1928* (London, 1929).

4 C. E. Whiting, *The University of Durham, 1832–1932* (London, 1932).

5 On engineering in the University of Glasgow, see James Small's contribution to the volume *Fortuna domus. A Series of Lectures Delivered in the University of Glasgow in Commemoration of the Fifth Centenary of its Foundation* (Glasgow, 1952), pp. 335–55.

6 The membership of the Institution rose from 288 in 1836 to 797 in 1856. The origins and development of this and other engineering associations are examined in detail in R. Angus Buchanan, *The Engineers. A History of the Engineering Profession in Britain 1750–1914* (London, 1989).

7 *University of Durham, Calendar, 1838–39* (Durham, 1838), p. 8.

8 *Ibid.*, p. 9.

9 *The King's College Calendar, 1840*, pp. 11–18.

10 On Cowper and Hosking, see the entries in the *Dictionary of National Biography*.

11 On Charles B. Vignoles, see K. H. Vignoles, *Charles Blacker Vignoles, Romantic Engineer* (Cambridge, 1982).

12 On Eaton Hodgkinson and on his cooperation with Fairbairn, see *Proceedings of the Royal Society of London*, 12 (1863), pp. xi–xiii.

13 On Woodcroft, see the *Dictionary of National Biography*.

14 Naturally, there were exceptions. Henry Moseley, for example, who was the first professor of natural philosophy at King's College, London, was competent technically as well as being a distinguished scholar. He was actively engaged in studies of the mechanical principles of engineering, and worked on the stability of ships.

15 On the new generation of 'scientific' teachers of engineering, see David F. Channell, 'The harmony of theory and practice: the engineering science of W. J. M. Rankine', *Technology and Culture*, 23 (1982), 39–52.

16 *University College, London, Calendar. Session 1866–7* (London, 1866), p. 22.

17 A workshop was opened at King's College in 1840, and a technician was

appointed. As the Calendar of the College put it (1846 edn, p. 38), 'students are introduced to wooden constructions, as roofs and bridges, and to the construction of machinery'. However, the equipment was inadequate, and it was only in 1856 that steam engines and machine tools made their appearance.

18 In 1840, the engineering classes at Durham were attended by eleven students, a figure which, four years later, had fallen to one.

19 In Scotland, William McQuorn Rankine experienced similar difficulties. In his evidence to the Devonshire Commission in 1872, he declared that, by the mid-1860s, attendances had began to improve; however, the average number of students at his engineering classes was no more than forty a year. See *Report [and Minutes of evidence] of the Royal Commission on Scientific Instruction and the Advancement of Science* [Devonshire] (London, 1872), Fifth Report, Minutes of Evidence [*c*. 958], pp. 19–25.

20 King's College had such a school from the start. With age of admission between 13 and 15, it had 500 pupils in 1846. See Hearnshaw, *Centenary History*, pp. 101–4 and 191–3. This example was subsequently followed by other institutions, notably Firth College, Sheffield, where a junior preparatory school was opened in 1889.

21 From the mid-1850s, there was a campaign for the reform of all types of military education. At about the same time, attempts were made to improve the preparation of civilian engineers destined for service in India. These two developments led to a tightening of standards in both syllabuses and examinations. Mathematics and classics remained the most important subjects, but greater emphasis was placed on civil engineering and railway construction. See Whitworth Porter, *History of the Corps of Royal Engineers* (London, 1889), and J. G. P. Cameron, *A Short History of the Royal Indian Engineering College, Coopers Hill* (London, 1960).

22 From 1869, Owens College announced in its calendar that the College was recognized by the Secretary of State for India in Council as 'possessing an efficient class for instruction in engineering with a view to the preparation of candidates for admission to the competitive examination for appointment in the Indian Public Works Department'. See *Owens College. Calendar 1868–9*; also for subsequent years.

23 William J. Reader, *Professional Men. The Rise of the Professional Classes in Nineteenth Century England* (London, 1966), and Harold J. Perkin, *The Origins of Modern English Society, 1780–1880* (London, 1969).

24 An example is that of Peter W. Willans (1851–92), whose high-speed steam engines made his company world famous. The son of the owner of a large textile mill in Leeds, Willans studied at a local grammar school before being apprenticed to Carrett & Marshall's foundry in Leeds and then to the renowned shipyards of John Penn & Sons in Greenwich; see his obituary in *Proceedings of the Institution of Mechanical Engineers*, 2 (1892), 224–5. A university degree was not altogether uncommon in the 1850s. Sir Andrew Fairbairn, a nephew of William Fairbairn and the owner and head of a successful factory for the production of textile machinery in Leeds, read for the Mathematical Tripos in Cambridge and graduated as 37th Wrangler in 1850.

25 John Nasmyth, the owner of one of the best-known mechanical engineering

works in Manchester, charged fees of between £150 and £300, depending on the type of instruction provided. See John Cantrell, *John Nasmyth and the Bridgewater Foundry. A Study of Entrepreneurship in the Early Engineering Industry* (Manchester, 1984), pp. 238–9. Among the most important centres for premium pupillage were the workshops of the railway engineering companies, such as the Great Northern Railway Co., and the Crewe works of the London and North Western Railway Co.

26 See *The Student's Guide to the University of Cambridge* (Cambridge, 1874), pp. 79, 85, and 69–103, and *The Student's Handbook to the University of Oxford* (Oxford, 1873), pp. 152–64.

27 Fleeming Jenkin, *Report [and Minutes of Evidence] of the Royal Commission on Scientific Instruction and the Advancement of Science* [Devonshire], First Supplementary and Second Report, Minutes of Evidence (London, 1872) [*c.* 536], p. 1,601.

28 For a critical assessment of the state pupillage and apprenticeship as a preparation for engineering careers, see A. P. M. Fleming and J. G. Pearce, *The Principles of Apprentice Training. With Special Reference to the Engineering Industry* (London, 1916). See also Charles More, *Skill and the English Working Class, 1870–1914* (London, 1980).

29 Ambrose Fleming, *Memories of a Scientific Life* (London, 1934), pp. 12–13.

30 L. T. C. Rolt, *The Mechanicals. Progress of a Profession* (London, 1967), and Buchanan, *The Engineers*.

31 His report, 'On the machinery of the Paris Universal Exhibition, 1855', was republished in William Fairbairn, *Useful Information for Engineers* (London, 1866), pp. 125–79. See also his autobiography, *The Life of Sir William Fairbairn, Bart.*, edited by William Pole (London, 1877), pp. 371–4.

32 By 1880, Beyer's contributions to the endowment of Owens College amounted to £108,900. See Joseph Thompson, *The Owens College. Its Foundation and Growth* (Manchester, 1886), pp. 294–6 and 551–67.

33 On Leeds, see A. N. Shimmin, *The University of Leeds* (Cambridge, 1954); on Sheffield, Arthur W. Chapman, *The Story of a Modern University* (Oxford, 1955). In 1886, Sir Andrew B. Walker offered University College, Liverpool, £15,000 (subsequently increased to £23,000) towards the organization of an engineering laboratory, so that 'nothing might be lacking to the new Laboratories in completeness of scope or of equipment' (*University College, Liverpool, Calendar 1900–1901*, p. xvi). The laboratories were opened in 1889. In addition, in 1886, Thomas Harrison had offered £10,000 for the endowment of a Harrison Chair of Engineering; see Thomas Kelly, *For the Advancement of Learning. The University of Liverpool, 1881–1981* (Liverpool, 1981).

34 For example, in 1889, Henry Brown offered Yorkshire College, Leeds, £5,000 for the founding of five or more scholarships for students in various branches of applied science. Similar initiatives were launched in Liverpool by Richard Moon, chairman of the London and North Western Railway Co. (1892), and E. Harland, a local shipbuilder (1895). By 1890, scholarships for engineering students were available in most university colleges.

35 David Allan Low (ed.), *The Whitworth Book* (London, 1926), pp. 7–14.

36 *The Whitworth Scholarships, and How to Obtain Them* (Manchester, 1883).

37 See Hearnshaw, *Centenary History*, pp. 289–90.

38 In 1887, the calendar of Owens College began to announce that 'some of the principal mechanical engineers in Manchester and the neighbourhood have signified their willingness to receive certificated engineering students of the college into their works, either as premium apprentices for a short term, or as ordinary apprentices without premiums'. In the same year, similar notices were published in the calendars of Yorkshire College, Leeds, and University College, Liverpool. A study of the gradual replacement of apprenticeship by higher technological education is Colin Divall, 'A measure of agreement: employers and engineering studies in the universities of England and Wales, 1897–1939', *Social Studies of Science*, 20 (1990), 65–112.

39 In the 1880s, the three-year course leading to a certificate of engineering at Owens College, Manchester, included pure mathematics, applied mathematics, physics, experimental mechanics, geometrical and mechanical drawing, and engineering. Engineering was divided into three parts: surveying and estimating (first year), applied mechanics (second year), and the theory and construction of machines (third year). Towards the end of the decade, engineering laboratory classes and courses in chemistry were added.

40 *Yorkshire College. Eleventh Annual Report, 1884–5*, p. 30.

41 On the Central Institution, later to become one of the constituents of the Imperial College of Science and Technology of London, see A. Rupert Hall, *Science for Industry. A Short History of the Imperial College of Science and Technology* (London, 1982).

42 For a detailed account of the development of these activities, see Isaac Todhunter and Karl Pearson, *A History of Elasticity and the Strength of Materials*, 2 vols. (Cambridge, 1893).

43 Alexander B. W. Kennedy, 'The uses and equipment of engineering laboratories', in *Institution of Civil Engineers, Minutes of Proceedings*, 88 (1887), 1–80.

44 In 1894, a modification in the by-laws concerning the qualifications for membership stated that candidates for admission 'must furnish evidence of training in the principles as well as in the practice of Engineering'; see *Institution of Mechanical Engineers. Proceedings* (1890), p. cxi. However, no clear indication was given as to the kind of theoretical preparation that was expected. This coolness towards examinations contrasts sharply with the more receptive attitudes of the Institution of Civil Engineers. For a comment on the contrast, see Joseph O. Marsh, 'The engineering institutions and the public recognition of British engineers', *International Journal of Engineering Education*, 16 (1988), 119–27.

45 Edward Ellington, 'Address by the President' (Ordinary General Meeting, 11 March 1911), *Institution of Mechanical Engineers. Proceedings*, (1911), 213–35.

2 The training and career structures of engineers in France, 1880–1939

André Grelon

During the last third of the nineteenth century, the need to produce highly trained engineers to meet the demands of industry became a subject of national concern in France. Very different solutions to the problem were advanced, and these duly engaged the attention of the government, business circles, and the universities. As a result, between the 1880s and 1914, a diverse array of engineering schools were founded in response to the individual needs of different sectors of industry.

In marked contrast with the dramatic growth of engineering schools in this period, their development became significantly restricted during the economic crisis of the 1930s. It is the purpose of this chapter to trace the history of the schools during this period of transition. I shall consider the problems raised by the training of engineers, the changes in the context of the debate, and the recurring questions (many of them still with us today) surrounding employment and careers in engineering

The development of engineering schools in France

The earliest French engineering schools were established in the eighteenth century to train civil and military engineers for employment in the service of the crown. Such a pattern was not peculiar to France. In both function and form, they were broadly comparable with schools founded at about the same time in the other monarchies of Europe, including Britain, Spain, the German principalities, and Sweden.

During the French Revolution, the system underwent a fundamental change: now, in 1794, a single school, the Ecole Polytechnique, was established by the National Convention to prepare all the senior members of the state's technical services. The engineering schools already in existence (such as the Ecole des Mines, the Ecole des Ponts et Chaussées, and the Ecole du Génie Maritime) were linked with the Ecole Polytechnique as *écoles d'application*, charged with providing practical training in the individual engineering specialities.

In 1829, in response to rising industrial demands, a group of academics working with a private entrepreneur, Alphonse Lavallée, founded a new school, the Ecole Centrale des Arts et Manufactures in Paris; the function of Centrale was to meet the critical need for engineers in industry. At a lower level, two *écoles d'arts et métiers* had already been established under Napoleon at Châlons-sur-Marne and Angers to train factory foremen and technicians, and similar establishments were opened elsewhere during the nineteenth century. The industrial expansion of the Second Empire created an awareness of new pressures, and, in response, evening classes and technical schools, directed specifically at providing a training for industry, were established in a number of provincial cities, such as Lyons, Lille, and Mulhouse.

The disaster of 1870–1 stimulated a national debate on the need to rebuild France's strength, with particular emphasis on training at all levels. As a result, during the last quarter of the nineteenth century, the university system underwent a process of fundamental reorganization culminating in the establishment of sixteen universities across the country. Several engineering schools were set up within the faculties of science of these universities, in a manner similar to the establishment of the *scuole di applicazione* in the Italian universities.

After the First World War, the demand for technical staff increased, but the recession of the 1930s soon put an end to the boom, and, for the first time in their history, engineers, as a professional group, faced serious unemployment. Their professional engineering organizations were mobilized for action, and they succeeded in persuading the government to initiate legislation to protect their status. The resulting law, restricting the use of the title 'ingénieur diplômé', came into effect on 10 July 1934. It is the law that still governs the organization of engineering schools to this day.

Of the interests that have been involved in the training of engineers in France, the most important has been the State. In contrast with Britain, the State in France has a long tradition of involvement in all aspects of education. Among the many government departments that have traditionally had a role in this training, the Ministry of Trade, Industry, and Agriculture, has been especially influential, being responsible for most technical training throughout the nineteenth century and up to 1920. The Ministry of Public Instruction, too, has played a key role, most notably during the Third Republic.[1]

In addition to the State, other political, economic, and social actors have contributed significantly to the training of engineers. In particular, many municipal authorities have collaborated successfully with the national educational service since the early days of the Third Republic. There is a parallel here, in both the style and the chronology of the process, with the decisive role of English municipal councils in the establishment of the 'red brick' civic universities.

Industry has generally been involved through local associations representing the interests of manufacturers, although both national confederations of employers and individual industrialists have also played a part. Understandably, employers' organizations have always taken the pragmatic view that where skills are being nurtured in scientific and technical training, they should be exploited, and that where the structure for such training does not exist, it must be called for and, where necessary, created by the employers themselves. This has happened when neither the state nor local government has felt able to take direct responsibility for the work or, in certain cases, when ideological interests, such as those of Catholic employers in northern France, have pointed to the need for an independent approach.

The university community has naturally had a central role in the process. The specialized institutes of applied science that began to emerge in the science faculties from the 1880s were largely the result of the enthusiasm of a generation of young academic scientists seeking to place the university at the centre of national life. In the 1880s and 1890s, the advocates of links with industry had everything in their favour, not least because they could be seen as proposing institutional change and modernization while presenting themselves as the heirs of a distinguished university tradition.[2]

There were also individuals who set up technical schools on their own initiative and for a variety of reasons. Such schools were usually located in Paris, and most of them had difficulty in gaining the recognition that went with belonging to the recognized hierarchy of engineering schools. Their

Table 2.1. *Engineering schools founded, 1880–39*

Subject	1880–1918	1919–1939
General engineering	5	2
Mechanical engineering, metallurgy	2	4
Electricity	9	2
Physics/chemistry	12	7
Aeronautical engineering	1	2
Building, public works, mining, geology	2	1
Textiles	3	0
Agriculture, food	5	4
Miscellaneous	3	1

founders were independent, had no position in the State, and were not bound by the authority of the employers' associations. Nevertheless, their schools gradually won acceptance as the qualifications of their graduates came to match more precisely the expectations of employers.[3]

A last group of participants in the process of establishing engineering training were the associations of former students of the various schools. These associations have been essential to the growth and advancement of the schools at which they trained, and there have always been strong bonds between the schools and their *anciens élèves*.

Structural unity and diversity

The number of participants involved in the training of engineers has clearly contributed to the complexity of this facet of French educational history. Before the progressive reforms of the universities by the Third Republic, on a model derived from Germany, advanced scientific teaching at universities was more notional than real. In contrast with Germany, faculties of science in France could offer nothing, in either their structure or their teaching activities, to which the new schools of engineering could usefully refer.

What then were the existing models? Essentially, there were two possible routes. The first was through the schools training professional men for the technical services of the state. The students who embarked on this higher training came from the secondary schools, with the inevitable corollary that social as well as purely intellectual criteria played a part in their selection. The curricula were intended to give a mastery of academic science and, thereby, a rational understanding of phenomena. It was thought important for student engineers to begin their training by obtaining an integrated and comprehensive view of the role of science in the processes of industry: only then were they in a position to choose whether to apply their knowledge in chemistry, metallurgy, or mechanical or civil engineering.[4]

The second route was through the developing network of *écoles d'arts et métiers*. The pupils in these schools came from the post-primary schools that were first created in 1833 (in principle, in every department) to provide pre-vocational training to children aged, typically, between twelve and fifteen. The course of study was based on the teaching of techniques and shop-floor practice, and it assigned a dominant role to workshop experience. Although science was not excluded, its place was a secondary one.[5]

Both of these routes developed steadily during the second half of the nineteenth century, but towards the end of the century a third type of institution began to appear, with features drawn from the other two. These new schools were intended to meet the industrial demand for engineers and technical and scientific staff specializing in the burgeoning sectors of what has been called the second industrial revolution. The courses combined formal theoretical work at a high level with the study of industrial applications, extended laboratory sessions, visits to factories, and lectures by practising engineers and industrialists. These schools took students from both secondary and post-primary education, though after a few years the students they admitted had all reached a standard comparable with that of the *baccalauréat*.[6]

Whichever model was followed, the administrative structure of all the schools was more or less the same; the spirit that infused them was derived from the military academies. The students of the *écoles d'arts et métiers* wore uniforms, just as *polytechniciens* did, and they formed a small exclusive community conscious of having being chosen by a tough competitive examination. This was both reflected in and fostered by a training of considerable intensity, with the pupils being confined within the walls of their schools, and with a meticulously determined routine of instruction that subjected all of them to the same demanding rhythm of study. The aim, in short, was to fashion students in a clearly conceived, pre-determined mould. The freer, more open model of the university, which might have proved attractive if it had emerged as a realistic alternative earlier in the century, was ignored.

The diploma question

Originally, the term 'engineer' did not carry with it any implication of a qualification; it was a grade in a military or civil service department organized in a hierarchy that extended from assistant engineers at the bottom to engineers-in-chief at the top. When it became clear, in the mid eighteenth century, that engineers needed systematic training, the solution that emerged was, as I have indicated, that of the specialized school, in which pupils were prepared for a career that would take them to the rank of engineer.[7] Hence, the subsequent establishment of the Ecole Polytechnique and its associated *écoles d'application* during the Revolution and the First Empire simply formalized a system that already existed. Graduates of Polytechnique would enter an *école d'application* for specialized training before their incorporation in a *corps d'Etat*, and they would acquire their identity as engineers gradually during their professional lives. They thus entered their careers not as 'engineers' but as *polytechniciens*, and they retained that label throughout their professional lives.

The question of diplomas arose with the founding of the Ecole Centrale des Arts et Manufactures in 1829. Now, for the first time, there was an institution which awarded an engineering diploma possessing a 'cash value' on the labour market. Industrial employers did not find it easy to accept the diploma. For they associated the title 'engineer' with specific duties and responsibilities corresponding to the various stages in the career structure that existed in the sectors or companies with which they were familiar. As a result, engineers from the Ecole Centrale had the task of winning recognition for their diploma as an automatic qualification for employment at engineer level. When the state accepted the diploma of the Ecole Centrale from its founders in 1857, it had no choice but to endorse the course of training and, for the first time, to give legal recognition to a diploma in 'civil' engineering.

In the same year as the Ecole Centrale des Arts et Manufactures became a state school, the Ecole Centrale of Lyons was established as a private institution, awarding its own engineering diplomas, graded first or second class according to the candidate's performance in the examinations.[8] About the same time, two of the leading state schools, the Ecole des Mines and the Ecole des Ponts et Chaussées were opened to students from outside the civil service. This new category of pupils received the same training as student engineers in state employment, though without the right to a civil service appointment. Inevitably, there arose the question of the type of diploma that was to be conferred on this new kind of student. But it was fifty years before the matter was settled by the Corps des Mines, and it took another twenty years for the Corps des Ponts et Chaussées to give its reluctant agreement.[9]

Until the end of the nineteenth century, it was only the élite of the technical schools – those that were subsequently to be termed the *grandes écoles* – with students drawn from the *lycées*, that awarded a full engineering diploma. The *écoles d'arts et métiers* and the institutions in the technical college tradition, whose students came through post-primary education or commercial and industrial schools, gave the lower qualification of the *brevet*.

In this way, the engineer's diploma became established as a higher qualification, though one that had no place in the traditional hierarchy of academic awards (the *baccalauréat*, *licence*, and doctorate), all of which remained the preserve of the university system and had national validity, so that a *licence* gained at Lille was of the same value and official status as one from Lyons. The system reflected the principles of the unified Université de France, and it was preserved even after the establishment of the sixteen regional universities in 1896. In contrast with the university system, there was no uniformity or national standard for the award of engineering diplomas. Each bore with it the status of the institution that conferred it, a status largely determined by the professional success of the institution's former students. For that reason a qualified engineer was always formally described as 'ingénieur de l'Ecole N . . .'.

A new law of 1897 allowed the universities to grant diplomas of their own. The science faculties, which at the time were especially active in establishing their associated institutes of applied science, were given the right, under the new arrangements, to award engineering diplomas. Each authorization was certified by an order from the Ministry of Public Instruction, which was published in the *Journal officiel* and so given official status. By 1907, comparable approval had been given for the diplomas of the *écoles d'arts et métiers*, which came under the Ministry of Trade and belonged to what I have described as the technical college tradition.

The process of gaining approval was less straightforward for private institutions that had no link with a ministry. While state institutions submitted their diploma programmes for validation by an external body – either the Ministry of Public Instruction or the Technical Education Council (Conseil Supérieur de l'Enseignement Technique) – there was no equivalent body to act on behalf of schools founded by individuals or private companies. Nevertheless, these schools were under constant pressure from their students, past and present, to award engineering diplomas on the completion of their studies. It was to this pressure that the Catholic Ecole des Hautes Etudes Industrielles in Lille eventually bowed. The Ecole had been planned as an institution to train the Christian factory-owners of the future, but it soon had to set up a third-year engineering course for students who were going on to salaried employment and who wanted to improve their career prospects. A similar development occurred at the Ecole Supérieure d'Electricité in Paris.

A first solution to the problem came with the Astier law, passed on 25 July 1919. Under this law, private colleges willing to submit their curricula to the Technical Education Council and to allow regular inspection could be given the status of being 'recognized by the state' and issue diplomas 'endorsed by the Ministry of Trade and Industry'. This bestowed semi-official recognition on their diplomas, although the ministerial endorsement did not amount to a declaration that they were on a level with engineering diplomas. The whole process was complicated by the decision of certain colleges to decline state recognition; in the case of Catholic schools, such a decision would be taken primarily on ideological grounds. The result, at all events, was a confusion and lack of clarity that persisted until well after the First World War.

As elsewhere in Europe, the need for legislation came to be felt very quickly during the economic recovery of the 1920s,[10] when businesses urgently needed to build up staffs depleted by the war. Existing schools increased their intakes, and many new technical courses were established, most noticeably correspondence courses, some of which exploited the profession's popularity with the young by offering 'engineering diplomas' after only a few months of study. Confusion between such diplomas and those of celebrated private schools such as the Ecole Supérieure d'Electricité was seen as intolerable. The smaller schools, and more particularly the correspondence courses, were condemned by the associations of *anciens élèves* for lowering the standards of training and thereby undermining the prestige of the engineering profession.

The economic crisis of the 1930s appeared to be the fulfillment of these warnings. As a result, after fifteen years of discussion among the interested parties, a coherent solution was proposed in the law of 10 July 1934 which attempted to safeguard the title 'ingénieur diplômé'. Under the law, a commission was established to advise on state engineering training and, above all, to determine which of the private institutions should have the right to award engineering diplomas. The results were to be enshrined in an official annual list of accredited state and private colleges, published by the commission.[11] By now, there was some feeling within the engineering organizations that not only the diploma but also the term 'engineer' needed protection. But the system has withstood the test of time and in all important respects it still works in the same way to this day.

It is worth noting that the French legislation came a few months after Belgium had passed a law (on 11 September 1933) on the use of the title of engineer. The timing is significant. For this was a period when engineering associations throughout Europe were demanding protective measures so vehemently that the International Labour Office's Commission Consultative des Travailleurs Intellectuels proposed a formal agreement under which 'member states undertake to legislate on the granting and applicability of the title of engineer, and particularly to ban its use if the legal requirements have not been met'.[12]

Employment

The pattern of development of the engineering schools from the 1880s and the part played by employers in establishing many of them suggest that there was a strong and persistent demand for trained staff in industry. Despite this, employers as a body did not give immediate recognition to engineering qualifications, nor did they grant the seniority that qualified engineers believed to be their right. Before a young diploma-holder could hope to be appointed to a senior position as an engineer, he had to undergo a long period of preparation. After passing the first hurdle, which was employment by the firm, he had to work his way up one grade at a time, and even when he reached his goal, there was no guarantee that the material rewards would match his expectations: salaries, in fact, generally remained low. In these circumstances, it is hardly surprising that engineers emphasized the importance of their contribution for good corporate management and set up bodies to defend their professional rights.

How did industrialists regard the technical diplomas held by applicants? There were several patterns. The diploma of the Ecole Polytechnique, which was not formally classed as an engineering diploma until 1937, gave its holders undeniable advantages, virtually guaranteeing that they would reach one of the most senior positions in a firm. On joining the management or the board of a company, a *polytechnicien* brought with him the contacts appropriate to the *corps* to which he was attached (Mines, Marine Engineering, Explosives, etc.) and a knowledge of the inner workings of ministries. Hence, companies found it profitable to recruit *polytechniciens* as a way of acquiring a range of influential connexions at the highest official level. This kind of recruitment from the civil service (known as *pantouflage*) was worth while only for large companies with national interests. It was natural, therefore, that the electrical companies in the area of Grenoble only began to appoint *polytechniciens* after they had been bought up by big Parisian companies.[13] But *pantouflage* had occurred ever since the early nineteenth century. The Compagnie de Saint-Gobain, for example, appointed a succession of *polytechniciens* from 1833. Typically, the new recruits joined the company about the age of forty, at a stage in their careers 'when public service had proved a disappointment'.[14] Hence, far from being new, the process merely became more marked in the course of the century.

As for the other engineering schools, there were two categories for employment purposes: those with a national reputation earned by long traditions, and the rest. The former were a mere handful. They included the Ecole des Mines and the Ecole des Pont et Chaussées, both of which had been producing engineers for employment outside the state sector since the mid nineteenth century, the Ecole Centrale des Arts et Manufactures, the Ecole des Mines at Saint-Etienne, the various *écoles d'arts et métiers*, and a few others. For the most part, these other schools (of which the écoles de chimie at Lille, Lyon, Bordeaux, and Toulouse, the Ecole d'Electricité Industrielle at Marseille, and the Ecole Textile d'Epinal are examples) served purely local needs, though a few of them seem to have harboured aspirations to the celebrity of the older establishments. Clearly the employment market was more extensive geographically for diploma-holders from the well-known schools. But, for the majority, who were trained in the area of their birth, the natural sequel was employment in local firms.[15] Here, incidentally, it is important to guard against the notion that all the institutions in Paris were national institutions and those in the provinces of merely local importance. For example, the four electrical schools that were founded in Paris between 1900 and 1905 drew their students from the region and served an area of employment confined to the Paris area. In contrast, the Institut Electrotechnique at Grenoble gained a reputation throughout France and internationally.

How, then, did an applicant come to join a firm? Most recruiting was done through personal contacts. The recommendation of a relative or friend assured the head of the firm of the applicant's good character – something essential in a future employee. Another method was placement by the administration of the school in response to requests from local industrialists or others with whom it had friendly contacts. It was for this reason that every school, whether public or private, had to rely on a network of employers ready to take on students who had gained its diploma. A further way was through the appointments service of the association of *anciens élèves*. In some large firms there were networks of former students of one school or another promoting the appointment of students or younger graduates. On the whole, however, employers distrusted such 'parallel' structures, which risked encroaching on the manager's task of making new appointments, so creating an unofficial alternative to the company hierarchy.[16] Finally, if more effective means were not available, a candidate could always fall back on a letter of application sent on his own initiative.

Which sectors of the economy offered employment opportunities to the holders of engineering diplomas? It is noteworthy that specialized schools had been established to teach across the whole range of the technology concerned. But, at first, these institutions did not all award engineering diplomas, and their intakes were often very small – a handful or a few dozen a year.

In time, however, the different branches of industry and business drew steadily increasing numbers of their technical staff from these schools, and this marks a definite change from the first period of industrialization. The point can be demonstrated by looking at the areas of employment of former pupils of the *écoles d'arts et métiers*, known as *gadzarts*, early in the twentieth century. Even if their schools did not officially award diplomas, *gadzarts* had come to be widely regarded as the all-purpose engineers of French industry, as table 2.2 shows very clearly.

Careers

The young graduate who had just found a post was hardly ever given the rank of engineer straight away, since it was an unwritten rule in industry that he had first to demonstrate the value of his qualifications in practice. In this, the heads of firms were drawing a sharp distinction between theory, however well mastered, and its industrial application. At Peugeot, for example, it was stated that 'the employer regards a diploma as no more than an encouraging mark of potential'.[17]

This attitude betrays a clear distrust, within the world of the factory, of those who held qualifications in what could, in fact, be learned only through long workshop experience: plainly the culture of business and manufacturing had not yet accepted the academic world as a valid element. In the old craft tradition, after all, the apprentice had to pass stringent tests before winning acceptance as a fully fledged practitioner and then going on to become a master of his craft. Hence it was natural that the new recruit was expected to start at the bottom of the ladder, even if he came from the Ecole Centrale. This seems to have been virtually universal practice, as the career guides of the time make abundantly clear. As one of them put it:

> It is only in exceptional cases that a young man straight from the rue Montgolfier [i.e. the Ecole Centrale] will be employed immediately as an engineer, that is as the properly qualified head of a major technical department. Putting it bluntly, he probably lacks the necessary practical qualifications, perhaps even the theoretical ones.[18]

There were two main ways of starting on a career. The more traditional one involved 'resolutely donning the workman's blue overalls'. Progress on this route was from workman to charge-hand, then to foreman, and many diploma-holders got no further. Others continued up the ladder as section managers, with subsequent promotion to chief engineer, and just a few finished as factory managers.

The second way, which became increasingly common as industries developed, was through what was customarily called the *bureau d'études*.

Table 2.2. *Employment of* gadzarts, *1904*

Industry	per cent
Fisheries, forestry, agriculture	0.2
Water, gas, electricity (town supplies)	5.6
Petrol, liquid fuels	0.1
Solid fuels, minerals	1.8
Mining, building materials	0.2
Metal production	1.8
Primary metal extraction, smelting, boilermaking	12.8
General mechanical engineering	21.7
Machinery, cars, naval and aeronautical construction	7.3
Electrical construction	0.9
Glass, ceramics, and building materials	1.6
Public works and buildings	5.6
Chemical industry, rubber, asbestos	2.4
Agriculture and food	1.6
Textiles, clothing, leather and tanning	2.1
Wood, paper, cardboard, carbon paper	2.7
Miscellaneous manufacturing	1.7
Transport	11.0
Trade	1.9
Banks, insurance, consultancy	7.5
Liberal arts and management	2.7
Armed forces	6.2
Other	0.6

Note: the data refer to 8,691 former pupils of the *écoles d'arts et métiers*. Note the large numbers in metallurgy and in transport, most of them in railways. In the armed forces, *gadzarts* were most numerous in the navy (175 officers and 240 chief, assistant, and pupil engineers). In addition, firms of engineering consultants employed a considerable number of *gadzarts*. The other sectors show the wide range of their careers.

Source: prepared from data in Paul Blancarnoux, *L'ingénieur des arts et métiers* (Paris, 1908).

In this area, there were three essential tasks, of different importance according to the industrial sector concerned: (a) as a planning department to draft projects, estimates, and reports; (b) as a laboratory, for carrying out research on processes, checking experiments, and analysing raw materials, products, and by-products; and (c) as a sampling service for the control of quality and prices. This range of work made the department a very satisfactory place for learning about industrial practice, and career guides sometimes offered quite lyrical descriptions: 'This research unit is the abode of thought; from it ideas pour forth . . . it is there that the life of the intellect has its source. It is the working place for engineers.'[19] Enthusiasm of this sort was significantly modified a few years later, when engineers found their careers at a standstill in the aftermath of the First World War. Now, the atmosphere of the *bureau d'études* was said to be 'too enclosed; its thinking is inclined to be narrow; its staff are apt to fall into a habit of thought that sees the workshop, the commercial department, and even . . . customers as existing for its benefit.'[20] Here, as on the factory floor, the new recruit had to put on the draughtsman's white coat and work at the drawing-board before he could expect any increase in responsibility or pay.

Apart from the workshop and the *bureau d'études*, there were two main areas open to engineers: the commercial department and management, both of which developed extensively in the late nineteenth and early twentieth centuries. The growth of the engineer's commercial role began well before 1914, but it became especially marked after the war, although even then it affected only a small proportion of technical workers. Career patterns resembled those of other employees: a young engineer started as a sales representative, before broadening his responsibilities and becoming a commercial engineer. Appointments of this kind were much sought after, since they were thought more agreeable than technical work: the surroundings were cleaner, the life more interesting, and there was more scope for personal relationships. Moreover, as a contemporary source put it, 'incomes are higher, and can be considerably higher, because they are related to the volume of business'.[21] The attitudes of the engineering associations to the development of the commercial role were mixed. On the one hand, the associations could only approve of an extension of the engineer's area of work, at a time when the profession had to face new competition from staff trained in commercial schools; yet it was a matter for regret that engineers should abandon technical work. If engineers had to relinquish their specialist tasks in order to advance their careers, factory owners would in the end be deprived of the inventive capacity of their technical staff and see the productivity of their businesses reduced.

Lastly, there was general management. The years between 1880 and 1930 were a time when management assumed a primary role in business, becoming the nerve-centre of the firm. The thinking of a writer such as Henri Fayol, in his *Administration industrielle et générale*, gave the strongest indication of the change.[22] The book provided a firm grounding in theory for the advocates of the French style of management and presaged the role that salaried managers were to play in the running of their firms. The general management of a company formed a complex system of services and called for a variety of skills: lawyers for litigation, accountants for the finance department, lawyers or former military officers for personnel management. To find a place in the system, engineers had to have undertaken financial, legal, or social and economic studies – a kind of training given only in certain of the most prestigious schools, notably the Ecole des Mines and the Ecole des Ponts et Chaussées in Paris. Positions in general management or administration were naturally coveted, and the criteria for obtaining them extended beyond technical qualifications, to embrace a much more diffuse range of social qualities, such as family connexions or social origins.

Young engineers embarking on their careers were strongly advised to move between the different departments in order to increase their familiarity with the firm's range of activities. But it was even more important for an engineer to be professionally mobile within his own field of expertise and, by moving between firms, to gain the breadth of experience essential for a position of responsibility when the time came. The generally informal nature of appointing procedures and of the legal ties between employee and company (contracts were a rarity) helped to facilitate such mobility.

In important respects, the First World War marked a watershed. Before 1914, young diploma-holders were often advised to apply their talents in small firms that gave them varied experience and more opportunity for exercising responsibility and taking part in managerial decisions. From the 1920s, however, guides to careers tended to assert that only larger firms could offer posts with a future and that, by contrast, continuity of employment in smaller businesses was too much a matter of luck. The reality underlying these assessments was the growing size of companies. The total number of industrial firms declined from 697,000 in 1906 to 525,000 in 1936, while the proportion of large companies increased markedly: those with between 200 and 500 salaried staff went up from 6.4 per cent to 8.7 per cent of the total, and those with over 500 rose from 10.6 per cent to 16.3 per cent. In these circumstances, it was natural for engineers generally to turn to the larger companies.

Of course, not all engineers enjoyed the same career prospects. Almost invariably, they started at the bottom of the ladder, but their chances of rising quickly in their firm and of attaining the highest positions varied greatly. *Gadzarts*, for example, did not invariably rise to the rank of engineer. For every Mattern, who became a factory manager and then technical director with responsibility for all the Peugeot works, there were many men of modest background who ended their careers as foremen, section heads, or workshop managers. It must be noted, however, that none remained workmen and all advanced more quickly and to higher positions than those without diplomas.[23] The hierarchy in this respect was unmissable. After the *polytechniciens*, those with the best prospects were former students of the Ecole des Mines and the Ecole Centrale: but by the late nineteenth century, even *centraliens* could not all hope to achieve the very highest rungs of the ladder.[24]

Conditions also varied considerably with the sector. Car manufacturing was well known as an industry for practical engineers, many of them self-taught. Some firms, like Berliet, did not employ diploma-holders, while Citroën showed a marked preference for *gadzarts* and, to a lesser extent, *centraliens*. In general, such men advanced slowly, and their qualifications were rather grudgingly recognized.[25] The textile industry was equally distrustful of engineers, preferring to employ self-taught men or those with diplomas but a lower level of formal training.

In electricity, the big generating and distribution companies, such as the Compagnie Parisienne de Distribution d'Electricité, took on qualified men from the *grandes écoles*, the Ecole Supérieure d'Electricité, and the electrotechnical institutes, giving them the rank of engineer after a short period of training. Diploma-holders of such schools as the Ecole Breguet and the Ecole Sudria started in junior posts, were kept longer working at routine manual tasks, and had less attractive career prospects. The union of electrical engineers summed up the situation of the industry as a whole in pessimistic terms:

> the engineer has none of the advantages that are necessary for a career in management. Length of service gives him no right to promotion, any more than does his value to the firm or his hard work. There are few senior posts open to him as a manager or departmental head ... The engineer without connexions or private means is often condemned to remaining trapped in a subordinate position.[26]

The position was more complicated for chemists, towards whom there was an unmistakeable prejudice in France. Although there was some improvement in the 1920s, chemists were often excluded from promotion anywhere except in the laboratory, and other engineers no better qualified were commonly chosen for posts that did not demand specifically chemical expertise. This was in sharp contrast with the chemical industry in Germany, where chemists were to be found at every level, including the boardroom.

Salaries

An analysis of the pay structure helps us to understand the types of career followed by engineers and to distinguish between their various aspirations and difficulties. It also throws light on such matters as their standard of living and hence on their position in the social hierarchy of their firms and of French society as a whole. Regrettably the information is scanty. In his monumental economic history of France between the wars, Alfred Sauvy contented himself with the statement that 'we are too poorly informed about the remuneration of staff and employees in the private sector to make any judgement'.[27] However, data do exist, and, though incomplete, they allow some conclusions to be drawn.

I take as an example the *gadzarts* employed by the Paris, Lyons, and Marseilles railway (PLM), for whom there are precise figures for the period up to 1914. Generally, *gadzarts* in the PLM started as labourers in the metal shop before moving on to work on locomotives as apprentice mechanics. Starting salaries reflected the ranking of students on leaving their particular school. Those placed first and second earned 6 francs a day; for those who were ranked between third and fifteenth, the daily rate was 5½ francs; those who were less well placed had to make do with 5 francs.[28] 'Six francs per working day – barely 150 francs a month – or the wages of an ordinary draftsman, even an eighteen-year-old labourer' was the rather embittered comment of one career-guide written by a *gadzart*.[29] Thereafter, *gadzarts* moved up through the three grades of fireman, then the four grades of mechanic, before reaching the rank of chief mechanic at an annual salary of 3,300 francs (275 francs a month). Further promotion was then possible through the four grades of assistant depot manager to a final position as depot manager, but only a tiny minority could hope one day to reach the rank of chief locomotive engineer. Of the 219 *gadzarts* employed by the PLM in 1909, only six became either assistant or chief locomotive engineers. Their salaries are not recorded, but the 92 assistant and depot managers earned between 3,600 and 7,000 francs a year (300 and 580 francs a month). This represented a four-fold increase in earnings by comparison with the level on entry.

Of course, there were also fringe benefits (such as administrative and lodging allowances for depot managers and free travel), but these were not substantial. It should be added that *gadzarts* earned less on the railways than in other sectors, although newly appointed electricians on the Paris Métro earned 200 francs a month, rising to 225 francs, while in the municipal technical departments the scale rose to ten times the starting pay. In these departments, 100 francs a month was normal for a general assistant, while city engineers, at the top of the hierarchy, in positions that were highly prized and rarely attained, could earn 1,000 francs.

Incomplete though they are, these figures deserve comment. A full-time craftsman in Paris at the time would earn an average of about 2,700 francs a year (225 francs per month),[30] so that there was only a narrow differential between his wage and the sum that an engineer with a diploma from one of the *écoles d'arts et métiers* could expect after fifteen or twenty years of service. The narrowness of the differential is significant, since before 1914 *gadzarts* established the norms for the salaries of practising engineers (except for graduates of the *grandes écoles*). They supplied the mass of the senior workforce, and the *écoles d'arts et métiers* served as a natural model for the other schools. The Ecole Breguet, for example, aimed to make its diploma-holders 'electrical *gadzarts*', while the Institut Chimique in the Faculty of Science at Lille set out to supply industry with '*gadzarts* in chemistry'.

Far more information is available for the post-war period, when engineers as a whole became increasingly aware that they formed a sector of the nation's manpower with particular interests to defend. They built up their professional associations and started to examine questions of salary. In such discussions two yardsticks were used repeatedly: first, how the salary compared with the incomes of labourers, and, secondly, how adequately it met their own and their families' needs. These measures were of course constantly combined, not to say confused, but they were part of a wider problem of status. It was taken as axiomatic that comparisons with labourers' pay should reflect the engineer's authority and his rank in the hierarchy of the firm. Could an engineer be in charge of workmen who earned almost as much as he did? What should be the norm for the pay differential between a manager and his subordinates? And how was recognition to be won for the specific title of engineer, in a way that would distinguish its holders from less qualified staff promoted from the rank and file, unless some differential was incorporated from the starting point on the salary scale?

These questions gradually developed into pay demands similar to those made by the trade unions, especially in 1936–7. When discussions touched on the question of how much an engineer must earn to keep himself and his family properly, the whole notion of needs was obscured by elusive considerations having to do with the social environment. Engineers had a position to maintain in society, and their standard of reference was middle-class life. During the depression of the 1930s, the fear of no longer having the means to realize their social aspirations grew into an obsessive dread of losing status,[31] and as this happened, it generated a widespread feeling among engineers that they had suffered a glaring injustice.

To assess the justness of this view, the pay of engineers has to be compared with that of skilled factory workers. In fact, the comparison is not easy. For workmen's wages were based on an hourly or daily rate, supplemented by overtime and other extra pay for night shifts, all of which could increase the basic wage by 10 per cent.[32] Engineers' salaries, by contrast, were calculated on an annual or monthly basis, and did not always include extra benefits, such as subsidized or free housing and profit-sharing schemes. These extras differed from one firm to another, so that the figures I have assembled must be taken as approximations, although they serve for the purposes of comparison. For workmen, the figure given for the monthly salary is based on a 48-hour week (the law passed on 23 April 1919 having established the eight-hour day) and a four-week month.

It would be beyond the scope of this chapter to reproduce all the evidence. But putting together the data for the period about 1925, it is evident that, as far as salary was concerned, the career of an engineer can be divided into three periods. In the first of these, from the time of appointment, he would earn between 700 and 1,000 francs a month. Thereafter, a position of responsibility in mid-career would bring in between 1,500 and 2,000 francs. Those who went on to become technical directors or factory managers were paid between 2,500 and 3,000 francs, or more, and at this level they often shared in the profits. Naturally, these figures varied with the size of firms and with the different sectors of industry. But in 1925, 63 per cent of electrical engineers and over 80 per cent of chemical engineers were still earning less than 2,500 francs a month.[33] About the same period, a metal-worker in the aircraft industry earned 624 francs a month (calculated from an hourly rate of 3.25 francs) and a craftsman 925 francs, while in the metal industry, a skilled worker in the Paris region was paid 753 francs (corresponding to 3.92 francs an hour).

In 1925 the Union Sociale d'Ingénieurs Catholiques (USIC) calculated a standard budget for an engineer with a wife and two children, compared with that for a working-class family of the same size. Assuming a similar expenditure on food, it was the cost of other items (especially clothes and housing) that put a strain on the engineer's budget. In theory, he needed 16,636 francs a year for his basic needs (without extras like holidays or buying a car), compared with 10,835 francs for a working-class family. To achieve this, he would require an income of 1400 francs a month, a figure which, as we have seen, far exceeded the earnings of young engineers at the time. According to the USIC, an average of seven years in the profession was necessary before that level of pay was attained.[34]

Defending professional status: the special role of the engineer

Pay claims, like other demands for material benefits, such as family allowances (for which the USIC began to campaign in 1922) or the extension to engineers of the social security benefits granted to executive staff by the law of 1928, were not properly a matter for the traditional engineering associations that gathered together the former students of the different schools. Consequently, a number of unions were formed between the wars. Though very diverse in membership and ideology, they shared a commitment to defending their common interests, and at the end of the 1930s they merged in a single confederation, the Fédération Nationale des Syndicats d'Ingénieurs (FNSI).[35] It has often been said that these engineering unions were weak in both numbers and influence when it came to confronting politicians and economic decision-makers. That judgement, however, needs to be qualified. Engineers were poorly equipped, by training and professional outlook, for collective action. They were used to giving their allegiance to their school and, as a result, they had to overcome an ingrained restraint that made it hard for them to work together as a socio-professional body. Moreover, their position in the hierarchy of their firms discouraged them from making overt demands on pay and other matters. Hence, they tended to remain isolated, trapped in small industrial units and unable to join easily in trade union activities.

Even so, though recently established, the unions succeeded in recruiting members. By the early 1930s some 10,000–11,000 engineers had joined the USIC, the Union Syndicale des Ingénieurs Français (USIF), the Chambre Syndicale des Ingénieurs, or one of the industrial unions, such as those for metallurgical or mining engineers. As the total number of practising engineers before the Second World War was between 50,000 and 60,000, union membership stood at 20 per cent of the total. Since the unions had come into existence after the First World War (the USIC dated from the nineteenth century but did not act as a union until 1918), their memberships are of some significance. A start was made in meeting the demands of the new unions in 1934, and the process continued under the government of the Popular Front in 1936–8.

So engineering unionism went its own distinctive way. While it could not follow the example of working-class militancy, it had gradually to move away from the attitudes and methods of the traditional old students' associations and make engineers conscious of the common problems they all faced. Initially, union activity took the form of measures to make the profession aware of its working conditions: hence the inquiries into engineers' incomes and way of life. The next task was to justify the claim for higher pay by insisting on the vital part played by engineers in industry. Here, the associations had a long tradition of extolling the engineer's mission, and the unions duly took over this rhetoric, while adapting it to the changing circumstances of modern industry. Inevitably, a variety of aspects of the mission were emphasized, but the ideal type that emerges from their accounts has three features in common. First, the engineer, by his training, was the 'technical man', the intermediary between scientific discovery and its application in industry; secondly, he was an 'organization man', concerned with rationalizing the production process and keeping down its costs; finally, he was the man of consensus who stood at the focus of often conflicting views and whose position in the firm enabled him uniquely to bring employer and workmen together in a spirit of shared endeavour.

Conclusion

The system of training for engineers that emerges from this study seems both near and remote. It is near to us in the sense that engineering training in France still bears the marks of its original organizational structure. These marks include the practice of creating small independent schools in response to the appearance of new technologies, instead of extending the functions of existing establishments; the existence of a wide variety of bodies involved in the establishment and development of such schools; and an institutional structure at once complex and slow to change. Likewise, a number of the social and other problems I have discussed remain central concerns of the engineering profession today. In many respects, however, things have changed quite fundamentally. It would serve no purpose to enumerate all the differences, but there is one that deserves special mention. The number of engineers in France in 1939 could be measured in tens of thousands, and even then they thought the profession overcrowded. Now the figure is over 600,000, yet the increase has not led to the proletarization of the profession, as was prophesied by the sociologists of the 'new working class' in the 1960s. Far from it. With the development of new technologies, engineers are in ever greater demand in all industries, and their incomes continue to rise.

Thus the same type of professional man has had to find his place in very different social and historical situations, and we in turn, as historians, must be careful not to derive our image of yesterday's engineers from our perceptions of the situation in which they find themselves today.

Notes

1 Charles Rodney Day, *Education for the Industrial World. The Ecoles d'Arts et Métiers and the Rise of French Industrial Engineering* (Cambridge, Mass., and London, 1987), chapter 3.

2 Robert Fox, 'Science, the university, and the state in nineteenth-century France', in Gerald L. Geison (ed.), *Professions and the French State, 1700–1900* (Philadelphia, Pa., 1984), pp. 66–145; Robert Fox, 'L'attitude des professeurs des sciences face à l'industrialisation en France entre 1850 et 1914', in Christophe Charle and Régine Ferré (eds.), *Le personnel de l'enseignement supérieur en France aux XIXe et XXe siècles* (Paris, 1985), pp. 135–49; André Grelon, 'Les universités et la formation des ingénieurs en France (1870–1914)', *Formation-Emploi*, nos. 27–8 (1989), 65–88; Terry Shinn, 'The French science faculty system, 1808–1914: institutional change and research potential in mathematics and the physical sciences', *Historical Studies in the Physical Sciences*, 10 (1979), 271–332.

3 André Grelon, 'Les origines et le développement des écoles d'électricité Breguet, Charliat, Sudria et Violet avant la seconde guerre mondiale', *Bulletin d'histoire de l'électricité*, 11 (1988), 121–43.

4 Eda Kranakis, 'Social determinants of engineering practice: comparative view of France and America in the nineteenth century', *Social Studies of Science*, 19 (1989), 5–70.

5 Day, *Education for the Industrial World*, first part.

6 Terry Shinn, 'Des sciences industrielles aux sciences fondamentales: la mutation de l'Ecole Supérieure de Physique et de Chimie (1882–1970)', *Revue française de sociologie*, 22 (1981), 167–82.

7 Antoine Picon, *L'invention de l'ingénieur moderne. L'Ecole des Ponts et Chaussées, 1747–1851* (Paris, 1992).

8 Max Leclerc, *La formation des ingénieurs à l'étranger et en France. Nos instituts techniques, nos grandes écoles* (Paris, 1917).

9 Georges Ribeill, 'Des ingénieurs civils en quête d'un titre: le cas de l'Ecole des Ponts et Chaussées (1851–1934)', in André Grelon (ed.), *Les ingénieurs de la crise. Titre et profession entre les deux guerres* (Paris, 1986), pp. 197–209.

10 International Labour Office, *Les conditions de vie des ingénieurs et des chimistes* (Geneva, 1924), Etudes et documents, series L: Travailleurs intellectuels, no. 1.

11 Grelon, *Les ingénieurs de la crise*, part II.

12 International Labour Office. *Commission Consultative des Travailleurs Intellectuels. Fourth session. Preliminary Report on the Protection of the Title and Professional Organization of Engineers and Architects by M. T. Nissot, Delegate of the Belgian Confédération des Travailleurs Intellectuels* (Geneva, 1933).

13 Henri Morsel, 'Le patronat alpin français et la seconde révolution industrielle 1869–1939', in Maurice Lévy-Leboyer (ed.), *Le patronat de la seconde industrialisation* (Paris, 1979), pp. 201–8.

14 Jean-Pierre Daviet, *Un destin multinational. La Compagnie de Saint-Gobain de 1830 à 1939* (Paris, 1988).

15 Pierre Cayez, *Crises et croissance de l'industrie lyonnaise, 1850–1900* (Paris, 1980), pp. 177–8.
16 Yves Cohen, 'Titre d'entreprise contre diplôme d'ingénieur. Les ingénieurs gèrent les ingénieurs entre les deux guerres', in Grelon, *Les ingénieurs de la crise*, p. 91.
17 Cohen, 'Titre d'entreprise', p. 77. Guides to careers pointed out that car manufacturers similarly regarded the diploma as a recommendation rather than a formal qualification.
18 Paul Blancarnoux, *Du choix d'une carrière industrielle* (Paris, 1904), pp. 319–20.
19 G. Valran, *Préjugés d'autrefois et carrières d'aujourd'hui* (Paris and Toulouse, 1908), p. 143.
20 *Guide général CARUS pour la jeunesse* (Paris, n.d. [1925]), p. 435.
21 Yves Mainguy, *La profession d'ingénieur* (Paris, n.d. [1943]).
22 Henri Fayol, *Administration industrielle et générale* (Paris, 1916).
23 Day, *Education for the Industrial World*; Patrice Bourdelais, 'Employés de la grande industrie: les dessinateurs du Creusot, formations et carrières (1850–1914)', *Histoire, économie et société*, 3 (1989), 437–46.
24 Georges Ribeill, 'Entreprendre hier et audjourd'hui: la contribution des ingénieurs', *Culture technique*, no. 12 (1984), 77–92.
25 Patrick Fridenson, 'Les ingénieurs et cadres de l'automobile en France au XXe siècle', in Pierre Joutard and Jean Lecuir (eds.), *Histoire sociale, sensibilités collectives et mentalités. Mélanges Robert Mandrou* (Paris, 1985), pp. 431–48.
26 'La carrière d'ingénieur électricien', in *Les dossiers de l'action populaire*, no. 553 (25 May 1930), 895–904.
27 Alfred Sauvy, *Histoire économique de la France entre les deux guerres*, 3 vols. (Paris, 1984), vol. 2, p. 234.
28 Compagnie du PLM, 'Conditions d'admission des élèves des écoles d'arts et métiers dans le service de la traction', 3 pp. (duplicated typescript), 21 June 1909.
29 Blancarnoux, *L'ingénieur des arts et métiers*.
30 Jean and Jacqueline Fourastié, *Pouvoir d'achat, prix et salaires* (Paris, 1977), p. 40.
31 Yoland Mayor, 'Une surproduction sociale: le technicien au chômage', *Annales d'histoire économique et sociale*, 41 (1936), 419–25 (421).
32 Fourastié, *Pouvoir d'achat*, pp. 41–2.
33 From *Guide CARUS*; *L'écho de l'USIC* (1922); Sauvy, *Histoire économique de la France*, vol. 3, p. 370; A. Rosier, *Du chômage intellectuel. De l'encombrement des professions libérales* (Paris, 1934).
34 *L'écho de l'USIC* (June 1926). This USIC inquiry has been analysed in Valérie Gamichon, 'L'U.S.I.C., Union Sociale d'Ingénieurs Catholiques, de cadres et de chefs d'entreprise, 1892–1965', Mémoire de maîtrise, Université Paris X, 1982, pp. 153–60.
35 René Mouriaux, 'Du Front Populaire à la rupture du tripartisme: le syndicalisme cadre dans le creuset de l'histoire', in Marc Descotes and Jean-Louis Robert (eds.), *Clefs pour une histoire du syndicalisme cadre* (Paris, 1984),

p. 115; René Mouriaux, 'Le syndicalisme des ingénieurs et des cadres. Histoire et historiographies', *Culture technique*, no. 12 (1984), 229–38.

36 This aspect of the engineer's role was especially emphasized by Catholic engineers and the USIC. See André Grelon, 'L'ingénieur catholique et son rôle social entre les deux guerres', in Yves Cohen (ed.), *Les chantiers de la paix sociale* (Toulouse: Privat, forthcoming 1994).

37 André Grelon and Françoise Subileau, 'Le Mouvement des cadres chrétiens et la Vie nouvelle: des cadres catholiques militants', *Revue française de science politique*, 39 (1989), 314–40.

3 Technical education and industrial performance in Germany: a triumph of heterogeneity

Wolfgang König

In the literature dealing with the history of education in Germany, it is a commonplace that the high standard of scientific and technical instruction contributed significantly to the country's development into a major economic power. The German universities and *Technische Hochschulen* are traditionally seen as the most important elements in a powerful educational system that produced the scientists and engineers needed by industry.

My chapter raises some objections to this view. First, it argues that the development of the *Technische Hochschulen* in the nineteenth century was more influenced by the striving for social prestige and the requirements of the public service than by the demands of industry: close cooperation between industry and the *Technische Hochschulen* took place for the first time only after 1900, that is at a time when Germany's economic development was already far advanced. Secondly, it argues that if we concentrate exclusively on the *Technische Hochschulen*, we cannot grasp the essential characteristics of the German system of technical education. The system was characterized by a heterogeneous structure composed of a large number of technical schools, in which the so-called *Technische Mittelschulen* (intermediate technical schools) played an important role both qualitatively and quantitatively, being rather better adapted in some respects to meet the demands of industry than the *Technische Hochschulen* were. With respect to the view that technical education should be considered as a major force promoting industrial performance, my final conclusion is that the strength of the German system lay, first and foremost, in its heterogeneous structure and in the large number of engineers who were produced.

German technical education in the early industrial period

In Germany, numerous technical schools, called *Gewerbeschulen* and *Polytechnische Schulen*, were established between 1821 and 1836 (see

Table 3.1. *Dates of the foundation of German technical schools (*Gewerbeschulen *and* Polytechnische Schulen, *later developed as* Technische Hochschulen*)*

1821	Berlin
1825	Karlsruhe
1827	Munich
1828	Dresden
1829	Stuttgart
1831	Hanover
1835	Braunschweig
1836	Darmstadt
1870	Aachen
1904	TH Danzig
1910	TH Breslau

table 3.1).[1] The main purpose of these foundations was to catch up with Great Britain in industrialization. Franz Schnabel, the German historian of engineering education, has pointed out that 'Konstitution und Maschine' (literally, constitutions and machinery, meaning respectively the liberal intelligentsia and the industrialists) were the most active interest groups that favoured the foundation of technical schools.[2] However, when the history of the various foundations is examined more closely, it emerges that the liberal bureaucracy in the different German *Länder* played a more important role.

One indication of the contribution of bureaucracy and government is that all the technical schools were established in the capitals. From the beginnings of technical education in Germany, in fact, a considerable discrepancy existed between goals and realities in the promotion of industry. In the case of most of the technical schools, there is no evidence of any substantial flow of graduates into the few modern industrial firms. Most of those who taught in these schools had no contact with trade and industry. Moreover, the German *Länder* were completely independent of one another as far as the conceptualization and realization of their plans for technical education were concerned. In each of them, the experiences of the older schools influenced the organization of the later ones, and each *Land* adjusted its school system to its own special needs. In this manner, a heterogeneous system of highly individualistic technical schools developed which can only be summarized here in a very cursory way.

In the different technical schools, there were two competing concepts of technical education. The concept of *technische Allgemeinbildung* (general technical training) made a virtue of necessity. Since most of the schools had only small teaching staffs, it was not possible to offer a separate course for each individual profession. *Technische Allgemeinbildung* was broadly conceived for the education of merchants, civil servants, and other professional men who had something to do with trade and industry, but not of engineers and entrepreneurs. The competing concept of *technische Spezialbildung* (specialized technical training) was designed, first and foremost, for the technical branches of the public services and only secondarily for private industry. On this conception, the technical schools had a departmental organization. Most of the departments, such as the *Bauschule* (department of architecture), *Ingenieurschule* (department of engineering), *Postschule* (department of postal services), *Forstschule* (department of forestry), and so on, were organized according to the requirements of the public service concerned. Other departments, like the *Handelsschule* (department of commerce) and, in particular, the *Gewerbeschule* (department of trade) offered training for private industry. But it was only from the 1840s, when the *Gewerbeschule* were divided into departments of mechanical engineering and chemical engineering, that the technical schools began to offer an engineering education in a modern sense. Most of their graduates entered one of the public services, where engineers were needed for such tasks as building railways, highways, canals, and dams. In some German states, however, only the lower level of technical servants were trained at these schools, while higher-status public servants were trained at the universities. For instance, in Hesse-Darmstadt, until 1866, upper-level engineers had to attend the university of Giessen, where an engineering programme existed until 1873.

The most important exception to this German system of technical education was the Prussian model, which was introduced by Christian Peter Wilhelm Beuth in the 1820s.[3] Peter Lundgreen has described the Gewerbeinstitut in Berlin, which was the central element in the model, as the prototype of the technical schools in the early period of industrialization ('Prototyp der frühindustriellen Technikerschule'). As I see it, the implication of such an interpretation is that the Prussian model was successful in supplying technicians for trade and industry. But the fact remains that the model was not adopted in most of the other German *Länder*.

The Prussian model exerted its greatest influence in Saxony, where a two-tier system of *Gewerbeschulen* was introduced. The system was similar in structure to that of Prussia, where the *Gewerbeinstitut* occupied the higher level and the *Provinzial-Gewerbeschulen* formed the lower one. The most distinctive characteristics of the Prussian *Gewerbeinstitut* were that the greater part of the training was given in workshops and that Beuth established and maintained contacts with trade and industry, with the intention of placing the graduates in suitable employment. Secondly, the Prussian model differed from that of other *Länder* in that it strictly separated training for the public services from training for private industry. Engineers who intended to enter a public service had to study at the *Bauakademie* until 1879, when the *Bauakademie* and the *Gewerbeakademie* merged to form the *Technische Hochschule* of Berlin. In this way, a varied and complex system of technical education came to exist in Germany in the mid nineteenth century. It offered a large number of schools, structured in a rather incoherent way that reflected the state of political disunion.

The development of the *Technische Hochschulen*

Between 1850 and 1900, the academic standing of research and teaching in the *Polytechnische Schulen* was raised.[4] This movement rested on a decidedly ambivalent attitude, within the *Polytechnische Schulen*, towards the universities. On the one hand, representatives of the *Polytechnische Schulen* attacked the universities on the grounds that they were detached from the real problems of life. On the other hand, however, they adjusted to the norms of the universities, with regard to their constitutions and their conception of science. It was symptomatic of this development that the *Polytechnische Schulen* were allowed to change their names to *Technische Hochschulen* between 1877 and 1890 (see table 3.2), and that, as *Technische Hochschulen*, they received the right to confer doctoral degrees between 1899 and 1901. The most important representative of this so-called emancipation movement (*Emanzipationsbewegung*), which struggled for a status equal to that of the uni-

Table 3.2. *Dates of the renaming of the German* Polytechnische Schulen *as* Technische Hochschulen

1877	Braunschweig
	Munich
1879	Berlin
	Darmstadt
1880	Aachen
	Hanover
1885	Karlsruhe
1890	Dresden
	Stuttgart

versities, was the Verein Deutscher Ingenieure (VDI), founded in 1856.[5] Through their membership of the VDI, the teachers in the *Polytechnische Schulen* and *Technische Hochschulen* managed to raise their social status as well. In the developments at the *Technische Hochschulen* during this period, social motivations were more important than the needs of trade and industry.

The *Technische Hochschulen* strove for constitutional privileges comparable with those possessed by the universities, notably, the right to elect their own rectors. They also strove for symbolic tokens, such as a golden rectorial chain and the right to use the title 'Magnifizenz'. However, more important for my present purpose was the upgrading of the entrance requirements and of the level of teaching. Immediately, the *Technische Hochschulen* adopted the standards of *Allgemeinbildung* which were enshrined in the general education offered by the humanistische Gymnasium, and the neo-humanistic concept of *Bildung*, which emphasized the importance of the old classical languages. The VDI reflected these ideals when it stated in 1886: 'We declare that German engineers have the same need with respect to their general education, and that they wish to be judged in the same manner as other professions for which higher scientific education is required'.[6]

In the first few decades after the founding of the *Gewerbeschulen* and *Polytechnische Schulen*, students embarking on their studies possessed a relatively low standard of primary education. Hence, a good deal of basic knowledge had to be conveyed, especially in mathematics, science, and the German language; this was done in the *Vorschulen* (preparatory schools) which were integrated into the *Gewerbeschulen*. When, during the nineteenth century, the entrance requirements were raised, these *Vorschulen* lost their function and were closed. In this respect, the Polytechnische Schule Zürich, founded in 1855,[7] became a model which from the start had no *Vorschule*, since its students were recruited from the excellent intermediate technical schools in Switzerland. In the German *Polytechnische Schulen*, most of the *Vorschulen* were closed between 1865 and 1880, and in parallel with this development, the number of obligatory terms of study was increased.

Henceforth, the *Polytechnische Schulen* and *Technische Hochschulen* recruited their students from the eight-year secondary schools (*Realschulen* and *Gymnasien*) which were dominated by the ideals of neo-humanism. As this happened, the graduates of the intermediate technical schools lost the right to enter the *Polytechnische Schulen*.[8] This development occurred even though the intermediate technical schools offered, quite apart from technical subjects, a better curriculum in mathematics and the sciences than the general secondary schools. As a result, through a series of reorganizations between 1870 and 1882, most of the intermediate technical schools in Prussia were transformed into general schools.

In this same period, however, the assimilation, by the technical schools, of the neo-humanist conception of *Bildung* was accompanied by the rise of the quite distinct concept of 'realistic' *Bildung*, which subsequently came to dominate and oust the humanistic concept. In place of the classical languages, the champions of this concept promoted mathematics, science, and modern languages. In particular, they claimed that the examinations of the *Oberrealschulen*, predominantly in mathematics and the sciences, and the *Realgymnasien*, largely focussed on modern languages, should be regarded as equivalent to the examinations of the *Humanistische Gymnasium*, as far as admission to the universities and *Technische Hochschulen* was concerned. Gradually, the movement achieved its aims. For instance, in Prussia, from 1870, graduates of the *Realgymnasien*, which at the time were called 'Realschulen I. Ordnung', and, from 1891, graduates of the *Oberrealschulen* were allowed to study modern languages and science at the universities. It was only some years later, in 1900, that equivalence was given to the *Oberrealschulen* and *Realgymnasien* by a conference in which the decisions were influenced by Kaiser Wilhelm II himself. Even after this conference, however, graduates of the *Realschulen* had to pass special examinations before embarking on such studies as theology and medicine. As a result, professors in the *Technische Hochschulen* discussed the possible counter-measure of requiring special examinations for the graduates of the *Humanistische Gymnasium*, on the grounds that their knowledge in mathematics and the sciences would not be sufficient. In the event, these special examinations were not introduced, although some *Technische Hochschulen* did allow the students coming from the *Oberrealschulen* to complete their studies more quickly than students from *Humanistische Gymnasien*.

The raising of the entrance requirements for the *Polytechnische Schulen* and the *Technische Hochschulen* was also influenced by the requirements of the technical branches of the public services.[9] For many years, only engineers who had attended a *Humanistisches Gymnasium* were allowed to enter the public service sector; and even after the equal status of the *Realschulen* was accepted at the school conference in Prussia in 1900, in certain other *Länder* – Mecklenburg, for instance – this requirement persisted. Throughout the nineteenth century, the social standing of engineers in the public services remained a focus of aspiration for engineers in private industry and for the technical schools. During the first half of the century, in fact, trade and industry in some German *Länder* were so underdeveloped that the *Gewerbeschulen* and the *Poly-*

technische Schulen could not have existed unless they had trained engineers for the public services. In several cases, the renaming of *Gewerbeschulen* as *Polytechnische Schulen* served to confirm that the technical schools had now become the main institutions for the training of engineers for this type of employment. One consequence was that the requirements of the public services influenced the development of the technical schools as well as the formation of the whole engineering profession. Historians have consequently spoken of a 'Berufskonstruktion durch den Staat', arguing that the engineering profession was designed by the state. As late as 1911, in the journal of the VDI, the *Zeitschrift des VDI*, complaints were voiced that the training in the *Technische Hochschulen* was unduly oriented to the public services[10] – a situation that was not helped by the fact that certain subjects relevant to important branches of private industry, such as textiles, were not taught at the *Technische Hochschulen*.

Just as the *Technische Hochschulen* absorbed their ideals of *Bildung* from the universities and the *Humanistische Gymnasien*, so the technical disciplines drew their standards of scientific methodology from the natural sciences and mathematics.[11] Engineering was regarded as an applied natural science standing at the interface between science and industry. The main objective of the theory of machines, for instance, was the construction of mathematical models representing the machines. At the *Technische Hochschulen*, devising these models entailed detailed calculations based on technological rules deduced from natural laws. The problem was, however, that the models, as well as the other premises of the calculations, were not at all exact, so that, in most cases, the results were only marginally relevant to the real tasks of engineering construction. In 1894, for instance, a critic cited the example of the progress in the construction of steam engines in recent decades, for which the mechanical theory of heat had been less important than the experiments, observations, and measurements of practising engineers.[12]

This 'overtheorization' of technology led to a widening gap between the theory of machines as taught in the *Technische Hochschulen* and the practice of machine construction in industry. The *Technische Hochschulen* accepted the development since it bestowed on them some of the social prestige associated with mathematics and the natural sciences, which assumed a new symbolic significance as the universities shifted their philosophical allegiance increasingly to positivism. This assimilation of the *Technische Hochschulen* to the model of the universities was encouraged and guided initially by the teachers in the *Technische Hochschulen*, who saw in it the additional advantage of being able to enhance their social status. This was also a period, after 1865, when these same teachers played a decisive role in the formulation of standards in technical education. For during the discussions within the VDI in the 1860s and 1870s, employers and industrial engineers alike declared that they were not competent to deal with such questions. In general, however, employers were convinced that technical education would have a beneficial effect on trade and industry. This became clear in the 1860s, for instance, when industrialists in the region of Aachen supported the plans to found a *Polytechnische Schule* through political addresses as well as by financial aid; by 1870, their support made it virtually inevitable that the *Polytechnische Schule* should be founded in Aachen and not in Cologne.

As the *Technische Hochschulen* continued to raise their entrance requirements and the theoretical level of their teaching, however, critical remarks from industry became more common. Whereas before 1865, it was above all the bureaucrats, and after 1865, the teachers in the technical schools who dominated the formation of the system of engineering education in Germany, the situation changed markedly in the 1880s and 1890s. Now, employers, managers, and industrial engineers began to take part in the debate. They complained that studies at the *Technische Hochschulen* lasted too long, that the graduates had a good education in the theory of machines, physics, and mathematics, but a rather poor one in economic subjects and production technology, and therefore that it took months, even years, before a graduate of a *Technische Hochschule* could work in a factory without assistance. Such a graduate would be well suited for work in the drawing or design office, but was not at all the right man for the workshops. In response to these criticisms, especially in the 1890s, reforms affecting teaching, research, and organization were undertaken which significantly changed the *Technische Hochschulen* as well as the general system of engineering education. Now, distinctive elements were introduced into the system – the very ones that foreign contemporaries saw as constituting the so-called German model.

Intermediate technical education and the market

About the middle of the nineteenth century, a consecutive system of technical education existed in Germany. Graduates of the intermediate technical schools could start work in industry or they could enter a higher technical school. From the 1870s, the intermediate technical schools were transformed into *allgemeinbildende Schulen* (general secondary schools): in Prussia, for example, in the 1870s and early 1880s, the *Provinzial-Gewerbeschulen* became *Realschulen*, and in 1902, in Bavaria, the *Indu-*

strieschulen became *Oberrealschulen*. In this way, governments met the demands of the teachers in the *Technische Hochschulen*, who wanted to enhance the *Allgemeinbildung* of the students they admitted and thereby also the social prestige of the *Technische Hochschulen* and the engineering profession. But the reforms had the effect of destroying the intermediate level in technical education. Technicians and engineers possessing qualifications at this level, which were in great demand in industry, were no longer produced, at least not in state schools, and through the 1880s and 1890s, industrialists, who now began to engage seriously in the promotion of technical education, urged that the gap in the system should be filled. About the turn of the century, the campaign had some effect. A number of new technical schools were created by the *Länder* and the cities and through private initiatives; these came to be known as *Technische Mittelschulen* (intermediate technical schools), a name that distinguished them from the *Technische Hochschulen*. The individual *Technische Mittelschulen* had names like Technikum, Polytechnikum, Maschinenbauschule, Baugewerkschule, among others.

The most important voice in the campaign for the foundation of new intermediate technical schools was that of the VDI.[13] It was also felt that the reforms would ease the pressure on the *Technische Hochschulen*, where there were large numbers of visiting students who left without taking the examinations. In 1888, the VDI published its 'Leitsätze zur Entwicklung Technischer Mittelschulen' (guide-lines for the development of intermediate technical schools). As part of these guide-lines, the VDI urged the foundation, by the state, of intermediate technical schools for mechanical engineering, in which managers as well as design engineers would be trained. On the entrance requirements for the *Technische Mittelschulen* there were two different opinions. One group argued for a rather modest level of theoretical requirements, allied to a more practical training in industry lasting three years. The other group, which finally prevailed, argued for a practical training of only two years and entrance requirements of a more demanding theoretical standard, equivalent to the so-called *Einjährige* – a certificate of education, obtained typically about the age of sixteen, that allowed the holder to complete his military service in only one year. Besides the shorter military service, the *Einjährige* was also proof that the candidate belonged to an upper social class.

The principles of the VDI's policy were subsequently accepted by the Prussian bureaucracy. The first intermediate technical schools conforming to them were established in Cologne and Dortmund, in the industrialized regions of the Rhineland and Westphalia. The school in Cologne, dating from 1891, was a municipal one that received financial support from the VDI for several years. It is notable that the entrance requirements of the Cologne school were not as severe as the majority of members in the VDI had proposed they should be: here the *Einjährige* was waived, and preparatory courses were introduced to improve the general education of the entrants. In Dortmund, the Prussian state took over a number of existing technical schools in 1893, uniting and reorganizing them in accordance with the principles of the VDI. Most of the graduates entered private industry or the Prussian railways as public servants. Practical training was an important part of the curriculum, and it was as an essential element of the school's policy that, in 1897, a new building was opened to house laboratories and technical apparatus. There were professors who complained that some *Technische Mittelschulen* were better equipped with technical apparatus than the *Technische Hochschulen*. The school in Dortmund was outstanding in this respect, and it became the model for other *Technische Mittelschulen* in Prussia.

Even after the reforms in Prussia and in other German *Länder*, the system of technical schools was very heterogeneous. First, there were higher-level *Technische Mittelschulen*: here, the entrance requirement was the *Einjährige*, although this was often replaced by entrance examinations, which gave pupils with lower qualifications an opportunity of entering. This type of school had been developed, as we have seen, as *Höhere Maschinenbauschule* (higher schools of mechanical engineering) in Prussia: the model for such schools was later adopted by other German *Länder* and extended to other technical branches, such as electrical engineering, civil engineering, and textile engineering. Secondly, there were *Technische Mittelschulen* at a lower level, in which the course lasted either one or two years. In these schools, the entrance requirement was the leaving-certificate of a primary school, allied to practical experience in industry for between three and six years.

The separation of higher from lower technical intermediate schools was strict, especially in Prussia. Initially, the VDI was opposed to the lower *Technische Mittelschulen* in Prussia and campaigned to have them converted into higher ones. To replace the lower *Technische Mittelschulen*, the VDI proposed another type of school that would specialize in training *Werkmeister* (foremen) for industry. It was intended that these so-called *Werkmeisterschulen* should offer a training of between twelve and eighteen months. After 1901, industry established some experimental schools along these lines, but the schools did not succeed. Over the next few decades, the *Höhere Technische Mittelschulen* developed into *Ingenieurschulen* and finally into *Fachhochschulen*, which today, together with the *Technische Hochschulen* and *Technische Universitäten* make up the two-tier system of engineering education in Germany. The

Niedere Technische Mittelschulen were transformed into *Höhere Technische Mittelschulen* or developed into *Technikerschulen*, which still exist.

At the end of the nineteenth century, the situation was further complicated by the fact that, in addition to the technical schools organized by the *Länder*, there also existed many private technical schools. These schools had been established since the 1870s to fill the gap in technical education left by the upgrading of the *Technische Hochschulen*. A second push to expand private technical education occurred about the turn of the century, with important consequences. Before the First World War, in fact, the private technical schools had more pupils than those under governmental control. Most of them were in the small and medium-sized German *Länder* in Thuringia and Saxony, where the state, for financial reasons, was unable to set up its own technical schools. They were attended by a large number of students from Prussia, who later went back into Prussian industry, which was suffering from a lack of *Technische Mittelschulen*.[14]

The private technical schools run by the towns, like those run by individuals, were more flexible than the state-schools. Whereas the state-schools oriented their curricula, at least in part, to the examination requirements of the public services, which changed rather slowly, the private schools adjusted their programmes to the demands of industry and tried to attract students by offering subjects that were not readily available elsewhere: for example, at a very early stage, they included lectures on automobile and aircraft technology. Because there was no control over the private technical schools, some 'black sheep' were known to be undemanding both in their entrance requirements and in their curricula, as a way of attracting as many students as possible. In reaction, during the years just before the First World War, the VDI and other organizations and committees cooperated with the most respected private schools in imposing standards and a form of state supervision for the private technical schools.

Reforming the *Technische Hochschulen*

In the 1890s, not only intermediate technical education, but also higher technical education, including research in the *Technische Hochschulen*, underwent a marked change. Against the overtheorization of the *Technische Hochschulen*, with their emphasis on mathematics and science, critics advocated methods such as demonstration, observation, and experimentation, for which the *Technische Hochschulen* were not at all well equipped. Such small mechanical workshops as existed were mainly used for the construction of demonstration apparatus for use in teaching, and instruction consisted primarily of theoretical lectures, demonstrations involving the use of models, and exercises in design. Visits to industrial firms provided the only means of obtaining any impression of the problems of engineering practice.

To improve the conditions for teaching and research in the *Technische Hochschulen*, laboratories were essential. Since the late 1860s, the *Technische Hochschulen* had housed institutions for the testing of materials. These institutions had been important for civil engineering but far less so for mechanical engineering. From the 1880s, therefore, engineering professors demanded the setting up of mechanical laboratories. In the wake of the exhibition at Philadelphia in 1876 and the World Exhibition in Chicago in 1893, German professors were eager to point out the high standard of the American machine-tool industry. After the Chicago exhibition, it was held that the high standard was, above all, a result of education and research, which was conducted in the mechanical laboratories of American engineering institutes. In addition, both industrialists and professors of engineering in Germany were disappointed by the research done at the Physikalisch-Technische Reichsanstalt (PTR), which was founded in 1887. At the PTR, basic research in physics had pride of place, while the technical department remained in the shadow of physics and was eventually closed. In these circumstances, in 1895, the VDI adopted the demands of the engineering professors and proposed the foundation of mechanical laboratories for all German *Technische Hochschulen*, to be used both for education and for research. Thereafter, the demands of the VDI were realized with remarkable alacrity by the governments of the various German *Länder*. Governmental spending for science and technology as a whole was increased, although the lion's share went to the *Technische Hochschulen*, which found themselves comparatively spoiled.

The establishment of laboratories for mechanical engineering at the *Technische Hochschulen* was a precondition for bridging the gulf that separated theory and practice. Now, it was possible to develop a specific methodology of engineering science comprising four important elements:

1. gaining technical experience in industry, and deducing technical rules from this experience;
2. deducing technical rules from natural laws;
3. methods of calculation, and;

4. systematic experimenting with machinery of a kind that was also used in industry.

The new laboratories were created, first and foremost, for teaching purposes. But both then and subsequently, when the laboratories were expanded to become true *Versuchsfelder*, they contributed to making the *Technische Hochschulen* better places for research as well. From the middle of the nineteenth century, teachers began to define research as a task of the technical schools. But until the end of the century, industry and the state bureaucracy looked upon the *Technische Hochschulen* as institutions for training rather than as settings for research. Indeed, before 1900, little research was done by the professors of engineering in the *Technische Hochschulen*. It was seen as more important that professors should cooperate, as consultants, with industrial firms and with the technical branches of the public services. This meant that research and development, sometimes supervised by the professors, took place within the firms themselves. This kind of cooperation was facilitated by the frequency with which, in Germany, the top positions in industrial firms were filled by managers who had had a technical education – a fact that made it relatively easy for professors to place their graduates in such firms. An early consequence of these bonds was that when proper research facilities were established in the *Technische Hochschulen*, about the turn of the century, the pace of cooperation in research between industry and the *Technische Hochschulen* quickened.

As a result of this development, recruitment to the posts of professors of engineering changed as well. During the nineteenth century, most professors were promoted from junior teaching positions in the *Technische Hochschulen*. By about 1900, however, besides the doctoral degree and the *Habilitation*, experience in industry was becoming an important criterion for appointment to a chair in engineering science. Another facet was that professors in the *Technische Hochschulen*, in particular in new disciplines like electrical engineering and applied chemistry, sometimes abandoned their academic positions for careers in industrial research and development. In this way, contacts and collaborations between industry and the *Technische Hochschulen* proliferated. For the *Technische Hochschulen*, the development was not without its problems. In particular, it became increasingly difficult to recruit highly qualified men, who could secure more attractive salaries in industry.

In marked contrast with its readiness to cooperate with the *Technische Hochschulen*, German industry at the end of the nineteenth century showed little interest in basic research. Apart from the critical attitudes towards the Physikalisch-Technische Reichsanstalt, to which I have already referred, this is reflected in the efforts of the mathematician Felix Klein, professor at the University of Göttingen, to establish a cooperation in basic research between the universities and industry.[15] Most entrepreneurs rejected the idea. Only at the universities of Göttingen and Jena did Klein's plan enjoy some success. There, industrial foundations and so-called 'applied institutes' were established, and Klein came to be regarded as a pioneer in securing industrial funds for the purpose of basic research in mathematics and physics, performed in the universities. In general, however, the promotion of basic research continued to be regarded as a responsibility of the state.

The mechanical laboratories were quite as successful in their educational function as they were for research. Through them, the *Technische Hochschulen* were able, in some measure, to attain the Humboldtian goal of the unity of research and education (*Einheit von Forschung und Lehre*). Accordingly, engineering education became more practical, a change that diminished the criticisms from industry. Furthermore, the *Technische Hochschulen* introduced a practical year for new pupils, which meant that before admission, school-leavers had to work one year in industry as unpaid trainees. At the *Technische Hochschule* in Stuttgart, the practical year, which at first was required only for the technical branches of the public service, was introduced for all students in 1883, and other *Technische Hochschulen* followed suit in about 1900. However, the practical year too became the object of perpetual reforms. On the one hand, there was always a shortage of trainee places, while on the other hand, there was constant criticism of the arrangements governing the practical year. Even so, professors were convinced that the practical year was one reason for the high quality of engineering education in Germany. When Gisbert Kapp, who worked in industry in Germany as well as in England, became the first head of the electrical engineering department at the University of Birmingham in 1905, he tried to introduce the practical year, but did not succeed.[16]

When, between 1899 and 1901, the German *Technische Hochschulen* received the right to confer doctorates, the most important of their social demands was fulfilled. Thereafter, the discussion within the *Technische Hochschulen* concentrated on the social status of engineers, educational reforms, and the implications of the proliferation of engineering subjects. Emphasizing efficiency and optimization as essential elements in both theory and practice, engineers regarded themselves as the best-qualified leaders for society in general.[17] In this context, all the arguments were advanced which were later to be used in the technocratic movement. The majority of the people involved in the discussions, however, called for additional subjects such as social sciences, law, and economics, which they saw as necessary in order to improve the education of engineers.

Another group of professors that worked to establish a new area of studies in engineering education took as its aim the fashioning of the 'administration engineer' (*Verwaltungsingenieur*), who would be trained in both mechanical engineering and non-technical subjects. Their efforts had a variety of goals. First, they sought to break the monopoly of the jurists in the general public services, an aim that failed completely. Secondly, they were intended to improve the position of the graduates of the *Technische Hochschulen* on the labour market and to provide new professional openings for engineers. Although the success of the efforts is not easily assessed, they indicate that academic engineers had problems on the labour market, and that their qualifications were regarded as too high for normal engineering work.

Another development, which ran counter to this attempt to include non-technical subjects in engineering curricula, was the growth in the number of technical subjects resulting from the institutionalization of new disciplines and the differentiation of older ones.[18] Between 1860 and 1910, the number of engineering subjects doubled about every two decades. Two periods stand out: the years from 1860 to 1880, when the number of civil engineering subjects in particular increased, and the decade 1900–1910, when there was a marked proliferation of specialist areas in mechanical engineering. Whereas the earlier of these periods was marked chiefly by a growth in the responsibilities of the public services, the second was far more influenced by the development of the German machine building and electrical industries. In this latter period, chairs were created for a number of technical and professional subjects, such as steam-engines (including turbines), combustion-engines, automobile technology, aviation, aerodynamics, and machine tools. In addition, general technical fields like thermodynamics, the principles of machines, and materials science were built up. And finally, new programmes of engineering studies corresponding to defined professional tasks, like administration engineering or laboratory engineering, were launched. All this differentiation and specialization resulted, first, from the developments in engineering science and, secondly, from the efforts of the *Technische Hochschulen* to produce graduates with specific qualifications related to the demands of industry.

The increasing number of engineering subjects made reforms of the curricula necessary, but it was also clear that all the new subjects could not be incorporated. It was the German Committee for Technical Education (Deutscher Ausschuss für das technische Schulwesen, or DAtSch) which discussed the matter most thoroughly between 1910 and 1914. The conferences of the DAtSch – which was founded by the VDI, along with other technical, professional, and industrial associations – were attended by employers, managers, industrial engineers, professors of engineering, and delegates of the departments of education of the German *Länder*. The DAtSch was opposed to the growing specialization of curricula and to an extension of any programme of study to more than four years. Hence the main question became how to concentrate the expanding body of subject-matter within a scheme of such restricted duration. However, the DAtSch always spoke up for the autonomy of the *Technische Hochschulen* and avoided giving specific recommendations on their curricula. The result was that the problem was postponed; even today, it remains unresolved.

Enrolments at the *Technische Hochschulen* rose from a minimum in 1885 to a maximum in 1902–3 and then stagnated until the First World War.[19] The stagnation resulted primarily from the fears of an overloading of the programmes of the *Technische Hochschulen*, from an excess of supply over demand on the labour market for engineers that began in the 1890s,[20] and, to a lesser extent, from the restrictive entrance requirements imposed by the *Technische Hochschulen* themselves. After the turn of the century, in fact, there was fierce competition for jobs between the graduates of the *Technische Hochschulen* and the graduates of the *Technische Mittelschulen*. Although we possess no exact figures on the extent of the oversupply of engineers, it seems likely that between 1900 and 1910 about 10,000 graduates of the *Technische Hochschulen* (*Diplom-Ingenieure*) entered the labour market. In addition, there were about 100,000 other engineers, a heterogeneous group consisting of graduates of the *Technische Hochschulen* and the *Technische Mittelschulen* and engineers who had acquired their qualifications in industry. New entrants to the profession found it particularly difficult to find a job and to start their career. Salaries were cut, and a widening gap developed between the graduates' social expectations and their realistic prospects.

In response, some professors of the *Technische Hochschulen* and the Verband Deutscher Diplom-Ingenieure (VDDI) – a new group of academic engineers, founded in 1909 – attempted to exclude the graduates of the *Technische Mittelschulen* from the engineering profession. For example, they strove to secure legal protection for the title 'engineer', which they saw as the preserve of academic graduates, while insisting that the graduates of the *Technische Mittelschulen* should have the title 'technicians'. The lobbyists argued that the graduates of the *Technische Hochschulen* in particular would be better trained for industry than the graduates of the *Technische Mittelschulen*. However, the attempts failed, in the face of vehement opposition from industrial engineers. It became apparent that industry was unwilling to reward the higher scientific qualifications of the graduates of the *Technische Hochschulen*: practical experience and individual performance were far more highly regarded and valued.

Conclusion: technical education and industrial performance

In conclusion, I have to concede that the subject of my chapter – the relations between technical education and industrial performance in Germany – has not been treated exhaustively. As in most of the literature on the topic, my comments have been chiefly concerned with the system of engineering education, whereas the demands of industry for the institution of technical qualifications have been covered rather more cursorily. This brings out the dilemma facing any historian of this aspect of German history. So long as we lack research on the careers of the technical intelligentsia or on the selection processes and recruitment of industrial engineers, the question regarding the relations between technical education and industrial performance cannot be answered properly. The remarks that follow, therefore, are necessarily hypothetical rather than definitive.

In the secondary literature, the role of technical education in general, and of the *Technische Hochschulen* in particular, is traditionally given a central place in attempts to explain Germany's industrial success in the *Kaiserreich*. This judgement accords with the assessment of contemporaries, especially in Germany, who were convinced that the country's superior system of technical education was crucial in her struggle for power and economic advancement. It should be borne in mind, however, that such arguments also had the effect of raising the prestige and social standing of both the engineers and the *Technische Hochschulen*. In other countries, especially in Great Britain, the judgements about German technical education were more varied, even contradictory. While one observer called the provision for the education of engineers in Germany 'a precise national weapon', another judged German engineers as 'disguised mathematicians'.[21] There are many indicators – and I have tried to give some – that lead me to believe that the influence of technical education on industrial performance was overestimated by contemporaries and is overestimated by historians today. In my view, we are justified only in stating that the German system of technical education was not a constraint on the development of industry.

In proposing this modification, I am conscious that the task of explaining the strengths and advantages of the German system of engineering education is merely being transferred to another level of analysis, which it is important, and possible, to broach. As I see it, the success of technical education in Germany and its importance for industry is based on factors other than those advanced by contemporaries and historians, who have emphasized, above all, the rather lofty scientific and theoretical character of the *Technische Hochschulen*. My own inclination is to stress two quite different elements.

The first is the horizontal structure of the German system for training engineers. Essentially, here, I am referring to the large number of technical schools. In 1910 there were eleven *Technische Hochschulen*, three mining colleges (*Bergakademien*), and many *Technische Mittelschulen* of very different kinds. The roots of this horizontal structure lay in the political disunion of Germany before 1871, and in the striving of each *Land* for its own system of technical education. Even after the *Reichsgründung*, the German *Länder* retained their cultural autonomy, so that the initial political weakness of Germany emerged as a source of strength in the system of technical education. Competition between the different technical schools raised the quality of the system as a whole.

The second element that I wish to bring out relates to the vertical structure of the German system. By this, I mean the vertical differentiation of the system of technical education into at least two branches: that of the *Technische Mittelschulen* and that of the *Technische Hochschulen*. This bipartite system had, and still has today, no parallels in other European countries: any comparisons between the German and other systems of technical education, in fact, is inadequate when the *Technische Mittelschulen* are excluded. If we concentrate solely on higher technical education,[22] the results of a comparative study of the various national systems are interesting, but they throw little light on the contribution of technical education to industrial performance.

In any quantitative comparison between the systems of different countries, the difficult decision has to be made as to what kinds of technical schools should be included or excluded. A pioneering study by Peter Lundgreen points to the problematic results that can emerge from such a comparison. In his study, Lundgreen compares the number of instructors and students of science and technology in France on the one hand and Germany and Prussia on the other in the period before the First World War.[23] His conclusion is that the differences were not very marked – a view that he cites as an argument against the traditional view that technical education in France was backward. Even leaving aside discussion of Lundgreen's conclusion, his data are derived on a highly questionable basis. For France, he includes the *écoles d'arts et métiers*, whereas for

Prussia and Germany, he disregards the *Technische Mittelschulen*, which, in fact, trained far more engineers than the *Technische Hochschulen*. The argument that the *écoles d'arts et métiers* demanded a significantly higher level of technical education than the *Technische Mittelschulen* is an unsatisfactory one,[24] since there was a strong similarity between the two types of schools, with respect both to the careers of their graduates and to the positions of these graduates within the engineering profession. In 1907, the *écoles d'arts et métiers* were given the right to bestow the title of *ingénieur des arts et métiers* on their best graduates. The measure was similar to that enshrined in the statutes of the VDI, which allowed most of the graduates of the *Technische Mittelschulen* to become members of the VDI and hence full members of the engineering profession.[25] If we take account both of the data given by Peter Lundgreen and of the considerations I have outlined here, it is hard to avoid the conclusion that at the turn of the century, many more engineers, per capita of the population, were being trained in Germany than in France – a result similar to the conclusion that Göran Ahlström draws from his comparison between Germany and Sweden.[26]

There is abundant evidence that the number of engineers entering German industry after a training in the *Technische Mittelschulen* was far higher than the number of engineers coming from the *Technische Hochschulen*.[27] The most striking (indeed, so far as I can see, the only) data are to be found in a statistical survey published by Reinhold Jaeckel in 1908 (see table 3.3).[28] As Jaeckel shows, the number of graduates of the *Technische Mittelschulen* in the Berlin electrical industry was twice the number of graduates from the *Technische Hochschulen*; in the machine-construction industry the disparity was as much as four times. However, more of the graduates of the *Technische Hochschulen* ended their careers in senior positions, although they always faced competition from those who had passed through the *Technische Mittelschulen*. For instance, twice as many of the leading shop foremen (*Oberingenieure*) and technical directors (*Betriebsleiter*) in the Berlin machine building industry came from the *Technische Mittelschulen* as came from the *Technische Hochschulen*. Moreover, it seems probable that the Berlin figures are flattering to the *Technische Hochschulen*. In the first place, in Berlin the electrical industry, with its higher educational requirements, was stronger than elsewhere in Germany. And secondly, in Prussia in general and Berlin in particular, there was a shortage of intermediate technical schools and engineers. In Berlin, it was not until 1909 that the first *Technische Mittelschule* opened its doors, at the urgent behest of industry. There is no doubt that in Berlin a vertically differentiated system of

Table 3.3. *The training of technical employees in Berlin industry, 1907–8 (given as percentages, with absolute figures in parentheses)*

	All engineers	Higher technical training (Technische Hochschulen)	Medium level of technical training, including self-educated engineers* (Technische Mittelschulen and Fachschulen)
All Industry	100 (3,265)	26.40 (862)	73.60 (2,403)
Machine Construction Industry	100 (1,840)	19.24 (354)	80.76 (1,486)
Electrical Industry	100 (1,209)	34.16 (413)	65.84 (796)

* 4.5 per cent were self-educated engineers. Approximately one third of the employees in the two groups had left their respective schools with no formal examination certificate.
Source: Reinhold Jaeckel, *Statistik über die Lage der Technischen Privatbeamten in Gross-Berlin. Im Auftrage des Bureaus für Sozialpolitik bearbeitet* (Jena, 1908), pp. 1, 4 and 36.

engineering education more nearly fulfilled the needs of industrialists than the *Technische Hochschulen* alone.

Together, these vertical and horizontal elements in German technical education made up a complex and diverse structure that successfully met the varied demands of scientific engineering, private industry, and the public services. There was no German system or exemplification of technical education in any sense that would imply simplicity and order. Also, there was no systematic coordination of technical education with industrial demand. The German system, as I have argued, was the consequence of competing forces and contradictory demands, and its success was a triumph not of planning and order but of heterogeneity.

Notes

1 I only mention the most important works on the special schools, which also serve as a guide to the older literature. For Braunschweig, see Helmuth Albrecht, *Technische Bildung zwischen Wissenschaft und Praxis. Die Technische Hochschule Braunschweig 1862–1914* [Veröffentlichungen der Technischen Universität Carolo-Wilhelmina zu Braunschweig, 1] (Hildesheim, 1987). For Stuttgart, see Jürgen Blum, Karl-Heinz Hunken, August Nitschke, and Gottfried Stute (eds.), *Die Universtät Stuttgart*, volume 2: Johannes H. Voigt (ed.), *Festschrift zum 150-jährigen Bestehen der Universität Stuttgart. Beiträge zur Geschichte der Universität* (Stuttgart, 1979); Gerhard Zweckbronner, *Ingenieurausbildung im Königreich Württemberg. Vorgeschichte,*

Einrichtung und Ausbau der Technischen Hochschule Stuttgart und ihrer Ingenieurwissenschaften bis 1900 – eine Verknüpfung von Institutions–und Disziplingeschichte, [Technik + Arbeit. Schriften des Landesmuseums für Technik und Arbeit in Mannheim, 2] (Stuttgart, 1987). For Aachen, see Hans Martin Klinkenberg (ed.), *Rheinisch-Westfälische Technische Hochschule Aachen 1870–1970*, 2 vols. (Stuttgart, 1970). For Berlin, see Reinhard Rürup (ed.), *Wissenschaft und Gesellschaft. Beiträge zur Geschichte der Technischen Universität Berlin 1879–1979*, 2 vols. (Berlin, 1979). For Hanover, see *Universität Hannover 1831–1981. Festschrift zum 150jährigen Bestehen der Universität Hannover*, vol. 1 (Stuttgart, Berlin, Cologne and Mainz, 1981). For Darmstadt, see Erwin Viefhaus, 'Hochschule-Staat-Gesellschaft. Zur Entstehung und Entwicklung der Technischen Hochschule Darmstadt im 19. und 20. Jahrhundert', in Helmut Böhme (ed.), *100 Jahre Technische Hochschule Darmstadt. Jahrbuch 1976–7* (Darmstadt, 1977), pp. 57–111, and *Jahrbuch 1978–9* (Darmstadt, 1979), pp. 35–102. For Dresden, see Rolf Sonnemann *et al.*, *Geschichte der Technischen Universität Dresden 1828–1978* (Berlin, 1978). Unfortunately, there are no books that can be equally recommended on the *Technische Hochschulen* of Karlsruhe, Munich, Breslau, and Danzig.

For guidance to other literature, see Wolfgang König, 'Stand und Aufgaben der Forschung zur Geschichte der deutschen Polytechnischen Schulen und Technischen Hochschulen im 19. Jahrhundert', *Technikgeschichte*, 48 (1981), 47–67; Lars U. Scholl, 'Die Entstehung der Technischen Hochschulen in Deutschland', in Walter Twellmann (ed.), *Handbuch Schule und Unterricht*, vol. 7, part 2: *Gesellschaft/Umwelt* (Düsseldorf, 1985), pp. 700–15.

2 Franz Schnabel, 'Die Anfänge des technischen Hochschulwesens', in *Festschrift anlässlich des 100jährigen Bestehens der Technischen Hochschule Fridericiana zu Karlsruhe* (Karlsruhe, 1925), pp. 1–44, and Franz Schnabel, *Deutsche Geschichte im neunzehnten Jahrhundert*, vol. 3: *Erfahrungswissenschaften und Technik* (Freiburg, 1954).

3 Peter Lundgreen, *Techniker in Preussen während der frühen Industrialisierung. Ausbildung und Berufsfeld einer entstehenden sozialen Gruppe*, [Einzelveröffentlichungen der Historischen Kommission zu Berlin, 16. Publikationen zur Geschichte der Industrialisierung] (Berlin, 1975).

4 Karl-Heinz Manegold, *Universität, Technische Hochschule und Industrie. Ein Beitrag zur Emanzipation der Technik im 19. Jahrhundert unter besonderer Berücksichtigung der Bestrebungen Felix Kleins* [Schriften zur Wirtschafts- und Sozialgeschichte, 16] (Berlin, 1970).

5 Karl-Heinz Ludwig und Wolfgang König (eds.), *Technik, Ingenieure und Gesellschaft. Geschichte des Vereins Deutscher Ingenieure 1856–1981* (Dusseldorf, 1981), and Kees Gispen, *New Profession, Old Order. Engineers and German Society, 1815–1914* (Cambridge, 1989).

6 Quoted in Ludwig and König, *Technik, Ingenieure und Gesellschaft*, p. 141.

7 Gottfried Guggenbühl, 'Geschichte der Eidgenössischen Technischen Hochschule in Zürich. Im Überblick dargestellt', in *Eidgenössische Technische Hochschule 1855–1955. Ecole Polytechnique Fédérale* (Zürich, 1955), pp. 1–257, and Klaus Urner, 'Vom Polytechnikum zur Eidgenössischen Technischen Hochschule': Die ersten hundert Jahre 1855–1955 im Überblick', in Jean-François Bergier and Hans-Werner Tobler (eds.), *Eidgenössische Tech-*

nische Hochschule Zürich 1855–1980. Festschrift zum 125jährigen Bestehen (Zürich, 1980), pp. 17–59.

8 Wolfdietrich Jost, *Gewerbliche Schulen und politische Macht. Zur Entwicklung des gewerblichen Schulwesens in Preussen in der Zeit von 1850–1880* [Berufliche Bildung und Berufsbildungspolitik, 10] (Weinheim and Basel, 1982).

9 Lars Ulrich Scholl, *Ingenieure in der Frühindustrialisierung. Staatliche und private Techniker im Königreich Hannover und an der Ruhr (1815–1873)* [Studien zu Naturwissenschaft, Technik und Wirtschaft im Neunzehnten Jahrhundert, 10. Forschungsunternehmen 'Neunzehntes Jahrhundert' der Fritz Thyssen Stiftung] (Göttingen, 1978).

10 *Zeitschrift des Vereines Deutscher Ingenieure*, 55 (1911), 1097.

11 Hans-Joachim Braun, 'Methodenprobleme der Ingenieurwissenschaft, 1850–1900', *Technikgeschichte*, 44 (1977), 1–18, and Wolfgang König, 'Science and practice: key categories for the professionalization of German engineers', in Melvin Kranzberg (ed.), *Technological Education – Technological Style* (San Francisco, 1986), pp. 41–7.

12 Adolf Ernst, 'Maschinenbaulaboratorien', *Zeitschrift des Vereines Deutscher Ingenieure*, 38 (1894), 1351–62.

13 The only comprehensive (though regrettably unsatisfactory) work concerning the technical intermediate schools is Gustav Grüner, 'Die Entwicklung der höheren technischen Fachschulen im deutschen Sprachgebiet. Ein Beitrag zur historischen und zur angewandten Berufspädagogik' (Habilitationsschrift TH Darmstadt, Braunschweig, 1967). Also recommended on individual schools are: Lothar Suhling, 'Die Entwicklung zur Fachhochschule', in *Fachhochschule Dortmund, 90 Jahre praxisbezogenes Studium in Dortmund 1890–1980* (Dortmund, 1980), pp. 9–131, and Günter Sodan (ed.), *Die Technische Fachhochschule Berlin im Spektrum Berliner Bildungsgeschichte* (Berlin, 1988).

14 On Prussian students at foreign *Technische Mittelschulen*, see *Zeitschrift des Vereines Deutscher Ingenieure*, 32 (1898), 557, and 46 (1902), 58–60.

15 Manegold, *Universität Technische Hochschulen und Industrie*.

16 D. G. Tucker, *Gisbert Kapp, 1852–1922* (Birmingham, 1973).

17 Ludwig and König, *Technik, Ingenieure und Gesellschaft*, pp. 269–75.

18 See, as an example, the tables in Klinkenberg, *Rheinisch-Westfälische Technische Hochschule Aachen*, which show the development of the sub-disciplines in engineering.

19 Frank R. Pfetsch, *Zur Entwicklung der Wissenschaftspolitik in Deutschland 1750–1914* (Berlin, 1974), pp. 174–6, and Lundgreen, in Rürup, *Wissenschaft und Gesellschaft*, p. 213.

20 Ludwig and König, *Technik, Ingenieure und Gesellschaft*, pp. 247–51.

21 Quoted in Manfred Späth, 'Die Technische Hochschule Berlin-Charlottenburg und die internationale Diskussion des technischen Hochschulwesens 1900–1914', in Rürup, *Wissenschaft und Gesellschaft*, vol. 1, pp. 189–208, especially pp. 192 and 197.

22 Göran Ahlström, *Engineers and Industrial Growth. Higher Technical Education and the Engineering Profession during the Nineteenth and early twentieth centuries: France, Germany, Sweden and England* (London and

Canberra, 1982); Peter Lundgreen, 'The organization of science and technology in France: A German perspective', in Robert Fox and George Weisz (eds.), *The Organization of Science and Technology in France, 1808–1914* (Cambridge and Paris, 1980), pp. 311–32, and 'Education for the science-based industrial state? The case for nineteenth-century Germany', *History of Education*, 13 (1984), 59–67.

23 Lundgreen, 'The organisation of science and technology in France', pp. 327–30.

24 Charles R. Day, *Education for the Industrial World. The Écoles d'arts et métiers and the Rise of French Industrial Engineering* (Cambridge, Mass., and London, 1987).

25 Ludwig and König, *Technik, Ingenieure und Gesellschaft*, pp. 250–1.

26 See Ahlström's chapter in this volume.

27 See, for instance, *Zeitschrift des Vereines Deutscher Ingenieure*, 31 (1888), 376 and 52 (1908), 712; also Georg Siemens, *Erziehendes Leben. Erfahrungen und Betrachtungen* (Urach, 1947), pp. 79–81.

28 Reinhold Jaeckel, *Statistik über die Lage der technischen Privatbeamten in Gross-Berlin. Im Auftrage des Bureaus für Sozialpolitik bearbeitet* (Jena, 1908).

Part II

Coping with the giants

Introduction

From an economic point of view, the countries considered in this section differed significantly from one another with respect both to the timing of their industrial development and to its pace. One of them, Belgium, provides an example of successful early industrialization, as early as that of Britain and France and earlier than that of Germany. Sweden's economy too had taken off by the mid nineteenth century. Italy and Spain, on the other hand, despite having regions of vigorous manufacturing activity by the second half of the nineteenth century, developed more belatedly than either Belgium or Sweden and lagged conspicuously behind the giants with which all four countries had to compete.

The reason why the nations in part II are grouped together is that, in very different ways, the development of their provision for higher technical education occurred through the adaptation of models that had already been pioneered in neighbouring countries, in particular France and Germany. In the event, the process of adaptation produced results that departed substantially from the originals. Hence, the systems that emerged are of considerable interest in their own right rather than as pale imitations of foreign practices. Nevertheless, they have not attracted the serious attention they deserve, if only because of the more prominent position of France and Germany in the world economy.

A point that emerges strongly from the chapters by Jean Baudet and Göran Ahlström is that the countries they discuss began not only to organize technical schools by the early nineteenth century but also, from the start, to address the problem of training for employment in manufacturing. The conclusion drawn by Baudet and Ahlström is that, in both cases, education was not an impediment to industrial take-off. Indeed, in Belgium the growth of education proceeded simultaneously with that of industry. It is not at all clear, however, that the growth can be interpreted as a simple response to industrial demand. For one of the most interesting points to emerge from Baudet's account is the extent to which regional rivalry affected the development of institutions of higher technical education. The rivalry was further heightened by religious conflict and by the running battles between the graduates of different schools. It seems that it was precisely this combination of pressures which provided the condition for diversification and specialization and which fostered a growth of new institutions from below that is very similar to what occurred in Germany – albeit on a different scale.

This does not seem to have happened in Sweden. The two main institutions of higher technical education, the KTH in Stockholm and Chalmers in Gothenburg, continued to supply well-educated men who gradually came to occupy senior positions in Swedish industry. However, as Ahlström suggests, this fruitful interaction did not produce the more specialized intermediate-level schools which manufacturers, from the 1890s, increasingly claimed were necessary. The reason for this failure to heed the call of industry, according to Ahlström, is to be found on the demand side: manufacturing in Sweden had not reached the 'critical' size that was necessary to stimulate a further development in technical education comparable with that which occurred in the German *Mittelschulen*.

The controversial question of the role of industrial demand as a trigger for technical education is highly relevant to the analyses of Italy and Spain. There, the need to prepare civil engineers for state service had resulted in a structure for engineering education that was in place by the beginning of the nineteenth century. But in the north of Italy and in the relatively advanced manufacturing areas of the Catalan and Basque regions of Spain, there were pressures of a new and different kind, arising from a politically motivated desire to stimulate modernization and to emulate initiatives that were taking place in the more heavily industrialized parts of Europe. In a way familiar in other national contexts, the initiative and, to a significant extent, the financial support came from local authorities and private patrons seeking to compensate for governmental indifference.

In both Italy and Spain, the initiatives aimed at providing instruction in mechanical and electrical engineering began to bear fruit in the 1890s, and they soon generated an ample supply of highly qualified engineers. A conspicuous weakness persisted, however, in the preparation of technical experts for middle-level careers. In both countries, this sector of the educational system remained untidy (as it also did virtually everywhere in Europe) and seriously underdeveloped. The fact is that even in the areas of Italy and Spain where manufacturing was most active, voluntarism proved to be an inadequate basis on which to build alternatives to the outdated educational systems under governmental control.

4 The training of engineers in Belgium, 1830–1940

Jean C. Baudet

Many of the traditions that Belgium inherited at independence in 1830 came from France. These traditions, however, were coloured by fifteen years of Dutch occupation and, even more crucially, by the fact that the country lay at the cross-roads of influences emanating not only from France but also from her other great neighbour, Germany. It was as a result of this location that Belgian engineering schools bore the marks of both the French and the German models, in sharp contrast with Sweden, for example, where the main influence was that of Germany alone. Another distinguishing characteristic is that Belgium, unlike Italy and Spain, had undergone early and very rapid industrialization. Indeed, it has been argued that Belgium was the first country in the world to adopt the new techniques invented in Great Britain, and that it was through Belgium that the industrial revolution reached the Continent.[1]

It was, in fact, a French writer living in Belgium, Natalis Marie Briavoinne, who coined the term 'industrial revolution'. In a paper read to the Académie des Sciences et Belles-Lettres de Bruxelles in 1838, on 'the progress of the industrial arts in the Belgian provinces from the late eighteenth century to our own times', he attributed this advance to the suppression of the craft-guilds at the end of the previous century. As Briavoinne argued, the pace of the expansion and modernization of manufacturing in Belgium had been remarkable. For instance, coal production had risen from about 2.5 million tonnes a year in the 1830s to an annual average of 22.7 million between 1901 and 1910. The production of pig-iron and cast iron had amounted to 234,176 tonnes in 1850 (at a time when the production of steel was still negligible); by 1912, more than ten times that amount of mild steel – 2,442,000 tonnes – was being produced. This rise in production far outpaced the rate of demographic expansion (the population rising from 3,785,814 in 1831 to 7,405,569 in 1920).

From the first half of the nineteenth century, therefore, Belgium needed engineers to push ahead with her industrial revolution. Here, the chronology is of interest. For the dates of the foundation of higher technical schools are a good indication of the way in which a society responds to the introduction of new techniques. The building of the first railway dates from 1835, with the factories of John Cockerill, the English-born Belgian industrialist, supplying the rails and engines. The chemical industry began producing soda and its derivatives in 1861, when Ernest Solvay discovered the ammonia-soda process for baking sodium carbonate. Electricity followed in 1869, with Zénobe Gramme's invention of the dynamo, and radio communications began in 1900, the year in which Maurice Travailleur established the Compagnie de Télégraphie sans Fils in Brussels. For such developments, Belgium certainly needed engineers and other highly trained technical experts, in addition to those who had long been required for government service and the army. Napoleon had established the Corps des Ponts et Chaussées in 1804 and the Corps des Mines in 1810, and the new Belgian administration was quick to reconstitute these bodies in 1831. A royal decree of 29 August 1831 established the mining department as a section under the Ministry of the Interior, with a staff consisting of three chief engineers, seven engineers, three assistant engineers, and twenty clerks of works. The Corps des Ponts et Chaussées was attached to the same ministry, employing ten chief engineers, twenty engineers, ten assistant engineers, and eighty clerks of works.[2] It was responsible for administering the communications infrastructure (roads and canals) and supervising the country's main source of wealth, the coalfields of Liège, Mons, and Charleroi.

In all these contexts, as well as in the army, there were careers to be made by qualified engineers from early in the nineteenth century. Yet, at the time, the country had no institutions for higher technical training. Most of the engineers who were employed when the Corps des Mines and the Corps des Ponts et Chaussées were originally set up had either studied abroad or been trained on the job. Jean-Baptiste Vifquain, one of the leading Belgian engineers of the first half of the nineteenth century, was typical in that he passed through the Ecole Polytechnique in Paris and, after leaving in 1814, went on to become inspector-general of the Ponts et Chaussées. His exact contemporary as a *polytechnicien*, Jean de Vaux, became inspector-general of the Corps des Mines and taught the practice of mining at the Ecole Spéciale at Liège from 1836 to 1844.[3] Alfred Belpaire, who became inspector-general of railways, posts, and telegraphs, was also educated in Paris: he graduated from the Ecole Centrale des Arts et Manufactures in Paris in 1840. Two other Paris-trained engineers were Rémi de Puydt, who was appointed chief engineer of the Ponts et Chaussées at the beginning of the Belgian Revolution and carried out major canal works on the Sambre and the Meuse, and Jean-Baptiste Masui, first secretary of the Ministry of Public Works, who rose

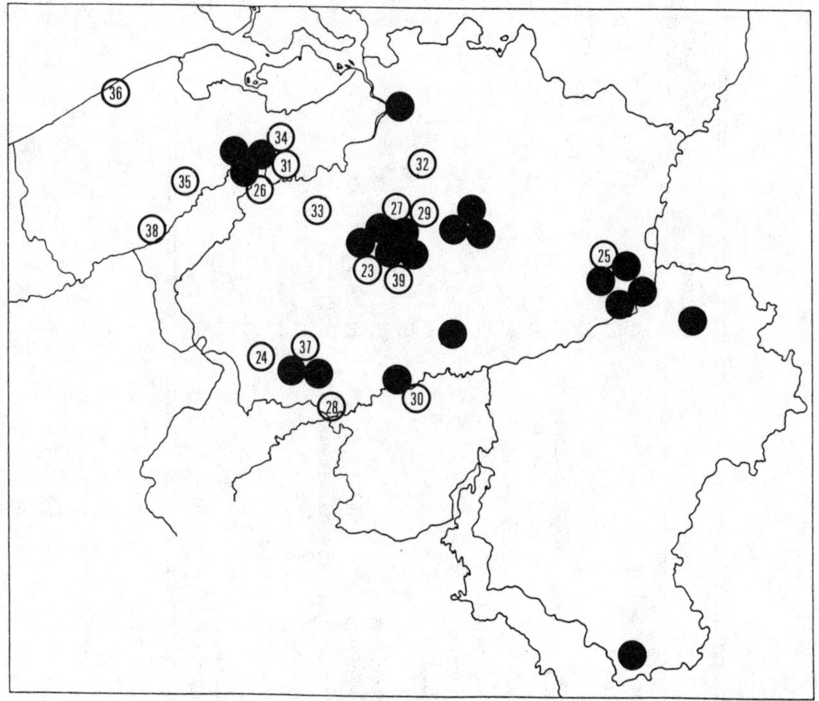

Engineering schools in Belgium, 1830–1940.
• Schools created between 1830 and 1900.
○ Schools created from 1901 (see table 4.1).

to be director-general of railways, posts, and telegraphs. Many more names could be added to this list, but those I have cited serve to show the attraction of a Parisian training in the eyes of young Belgians aspiring to technical careers.

No sooner had independence been achieved, however, than new initiatives in higher education began to be launched. The Ecole Royale Militaire was founded in Brussels in 1834; the law on public education and state-funded universities (the *loi organique* of 27 September 1835) made provision for courses at Ghent, to train engineers for the Corps des Ponts et Chaussées, and at Liège, for engineers going on to the Corps des Mines. Three years later, the Ecole des Mines at Liège and the Ecole du Génie Civil at Ghent were officially inaugurated, by separate royal decrees both dated 10 October 1838. They produced few graduates, but they represent the beginnings of Belgian higher technical education.

Table 4.1. *Engineering schools in Belgium, 1900–40*

Number[1]	Year	Location	Title	Language	Administration[2]
23	1903	Brussels	Ecole supérieure de Commerce Solvay	Fr	B
24	1905	Saint-Ghislain	Ecole communale de sucrerie	Fr	A
25	1906	Liège	Institut technique	Fr	C
26	1907	Ghent	Ecole technique supérieure de brasserie/Hogere technische brouwerijschool	Fr/Fl	C
27	1911	Brussels	Institut supérieur de Commerce Cooremans	Fr	A
28	1911	Erquelinnes	Ecole catholique des arts et métiers	Fr	C
29	1915	Brussels	Ecole centrale des arts et métiers	Fr	C
30	1919	Charleroi	Ecole spéciale de techniciens	Fr	A
31	1920	Ghent	Institut agronomique	Fl	A
32	1921	Malines	School voor technisch ingenieurs	Fl	C
33	1926	Alost	School voor technisch ingenieurs	Fl	C
34	1926	Ghent	Ecole industrielle supérieure/Hogere nijverheidsschool	Fr/Fl	A
35	1928	Deinze	School voor technisch ingenieurs	Fl	C
36	1928	Ostende	School voor technisch ingenieurs	Fl	C
37	1929	Mons	Ecole Saint-Luc	Fr	C
38	1929	Courtrai	School voor technisch ingenieurs	Fl	A
39	1930	Brussels	Institut national des industries de fermentation	Fr	A

[1] See map 4.1

[2] A: State or local authority
B: Private
C: Catholic

The originality of the Belgian system

In that France provided the main model for higher technical education, Belgium was not unlike many other parts of Europe. In Belgium, however, there was no wholesale adoption of the French system; indeed, from the start there were considerable variations. Most obviously, none of the three schools mentioned above had the status or prestige of the Ecole Polytechnique. There were, of course, the members of the various *corps* of engineers holding state appointments: much as in France, young men would enter their *corps* after a training based on advanced mathematics that was not unlike that of the Ecole Polytechnique. But whereas the Polytechnique provided the only means of access to the army and the civil service, engineers in Belgium, even though there were fewer of them, were prepared in the three separate schools at Ghent, Brussels, and Liège. In a gesture towards some degree of centralization along French lines, a plan to unify these schools in a single Polytechnique at Brussels was proposed at the time of independence, but it came to nothing.

One of the administrative characteristics that the Belgian schools shared with the Ecole Polytechnique and the other French *grandes écoles* was their independence of the university system. Indeed, during the whole nineteenth century there were only four universities in Belgium: these were the state universities at Ghent and Liège, the Catholic University at Louvain, and the 'Free' University of Brussels, established by leading figures in anti-Catholic circles.

The choice of Liège as the location for the Ecole des Mines was natural. The Belgian coalfields are all in the Walloon provinces, and mining engineers trained at Liège would expect, and be expected, to make their careers in the southern half of the country.[4] Pupils studying at the Ecole des Ponts et Chaussées in Ghent, on the other hand, would be likely to take up appointments anywhere in Belgium. Since Ponts et Chaussées engineers outnumbered mining engineers by three to one, it was inevitable that, as a result of this division between the schools, Ghent should be disproportionately influential. This in turn had its effect in the higher levels of the civil service, where former pupils of the Ghent schools were particularly active in maintaining a network of influential contacts. As a result, there emerged a pattern of regional rivalries that have not yet been fully studied by historians of nineteenth-century Belgium.

Perhaps the most important departure from the French model lay in the work done by the Ecole des Ponts et Chaussées and the Ecole des Mines in training engineers for private industry. Like the Ecole Polytechnique in France, with its associated *écoles d'application*, both institutions had been founded to prepare army officers and civil servants. This was natural enough. For, at the time, industry had little need for highly trained engineers: the technologies in use did not call for advanced theoretical knowledge, and throughout the nineteenth century many factories worked perfectly well without employing any engineers at all. In France, it was private initiative that led to the creation of the Ecole Centrale des Arts et Manufactures in 1829 to train engineers for industry; in Belgium, that task was undertaken by special sections established in the 1830s within the same schools that trained for the civil service. As we shall see, by 1836, the schools at both Ghent and Liège had launched courses in subjects related to manufacturing.

Before moving on to a more detailed examination of these developments, it is important to mention one other important institution, the Musée d'Art et d'Industrie in Brussels. This was opened in 1830, before the end of Dutch rule. Following independence, a royal decree of 24 September 1832 laid down that measures should be taken to allow the Musée de l'Etat to deal with 'the latest developments in physics, chemistry, the arts, and industry'.

In the early years of independence, therefore, Belgium possessed four schools for advanced technical education, all of them administered by the state. Thereafter, new institutions were to appear with increasing speed. The diversity of these foundations, whether we consider their origins, their administrative affiliations, or their curricula, reflects a corresponding and growing diversity within Belgian society. On the eve of the Second World War, there were forty such schools, compared with four in 1835: in the course of a century, the original number had multiplied ten-fold, even allowing for some mergers and closures. How had this come about?

The first generation: 1836–65

In Belgium, as in many other countries, a belief in the contribution of education to industrial performance led to the establishment of technical schools before industrialists voiced any explicit demand for engineers and other experts. Belgian industry, however, was making rapid progress in the mid nineteenth century, and in due course this did serve to promote the growth of technical training in a wide range of subjects. The growth was also fostered to a large extent, by keen competition between state provision and private ventures, and by a similar rivalry between religious and regional bodies.

The potential demand for courses in specialist industrial subjects was soon apparent to private enterprise. In this, once again, France provided a stimulus as well as a model. In 1836, Théophile Guibal and Adolphe Devillez, who had both studied at the Ecole Centrale des Arts et Manufactures in Paris, gained the approval of the province of Hainaut for the opening of a school of mining and metallurgy at Mons to prepare mining engineers. It was the first such school to be established as private initiative, although it did receive some financial support from public funds. Clearly the development of coal mines, the metallurgical industry, and mechanical engineering in the Sambre valley, which was the main rival to the area around Liège, made industrialists aware of the need for a school comparable with the one that existed at Liège. Yet it is important to notice that the Mons engineers did not qualify, as those who had studied at Ghent and Liège did, for appointments in any of the state *corps*.

The state technical schools also responded to the need to train engineers for work outside the civil service, and in the same year (by decrees dated 26 and 27 September 1836) the Minister of the Interior reorganized the courses at Ghent and Liège to permit this extension. The Ecole des Ponts et Chaussées at Ghent was renamed the Ecole du Génie Civil, while the Ecole des Mines at Liège became the Ecole des Arts et Manufactures et des Mines. The courses were extended from three to four years, two for basic study, followed by two in specialized subjects. Ghent offered three alternative areas of specialization: roads and bridges, industrial arts and manufacturing, and civil architecture. Liège offered mining and arts and manufacturing. This hybrid structure was unsuccessful, and a royal decree of 1 October 1838 divided each of the schools, so as to create two schools in Ghent (the Ecole Spéciale du Génie Civil and the Ecole des Arts et Manufactures) and two in Liège (the Ecole Spéciale des Mines and the Ecole des Arts et Manufactures). The introduction of the adjective 'spéciale' in the titles of two of these institutions was highly significant. It meant that the diplomas of the schools concerned, unlike those of the other two, were qualifications for entry to the state engineering *corps*.

A further order by the Minister of the Interior, on 23 February 1843, established a section of mechanical engineering at the Ecole des Arts et Manufactures in Liège. A distinctive feature of this section was that the *diplôme d'ingénieur-mécanicien* was awarded after a course lasting three years, as opposed to the four years that were required in other engineering courses. The syllabus was also significantly different in that mathematics was not taught in any great depth. Mathematical instruction, in fact, consisted of just a single course in descriptive geometry. Also a great deal of time was devoted to drawing and workshop practice. In these respects, the Ecole des Arts et Manufactures displayed the same vocational bias as the Ecole des Mines et de Métallurgie at Mons. Inevitably, the emergence of this new type of curriculum for engineers had important consequences. For the term 'ingénieur' now came to designate two different kinds of graduate: one who had passed through a course lasting at least four years, with a strong component of advanced mathematics, the other whose formal education had been completed in three years, with a very modest amount of mathematics but with substantial practical experience.

Needless to say, the shorter, industrially oriented diplomas did not have the status of the more established qualifications. The point is clearly illustrated by the numbers and types of engineering diplomas awarded by the schools in Liège from 1841 to 1868.[5] Four grades of diploma were available. They were those of *ingénieur honoraire* in mining engineering, *ingénieur civil* in mining, *ingénieur civil* in arts and manufacturing, and *ingénieur civil mécanicien*. Since the diploma of *ingénieur honoraire* in mining engineering was a condition for entry to the Corps des Mines, the choice of both the school and the course of study was primarily dictated by the student's intended career: a young man aiming to become a colliery engineer or to work in the metallurgical industry was more likely to opt for one of the courses leading to the diploma of *ingénieur civil*, whereas anyone hoping for a civil service career was bound to take the longer route and become an *ingénieur honoraire* in mining. Table 4.2 shows that in the early 1840s more than half the students chose the course leading to the qualification for the Corps des Mines, whereas by the late 1860s fewer than a third of the students in higher technological education did so. The trend became still more marked as the industrialization of the country progressed, causing new schools to be established to meet the growing demand for technical expertise.

Table 4.2. *Engineers graduating from the engineering schools of Liège, 1841–68*

	Ingénieurs honoraires des mines	Ingénieurs civils	Total
1841–44	17	10	27
1845–48	21	26	47
1849–52	11	34	45
1853–56	11	35	46
1857–60	29	97	126
1861–64	81	136	217
1865–68	69	167	236
1841–68	239	505	744

There is no doubt that by the middle of the nineteenth century a clear distinction had emerged in Belgium between engineering careers in the civil service and those in the private industrial sector, and between the corresponding types of educational background. While the higher social status of the former was 'confirmed' by a lengthy course of study and a sophisticated mathematical preparation, access to the latter was achieved after a shorter preparation in which there was a greater emphasis on workshop instruction. Not surprisingly, these differences fuelled considerable rivalry between the groups involved. In fact, it was in this period that professional organizations were set up with the explicit purpose of protecting or, in the case of the industrial engineers, enhancing the status and occupational opportunities of their members. An association of engineers trained at Liège was formed in 1847, followed in 1851 by the Association des Ingénieurs Honoraires des Ponts et Chaussées (for graduates of the Ghent School) and, two years later, by an association of engineers who had been educated at Mons. There is a close parallel here with France, where the Société des Ingénieurs Civils de France was founded in Paris in 1848, bringing together the graduates of the Ecole Centrale to contest the Polytechnique's monopoly on state appointments.

In this same period, the school at Mons was reconstituted by royal decree (23 August 1845) and in 1852 the Ecole Spéciale de Commerce of Antwerp was established in 1852 (by a royal decree of 29 October) to give 'special instruction in the theory and practice of commercial science'. Graduates of the Antwerp institute were not yet accorded the rank of *ingénieur commercial*, but the school was a natural addition to the list of new institutions for the training of business managers, since commerce, like technology, had no place in the universities. The position of agriculture, for which a state-run Institut Agricole was created at Gembloux in 1860 (decree of 18 July 1860), was similar.

One of the most striking developments of the period was the involvement of the Roman Catholic Church in the promotion of higher technical education. In 1863 a general council of Belgian bishops at Malines decided to found the Ecole Spéciale du Génie Civil, d'Industrie et des Mines at Louvain. The school was not a faculty or part of the Catholic University of Louvain, which dated from 1834, but it was 'attached' to its faculty of science.

Thus eight technical schools were established between 1836 and 1865, six by the state, one by the province of Hainaut (on the private initiative of two engineers), and one by the Catholic Church. In addition to the traditional subjects of construction, mining, and arts and manufacturing, they were now training specialists in mechanical engineering, commerce, agriculture, and applied zoology.

The second generation: 1866–95

Despite the development of the railway system and the resulting industrial expansion, the years 1836–65 had been marked by consolidation and by the diffusion of the technical achievements of the previous generation. What had happened, in fact, was a continuation of the first industrial revolution and of the age of the steam engine (the spread of the railway hardly constituting anything we can call a true technological revolution). Hence, it is not surprising that, apart from the introduction of teaching in commerce and agriculture, the engineering schools whose foundation I have described were not different in kind from those of the earlier period. The generation of schools founded between 1866 and 1895, however, was closely linked to the second industrial revolution, the age, above all, of electricity but also of chemistry, in particular of the synthetic dyes which so added to the complexity of the textile industry.

The importance of these sectors is clearly reflected in the transformation of existing schools as well as in new foundations. When, in 1873, the Free University of Brussels established its own Ecole Polytechnique, provision was made not only for instruction in the traditional branches of engineering – civil, mining, and mechanical – but also for courses in metallurgy and chemistry. Five years later, the Catholic authorities founded the Ecole Supérieure d'Agriculture at Louvain, despite the university's unwillingness to cooperate and hostility from some teachers in the faculty of science.

Perhaps the most remarkable of the second-generation foundations was an institution devoted specifically to the teaching of electrical technology. This was the Institut Electrotechnique Montefiore, opened in Liège in 1883 and therefore one of the pioneers of its kind in Europe, second only to the section for electrical engineering that was inaugurated at the Technische Hochschule of Darmstadt in 1882. Like so many other initiatives that were triggered by the 'electricity mania' of the early 1880s, the school was private. It was, in fact, a wealthy Belgian industrialist and graduate of the Ecole des Arts et Manufactures at Liège, Georges Montefiore, who promoted its opening and endowed it. In important ways, this first venture into the advanced teaching of electrical technology in Belgium was a product of the Exposition Internationale d'Electricité of 1881 in Paris, where Montefiore, an international figure with interests in Italy was well as in the Liège area, had been a member of the organizing committee.

The structure adopted by the Institut Montefiore was unusual in that it provided one-year courses entirely devoted to electrical engineering, and admitted mainly (though not exclusively) men students who had already completed a course of instruction in one of the traditional branches of engineering. Just as the emergence of new specialities provided a stimulus for the opening of new schools, so those that were already in existence also embarked on the creation of new sections and courses. In 1887, for example, an Ecole Supérieure de Brasserie was established at Louvain for the instruction of technical employees for the local brewing industry. The creation of this school was largely the work of Jules Vuylsteke, who studied engineering in Louvain. The new institution had the same relationship with the Catholic University as the Ecole du Génie Civil and the Ecole d'Agriculture. Another specialized school was the Ecole Sucrière Belge, founded by the city of Liège at Glons in 1889 to serve the sugar industry; this school awarded its first diplomas in sugar manufacture and in industrial, electrical, and electromechanical engineering.

The year 1890 is an important date in the history of Belgian engineering. As I have mentioned, the schools at Ghent and Liège had a monopoly on entry to state appointments, and this privilege was naturally the source of much dissatisfaction among the graduates of other, lower-ranking schools. Eventually the protests culminated in the law of 10 April 1890 governing the hierarchy of academic qualifications. Although the protest movement has still been little-studied, there is no doubt that engineering associations played a decisive role in ensuring that the academic qualifications of *ingénieur civil des mines* and *ingénieur des constructions civiles* were added to the existing ones of *candidat* and *docteur*. More importantly, the new law gave the schools at Brussels and Louvain, as well as those at Ghent and Liège, the right to grant the qualifications, and it bound all four schools to their local universities, with the titles of 'faculties of applied science'. The school at Mons was also allowed to give the qualifications, but the process of integration did not extend to the special engineering courses offered by other technical schools. Hence, the qualifications for such categories as mechanical, commercial, agricultural, and industrial engineers, brewers, chemists, metallurgists, electrical engineers, and sugar makers all remained outside the official structure of 'university' instruction. The tag 'university', in fact, came to acquire a special meaning. Originally university education and higher education were one and the same thing. Now the idea grew up that there were two levels of higher education. One was given in the universities proper, while the term 'non-university' was used to designate the wide range of other schools and institutes.

The emergence of this two-tier structure did not prevent the further expansion of the lower-status technical schools. In fact, such schools continued to proliferate. A good example is the Institut Meurice-Chimie at Charleroi, founded in 1892 to train graduates in chemistry and technology – graduates who, in the twentieth century, were to be given the title *ingénieur-chimiste*. Established by Albert Meurice, a young engineer from the agricultural institute of Gembloux, the Charleroi school moved to the Brussels area in 1894. Also in Brussels, there was an Ecole Supérieure de Commerce, founded in 1893 by Catholic circles. About the same time, the instruction of engineers for the textile industry was taken in hand by the Ecole Supérieure des Textiles at Verviers, established in 1894, with some initial support from the University of Liège. This school had roots that went back to 1855, when the Verviers Chamber of Commerce set up a weaving school to train skilled workmen rather than engineers. Twenty years later, a local manufacturer, Victor Deheselle, offered the town of Verviers a substantial sum for the creation of an engineering school to be attached to the one that already existed for weaving. In the event, it was only in 1890 that the local council took a decision on the offer, and it was for this reason that the new school did not open until 1894. It was the first time that an engineering school was established in Belgium with an attachment to an existing institution at the secondary level, though the formula was to be repeated often in the twentieth century.

There were two further developments in 1895. The first occurred at Ghent, where the Ecole Supérieure des Fermentations (Hogeschool voor de Gistingsbedrijven) was established; here, in the first Belgian engineering school to teach in Flemish as well as French, refrigeration and flour milling engineers and specialists for the sugar, dairy, and other food industries were trained. The other development was the foundation, at Seraing, of the Congrégation des Aumôniers du Travail, a chaplaincy for workers that aimed to 'bring the working population back to Christianity'. Until then, the only Catholic engineering schools had been those connected with the University of Louvain. Moreover, their promoters had been generally associated with the right wing of the Catholic party, and they had served a broadly middle-class student body. The Aumôniers du Travail, by contrast, stood more markedly to the left. They directed their attention to the working classes and set out, at least initially, to offer training for workers and foremen only. Their first school, financed by Edouard Otlet, a rich senator from Luxembourg, was the Institut des

Arts et Métiers at Pierrard-Virton, which opened in 1900, admitting thirteen students.

The pattern of expansion in the years up to 1895 is clear. It reflected, in part, the increasingly important contribution of private initiatives, involving either rich industrialists near the end of their careers, like Montefiore, or enterprising young engineers, like Meurice. But the growth was also in part a consequence of the development of new specializations. Engineers were now in demand in the electrical, chemical, textile, and agricultural and food industries. Leading factories set up their own laboratories, providing openings for chemical engineers, while work-places made steadily more use of electricity for lighting and power, so creating opportunities for electrical engineers.

The third generation: 1896–1925

The impetus of the second generation of schools was carried over into a third generation that began to emerge, with ever-increasing rapidity, in the improved economic circumstances of the late 1890s. An early product of the new confidence was the proposal for a school for advanced commercial studies at Mons that was made in March 1899 by Henri Dutrieux, an engineer in the state railway administration. Several industrialists, notably Raoul Warocqué, rallied to the call, offering support and capital, and in October 1899 the first students, fifty-two in number, were admitted to the school, which took the title of the Institut Commercial des Industriels du Hainaut. The first class of *licenciés* in *sciences commerciales* graduated in August 1903. The Mons school complemented the Institut des Arts et Métiers at Pierrard-Virton, which had been in existence since 1900. In 1903, provision for commercial education was further strengthened, when the industrialist Ernest Solvay offered the Free University of Brussels the funds for another Ecole Supérieure de Commerce to train *ingénieurs commerciaux*. While the graduates of Antwerp and the Ecole Saint-Louis in Brussels were given the title of *licenciés*, like those of Mons, the new school used the term *ingénieur commercial* and introduced technology and industrial organization as major components of the new programme. Former pupils of the Ecole de Commerce Solvay formed an association in 1910.

In a quite different sector, on 29 July 1905, the town council of Saint-Ghislain gave its formal approval to the programme of the Ecole Professionelle Communale de Sucrerie.[6] It was actually taking over a private institution established in about 1894 by Alfred Molhant, a chemical engineer who had taken his diploma at the Ecole des Mines at Mons. The 'Molhant courses', which were given at Mons before transferring to Saint-Ghislain, provided advanced training for operatives in the sugar industry. On accepting responsibility for the institute, the new administrators of the Saint-Ghislain school did what they could to raise the level of instruction. As part of the process, the title of the school was changed, in 1906, to the Ecole Professionnelle des Industries Chimiques, and five years later it became the Institut de Chimie de Saint-Ghislain. Until 1933 it awarded the qualification of *licencié en sciences chimiques*, and thereafter that of *ingénieur technicien*.

Like the Institut Meurice-Chimie, the Institut de Chimie de Saint-Ghislain engaged not only in teaching but also in the provision of laboratory analysis and consultancy services for local industries. By the turn of the century, therefore, industrialists were promoting the establishment of engineering schools not only to train the staff they needed in growing numbers – staff who, also, possessed ever higher scientific qualifications – but also to provide centres for qualify control and testing. At the same time, the old-established engineering schools embarked on the building of workshops and laboratories and formed major collections of machines.[7] This emphasis on practical work in the training of engineers represented an explicit attempt to ape the technical schools of Germany, with the result that the French model in engineering training became increasingly overlaid with elements from the German tradition.

Catholic contributions to technical education continued to grow apace. An Institut Technique (renamed a few years later the Institut Gramme, in honour of the inventor) was created by the Jesuits at Liège in 1906; it awarded the title of *ingénieur technicien*. Another foundation that owed its existence to Catholic support was the Ecole Technique Supérieure de Brasserie, founded at Ghent in 1907. Like the Institut des Fermentations, it had French and Flemish sections and bore the alternative name of Hogere Technische Brouwerijschool. The year 1911 saw the foundation, by the city of Brussels, of the Institut Supérieur de Commerce Lucien Cooremans and, at Erquelinnes, of a Catholic Ecole des Arts et Métiers.

The First World War had predictably disturbing consequences. But while the universities were closed, the occupying authorities took little interest in the advanced technical schools, which increased their intakes considerably. For example, at the Institut de Chimie at Saint-Ghislain student numbers rose from twenty-seven in 1914 to sixty two years later. In 1915, this situation prompted Paul Daubresse, a professor at the University of Louvain, to convert the Ecole Centrale des Arts et Métiers in Brussels into an engineering school awarding the qualification of *ingénieur des arts et métiers*.[8] Until then, it had been a secondary school, originally founded by the Jesuits in 1898 as the Ecole Notre-Dame du Travail to provide evening classes for workmen.

One of the first major reforms after the war was that of agricultural engineering studies, in 1919. By a new law of 15 November, the qualification of *ingénieur agricole*, which had been given at Gembloux after a three-year course, was replaced by that of *ingénieur agronome*, for which four years of study were required. In the same year, the province of Hainaut established the Ecole Spéciale de Techniciens, which offered advanced courses as part of the Université du Travail at Charleroi.[9] Three years later, this became the Ecole Spéciale d'Ingénieurs Techniciens, with departments of mechanical, electrical, and chemical engineering.

In the aftermath of the war, Flemish nationalism assumed unprecedented strength. Except in the two engineering schools in Ghent, all advanced teaching throughout the country was still given in French, and nationalists now demanded that it should also be given in Flemish. This was the background to the establishment, by a royal decree of 26 May 1920, of the Flemish-speaking Institut Agronomique de l'Etat, as a subsidiary to the Gembloux institute and as part of the legislative measures establishing the qualification of *ingénieur agronome*. Finally, in 1921 a 'section technique supérieure' for the training of technical engineers (*technisch ingenieurs*) was added to the Flemish Ecole Technique Catholique at Malines.

The fourth generation: 1926–40

For the study of engineering training, the years from 1926 until the Second World War can be divided into two parts separated by the crisis of the 1930s.

Whereas seven engineering schools were established in Belgium between 1926 and 1930, there was not a single new foundation for the next ten years. The reason for this lies in the economic circumstances, which led to widespread unemployment among engineers. Another result of the depression was the law of 11 September 1933 restricting the use of the various qualifications of *ingénieur*. Under the law, which imposed order amid the mounting proliferation of qualifications, only the four titles of *ingénieur civil, ingénieur technicien, ingénieur agronome*, and *ingénieur commercial* were given legal recognition.[10]

In this period, too, the Flemish movement continued to make its mark, as it had done ever since the war. A Catholic Flemish-speaking school for the training of *technisch ingenieurs* opened at Alost in 1926, and in the same year Ghent established its Ecole Industrielle Supérieure (Hogere Nijverheidsschool) for engineers, with both French and Flemish sections. The Catholic Church was responsible for starting two other Flemish-speaking technical engineering schools, at Deinze and Ostend, both in 1928, and in 1929 it inaugurated a French-language school at Mons, the Ecole Saint-Luc, later the Institut Reine Astrid des Arts et Métiers Saint-Luc. Finally, two colleges were opened by provincial governments: a Flemish engineering school at Courtrai in 1929 and the Institut National des Industries de Fermentation in Brussels in 1930, which awarded the diploma of *ingénieur* in fermentation technology.

The period was a particularly busy one for legislation affecting engineers. The law of 1890 on the status of academic qualifications was superseded by the Act of 21 May 1929, with two main results. First, the division of university courses into the two cycles of the *candidature* and the *doctorat* was replaced by the tripartite structure of *candidature, licence*, and *doctorat*. The only exceptions were in medicine, pharmacy, law, and engineering, where the two-fold structure was retained, on the grounds that the main consideration was entry to professions rather than academic study. Secondly, the two legally recognized engineering diplomas (*ingénieur civil des mines* and *ingénieur des constructions civiles*) were replaced by a single qualification, that of *ingénieur civil*, awarded in nine categories: architecture, construction engineering, naval construction, and chemical, electrical, textile, mechanical, metallurgical, and mining engineering.

There was also legislation on engineering studies outside the universities, notably the royal decrees of 5 July 1933, on the status of the *ingénieur technicien*, and of 30 October 1934, establishing the title of *ingénieur chimiste agricole*. The Act of 11 September 1933, mentioned above, tackled a rather different problem by establishing a completed system of protection for the titles delivered by the universities and by the engineering schools – a system distinct from that which protected the professional titles covered in other legislation.

Although a detailed study of this legislation would be inappropriate here, it is worth remarking that what I have called the fourth generation, of the post-war period (or, more specifically, of the period that followed the years of euphoria and spiritual malaise immediately after the First World War), was notable for the brisk parliamentary activity that culminated in the legislation for the protection of the engineering profession. This activity and its fruits showed that engineers could call on the support of strong pressure groups, and that the university and engineering school authorities, for their part, were well able to look after their own interests.

Here, four dates are important. The first is 1885, when the Société Belge des Ingénieurs et des Industriels was formed, with aims that were scientific and not concerned with diplomas and titles. The best-known president of this association was an industrialist without engineering qualifications, Ernest Solvay, who held office from 1904 to 1906. The second date is 1926, when graduates of Ghent, Liège, Louvain, Brussels, Mons, and the Ecole Militaire set up the Fédération des Associations Belges d'Ingénieurs Diplômés par les six grandes écoles de niveau universitaire (FABI), with the clear purpose of distinguishing themselves from the rest of the profession. The third date is 1928, which marked the foundation of the Vlaamse Ingenieursvereniging, a Flemish association of engineers, whose goal was the pursuit of nationalist objectives as well as the protection of professional titles. The last is 1933, when the Union Nationale des Ingénieurs Techniciens (UNIT), a body concerned almost entirely with diplomas, was established.

This sequence of events gives a flavour of the changes in professional concerns that came about between 1885 and the late 1920s. For a full understanding, however, it would be necessary to analyse Belgian society as a whole during the period and to embark on a study that would lay bare the roots of the institutions, conflicts, and aspirations of our own day.

Conclusion

It is beyond question that the pace at which engineering schools were founded in the century 1830–1930 reflected rather precisely the advancing industrialization of Belgium, although after the First World War the process was accelerated by social change and by deep tensions, such as those between Catholics and socialists, and between Flemish and French-speaking areas. But can all the schools be considered in the same category? With such a variety of administrative structures and such a wide diversity of aims on the part of those who founded them, and with local conditions differing so markedly between areas as far apart as Ostend and Virton, some attempt at classification has to be made.

Leaving aside the commercial and agricultural schools (eight in all), the remaining thirty schools were clearly distinguished from one another by the legislation of 1933. The oldest, which were all founded before 1873 and which awarded the diploma of *ingénieur civil*, were put in one category, while those that offered the qualification of *ingénieur technicien* were placed in another. Eventually, all the various engineering qualifications we have seen coming into existence were themselves divided between these two simple categories.

At this point, the historian must make way for the sociologist in assessing the social forces that produced the two-fold division of schools and qualifications. First, there were the associations of former students. These merged into two federations: the FABI (the Fédération des Associations Belges d'Ingénieurs Diplômés, supported to some extent by the Vlaamse Ingenieursvereniging) and the UNIT or Union Nationale des Ingénieurs Techniciens. It is no surprise that the older and better-organized associations, essentially those in the Fédération, gained more favoured status.[11] The diploma of *ingénieur civil* was legally classified as an 'academic' degree and hence superior to that of *ingénieur technicien*. It carried greater weight as a means of access to a number of professions, in particular to the state services, and it carried higher social prestige.

Secondly, there were the leading engineers within the schools, engaged in one of the decisive battles in what historians have called the 'guerre scolaire'.[12] Former students and school administrators alike had an interest in the reputation of their institutions. Industrialists, on the other hand, were led by the demands of technical rationalization to think of engineering schools as suppliers like any others, though suppliers of a fourth component of production, scientific and technical knowledge, that had no place in classical economics.

What were the relations between industrial employers and the Belgian engineering schools? Or, more generally, what was the link between the expansion of industry and the constantly rising number of engineers? Was it the growing supply of engineers that stimulated the remarkable economic development of a small country wedged between Germany and France, or was it industrial growth that created the demand for more engineers? So far, it is impossible to give more than a tentative answer, and my comments should be read accordingly.

Engineers launched businesses in new sectors such as electrical machinery and installation, fine chemicals, and radio communications, and transformed traditional industries like glass manufacture and construction in steel. It is not at all clear, however, whether these were spontaneous developments or whether industrial employers as a body were aware that the opening of advanced schools would in time transform the economies of whole regions. After the First World War, the key policy-makers knew very well that technological innovations would revolutionize production and hence society as a whole, but it is by no means certain that the future scope of the changes that were afoot was grasped by even the most far-sighted employers before 1914.

Perhaps the most distinctive characteristic of the development of Belgian engineering education was the foundation, early in the twentieth century, of schools specifically intended for working-class students. In this movement the lead was taken by the Catholic Church, followed soon afterwards by the socialists. Yet a variety of social forces combined to distinguish these new institutions from the older establishments, as the legislation of 1929 and 1933 shows very clearly. It was as though Belgian society was frightened of going too far, as if it was determined to keep knowledge and power as a preserve unsullied either by practice or by the masses of society. It was the great failure of Belgian society (as of all Europe, for similar divisions were to be found virtually everywhere) that, far from resolving the inner tensions of the system, it persevered with a 'split-level' system for training engineers.

This opposition between knowledge and power on the one hand and practicality and the masses on the other, is of course no new discovery.[13] Indeed, recent studies of the engineering profession, especially in Belgium, have shown that, in the sociology of knowledge, we find the concepts we need for the examination of the opposed and often conflicting categories of scientist and engineer, employer and engineer, and engineer and worker. They have also shown that the opposition between theory and practice (which is fundamental to these groupings and to Western thought as a whole) lies at the heart of the problems raised by the training of engineers and the legitimation of their authority. We have here a powerful lever for understanding the systems of ideas, concepts, and values that help to structure industrial societies.

Between 1918 and 1940, social relations in Belgium crystallized in what should be the most dynamic activity of a modern society, the application of science to industrial production, taking the form of the two-fold system of training for engineers I have described. The sons of middle-class parents were given a training that favoured abstract knowledge and clothed itself in the dignity of the academic gown; they could become *ingénieurs civils* and rise to the highest appointments in the civil service. Those from working-class families, or the most 'deserving' of them, were offered practical training in schools that lacked prestige: posts as *ingénieurs techniciens* were open to them, but the higher civil service was not.

At the time, also, no one questioned the superiority of French to what was dismissively regarded as the Flemish *patois*. Although Flemish-speaking colleges for *ingénieurs techniciens* and *ingénieurs agronomes* were established, it was unthinkable that *ingénieurs civils* should receive their training in that language. It is true that Flemish was introduced at the University of Ghent in 1930, but many more years were to pass before the language was used in the instruction of *ingénieurs civils*.

Notes

1 On Belgian industrialization, see Jan Dhondt and Marinette Bruwier, 'The Industrial Revolution in Belgium and Holland', in *Fontana Economic History of Europe*, vol. 4 (London, 1970); Pierre Lebrun, Marinette Bruwier, Jan Dhondt, and Georges Hansotte, *Essai sur la révolution industrielle en Belgique 1770–1847* (Brussels, 1979). See also René Leboutte, 'Bibliographie générale d'archéologie industrielle', *Technologia*, 9 (1986), 93–103.

2 See Jean C. Baudet, 'Pour une histoire de la profession d'ingénieur en Belgique', *Technologia*, 7 (1984), 35–62; *Les ingénieurs belges, de la machine à vapeur à l'an 2000* (Brussels, 1986); *Introduction à l'histoire des ingénieurs* (Brussels, 1987).

3 André Lederer, 'Jean-Baptiste Vifquain', *Technologia*, 4 (1981), 19–25.

4 Alphonse Le Roy, *Liber Memorialis. L'Université de Liège depuis sa fondation* (Liège, 1869).

5 Nicole Caulier-Mathy, who has examined the careers of ninety-three engineers in the *Corps des Mines* between 1815 and 1850 and between 1918 and 1940, has argued that their social background was mainly *bourgeois*, and that aristocratic families were generally not attracted to this branch of the public services. His figures show that 56 per cent of the engineers he studied came from the province of Liège and 23 per cent from the province of Hainaut. See Caulier-Mathy, 'Les ingénieurs de l'administration des mines 1815 à 1850', contribution to the conference on the history of Belgian engineers organized by the Société Royale Belge des Ingénieurs et des Industriels (Brussels, 25 November 1985).

6 G. Hainaut, 'L'Institut de Chimie de Saint-Ghislain (1905–1980)', *Annales du Cercle Historique et Archéologique de Saint-Ghislain*, 3 (1982), 563–74.

7 For example, the Institut de Mécanique was established at the University of Brussels in 1899 through the efforts of Lucien Anspach, who taught mechanical engineering. Apart from the caretaker's quarters, the buildings consisted simply of a hall for boilers and a machine room. One of the teachers, Professor Charles De Keyzer, later recalled that 'a series of lessons was . . . given to make students familiar with different kinds of engines for driving machinery. We are indebted to the kindess of factory owners who allowed this instruction to be given at their works.' See Goblet d'Alviella, *L'Université de Bruxelles pendant son troisième quart de siècle* (Brussels, 1909), pp. 121–6. The first research laboratory in a Belgian engineering school seems to have been the 'laboratoire spécial de recherches chimiques', established by a ministerial decree of 12 January 1864. This was open to final-year students who had shown a special aptitude in chemistry. See Le Roy, *Liber Memorialis. Université de Liège*, col. 1047.

8 Jean C. Baudet, 'Pour une histoire de la formation des ingénieurs en Belgique', *Technologia*, 2 (1979), 71–88.

9 Paul Pastur, a socialist and permanent representative of the province of Hainaut, established the Ecole Industrielle Supérieure (which was, in reality, a secondary school) at Charleroi in 1903. The socialists followed left-wing Christians, much of whose ideology they shared, in involving themselves in working-class education. The better-off, as they argued, could afford to base

their education on the classical languages, with no thought for their practical value, but the education of children from working-class families had to be vocational and have as its aim the improvement of the technical knowledge of factory workers. In 1911, the Ecole Industrielle at Charleroi was renamed the Université du Travail, although there was no pretence that the institution was of university status. It remained a large assemblage of specialized schools at secondary level.

10 René Brion, 'La querelle des ingénieurs en Belgique', in André Grelon (ed.), *Les ingénieurs de la crise. Titre et profession entre les deux guerres* (Paris, 1986), pp. 255–70. It is noteworthy that the French law regulating the 'award and use of the title *ingénieur diplômé*' dates from 10 July 1934. Spain had passed similar legislation by a decree dated 14 March 1933. The volume edited by Grelon is a valuable study of the period in which legislation was prepared to protect the qualified engineers of Europe.

11 In the nineteenth century, the engineering schools were drawn closer to the universities. However, it is impossible to say whether it was the universities which, in the end, recognized how the establishment of new faculties of applied science would increase their power – both financially (through increased governmental subsidies and support from industry) and in prestige (with industrial success winning technicians the social acceptance to which they aspired) – or whether the engineering schools were attracted by the prospect of belonging to institutions that were highly regarded in Belgian society.

At the beginning of the twentieth century, Belgian engineering schools combined the German model of development with that of France. Thanks to the work of Peter Lundgreen, we can understand the importance, for the German Technische Hochschulen, of being granted university status in the late 1890s. See Peter Lundgreen, 'De l'école spéciale à l'université technique. Etude sur l'histoire de l'Ecole supérieure technique en Allemagne avant 1970 et regard sur son développement ultérieur', *Culture technique*, no. 12 (1984), 305–11. See also Heiner Stück, 'L'émancipation des écoles supérieures techniques et la professionalisation des ingénieurs en Allemagne au XIXe siècle', in Grelon, *Les ingénieurs de la crise*, pp. 271–89.

12 In their studies of educational debate in Belgium, historians have tended to place special emphasis on primary and secondary schools. They have analysed perceptively enough the ideological conflict between 'free' (Catholic) schools and 'official' instruction, but they have been less successful in establishing a clear perspective on the dispute over the language that should be used in instruction. They have generally done little to trace the course of the dispute in higher education, where it had the effect of separating the universities from non-university institutions, perhaps because it is in the universities that they themselves were trained.

13 The 'sociology of knowledge' goes back to Condorcet, since whom there has been a continuing tradition passing through Lucien Lévy-Bruhl, Max Scheler (who identified the multiplicity of types of knowledge and the link between these diverse types and social structures), Karl Mannheim (who studied the reciprocity of 'conditioning' between knowledge and social groups), and Georges Gurvitch (who schematized the results of nearly two centuries of

research with great clarity). Gurvitch defined the subject as the study of 'the functional correlations to be established between . . . the different systems of knowledge and social frameworks'; see his *Traité de sociologie* (Paris, 1960), II, p. 120.

5 Technical education, engineering, and industrial growth: Sweden in the nineteenth and early twentieth centuries

Göran Ahlström

Interest in determining the causes of economic and industrial growth has increased significantly since the Second World War. This is a result not least of the recognition, by historians and economic analysts, of the residual or 'technic' factor. It has come to be generally agreed that a country's economic growth is explained to a large extent by factors other than inputs of physical capital and labour.[1] Investments in education, both general and technical – i.e. in 'human capital' – are now seen to be of great importance. So too is the contribution of the engineer, especially at the stage of innovation, when basic research and new inventions are put to economic use. It is my premise, in fact, that the provision of a thorough theoretical and practical education is necessary and has been so at least from the period in the later nineteenth century when the science-based industries assumed a leading position in manufacturing.

It is also well established that the economic and industrial growth rates of Sweden from the middle of the nineteenth century to the present, at least until the 1970s, have been among the highest in the world.[2] Yet even in this specific case it is difficult, probably impossible, to measure the importance of the engineer, and *a fortiori* of specific types of engineer, in the process of industrial growth. Nevertheless, comparative analyses of different industrial countries, concerning the numbers of engineers, the functions they perform, and so forth, do suggest certain conclusions about their role.

As I emphasized in my book *Engineers and Industrial Growth*,[3] the relevant starting-point in such an analysis on an aggregated level must be the number of engineers with specific qualifications in a given country, allied to a discussion of the demand for engineers and the careers they pursued. In such a discussion, considerable weight has to be attached to cultural and social factors. Society's way of responding to and forecasting the industrial need for technical competence – an aspect closely related to the supply side – is also of great importance. In these respects, to which I shall return, and in the comparative perspective, Sweden stands out as a successful case.

The literature on this aspect of the Swedish story has been anything but plentiful. Indeed, apart from a number of monographs on Swedish technical universities and some public reports, it is only recently that social historians and historians of education have begun seriously to consider Swedish developments.[4]

Swedish and European technical education

It is essential to distinguish between the institutionalized structures of education corresponding to various occupational levels in industry, private or public. Three such levels can be identified during the nineteenth century, and in Sweden, as elsewhere on the Continent, a hierarchy of technical schools was accordingly established.[5] At the top were the highly qualified engineers who had received an education in a technical university or similar, destined for leading positions in industry and administration in the private and public sectors. Next came those educated in a technical secondary school or a comparable institution. Engineers in this category were suited to jobs at a dependent and middle level or to leading positions in the minor sectors of industry. At the lowest level were the products of technical education – vocational training – for operatives of various kinds. In this chapter, I consider only students and graduates destined for the top and middle positions, i.e. those coming from the technical universities and the technical secondary schools or colleges[6] – a choice that does not imply any underestimation of the importance of the technical education for workers.

In Sweden, as throughout continental Europe, observers recognized at an early stage the importance of technical education and qualifications for people in leading positions.[7] France has always been recognized as a leader in institutionalized education, followed (during the nineteenth century) by Austria, the German states, and, among others, Sweden. The institutions that resulted in Germany, notably the *Gewerbeinstitut*, developed into technical universities, while educational provision for students aspiring to positions in the middle range was not made until later. Germany was particularly successful and she set the general pattern for the system of technical instruction in Sweden,[8] while France seems to have 'forgotten' the middle level, with implications for her industrial performance.[9] In my view, the French case would reinforce the conclusion that an institutionalized technical education for all occupational levels is an indispensable condition for success.

During the nineteenth century, the Kungl. Tekniska Högskolan or The Royal Technical University in Stockholm (KTH) was, strictly speaking, the only technical university in Sweden. And even it received its formal title only after fifty years of existence. Its original statutes date from 1826, when it was given the title Technological Institute. That institute had grown from the Mechanical School, which was founded in Stockholm in 1798 and which in its turn goes back to the Laboratorium Mechanicum (later the Royal Model Chamber) founded in 1697 by Christopher Polhem, 'the father of technical education' in Sweden.[10]

Whatever the formal position may have been, however, we have also to take account of two other institutions, both of which were in effect technical universities. The Chalmers Institution in Gothenburg was founded in 1829, thanks to a donation of 1811 by William Chalmers (a Swedish-born son of English parents) for the establishment of a trade school. The Chalmers School provided a technical education that was of equal standing with that available at the KTH: indeed, until the middle of the century, its syllabus had a strongly 'scientific' profile. Nevertheless, it was not until 1937 that the Chalmers school was granted the title of Chalmers Tekniska Högskola (Chalmers Technical University), a name that was attached to the school's upper divisions. Two years later, joint statutes for the technical universities in Stockholm and Gothenburg came into force.

In the philosophy of technical education, therefore, a distinction is visible here between the two institutions during the first half of the nineteenth century. In both cases, education was geared to what were seen as society's industrial needs. For example, in the case of the technical university in Stockholm, the first statutes (rather similar to those at the Polytechnisches Institut of Vienna) stated that the purpose of the school was 'to collect and purvey knowledge and information necessary in order to run . . . crafts and industry successfully'. But this raised the question how such a goal could best be obtained: by an educational philosophy founded on 'learning by doing', apprenticeship, and 'trial and error', i.e. with an emphasis on practical learning, or by a more scientific training founded on a thorough knowledge of mathematics and the application of an up-to-date command of physics, chemistry, and other 'pure' sciences.

While at Chalmers it was recognized from the beginning (notably by Carl Palmstedt, professor and director of the school) that scientific principles were essential elements in the best technical education, in Stockholm the education provided at the Institute was extremely elementary throughout the first two decades. In fact, the original statutes of the Technological Institute stated explicitly that instruction should 'generally' be popular and practical rather than severely scientific.[11] As a result, there were soon internal quarrels concerning the Institution's main function, the sort of education it was to offer, and its methods. The director, G. M.

Schwarz, 'Sweden's first *teknolog*', was against theory, arguing that education at the Institute should be free from anything that could be called 'scientific'. Despite work by committees and proposals for improvements, the Institute had to wait until the mid-1840s for a radical change that promoted a specifically scientific orientation, with mathematics as the basic subject. Then, new statutes aimed at increasing the degree of specialization, were passed (in 1846) and put into effect in 1848. It was from this time that the school emerged as a true institution for higher technical education. As the statutes put it, the Institute was to be 'An institution of education for young men who pursue some kind of industrial occupation which cannot be properly performed without a knowledge of nature, especially of chemical and mechanical knowledge of a technical kind'.[12] Now, in accordance with this principle, mathematics became the basic subject at the Institute.

In the school's subsequent development during the nineteenth century, the move of the upper division of the Falun Mining School to Stockholm and its amalgamation with the Technological Institute were of special significance. The move resulted, in 1867, in the adoption of new statutes which led to a division into four *fackskolor* (specialized schools for different branches of industry): one for machine construction and mechanical technology, one for chemical technology, one for mining science, and one for civil engineering. The scientific character of the education was explicitly emphasized. The courses were said to be 'for young men who want to pursue some kind of technical profession, requiring a sufficient *scientific education*'.[13]

It is obvious that in the mid nineteenth century anyone in Sweden who sought an internationally reputable technical education could find it in these institutions. However, apart from a few minor examples, an institutionalized structure of lower technical education was non-existent before the 1850s. In retrospect, this is not surprising. As the Committee of 1907 which reported on this sector of Swedish education explained: 'When at the turn of the century in 1900 the need for technical instruction grew, as a result of industrial development, it was quite natural that the extensive technical knowledge demanded by those holding the leading positions within large-scale industry should be satisfied first'.[14] In this context, the Committee mentioned developments in Austria and Germany as well as in Sweden, continuing:

> When the oldest technical institutions had developed into 'universities' with a main duty of serving the interests of larger industrial firms, there emerged a need for specific schools in which those in small concerns and in craft occupations . . . could acquire limited but specially adapted technical instruction . . . it was in this respect that the first notable efforts were made about the middle of the nineteenth century.

Another incentive for the mid-century reforms was the fact that the technical universities required a new type of preparatory school, in which 'real' subjects, i.e. disciplines in the areas of mathematics and natural science, were central. In accordance with these views and inspired by the German *Gewerbeschulen*, technical secondary schools now began to be introduced into Sweden. Four schools, named *tekniska elementarskolor*, were opened in the 1850s – at Malmö (1853), Borås (1856), Örebro, and Norrköping (both 1857) – and in 1901 a fifth school was added, in Härnösand. These schools were to give a complete technical education for a specific level of occupation, while also providing entrance qualifications for the technical university.

The plan for Swedish technical education, which in the main was realized, was presented in 1850 by L. J. Wallmark, director of the technical university in Stockholm. It is said to have opened a new era in the history of Swedish technical education.[15] The importance of an education for each of the three levels to which I referred earlier was explicitly emphasized. In the industrial context of the time, the technical secondary schools worked satisfactorily for several decades, but in the 1870s it was thought necessary to reform them as part of a wider reorganization of the country's entire provision for technical education.[16]

The main reason for change was the content of the instruction in the technical secondary schools. Hitherto, these schools had provided only a general education, and it was now considered important to give their curricula a more markedly technical character. In the Committee of 1907 the point was made in these terms: 'It is remarkable that the education at our "technical elementary schools" in its oldest form had, to a large extent, a general mathematical and scientific character, and [that] the schools were only to a minor extent recognizably technical schools'.[17] Drawing on an international comparison, the Committee observed that in Austria and Germany, towards the end of the 1860s, it was realized that the *Realschulen* and *Gewerbeschulen* could not fulfil their double function of educating both for direct entry to industry and for further study in higher technical institutions. On the one hand, the education was not professional enough for smaller firms, and, on the other, it was not advanced enough for the rising entrance qualifications in the technical universities. The Swedish problem was very similar. In the new regulations of 1877, it was emphasized that the duty of the technical secondary schools was to provide elementary *technical* knowledge (the italics are in the original document) for youngsters who wanted to be educated for industrial employment. To realize this goal, a separation of the technical subjects into *fackavdelningar* (specializations) was made. The old function of education, to prepare for entrance to the technical university was abandoned. That task was taken over by the natural science 'branch' at the general secondary school.

It is clear, then, that from the 1850s three levels of education, corresponding to distinct general levels in the occupational hierarchy, were established, along the general lines of the German system. Thereafter, in the 1870s, in accordance with a rising demand and a more urgent call for quality from industry, further organizational changes were made: the most notable improvements, dating from 1877, concerned the technical education of engineers and technicians for small-scale industry and for positions in the middle range. In principle, the formal organization that was established in the 1870s existed until the 1920s.[18] On the highest level were the technical universities in Stockholm and Gothenburg; next were the technical secondary schools, including Chalmers' elementary section; while the third level was represented by various training schools. Towards the end of the 1890s there were about thirty-five schools in this last category; by 1908–9 there were sixty-six of them.[19]

Generally, the system of technical education in Sweden during the nineteenth century met quite satisfactorily industry's demand for qualified engineers and technicians. But by the beginning of the twentieth century, critical voices were beginning to be raised. Again, most of the criticisms concerned the education of engineers for middle-range positions, and again they were inspired by perceptions of German technical education – a point to which I return in the section 'Demand and career patterns'.

Numbers of engineers

One difficulty in assessing the importance of the engineer in the growth process in earlier periods has been our rather scanty knowledge of the number of active engineers and their occupations in society at various times. In *Engineers and Industrial Growth*, I tackled the problem by estimating the numbers of highly qualified engineers in France, Germany, and Sweden, admitting to this category all those with an education from the schools that were either already, or were later in the nineteenth century to become, technical universities. I showed that about 1850 there were roughly 600 graduates in Sweden with qualifications from the KTH and Chalmers. If we include the military engineers qualifying at Högre Artilleriläroverket och Artilleri-och Ing. Högskolan at Marieberg (a military engineering school founded in Stockholm in 1818), this figure has to be doubled. If in addition we include students at the KTH and

Chalmers who only attended occasional courses, the total figure for technicians and engineers who received some form of education in these schools rises, by the mid-century, to around 1800.

One important school, the Marieberg school in Stockholm, was not included in my study, despite the fact that in the literature it has been regarded as the only real technical university in Sweden before the reorganization of the KTH in 1876[20] and as a Swedish counterpart to the French Ecole Polytechnique.[21] The reason for the omission of this school was its marked military orientation: its original function was that of a higher educational institution for officers in all branches of the army.[22] A further complication was that, from 1842 until 1869 the school also educated 'civil engineers', i.e. non-military engineers for public works (a form of training taken over by the KTH in 1869), and that it was not possible to distinguish these engineers from the military ones. However, the education of 'civil' engineers was only marginal in the school's total activity, and the underestimate is correspondingly small.[23]

The growth in the number of graduates from KTH and Chalmers and the corresponding increase in the stock of engineers with an education from these two universities from the 1850s can be observed from table 5.1. As the table shows, the average number of graduates produced in each year doubled between the 1860s and the 1890s – from about 50 to 100 – and by the 1910s KTH and Chalmers had a combined annual output of over 150 highly qualified engineers. Accordingly, the stock of such engineers increased from between 700 and 800 in the 1850s, to 1500 in the late 1880s and 2000 in the late 1890s. By the First World War, there were almost 3,500 engineers in Sweden who had been educated at one or other of the two technical universities.[24]

To these figures we must also add the engineers who had graduated from the technical secondary schools and (from 1877) from the elemen-

Table 5.1. *Number of engineers graduating from the KTH and Chalmers; 10-year annual averages*

	Graduates (flow)	Number of engineers (stock)
1850s	32	720
1860s	46	980
1870s	65	1,230
1880s	61	1,470
1890s	100	1,860
1900s	144	2,650
1910–14	154	3,320

tary section at Chalmers. However, calculations comparable with those for the graduates from the technical universities have not been attempted. The main reason is that a good deal of double-counting would be inevitable, since, as I have already observed, the technical secondary schools, from their inauguration in the 1850s until 1877, also served as preparatory schools for the technical universities.

Nevertheless, it is possible to give some estimate of the total number of engineers in Sweden at the beginning of the twentieth century. The essential evidence is provided by an inquiry, made in 1908 by the Committee that had been appointed in the previous year, into the number of technicians in private and public industry in Sweden. This evidence shows that the engineers who had graduated from Sweden's technical universities made up rather more than 40 per cent of the total, while those from the technical secondary schools or colleges accounted for about 30 per cent, with the rest – including those who had received their technical education abroad – coming from schools that formed 'technicians'.

As table 5.1 indicates, the number of practising KTH and Chalmers engineers in 1908 was about 3,000.[25] The percentages given for the various types of technicians identified in the 1908 investigation gives us, for the number of practising engineers in Sweden at that time, a figure of about 2,200 who had been educated in the Swedish technical colleges and about 2,000 'technicians' with other qualifications, including roughly 750 educated outside Sweden. If, for statistical purposes, we omit those who had received their technical education abroad as well as those in the third category above, we arrive at a rough estimate of 1,000 for the number of engineers in Sweden who, about 1880, had been educated at a technical secondary school or college. By the early 1890s, the number had risen to about 1,500, and just after the turn of the century, it stood at approximately 2,000.

These figures assume their full significance when they are compared with those for Germany. From this comparison, a conspicuous quantitative difference emerges. For although the number of graduates grew substantially in Sweden during the nineteenth century, the number of qualified engineers in society as a proportion of the economically active male population was lower than in Germany. If we take only engineers trained in the technical university, it was not until the First World War that Sweden attained the figure of 2.0 per thousand – a figure that Germany achieved as far back as the early 1880s. When engineers from technical colleges and comparable schools are included, the difference between Germany and Sweden in this respect becomes even more marked. According to K.-H. Ludwig's study *Technik und Ingenieure im*

Dritten Reich, the number of engineers in Germany at the turn of the century who had been educated in one of the *Fachschulen* – technical secondary schools/technical colleges – together with other 'engineers' was between three and five times the number of engineers who held the highest qualifications.[26] In Sweden, by contrast, as the investigation in 1908 indicated, the ratio between 'technical university engineers' and other engineers/technicians was only 1:1½. This gives a total density of engineers in Sweden in the early twentieth century that was probably, at the most, between one third and one half of the figure for Germany.

Demand and career patterns

Of course, technical education does not by itself create a modern industry. There must also be a demand for engineers and technicians. Here, the main reason for the low density of engineers in Swedish society, relative to Germany, was probably not a lack of demand for qualified engineers and technicians, although, as I shall show, such arguments have been advanced. As was pointed out by the Committee of 1890 which considered the expansion and reorganization of the technical university in Stockholm, a steady stream of inventions and new areas of application for the technical sciences had created a 'lasting increased need for persons with a thorough technical education'.[27] That the demand for engineers with the highest qualifications ran strongly through the later decades of the nineteenth century and the early twentieth century has also been stressed.[28] According to a public inquiry of 1919, established to ascertain the distribution of engineers in various sectors and the need for technical skills in the Swedish economy, a growing shortage of qualified engineers was beyond question. The small increase in the number of employed engineers with an education from KTH and Chalmers was particularly noticeable with regard to the period covered by the inquiry (1910–19).[29] Commenting on the appointment of the committee for this inquiry, the head of the ministry said that within professional circles it had been emphasized 'for a long time' that fewer engineers were being educated than were required to meet the needs 'not only of our present industry, but more particularly to create suitable conditions for new industry'. The first 'parent' of this opinion was said to be Svenska Teknologföreningen (The Swedish Association of Engineers and Architects or STF), and a similar view had been expressed, in an address to the government, by Sveriges Industriförbund (The Swedish Association of Industries).[30] However, most of the criticisms of the Swedish system of education from the 1880s onwards were directed against the middle and lower levels of technical education. Development in this area had been far from satisfactory.

So it was that while the Swedish reforms of the 1870s (based on the German pattern) marked the end of a phase of development, Germany's own system of technical education for the middle and lower levels entered an important new phase of development.[31] Already, about 1880, it was found in Germany that the *Gewerbeschulen*, for example, were not successful, and society had reacted very quickly to this failing. With the support of the government, municipal communities, craft and industrial societies, and private individuals, specialized schools for specific industrial activities and professions were created. The reforms were supported by a national *Gewerbeordnung* whose importance was endorsed by, among other organizations, the German national engineering organization, Verein deutscher Ingenieure (VDI).[32]

Comparable changes did not occur in Sweden. The Swedish Committee of 1907 found it remarkable that it had only recently come to be generally recognized in Sweden that something must be done about the number and quality of technicians for middle- and lower-range positions. As the committee's report put it: 'By comparison with the progress of our industry, the development of lower technical education in the country over the last thirty years appears slight'.[33] It was considered of specific interest to study the relative numbers of technicians and workshops or factories and workers in the various industrial sectors. On average, for the year 1908, it was found that throughout industry, there were between four and five factories and about 130 workers for every technician. In mining, the relative number of technicians was higher: one to every 60 workers.

It has to be emphasized that the number of factories per technician is calculated as an average for all industry (excluding mining) and that the figure is based on an underestimate of the total number of technicians. The committee also stressed that more than half (54 per cent) of the individuals with formal technical qualifications were active in what it called 'true' mechanical and allied industries, where the average was one technician in each factory. Nevertheless, in the committee's words: 'technical education has not yet fully assumed the right to manage our industry'. The situation was further aggravated by the fact that the majority of the technicians worked in drawing departments, laboratories, and business offices, which meant that the proportion of educated engineers in managerial positions was even smaller, by comparison with the number of factory-workers, than the raw data would suggest.

In discussing the causes of its findings, the committee took account of the possibility that many employers had no proper understanding of the value of a technical education. This was reflected, according to the committee, in the tendency of many graduates from the technical secondary schools to find jobs abroad. But the committee concluded that the main cause was that Sweden 'for many industrial fields lacks specialized education [*fackundervisning*], and the specialized education that is given is not consonant with present industrial needs, owing to bad or weak equipment and obsolete organization'. However, these criticisms of lower technical education raise the more general question: what careers did the country's qualified engineers enter?

For the first half of the nineteenth century, information is scanty. It is only for the first decade of Chalmers graduates (1829–39) that their occupational fields are known. But it is clear that engineers went on to all types of occupations, as is the fact that the areas in which the majority of engineers made their careers were industry and craft activities: more than half of the Chalmers engineers were active in these fields.[34]

For later periods, the information is better. The occupations of the engineers who qualified at KTH between 1850 and 1880 have been studied, as well as (in the investigation referred to above) the technicians in employment in 1908. It is obvious from table 5.2, which summarizes these results, that qualified engineers were active in every branch of the economy, but it has to be observed that a particularly high proportion were active in mining and in mechanical and other industrial sectors. The figure for 1880 is approximately 45 per cent of the KTH engineers, for 1908, it is over 60 per cent. About three-quarters of the Chalmers and college engineers were in these fields at the latter date. Also notable is the rather high proportion of engineers active in railways and hence working in the building up of the country's infrastructure.

The 1908 study also shows that qualified engineers were frequently to be found in senior positions. This was most evident for the KTH engineers, less so for engineers who had come from the technical secondary schools. The contrast is brought out clearly in table 5.3.

Most earlier studies of Swedish engineers have not taken account of the age structure of the individuals, i.e. the pattern of careers over time. However, this pattern has been thoroughly studied by Rolf Torstendahl in his *Dispersion of Engineers in a Transitional Society. Swedish Technicians 1860–1940* (1975). Torstendahl examined technicians' careers at three points: 1–2 years, then 14–16 years, and finally about 29–31 years after graduation. The main investigation covered the graduates who emerged from the schools between 1881 and 1910. This gave a total of 4,396 qualified engineers: 2,015 from KTH, 972 from Chalmers, and 1,409 from the technical secondary schools.

Table 5.4 contains some of the results of Torstendahl's work. As the

Table 5.2. *Occupation of graduates from the KTH (1880, 1908), Chalmers, and technical secondary schools (TES) (1908)*

Industry/Field of occupation	KTH				Chalmers		TES	
	1880	%	1908	%	1908	%	1908	%
Mining	62	8.4	132	13.6	29	5.7	66	6.0
Engineering	172	23.2	254	26.1	199	39.4	412	37.8
Wood, pulp and paper	24	3.2	57	5.9	46	9.1	105	9.6
Chemical	23	3.1	42	4.3	15	3.0	21	1.9
Mineral	2	0.0	34	3.5	34	6.7	46	4.2
Other industries[a]	42	5.7	87	9.0	45	8.9	161	14.8
Building and Construction	56	7.6	105	10.8	81	16.0	64	5.9
Railways	119	16.1	196	20.2	48	9.5	122	11.2
Telegraph	6	0.0	32	3.3	5	1.0	10	0.9
Various[b]	234	31.6	33	3.4	3	0.6	79	7.2
	740		972		505		1,091	

[a] Including food, textile, leather and rubber, consultancy, and unspecified.

[b] Including national defence, state administration, education, others, and unknown occupation.

Sources: *Industritidningen Norden* (1881) pp. 39ff, C. G. Rystedt's article 'Teknologernas verksamhet och öden' (Rystedt's register of KTH graduates 1850–1880); 'Den lägre tekniska undervisningen i Sverige' (Lower technical education in Sweden) *Bihang till Riksdagens Protokoll* (1918), pp. 485ff.

Table 5.3. *Job position in 1908. Engineers graduated from the KTH, Chalmers, and TES*

	KTH		Chalmers		TES	
	Number	%	Number	%	Number	%
Level I	352	36.2	142	28.1	232	21.3
Level II	451	55.7	263	52.1	383	35.1
Level III	79	8.1	100	19.8	476	43.6
	972		505		1,091	

Note: Level I denotes independent leading positions in management and similar. Level II positions at a dependent and middle range, where a qualified technical education is required. Level III includes persons in lower positions, such as foremen, draughtsmen, etc.
Source: See table 5.2.

Table 5.4. *Engineers graduated from the KTH, Chalmers, and TES (Borås, Malmö), 1881–1910, employed in the metal industry, building trade, consultancy engineering, and railways at different stages in their careers (%)*

	Percentage of graduates in these branches after certain years		
	C1 (1–2 yrs)	C2 (14–16 yrs)	C3 (29–31 yrs)
KTH	71.1	61.5	58.7
Chalmers	68.2	63.2	59.2
TES	71.8	62.9	60.5

Source: R.Torstendahl, *Dispersion of Engineers* (1975), p. 99.

table shows, the four dominant sectors were the metal industry, the building trade, engineering consultancy, and railway engineering and management. Moreover, these sectors remained dominant over time, giving a strikingly stable occupational structure at a macro level. Finally, the study indicates that the engineers – KTH and Chalmers as well as 'college' products – attained leading positions rather quickly.

Table 5.5 gives a break-down of individual careers in the private sector. A high proportion of the engineers were active in this sector. This is obvious from Torstendahl's study. As table 5.6 indicates, it is also clear that the preference for the private sector was more pronounced among engineers from Chalmers and the technical secondary schools than among those who had graduated at the Stockholm technical university.

Table 5.5. *Positions in private business, after certain number of years in a career. Engineers graduated from the KTH, Chalmers, and TES (Borås, Malmö), 1881–1910*

	Percentage of group at work in Private Business				
	Business leaders	Employees	Consultant engineers	Unspecifiable	Group size
1. 1–2 years					
KTH	2.8	80.6	16.3	0.3	870
Chalmers	1.0	88.0	10.6	0.5	407
TES	1.9	82.4	15.4	0.4	485
2. 14–16 years					
KTH	27.8	54.4	16.8	1.0	915
Chalmers	19.8	63.9	15.4	0.9	460
TES	17.3	70.8	11.5	0.5	427
3. 29–31 years					
KTH	40.5	40.5	18.3	0.6	820
Chalmers	32.7	47.3	18.0	2.0	395
TES	29.0	57.8	12.7	0.0	367

Source: Torstendahl, *Dispersion of Engineers* (1975), p. 217.

Finally, table 5.7 shows that the percentage of Chalmers and college engineers going into the private sector was similar to the corresponding proportion of the members of Svenska Teknologföreningen; about 1910 it stood at approximately 70 per cent.

The most obvious conclusion that emerges from this discussion is that in the second half of the nineteenth century highly qualified engineers were dispersed across all fields, but that a clear majority of them opted for industry, mostly in the private sector. The choice reflected contemporary evaluations of the hierarchy that was seen to exist in industry and more widely in the economy, and it was vindicated by the tendency for engineers of this calibre to reach senior positions fairly rapidly. A similar pattern is observable among academically less qualified engineers, i.e. those who had graduated from the technical secondary schools. Although about one fifth of this group in the early twentieth century held managerial or other senior posts, the majority were to be found in middle and lower positions. It seems likely that college engineers who achieved managerial status did so, for the most part, in small companies.

Table 5.6. *Distribution of engineers into public and private sectors after certain years from graduation. Graduates of the KTH, Chalmers, and TES, 1881–1910*

	Public sector	Private sector	Non-sectorised specified occupation	Unspecified occupation	Total number
1. 1–2 years					
KTH	32.7	62.0	1.0	4.2	1,378
Chalmers	23.6	72.7	1.3	2.5	556
TES	12.7	79.2	2.1	6.1	1,023
2. 14–16 years					
KTH	37.3	57.2	3.1	2.4	1,558
Chalmers	24.7	69.6	2.1	3.5	662
TES	20.9	71.2	4.5	3.4	597
3. 29–31 years					
KTH	38.0	54.3	5.5	2.2	1,476
Chalmers	25.8	64.2	6.5	3.5	598
TES	20.8	60.2	5.3	7.6	903

Source: Torstendahl, *Dispersion of Engineers* (1975), p. 155.

The professionalization and social status of engineering

It is clear that engineering as an 'art' existed long before engineering as a 'profession' and that at the beginning of the nineteenth century it was only in France that engineering was 'clearly and definitely established as a learned profession'.[35] In other continental countries, in Scandinavia, and in England, the process of professionalization got under way with very different degrees of intensity.

A central distinction that has emerged in the theoretical literature on professionalization is the one between occupation and 'profession'. On this analysis, a profession is defined as an occupation whose members possess a high degree of *specialized*, *theoretical knowledge*, are expected to carry out their tasks while taking account of certain *ethical rules*, and are bound by a strong *esprit de corps* arising from a common education and adherence to particular doctrines and methods.[36]

In Germany, professionalization advanced rapidly during the nineteenth century through the country's institutions of technical education and such organisations as the national Verein Deutscher Ingenieure, founded in 1856. The VDI was the successor of the association formed ten years earlier by former students at the Berlin Gewerbeinstitut, later the Technische Hochschule of Berlin, and, as Wolfgang König's contribution to this volume shows, it made an important contribution to furthering the professional interests of engineers in German society. Swedish developments in this area followed a pattern similar to that in Germany, though somewhat more slowly. Specialized, theoretical knowledge was purveyed, from the 1820s, by the forerunners of the technical universities in Stockholm and Gothenburg and, from the 1850s, by the broader system of engineering education. It was about 1860 that the Swedish Association of Engineers and Architects – Svenska Teknologföreningen or STF – was founded. Although the STF takes 1861 as the year of its formal foundation, it had its roots in the 1850s, notably in a student organization at the technical university in Stockholm. The Stockholm Ingenjörsföreningen, founded in 1865, was also important. It emerged as an élite group, consisting of those who were regarded as the most prominent of Sweden's technicians.

The Ingenjörsföreningen also maintained close contact with scientific

Table 5.7. *The Swedish Association of Engineers and Architects. Distribution of members in fields of occupation according to the 1909 register of members*

		Abroad		
Occupation or activity	In Sweden	In Europe	Non-Europe	Total
In governmental service[a]	318	–	–	318
In municipal service[b]	150	–	2	152
Ironworks and mining	154	7	4	165
Other industries	507	45	27	579
Engineers in private business[c]	151	4	5	160
Architects in private business[d]	93	–	–	93
Private railways and trams	47	–	–	47
Teachers	69	–	–	69
Insurance	25	–	–	25
Businessmen	13	–	–	13
No information[e]	174	24	7	205
	1,701	80	45	1,826

[a] Public railways, telegraph, marine corps, civil engineers, the board of pilotage, patent and registration office, and hydro-electric power board.
[b] Engineers for public works or geodetic assessment and town architects.
[c] Keepers of patent agencies and entrepreneurs in civil engineering.
[d] All architects in non-public sector.
[e] Including retired engineers and members on travels for the purpose of studying.
Source: G. Holmberger, *Svenska Teknologföreningen 1861–1911* (Stockholm, 1912), Appendix VIII, p. 266.

research and technical education. Of its total membership of 95 in 1865, about 80 per cent had received a theoretical education, and a quarter were graduates of the technical universities in Stockholm and Gothenburg.[37] In 1891 the Ingenjörsföreningen was amalgamated with Svenska Teknologföreningen. This further increased the importance and strength of the latter organization, which had fulfilled the role of a national association since the later 1880s. It became a 'point of support in the efforts of engineers to win recognition, on the national as well as the local level for technical and industrial points of view'.[38]

However, the process of professionalization in Sweden was well under way as early as 1870, and the activities within the two organizations I have mentioned were not limited to purely technical problems. In making this point in his work on Swedish engineers, Nils Runeby stresses that the new professional élite emerged first from a background in science. Confident of his own competence, the qualified engineer also claimed his place – and a corresponding responsibility – in society.[39]

Hence, in a manner that paralleled Sweden's industrial development, the prestige and social standing of engineers rose too. With his technical qualifications, the engineer came to represent a new élite and, in a way, became the symbol of the industrial epoch and a new culture: to quote Gunnar Eriksson, he was 'standing at the line where industrialization and science met'.[40] As in Germany, the struggle for the right to grant the doctorate to candidates in higher technical education marked the culmination of the process of social aspiration. It was believed that once this was achieved, the qualified engineer would receive the respectability in society he deserved, as well as the protection he needed against the less qualified. Runeby has convincingly interpreted these views as an expression of the close relations that existed between purely scientific aspirations and academic ideas of status and professionalism: 'The men of the "new" élite sought their social acceptance by joining the "old" one'.[41] In Germany the corresponding process culminated in the late 1890s, while in Sweden the right to confer the PhD in engineering was not granted until the 1920s: in 1927 at KTH, and at Chalmers ten years later.

In addition to professionalization, the social status of an activity may be measured by the social background of the individuals engaged in it. Unfortunately statistics concerning the socio-economic background of the students at the Swedish technical universities and technical secondary schools are not readily available for the nineteenth century, and I know of no study of the period that treats the question. However, there is no reason to assume that the profile of socio-economic backgrounds in Sweden differed significantly from that in Germany. It seems probable that students were largely recruited from the middle class, but also to a growing extent from the highest social groups.

Table 5.8. *Students who started their studies at the Swedish technical and classical universities after finishing secondary school, 1902/04 and 1924/26. Students divided according to father's occupation*

	KTH/Chalmers		Lund/Uppsala Univ.	
Social group	1902/04 (%)	1924/26 (%)	1902/04 (%)	1924/26 (%)
(a) I	50.2	60.2	55.6	43.9
(a) II	43.4	26.9	37.9	44.1
III	6.4	12.9	6.5	12.0
(b) I	39.4	40.1	51.9	38.7
(b) II	54.1	47.0	41.6	49.3
III	6.4	12.9	6.5	12.0
Number of students	279	394	1,121	2,025

Note: By calculations according to the (a) method, engineers and accountants belong to social group I, while according to (b), they belong to social group II.
Source: P. Dahn, *Studier rörande den studerande ungdomens geografiska och sociala härkomst* (Lund, 1936), table 148, p. 385.

A study of the social backgrounds of students who entered the universities and various specialized schools after the *studentexamen* (the secondary school leaving examination, roughly equivalent to the *baccalauréat*) in the first quarter of the twentieth century confirms this assumption.[42] The results with regard to the technical and classical universities at the turn of the century and in the mid 1920s are given in table 5.8, which brings out the very similar social backgrounds of students in the two types of institution.

About 1900, social groups I and II accounted for almost 95 per cent of the total number, and whatever criteria are used, between 40 and 50 per cent of the students at the KTH and Chalmers belonged to the upper class (social group I) – a proportion that still stood somewhere between 40 and 60 per cent in the mid 1920s. At the turn of the century, only about 5 per cent came from the lowest social groups: by the 1920s, this proportion had doubled, at both the technical and the classical universities.

The proportion of students at the technical secondary schools who came from the lowest social groups was higher, standing at about 10 per cent in 1895 and at over 20 per cent in 1910, as table 5.9 shows. It is noticeable, however, that in the mid 1890s more than one third of the students, perhaps 40 per cent, belonged to social group I. By 1910, this proportion had declined to between a quarter and a fifth. Yet the

Table 5.9. *Students at the technical secondary schools, 1895 and 1910 (autumn semester). Students divided according to father's occupation*

Social group	1895 (%)	1910 (%)
(a) I	41.8	24.5
(a) II	49.6	54.3
III	8.6	21.2
(b) I	34.7	19.1
(b) II	56.7	59.7
III	8.6	21.2
Number of students	268	335

Note: By calculating according to the (a) method engineers and accountants belong to social group I, while according to the (b) they belng to social group II.
Source: P. Dahn, *Studier rörande den studerande ungdomens geografiska och sociala härkomst* (Lund, 1936), table 81, p. 246.

predominance of middle- and upper-class origins, even in the somewhat lower technical schools (where the proportion in social groups I and II was about 80 per cent), is obvious.

A recent study of industrial managers in Sweden confirms these conclusions.[43] To a very minor extent, the managers in 1880 came from families in the lowest social group. One third had received an academic education – including KTH and Chalmers – and more than 10 per cent had received post-secondary education of some sort. Over one third (36 per cent) of the total number were products of technical education. It follows that, with very few exceptions, industrial leaders around 1880 were 'educated men' and came from the 'upper class'. However, the sample of only about 100 individuals, is too small to allow broad generalizations. Nevertheless, it is clear that the owners and managers of leading Swedish big business at the turn of the century had received an education that was far superior to that of most of their fellow-countrymen.

So it would appear that the status bestowed by a technical education in nineteenth-century Sweden was high. It probably had been so since the middle of the century, and there is no doubt that it was rising. A career as an industrial engineer was socially respectable in Swedish society long before the twentieth century, and the recruitment and selection of students wishing to enter technical education presented no significant difficulty.

Swedish industrial performance and technical education

The availability of capital and that of workers for various levels of occupation and of markets – factors that are constantly created in an industrial society – constituted the preconditions for modern industrial production. During the late eighteenth century and the nineteenth century, these preconditions were established in various ways in such nations as Britain, France, Germany, and Sweden.[44] Naturally, it is difficult to establish exactly when a process of industrialization starts in a particular country, but it seems plausible that Sweden's industrialization was well in train by the middle of the nineteenth century. The 1850s was also the first decade in which Sweden experienced a boom in the business cycle which had its origin in the industrial sector: in this case, in the wood and timber industry and its associated exporting activities.[45] Nevertheless, manufacturing industry's share of the GNP remained low, even in the boom of the 1870s. The main economic characteristic of the 1870s, in fact, was the heavy investment across the whole range of industrial activity and in the infrastructure, notably railways.[46]

From the 1880s, Swedish industrial production became more oriented to processing and improved quality. Exports became more differentiated, and manufactured products such as pulp, paper, and engineering tools and machinery, not least from the electrical industry, became important. But it was only in the last decade of the century that the break-through of 'modern' Swedish industrial society occurred. Thus the boom of the 1890s, which constituted the third period of significant growth in the Swedish economy during the second half of the nineteenth century, substantially increased the industry's share both in production and in the number of employees. The industrial production of consumer goods for the domestic market increased greatly, and the resulting expansion was of the same magnitude as that of the capital goods and export industry.[47] The emergence of a new Swedish export in the 1890s, iron ore, meant that the pattern of exporting was affected once again, but, as in the mining and iron industries, the technical and management characteristics of this product were far higher than in the case of, for example, sawmill products.

As I mentioned in my introductory remarks, the overall growth rates of the Swedish economy from the second half of the nineteenth century were among the highest in the industrial world. The growth of total industrial production (value added at fixed prices) between 1868 and 1912 was 4.9 per cent per annum,[48] which implies a doubling of production every fourteenth year. This could be seen as one result of an institutionalized system of technical education of high quality, capable of providing industry with the manpower it needed. However, it is impossible to prove such a causal link. Among other things, various types of engineers in society and the detailed profile of industrial growth have to be considered. As I have just indicated, this points to the need for an examination of the structure of Swedish industry, in particular of the importance of science-based and knowledge-intensive industry, and of its size-structure.

Unfortunately, no studies of this latter aspect of Swedish industry as a whole exist for the period before the 1870s.[49] But it is known that the 1820s marked the first phase in the growth of industrial production, more especially for the domestic market, and that this process was particularly evident in the textile industry, although it made its mark across the whole spectrum of manufacturing industry. This development culminated in the 1850s and 1860s with a more general break-through of factory industry. In textiles, this meant a substantial increase in factory size: in the mid-1820s, the average number of workers per factory was about 20, whereas by 1860 it was 100.[50] In manufacturing industry as a whole the pattern was more diversified.

In the twenty or so factories in manufacturing industry at the middle of the nineteenth century which had no connexion with the important Swedish mining and iron industry, about 1,500 workers were employed, almost one third of them at the Motala *verkstad*.[51] While the older factories in the mechanical sector expanded considerably during the 1850s and 1860s, a large number of smaller factories in the same sector were also established during these decades. Consequently the size structure of Swedish industry became very skewed. But the most prominent feature was the dominance of the large companies. In the early 1870s, almost 80 per cent of the total labour force in Swedish industry worked in establishments with more than 100 workers. Ten years later, the proportion had fallen to just below three quarters – a consequence of the establishment of new smaller factories. By the late 1880s, however, the proportion had risen again to 80 per cent. In the late 1890s, it was more than 90 per cent, and on the eve of the First World War, it was roughly 95 per cent.

The development of big industry becomes even more pronounced when we examine the proportion of establishments with more than 500 workers. This proportion increased from less than 20 per cent in the early 1870s to approximately one third about 1890, and thereafter to 50 per cent at the turn of the century and progressively to an even higher proportion by the time of the war.[52]

The Swedish technical universities and colleges were comparatively successful in meeting industry's demand for technical personnel. A large supply of trained manpower was considered of great importance, and the number of qualified engineers in Sweden grew substantially during the century. According to my calculations, the number of highly qualified active engineers (stock) at the time of the First World War was almost 3,500, while a rough estimate of the total number of engineers with formal qualifications at that time gives a figure of almost 9,000.

Does this mean that one explanation of the rather impressive growth and performance of Swedish industry is to be found in the development of the country's institutions of technical education, and that qualitatively as well as quantitatively the supply of engineers was 'optimal'? Are we also to conclude that Swedish society provided unusually favourable conditions that eased the transition from an agricultural to an industrial society? I have emphasized at several points that the prototype for Sweden in these respects was Germany and that, socially and culturally, the patterns of development in the two countries were (allowing for a time lag) similar. However, as a proportion of the economically active population, the number of highly qualified engineers in Sweden was significantly lower than in Germany, a fact that becomes even more pronounced if we also take account of engineers with lower formal technical qualifications. Such an observation is not compatible with the notion of an 'optimal' situation.

Public inquiries into technical education in Sweden in the early twentieth century stressed a 'shortage' of engineers, both the highly qualified and those with lower qualifications, which of course is the same as saying that the supply of engineers was too small.[53] It may be, however, that the higher proportion of engineers in German society merely reflects a different industrial structure, with an earlier, and broader, development of knowledge-based industry. On these issues we can only speculate.

It seems more important, for the moment, to emphasize the positive features of the Swedish case. In any analysis of the country's growth, a number of factors must be taken into account, not least economic policy and the development of international and domestic markets. As other contributions to this volume show, monocausal explanations have no place in economic history.

The major conclusion is, however, that in an international perspective, Sweden in the nineteenth and early twentieth centuries stands out as a success story in European educational history. It was understood from an early stage that a workforce well supplied with formal technical qualifications was essential for an industrializing society. And that appreciation of the importance of education was turned from precept into practice with remarkably few mistakes.

Notes

1 See, for example, Moses Abramovitz, 'Resource and output trends in the United States since 1870', *American Economic Review. Papers and Proceedings* (May 1956), 5–23; Robert Solow, 'Technical change and aggregate production function', *Review of Economics and Statistics* (August 1957), 312–20; and Edward Denison, *The Sources of Economic Growth in the U.S. and the Alternative before us* (New York, 1962), and *Why Growth Rates Differ* (Washington, D.C., 1967).

2 See, for example, Angus Maddison, *Phases of Capitalist Development* (Oxford, 1982), tables 3.1 and 3.2, and Brian R. Mitchell, *European Historical Statistics 1750–1970* (London, 1975), table E1.

3 The full title is *Engineers and Economic Growth. Higher Technical Education and the Engineering Profession during the Nineteenth and Early Twentieth Centuries: France, Germany, Sweden and England* (London, 1982).

4 See Gunnar Eriksson, *Kartläggarna. Naturvetenskapernas tillväxt och tillämpningar i det industrielle genombrottets Sverige 1870–1914* (Umeå, 1978); Nils Runeby, *Teknikerna, vetenskapen och kulturen. Ingenjörsundervisning och ingenjörsorganisationer i 1870-talets Sverige* (Uppsala, 1976); and Rolf Torstendahl, *Teknologins nytta. Motiveringar för det svenska tekniska utbildningsväsendets framväxt framförda av riksdagsmän och utbildningsadministratörer 1810–1870* (Uppsala, 1975), and *Dispersion of Engineers in a Transitional Society. Swedish Technicians 1860–1940* (Uppsala, 1975). Mention should also be made of Boel Berner, *Teknikens värld* (Lund, 1981); Hans DeGeer, *Rationaliseringsrörelsen i Sverige* (Stockholm, 1978); and Bosse Sundin, *Ingenjörsvetesnkapens tidevarv* (Umeå, 1981).

5 See David S. Landes, *The Unbound Prometheus. Technological Change and Development in Western Europe from 1750 to the Present* (Cambridge, 1972), p. 150, and Torstendahl, *Teknologins nytta.*

6 The term 'technical university' is used throughout this discussion, even though, in the cases of Germany and Sweden, it is strictly valid only from the second half of the nineteenth century. As I use it, the term 'technical college' is equivalent to 'technical secondary school'.

7 England was an exception. See Ahlström, *Engineers and Industrial Growth*, chapter 3.

8 I use 'Germany' to denote the German states collectively throughout the nineteenth century, although the title was not formally applicable until after 1871. On the success of the German system, König passes a rather different judgement in his contribution to this volume.

9 See Ahlström, *Engineers and Industrial Growth*, chapters 2 and 4.

10 Torsten Althin, *KTH 1912–62. Kungl. Tekniska Högskolan i Stockholm under 50 år* (Stockholm, 1970), p.12.

11 A comparison with the Polytechnical Institute in Vienna is interesting. The statutes of the Vienna school date from ten years before those for Stockholm, and the latter resembled them in several ways. The Vienna statutes stated explicitly that the main task of the Institute was to provide a '*scientific*' education (the italics appearing in the original text). By doing so, they forestalled criticism from the craft guild, which might otherwise have perceived a threat of competition with its privileges. In Stockholm, what was foreseen in Vienna actually occurred; see Ahlström, *Engineers and Industrial Growth*, note 48 (pp. 68–9).

12 See Pontus Henriques, *Skildringar ur Kungl. Tekniska Högskolans historia* (Stockholm, 1917), vol. 1, p. 219. It was also stated that, whenever governmental departments required, the school was obliged to comment on matters concerned with industry and craft practices and to supply craftsmen in the private sector with advice and information. This function as an advisory institution had been one of the institute's dual aims since its foundation.
13 'Scientific education' is italicized here.
14 *Utlåtande och förslag till den lägre undervisningens ordnande*, p. 1 [Committee of 1907]: printed in *Bihang till Riksdagens protokoll vid lagtima Riksdagen i Stockholm 1918.*
15 Victor Adler, *Om det tekniska undervisningsväsendet i Sverige* (Stockholm, 1897), p. 45.
16 See *Betänkande och förslag angående den lägre tekniska undervisningen i riket* [Committee of 1872]: printed in *Bihang till Riksdagens protokoll vid lagtima Riksdagen i Stockholm år 1876.*
17 Committee of 1907, pp. XXVI and 3.
18 See Rudolf Anderberg, 'Grunddragen av det svenska tekniska undervisningsväsendets historia', *Ingeniörsvetenskapsakademien. Meddelande*, no. 5 (1921), 71.
19 Adler, *Om det tekniska undervisningsväsendet i Sverige*, p. 1, and Committee of 1907, p. 30.
20 Torsten Gårdlund, *Industrialismens samhälle* (Stockholm, 1942), p. 228.
21 Lars J. Wallmark, *Om tekniska elementar-skolors inrättande i Sverige* (Stockholm, 1851), p. 6.
22 P. Sylvan and O. Kuylenstierna (eds.), *Minnesskrift med anledning av K. högre artilleriläroverkets och krigshögskolans å Marieberg samt Artilleri-och ingenjörshögskolans etthundråriga tillvaro, 1818–1918* (Stockholm, 1918), p. 17.
23 Torstendahl, *Teknologins nytta*, p. 20.
24 The method of calculation is described in chapter 3. Calculated annual averages (for five-year periods) are given in table 2.1, with annual figures in the Appendix.
25 This figure is twice the number found in the investigation, but it must be the more realistic figure for the *total* number of qualified practising engineers at the beginning of the twentieth century. For a discussion of the relevance of my calculations, see Ahlström, *Engineers and Industrial Growth*, p. 71 (footnote 64). The importance of foreign students at the technical universities as well as of engineers with a foreign education working in Sweden is also considered; see *ibid.*, pp. 21 and 26 (footnote 32).
26 Karl-Heinz Ludwig, *Technik und Ingenieure im Dritten Reich* (Dusseldorf, 1974), p. 19 (note 6). See also Ahlström, *Engineers and Industrial Growth*, p. 70 (note 59).
27 *Betänkande och förslag till utvidgning och omorganisation av Tekniska Högskolan* (Stockholm, 1891), p. 70.
28 Jan Wallander, 'Ingenjörerna i studentbetygen och i verkligheten', *Teknisk Tidskrift* (1944), p. 988.
29 The Committee of 1919 for the reorganization of Chalmers. Cited hereafter as *SOU* 1935:52 (*Betänkande i anledning av tillströmningen till de intellektuella yrkena*), pp. 258–62.

30 *Ibid.*, p. 263.
31 Committee of 1907, p. 6.
32 *Ibid.*, pp. 9–10 and 29.
33 *Ibid.*, pp. 30ff.
34 See Ahlström, *Engineers and Industrial Growth*, table 2.6 (p. 49).
35 See Frederick B. Artz, *The Development of Technical Education in France, 1500–1850* (Cambridge, Mass., 1966), p. 161. For a discussion of such concepts as 'engineer', 'engineering', 'technology', and 'professionalization', see (in addition to my comments here) Ahlström, *Engineers and Industrial Growth*, chapter 1.3.
36 The criteria that should be applied and the decision about the best method of analysis raise sophisticated sociological problems that cannot be considered in this context. With regard to the choice of the method of analysis, however, it seems reasonable to choose a gradualistic method, in which all the occupations are considered to be more or less professionalized. 'What is or is not a profession is determined by the intersection of the scale of professionalization at some point, the occupations above this point being denoted as "professions"'. See Bengt Abrahamsson, *Militärer, makt och poltik* (Stockholm, 1972), pp. 10ff. This seems preferable to a typological method, which attempts to define criteria by which 'professions' can be distinguished from 'non-professions'.
37 See Runeby, *Teknikerna, vetenskapen och kulturen*, pp. 88ff.
38 G. Holmberger, *Svenska Teknologföreningen 1861–1911* (Stockholm, 1912), p. 120.
39 Runeby, *Teknikerna, vetenskapen och kulturen*, p. 100.
40 Eriksson, *Kartläggarna*, p. 73.
41 Runeby, *Teknikerna, vetenskapen och kulturen*, p. 180.
42 See Paul Dahn, *Studier rörande den studerande ungdomens geografiska och sociala härkomst* (Lund, 1936).
43 Sune Carlson, 'Ett sekels industriledare', *Skandinaviska Enskilda Banken Kvartalsskrift*, no. 2 (1986). Carlson's findings for the year 1880 are discussed in Lennart Jörberg, *Svenska företagare under industrialismens genombrott 1870–1885* (Lund Studies in Economics and Management, no. 2) (Lund, 1988), p. 28.
44 Economic historians have debated these issues for more than a decade. The research in and on Sweden is surveyed and discussed in Lennart Schön, *Industrialismens förutsättningar* (Lund, 1982).
45 See Schön, *Industrialismens förutsättningar*, p. 15.
46 It should be mentioned that W. W. Rostow, in his book *The Stages of Economic Growth* (Cambridge, 1971) dates the Swedish "take-off" to the years 1868–90 (table 1, p. 38).
47 See Lennart Jörberg, *Growth and Fluctuations of Swedish Industry 1868–1912* (Lund, 1961), and 'The Nordic countries 1850–1914', in *The Fontana Economic History of Europe*, volume 4, part 2. Also Schön, *Industrialismens förutsättningar*.
48 Lennart Schön, *Historiska nationalräkensper för Sverige. Industri och hantverk 1800–1980* (Lund, 1988), Table I.14.

49 The only branch of Swedish industry that yields information on this matter is treated in Lennart Schön, *Från hantverk till fabriksindustri. Svensk textiltillverkning 1820–1870* (Lund, 1979).

50 The figures are for cotton-weaving factories. For woollen factories, the average figure about 1860 was only 32. See Schön, *Från hantverk till fabriksindustri*, Appendix, p. 179.

51 See Gårdlund, *Industrialismens samhälle*, p. 33.

52 In the early 1870s, establishments with more than 100 workers were already responsible for almost 90 per cent of the total value of production, a proportion that had risen to over 95 per cent by the early twentieth century. In the 1890s, establishments with more than 500 workers produced more than 50 per cent of the total value of production, a figure that exceeded 60 per cent in the 1910s. My statistics are taken from Jörberg, *Growth and Fluctuations of Swedish Industry*, page 134 (table).

53 It is sometimes stated that in England there was a 'lack' or 'shortage' of qualified engineers in industry, as well as in government and the public sector. It must be stressed, however, that from a purely economic point of view it is incorrect to use such terminology when such engineers were not in demand. I discuss the point in chapters 1.2 and 3 of my book, *Engineers and Industrial Growth*. There, I emphasize that in such circumstances, the term 'unmet need' is preferable. That term was coined by John Jewkes in his article 'How much science?', *The Economic Journal*, 70 (1960), 1–16, in which he developed the view that not only the supply of engineers but also the demand for them was inadequate.

6 Industrialization and technical education in Spain, 1850–1914

Santiago Riera i Tuèbols

It seems unnecessary to insist on the fact that the industrialization of any country and its provision for technical education are closely related. Here, Spain is no exception. Despite the existence of two important centres – Catalonia, with its powerful textile industry, and the Basque Country, where iron and steel and heavy industry were dominant – the difficulties that beset the process of Spanish industrialization throughout the nineteenth century were accompanied by corresponding difficulties in attempts to establish a supporting system of technical education. Neither industrialization nor technical education, in fact, developed in a wholly satisfactory way, in spite of the valiant efforts of a liberal bourgeoisie intent on consolidating its power.

Throughout a complicated history, political and social factors, as well as the attitudes of the ruling class, have decisively influenced Spain's economic development. Consequently, technical education has found itself constantly embroiled in a maze from which escape has been exceedingly difficult. The aim of this chapter is not only to describe how all this happened within the framework of industrialization, but also to attempt some kind of explanation.

The origins of technical education: the Escuela de Ingenieros de Caminos and other schools

The origins of the first engineering school in Spain, the Escuela de Ingenieros de Caminos y Canales, are distinctively French. The founder of the school, Augustín de Betancourt, had studied in Paris from 1784 until 1791, at the Ecole des Ponts et Chaussées, where he was the senior member of a group of Spanish scholarship-holders supported by the monarchy. Impressed by the Parisian school, Betancourt proposed to the Earl of Floridablanca the establishment of a similar institution in Spain. As a result, the Real Gabinete de Máquinas de Madrid was created in

1792, using the scale models, plans and memoirs accumulated by the Spanish scholarship-holders during their stay in the French capital. This institution, conceived initially as a laboratory, was to become, in 1802, the Escuela de Caminos y Canales.[1]

At its foundation, the Escuela de Caminos y Canales offered two courses, preceded by an entrance examination.[2] We know that Betancourt was farsighted enough to have two books translated in advance, so that they would be available by 1802. These were the *Geometría descriptiva* of Gaspard Monge and the *Tratado de mecánica elemental* by Louis B. F. Francoeur. We also know that he was helped in planning the new school by two important Spanish scientists, José Chaix and the Creole José Mª Lanz. The text book by Lanz, *Essai sur la composition de machines*,[3] to which Betancourt contributed, was commonly to be found in the libraries of the schools that I shall discuss below. And others who were associated with the Escuela likewise translated French works that were subsequently used by professional engineers and teachers at the Escuelas de Ingenieros. This is true, for example, of the *Traité du calcul différentiel et du calcul intégral* by Sylvestre F. Lacroix, translated by Francisco Travesedo, who was professor at the Escuela de Caminos y Canales, the Reales Estudios de San Isidro, and the University of Madrid.

The so-called War of Independence of 1808–14 brought this first experiment to an end, and it was not until the three years of liberal rule between 1820 and 1823 that the Escuela de Caminos y Canales was resurrected, though the new foundation too succumbed with the collapse of the liberal experiment. However, after the death of Fernando VII, in September 1833, a third attempt finally achieved success. At the beginning of this third stage – the Escuela de Caminos y Canales was reopened in November 1834 – it is surprising to note the absence of Betancourt's companions and disciples, who had still been teaching in the second Escuela in the twenties. Even so, the French influence persisted,[4] recalling the earlier close links with French science, notably through the stay in Spain of the well-known chemist Joseph-Louis Proust – in Vergara (1777–80), Segovia (1788–99), and eventually Madrid (1799–1806) – as well as François Chabaneau's discovery of a method for the purification of platinum, made while he was working at the Real Seminario Patriótico de Vergara towards the end of the eighteenth century.

In fact, these were not the only bonds with France. In Catalonia, there were already close associations in the late eighteenth and early nineteenth centuries. First, the successive visits of Pierre André Méchain, Jean-Baptiste Biot, François Arago, and others involved in the measurement of the length of the arc of the meridian through Dunkirk and

Barcelona, brought a number of Catalan scientists, such as Francesc Salvà, Francesc Santponçs, and Antoni Martí i Franquès, into contact with French science: in some cases, especially that of Martí i Franquès, it meant the dissemination of their works in Europe.[5] It should also not be forgotten that the Catalan region now belonging to France was part of Catalonia until the Treaty of the Pyrenees (1659), and that it was common for Catalans from the Peninsula to study in Montpellier, Toulouse, and Perpignan. In addition, Francesc Carbonell, the first director of the Escuela de Química established by the Barcelona Chamber of Commerce (Junta de Comercio de Barcelona), obtained his doctorate in medicine in Montpellier in 1801. There he was influenced by Jean-Antoine Chaptal, who was to determine his future orientation in chemistry. The second director, Josep Roura, was a frequent visitor to France, from where he introduced several of the latest scientific and technical developments, among them gas lighting, which was first tested in 1826 in Barcelona.

It should be noted that the creation of the Escuela de Ingenieros de Caminos y Canales was not an isolated attempt to launch modern technical education in Spain. As early as 1777, when the German Enrique C. Storr was appointed director of the mines in Almadén, he was required to teach mineralogy; this was the first move to institutionalize the subject. Later, in 1798, José Clavijo Fajardo, who was then director of the Real Gabinete de Historia Natural, appointed Christian Herrgen to head a specialized course in mineralogy that soon became deservedly famous. Four years later Herrgen proposed a curriculum that marked the beginning of a true *Escuela* for professionals. The War of Independence, however, was to interrupt what would have been a promising start, and it was not until 1825 that the Dirección General de Minas was established and only in 1835 that the Escuela de Ingenieros de Minas was set up as a separate entity in Madrid. It was later followed by the Escuela de Ingenieros de Montes (1843) and the Escuela General de Agricultura (1855).[6]

The first institution offering technical education directly linked with industry was the Real Conservatorio de Artes, which was established by Royal Decree on 18 August 1824, to incorporate and replace the old Gabinete de Máquinas. We know that in the hope of attracting a scientist of appropriate calibre, Lanz, then in Paris, was offered a professorship at the Conservatorio, although he probably did not take it up.[7] Likewise, it is certain that the second professor at the Conservatorio, Antonio Gutierrez, took advantage of visits to France – in 1827 his absence lasted the whole academic year – to maintain contact with Abraham-Louis Breguet, Félix Savart, and Jean Peltier. Members of the Sureda family, who played an important role in the institution, also kept in touch with scientists and centres of research abroad. One of them, Josep, moved to Saint Petersburg, where he spent several months at the invitation of Betancourt, who was already there, trying to operate a silk-spinning machine he had invented.

The Real Conservatorio de Artes also created chairs in Valencia, Seville, and Malaga, but not in Barcelona, where the Escuelas of the Chamber of Commerce offered modern technical education.[8] It is in these *Escuelas* and, to a lesser extent, in the Conservatorio de Artes and its auxiliary chairs, all established with the specific aim of training technicians to advance the country's industrialization, that the antecedents of the *Escuelas de Ingenieros Industriales* are to be found.

The Escuelas de Ingenieros Industriales

At the end of the 1840s, the liberal bourgeoisie in Spain was engaged in a struggle for political power. In marked contrast with what occurred elsewhere in Europe, the objective was never fully achieved. Yet already in the thirties feudalism had been abandoned, textile manufacturing had been modernized (notably in the Catalan cotton industry), a steel industry had been established (albeit with difficulty), and agricultural output had been growing. Moreover, the construction of the railway network had begun, with the aim of creating a sub-structure for the national market that was indispensable if industrialization was to succeed. What had been achieved, however, was to be interrupted by the crisis of 1866.

The bourgeoisie, which was trying to carry through both a bourgeois and an industrial revolution (by associating its quest for political power with dreams of modernizing the country) was aware that in order to achieve its goals, well-trained technicians were indispensable. These men required the solid theoretical and practical background that would enable them to plan and run the new industry. The vision was not entirely new. It had already been put into practice at a regional level by the Chamber of Commerce in Barcelona. Educational reform was to be initiated with the Act of 1845 which brought changes in secondary and university education. The number of universities was reduced to ten: at Barcelona, Granada, Madrid, Oviedo, Salamanca, Santiago, Seville, Valencia, Valladolid, and Saragossa. Law was to be taught in all of them, medicine in five, while only two provided a full course in pharmacy. Moreover, a doctorate could only be obtained in Madrid, which thus became the most prestigious university. But there was no mention of technical education. When the Royal Decree of 4 September 1850, drawn up by the Minister of Commerce, Education, and Public Works, Manuel de Seijas Lozano, remedied the matter five years later, the omission was explained as follows:

> Before setting up industrial schools, it was necessary to have in place the institutions that were to be the basis for them; and before promoting education, it was necessary to train the teachers who would be responsible for conducting it. Each reform has its due time and it is of no avail to wish to advance it prematurely.[9]

Despite these claims, the reality that was introduced by the Decree of 1850 was to be very different. For most of the lecturers who made up the staff of these schools had been trained abroad, as was the case at the Real Instituto Industrial de Madrid, or they came from institutions outside the University, as was the case in Barcelona, where the *Escuela* of the Chamber of Commerce had to provide the newly established Escuela Industrial not only with lecturers but also with premises and equipment.[10] Even so, the Decree marks the beginning (at least in principle) of a training in industrial engineering aimed at fashioning local technicians and hence at avoiding the need to 'search in foreign countries for people capable of practising them [the liberal professions, here engineering] with the full range of requisite knowledge'. It was a claim which also was not to be fulfilled, as I shall show below.[11]

The Royal Decree in question established a stratified educational system of a kind that commended itself naturally to the liberal bourgeoisie. It had three levels – elementary, intermediate, and higher – which fostered, or at least did not prevent, a degree of vertical mobility, if only in principle. The elementary level provided a basic training; while the intermediate level, which lasted three years, provided a substantial technical education. Entrance to this latter level was possible on completion of the elementary course; alternatively, it could be achieved either via the ordinary primary schools or by passing an entrance examination consisting of tests in grammar, mathematics, and drawing. To enter the higher-level course, which lasted two years, successful completion of the intermediate level was compulsory. At this higher level, two specializations were possible: in mechanics or chemistry.

Among the schools that were established, the *Escuelas* of Seville, Barcelona, and Vergara offered the first two levels, whereas the one in the capital, the Real Instituto de Madrid, also offered the higher level. Since the degree at the higher level could only be obtained by going to Madrid, with the financial costs that this involved, and since at the end of the intermediate level candidates were offered the opportunity of attending a further course and obtaining a qualification as a second-class industrial engineer, the number of first-class or higher industrial engineers was limited.

The Royal Decree of 20 May 1855, while not substantially modifying the earlier one of 1850, established that the purpose of the elementary level would be to convey knowledge of a type appropriate to workers, whereas the intermediate level, now retitled 'professional', was intended to train the technicians of industry. The role of the higher level was to prepare the teaching staff on whom the elaborate stratification of technical education depended.

Two years later, the Law on Public Education of 9 September 1857 extended the right to train engineers at the higher level to the *Escuelas* in Barcelona, Seville, and Vergara, as well as to those in Valencia and Gijón which had been established in 1855. In this way the privileged position of the *Escuela* in Madrid was brought to an end. Similarly the courses taught at the Escuelas de Ingenieros de Caminos, Minas, Montes, Agrónomos, and Industriales were formally classified as higher studies. In the following year, by a decree of 20 September 1858, the structure of higher education was formalized: now, it was necessary for candidates to study for three years at a faculty of science and then pass an entrance examination before beginning the further three-year programme at their chosen Escuela Superior.

Minor modifications were made in the intervening years up to 1868, the year in which the decrees of 21 and 24 October altered the previous regulations. In order to go on to the three years of higher education at the Escuelas de Ingenieros Industriales it now became necessary either to pass the courses taken at one of the faculties of science or, alternatively, to pass an entrance examination in these same subjects. This curriculum was to last until 1902.[12]

In conclusion, it must be noted that by 1867 all the other technical schools had closed, leaving Barcelona as the only Escuela Superior de Ingenieros Industriales until the Escuela in Bilbao opened in 1899. It is significant that the existence of the Escuelas de Ingenieros Industriales was justified only where industrialization was taking place rapidly. The Madrid school was to re-open only in 1901, in principle with the aim of supplying engineers for the state administration.[13]

The professional status that was accorded by the new structure was initially very low. The decree of 20 May 1855 specified that the titles established by this decree did not confer the exclusive right to practise the industrial profession; they were seen as a gauge of the ability and aptitude of industrial, mechanical, or chemical engineers, who would be employed by the Government according to their specializations. In fact, industrial engineers and the professional associations they established (in Madrid in 1861 and Barcelona in 1863) fought ceaselessly for the right to define their privileges and authority, which often entailed disputes with architects and, especially, mining engineers.[14]

Influences on technical education

If we compare the plan of 1858 for technical education that was formulated in the wake of the law of 1857 with the one that governed the Ecole Centrale des Arts et Manufactures in Paris in 1850, we find both differences and similarities. The most striking differences are that in Spain it was essential to have previously studied a number of specified topics in a faculty of science and that two fields of specialization, mechanics and chemistry, were available. On the other hand, the length of the course was the same, and there existed a remarkable similarity in the subjects that appeared in the curricula of the two schools.

The most obvious point of similarity was that of textbooks. When the *Escuelas* in Barcelona, Seville, Vergara, Gijón, and Valencia began to offer courses at the higher level, the Ministry of Development, in particular industrial development (Ministerio de Fomento) published a Royal Decree (dated 15 October 1861 and published in the *Gaceta de Madrid* on 20 October 1861) which specified the textbooks that were to be used for the courses in agricultural and industrial engineering as well as in architecture. The list for the first of these included a total of twelve works, of which six were French. The corresponding proportion of French items for industrial engineering was much higher: eighteen out of twenty-two books were of French origin, either in translation or in the original. In the Escuelas de Arquitectura, seventeen out of the twenty-nine works listed were French.[15] The French influence, therefore, was pervasive; indeed, it amounted to virtual dependence. But why was the French model favoured, when England, Scotland or Germany might, on the face of it, have been equally appropriate choices?

It seems that the Spanish authorities turned to France for at least three reasons: first, the prestige of French scientific and technical educational institutions; secondly, the presence of French capitalists in Spain, who often brought with them technicians and equipment from France; and thirdly, the geographical proximity, which meant that some of the first teachers at the Real Instituto had been educated in Paris[16] and that Catalan industrialists and engineers kept in close contact with their French colleagues and travelled to France both to improve their knowledge and to search for ideas and patents.

That the country later looked towards Germany is partly shown by the so-called 'university questions' that were raised and discussed by the *Krausistas* (followers of the German philosopher Karl C. F. Krause) in Spain during the 1860s and 1870s. The *Krausistas* were criticized, and some were even dismissed, for defending the use of 'live texts' instead of 'dead texts', as they used to call the textbooks imposed by the ministry. In fact, they were defending the principle of free teaching and, interestingly for my purpose, signalling a new admiration for the German model of university education.[17]

With respect to technical education in particular, it has to be borne in mind that in the second wave of industrialization, at the end of the century, the chemical and electrical industries were to play a leading role. It is well known that the former in particular was an industry in which Germans were dominant. Hence it is not surprising that towards the end of the century, a German model found favour, in Spain, as technical education was renewed with a view to introducing and developing the technological innovations that were now spreading through Europe. Significantly, in the inaugural addresses at academic courses, both in the universities and in the Escuelas de Ingenieros, as also in scientific and technical journals, criticism of technical education was common. The poor quality of practical instruction in laboratories and workshops was deplored, and the German system was praised as one in which theory and practice were fruitfully combined. This change in the favoured model in education was a virtually inevitable consequence of Germany's emergence as the undisputed pacemaker in the leading industrial sectors. In the event, however, the consequences of the new admiration for German education materialized rather slowly, because of an inherent Spanish reluctance to change, and the modification of the curricula was only completed in 1902.

Industrial development in the nineteenth century

I have argued that the industrialization of Spain was carried through under the powerful influence of industrial engineers, a professional group created for the purpose. This does not mean, however, that no other engineers had a role. The contribution of mining engineers in extracting and processing minerals, for example, is beyond question, though its exact nature is still obscure. Civil engineers, too, made a crucial contribution to the process of modernization, initially obtaining the most senior posts that were available to local professional staff in foreign railway construction companies.

Following the efforts of the enlightened monarchy of the eighteenth century to modernize the country and the promising moves towards industrialization made by the Catalan bourgeoisie, the year 1808 marked an interruption in these processes, which did not end until the late 1820s. Thereafter, the process of industrialization in the nineteenth century fell into two distinct phases. The first reached its climax in the fifties, and then lost momentum in the sixties, coming to an end in the crisis of 1866, when Catalonia led the way in developing the cotton industry. The second occurred at the end of the century.

The first phase began to take shape with the Alienation Law (Ley de Desamortización) of 1835, which attempted to repair the Spanish economy after the ravages of the War of Independence and the loss of the country's colonies. Through this law, land belonging to the Church became the property of the bourgeoisie, but at a highly profitable price for the latter, as the state agreed to be remunerated with consolidated debt bonds, which had lost much of their face value. However, attempts to create a class of small property-owners based on the French model and to create a system of capitalist exploitation based on the Prussian model both failed and, as a result, the agricultural problem was to remain a serious one.

The first wave of development was also marked by laws governing railways (the Ley de Ferrocarriles of 1855) and banking (the Ley de las Sociedades de Crédito y Bancos de Emisión of 1856). Both of these laws favoured the arrival of foreign capital, brought by such figures as the Rothschilds, the Péreires, and the Prost-Guilhous. It was under the protection accorded by the Ley de Ferrocarriles that the railway network was built up – a process which the law fostered by sanctioning all sorts of privileges for the concessionary companies established before 1864. These privileges included important discounts on import duties for mobile and fixed equipment as well as for the coal consumed, both during the construction of the lines and in the decade that followed. The construction of the Spanish railway system undoubtedly represented a missed opportunity for the development of the nation's industry. Moreover, having been developed in many places under pressure from local political and private interests, the system was inadequate and disorganized, with the added difficulty of the lack of a market to supply.

It was during this first stage that the Catalan cotton industry was modernized: between 1835 an 1860, for example, 99 per cent of all spinning and 45 per cent of weaving came to be mechanized. Yet it was a modernization that lacked coherence. It was achieved by the assimilation of the new technologies that were becoming available throughout Europe, although a number of innovations by Catalan technicians and engineers were also incorporated, such as the loom for the manufacture of silk velvet which Jacint Barrau patented and then sold to the English company Lister & Co., and the improved version of the same loom by the engineer Ferran Alsina, who used it in the production of cotton velvet. Later, at the beginning of the twentieth century, there came the innovation of stretching in the spinning process, due to Ferran Casablancas. However, it seems that, with few exceptions, Catalan employers in the textile sector preferred to modernize their factories using English equipment and under the direction of foreign technicians. In dyeing and printing, the dominant influences were French, introduced by skilled workmen from Mulhouse and local operatives who were sent to Mulhouse to improve their skills. A typical case is that the engineer José Vallhonesta, who brought to Spain the modern techniques of textile dyeing he had learned in Paris from Michel-Eugène Chevreul at the Gobelins factory.[18]

Despite its initial success, the textile sector in Catalonia was hampered by a serious shortage of coal and iron ore. The shortage could be remedied by exploiting hydraulic power from rivers or settling near the port of Barcelona, where imported coal arrived. But it constituted a serious weakness in Catalan industrialization, by making it dependent on the steel industry of northern Spain. In fact, the centre of Spanish metallurgy was at first closely linked with the profitable activities of mining and processing in Andalusia (some of the earlier blast furnaces and reverberatory furnaces for civilian, non-military purposes, being located in Rio Verde and Malaga). But in the mid-century the centre moved to Asturias, a region rich in coal beds, and subsequently the lead passed to the Basque Country, where abundant iron ore reserves ensured a peak of prosperity between 1880 and 1913.[19] During these thirty-three years, 91 per cent of the iron ore extracted in the Basque Country was sent to Britain in the boats which, on their incoming voyage, brought coal from Wales or Durham. Thus, what might have become an important Gijon–Bilbao axis became a Bilbao–Cardiff one. In this process, the main cause was clearly the state of transport in Spain, which meant that in the port of Cadiz coal from Newcastle was cheaper than coal from Sama de Langreo in Asturias.

The shortages of coal and minerals did not prevent the appearance of major machine-building companies in Catalonia. Nuevo Vulcano, founded in 1835, built the first steam-powered tug in 1849; Alexander y Hnos, creared in 1849, built the first stationary steam engines between 1840 and 1850; and La Maquinista Terrestre y Marítima established itself, from 1855, as the leading builder of bridges, steam engines, and, later, railway equipment. These manufacturers, which were all located in Barcelona, like the Seville company of Portilla & White, were founded, in about 1856, under the influence of large European companies. But all three of them had to engage in a long struggle against a tendency towards an excessive diversification of their products, made necessary by the weakness of the domestic market and by the competition from the foreign equipment, which, in the case of the railways and the merchant fleet and navy, was favoured by Spanish governments until the fiercely protectionist customs duties imposed in 1891 and 1906. The approval by the government, in 1908, of a programme of shipbuilding to be carried through by Spanish companies had the effect of reinforcing the protectionism that pervaded this important field.[20] Without going into the free-trade vs protectionism controversy, which I believe was resolved wrongly with the belated and extremely slow introduction of protectionism, it can be said that the companies I have mentioned recognized and often protested against the situation in which they found themselves.

Another important sector was gas and electricity. After the first attempt at gas lighting in the streets of Barcelona in 1826, it was fifteen years before the city council gave Charles Lebon the concession to install gas for street lighting. Once he had permission, Lebon not only built a modern factory in Barceloneta (a district of Barcelona) but also extended the enterprise to other Spanish cities: Valencia (1843), Granada (1866), Cádiz (1867), and Puerto de Santa María (1871).

In gas, foreign, and in particular French influence was always considerable. For example, in Madrid, after an attempt by an English company, it was the Péreires who promoted the Madrid Gas Street Lighting Company (Sociedad Madrileña de Alumbrado por Gas), which was managed by the French but with factories in the capital. Between 1859 and 1863 the Compañía General de Crédito, under the management of Alfred Prost, proceeded to set up factories in Valladolid, Pamplona, Burgos, Jerez, Cartagena, and Alicante. A company from Lyon established itself in Bilbao in 1844 and subsequently handed the enterprise over to the town council, as usually happened. In Saragossa the initiative was taken by the Lyon banking firm, Crédit Lyonnais, in 1865. In Santander, by contrast, it was (unusually) the English company Manby Wilson that supplied the city with gas, though even this activity passed into the hands of Lebon in 1867.[21]

With regard to electricity, a crucial event was the visit of Ramón de Manjarrés, the director of the Escuela de Ingenieros Industriales in Barcelona, to the Vienna Exhibition of 1873. There, Manjarrés saw Gramme's dynamos and ordered some of them from the Dalmau company. These were used in the first experiments in the physics laboratory of the Escuela in 1874 and 1875.[22] Thereafter, the pace quickened. On 28

September 1875 Maquinista installed the first electric arc lamps, and by the following year Batlló y Hnos had already installed five arc-lighting system.

It seems that as early as 1880 the Dalmau company, for which the engineer Narcis Xifra worked, installed the first power station in Spain.[23] In the following year the company became the Spanish Electricity Company (Sociedad Española de Electricidad or SEE), which installed the first electrical street lighting in Spain (in Barcelona in 1882) and, two years later, the first long-distance transmission line, from Sarría to Sants, over 8km. However, unexpected economic difficulties brought the SEE under British control in 1890. At the outset, the electrical sector had appeared a promising one: the example of the SEE, which functioned exclusively on Catalan capital and was considered by *L'électricien* to be the world's sixth largest electrical supply company, is significant. But soon it was impeded by the subordinate position of Spanish capitalism during the industrialization process. From 1890 onwards the history of the electricity companies became more intricate and, while it goes beyond the scope of this paper, it is sufficient to say that towards the end of the century there occurred a proliferation of supply companies through Spain that were eventually to be centralized.

Another notable company of this period was Planas, Flaquer y C*ia*, which carried out the improvement and extension of electrical street lighting in Girona in 1886 using for the first time in Spain, a transformer (a piece of machinery that was to be routinely manufactured by the same company from 1894). In 1895, Planas, Flaquer y C*ia* provided lighting equipment, made in its own factories in Catalonia, to illuminate the Teatro Real in Madrid.[24]

It is not clear to what extent the results obtained in the last two decades of the century depended on the instruction in electricity that had been available in engineering schools from as early as 1858: we simply do not know enough about the curricula and teaching practices to determine whether the introduction and dissemination of scientific theories preceded their practical application or whether it was the need for modernization that stimulated the development of electrical instruction. What is certain is that the time-lag between innovations and discoveries pioneered elsewhere in Europe and their diffusion in Spain via Catalonia was less marked in the case of electricity than in any other area of industrialization. Nevertheless, as the sector developed in Europe, so the lag became longer, reflecting an increasing level of technological dependence. The exploitation of foreign patents became more common, and routinely (though not invariably) basic products manufactured with local raw materials were imported. The result was a rise in prices, with a consequential effect in the loss of part – sometimes an important part – of the domestic market.[25]

Even so, electricity remained a sector in which there was an above-average increase in the number of industrial engineers employed at the turn of the century (see table 6.3., p. 158). This may be because the sector was a product of the second wave of industrialization, which was more scientific in character than the first and was therefore more clearly linked with the professional training of industrial engineers.

The fact that as the degree of technological dependence became more marked, the number of engineers in the sector increased and small- and medium-sized companies became ever more numerous at the expense of large companies, demonstrates clearly the contradictions and difficulties in Spain's modernization, even in those sectors which, for various reasons, seemed initially most promising.

Technical education and the funding of the Escuelas

The complex process I have described exercised a powerful influence on technical education. The law of 22 December 1868 permitting the exploitation of mineral resources was preceded by the regularization of the entry requirements for the Escuela de Ingenieros de Minas, and it was followed, on 24 October 1870, by new regulations governing the curriculum. The anxiety that existed over the curriculum is shown by the decision, taken in 1890, to abolish the regulations of 1870 and to substitute new ones. On 23 February 1901 these were also superseded; the new regulations remained in force until the final modification in the period I have discussed occurred on 30 July 1910. It is significant that a new Royal Decree on 9 November 1912 established a research laboratory for metallography in the Escuela. It was believed that the laboratory would encourage the kind of practical teaching whose absence had been so vehemently deplored as part of the recurring complaints about the excessively theoretical nature of technical education. But the laboratory was also seen as a vehicle for controlling the quality of the ore extracted from Spanish deposits and for seeking improvements in processing technique.

Despite all these initiatives, the government remained loyal to a liberalism of a characteristically nineteenth-century kind by avoiding (until the 1930s) any precise definition of the authority of industrial engineers. The repercussions of this failure were unmistakable in the recurring arguments with mining engineers, who, along with industrial engineers, were the senior technical employees most directly involved in industry.

The fact that from 1867 to 1899 the Escuela in Barcelona was the only one of its kind in Spain shows how strongly the process of industrialization was influenced by the profession of the industrial engineer and therefore the teaching in the related schools. More specifically, it indicates the distinctive view of the role of industrial engineers that was current among the Catalan administration and industrial bourgeoisie. In Madrid, the industrial engineer's function was to train a body of employees for the Administration, despite the very different aims that were stated at the start; in Barcelona, an industrial engineer was seen as an indispensable contributor to the country's industrialization. Since it was the central government in Madrid that legislated, this contrast is probably the reason for the highly theoretical background of the engineers – a background that prompted Lucas Mallada, a well-known practising engineer, to say at the Engineering Congress in Barcelona on the occasion of the Exposición Universal in 1888: 'What is needed is a little less science and a little more art'.

Another question is the funding of the *Escuelas*. If we limit ourselves to a well-known example, the Escuela de Ingenieros Industriales de Barcelona, it is obvious that the State, apart from meeting the initial building and installation costs, contributed nothing beyond a fixed sum of 15,000 pesetas. The city council also contributed a fixed amount of just over 24,000 pesetas, more than the State, while the remaining funds came from the provincial council (Diputación de Barcelona). The amounts contributed from these different sources at three significant periods are summarized in table 6.1.

It should be stressed that although the provincial council did not contribute anything in 1902, it had not stopped doing so. It is simply that in that year the *Escuela*'s own income, which had increased considerably since 1867–8, was sufficient, in conjunction with the subsidies from the State and the city council, to cover the normal running of the school. In fact, the average annual subsidy from the regional authorities in the decade 1880–90 was rather high: between 30,000 and 40,000 pesetas.

Table 6.1. *Sources of income of the Escuela de Barcelona* (in pesetas)

	1867–8		1880–1		1902	
Own income	1,505	(3.1%)	5,286	(6.7%)	36,202	(48.0%)
City council	24,100	(50.3%)	24,100	(30.7%)	24,100	(31.9%)
State	15,000	(31.3%)	15,000	(19.1%)	15,000	(19.9%)
Provincial council	7,233	(15.1%)	33,929	(43.3%)	–	(0.0%)
Totals	47,838		78,325		75,330	

Over the longer period from 1870 to 1910, by contrast, it was between 10,000 and 20,000 pesetas.[26]

It is clear that the State effectively entrusted to the Catalan bourgeoisie, through its regional institutions, the task of providing the main support for the *Escuela*. Significantly, the Catalan industrial bourgeoisie succeeded in providing the funding, whereas the other *Escuelas* disappeared from the map. It cannot be emphasized too strongly that this is an illustration of the direct relationship that was perceived to exist between industry and technical education.

Even so, the sums devoted to technical education were small by comparison with those in other developed countries. The shortage of laboratories, workshops, and equipment was one of the most worrying consequences of this. But the regenerationist atmosphere created by the loss of the last colonies, in Cuba and the Philippines, in 1898 also affected education. Men such as Josep Serrat i Bonastre in engineering asked not only for urgent reforms of the curricula but also for a careful consideration of the practical training of future teachers and of the needs of the schools for better equipment.[27] This is in tune with the views expressed in Italy when the Politecnico of Turin was set up in 1906. Moreover, in both countries, the view was expressed in the aftermath of an examination of the German model of technical education.[28]

By 1914, the curricula for industrial engineers had been modified. The curriculum of 1902, which replaced that of 1858, envisaged the setting up of an entrance examination, a five-year course, and a final examination. Five years later, in 1907, further slight modifications were introduced, including the extension of the course by one year.

Students at the Escuelas and the work of industrial engineers

Although no reliable data exist concerning the total number of engineers who graduated from the *Escuelas* in Spain during the nineteenth century, there is information covering limited periods. So far, I have been able to assemble three sets of figures, all related to the end of the period analysed. These cover mining engineers (Madrid), industrial engineers (Barcelona), and civil engineers (Madrid).

The data collected, grouped in five-year periods, are summarized in table 6.2. The number of fifty mining engineers included in the first five quinquennial periods has been obtained by dividing up the 237 engineers who graduated between 1877 and 1900 evenly over the twenty-four years of the period in question and multiplying the yearly average by five.[29]

Table 6.2. *The number of graduates from the Escuelas, 1876–1915*

	Mining engineers	Industrial engineers	Civil engineers
1876 –80	50	67	–
1881 –5	50	130	–
1886 –90	50	169	–
1891 –5	50	142	–
1896 –1900	50	176	–
1901 –5	59	278	57
1906 –10	114	293	74
1911 –15	129	173	147

Some tentative conclusions can be drawn from the table, although the incompleteness of the data makes this difficult. First, there is an unmistakable tendency towards a growth in the number of engineers in all three specialities. The exception in the five-year period 1911–15 for industrial engineers, which shows a decrease of 6.8 per cent compared with the previous period, can be attributed to the regular functioning of the *Escuelas* in Bilbao and Madrid and the redistribution of students who until then had been obliged to study in Barcelona. This growth has also to be linked with the increasing pace of development in the country generally. Industrialization, after all, requires well-trained technicians, and well-trained technicians in turn give an impulse to industrialization. On the other hand, an analysis of the annual, as opposed to the quinquennial data reveals very plainly the ups and downs of economic trends. These include, for example, a slight decrease in the number of graduates in the late 1910s, due to the First World War. In the case of civil engineers, despite these yearly variations, changes are less evident because of the highly selective character of the course and the close links that existed between the professional body and the national administration.

The analysis of the development of the different industrial sectors and of technical education leads directly to the question where engineers worked during the nineteenth century. Here, an answer can only be attempted, and then with caution, for the professional group that was at once the largest and the one most directly involved in industrialization, that of the industrial engineers.

For the statistical information used in these maps and in table 6.3, I have relied on the yearbooks of the Asociación de Ingenieros Industriales de Barcelona and of its equivalent in Madrid, the so-called Asociación Central, both of which at the time were independent. On these sources, a number of points have to be made. First, for the former, data for only three years are available (1888, 1895, and 1912), and, for the latter, there is information for only two years (1885 and 1913). Secondly, the fact that in 1887 a small number of members left the Catalan Association for the Asociación Central (forming a section within the Asociación Nacional de Ingenieros Industriales, a state level collective supported by the Asociación Central, and so creating a division that lasted until the end of the century) serves to distort the data. Thirdly, I am aware that the grouping by sectors is debatable. However, for all these imperfections, the data serve at least as a rough guide.[30]

From the imperfect evidence in table 6.3, certain trends emerge. The first is the decline in the number of industrial engineers employed in the textile industry in both the Catalan and the Central Associations. Secondly, there was a significant increase, both in absolute and percentage terms, in the sectors of water, gas, and electricity; this was a consequence, I believe, of the growth of the electrical sector referred to earlier. The significance of this sector appears all the greater if we consider that having been included in the gas sector, its growth equalled and then surpassed that of gas.

The chemical industry is another interesting case. While in the Catalan Association the percentage of engineers employed in the industry declined, there was a slight increase in the Central Association. This apparent anomaly is explained by the development of oil refineries (at Bilbao, Alicante, Seville, and Vigo) and above all by the creation of artificial fertilizer factories in Valencia. More generally, however, the small number and percentage of engineers employed in the sector can be explained by the assimilation of Spanish chemical companies by foreign firms. Another obvious trend was the gradual decline in the number of engineers employed in transport, owing to the consolidation of the railway network.

A final illustration of the relationship between industrial engineers and Spain's economic development is given by the map indicating the number of engineers working in each province in 1883.[31] The figures for the first five provinces are given in table 6.4. However, if we make the calculation by regions, rather than by provinces, the total numbers of engineers working in them are as in table 6.5.[32]

The conclusion that emerges is a rather predictable one for the leading industrial regions, Catalonia had the highest number of engineers in absolute terms, the highest percentage, and the highest number of engineers per 100,000 inhabitants (twice as many as in any other region). New Castile, with Madrid as its main city, was in second place: here, the concentration of professional engineers was a result of their engagement in the State administration rather than in industry – a situation that prevailed until significant industrial activity began to appear there in the twentieth century.

Table 6.3.

	Asociación catalana						Asociación central (State level)			
	1888		1895		1912		1885		1913	
	N.	%	N.	%	N.	%	N.	%	N.	%
Agriculture and mining	–	–	2	1.1	5	1.8	9	2.4	12	1.6
Textile industries	13	12.4	14	8	13	4.8	19	5.1	18	2.4
Chemical industries	5	4.7	3	1.7	6	2.2	12	3.2	32	4.3
Metallurgy and mechanical engineering	24	22.8	41	23.4	57	21.2	48	12.8	101	13.5
Other process industries	3	2.8	7	4	4	1.5	14	3.7	38	5.1
Water, gas and electricity	5	4.7	8	4.6	24	8.9	16	4.3	61	8.1
Transport	29	27.6	18	10.3	11	4.1	60	16	93	12.4
Education	9	8.6	10	5.7	29	10.8	55	14.7	76	10.2
Administration	8	7.6	6	3.4	29	10.8	83	22.1	179	23.9
Liberal professions	7	6.7	60	34.3	83	30.9	43	11.5	106	14.2
Others	2	1.9	6	3.4	8	3.0	16	4.3	32	4.3

Table 6.4. *Engineers working in the main provinces, 1883*

	Number	Per cent
Barcelona	155	31.76
Madrid	84	17.21
Seville	24	4.91
Valencia	16	3.28
Cadiz	14	2.87

If we examine the first two columns in table 6.5, Andalusia stands ahead of the Basque Country because of its mineral wealth, as well as its sugar industry, although its mid-century prosperity was a thing of the past. On the other hand, if we consider the concentration of professionals per 100,000 inhabitants, the figure for the Basque Country, including Navarre, is almost twice that for Andalusia, whereas if we exclude Navarre, the figure for the Basque Country rises to 4.88 engineers for 100,000 inhabitants.

It is clear that at the end of the century there were just two centres of industrialization in Spain: Catalonia and the Basque Country. These two centres, the former a century old, the latter more recent, recruited most of the engineers employed by industry. Other engineers, such as civil engineers, were almost all employed by the State. It would be interesting to analyse the case of mining engineers, but the information on their careers is, as yet, too scanty.

Modern technical education and the Mancomunitat in Catalonia

In 1901 a sector of the Catalan bourgeoisie began working for the integration of Catalonia with the wider economy and culture of Europe, and for giving the Spanish monarchy a constitutional and democratic character while continuing the still incomplete process of modernization. To these ends, they sought to develop a practicable programme of economic development and technical education. The programme was reinforced by a strong Catalan nationalism, which was part and parcel of the political reform movement, but in the end it foundered. The causes of this failure lie in the contradictions inherent in the movement's bourgeois roots and the tensions between the political and economic power of the centre and that of the periphery, tensions that were symbolized by the eternal struggle between Barcelona and Madrid.

Table 6.5. *Spanish engineers working in the regions, 1883*

	Number	Per cent	Number of engineers per 10^5 inhabitants
Catalonia	177	36.27	10.10
New Castile	90	18.44	5.53
Andalusia	63	12.91	1.92
Basque Country (inc. Navarra)	27	5.53	3.58
Old Castile	24	4.92	1.96
Valencia	23	4.71	1.67
Asturias	13	2.66	2.25
Aragon	11	2.25	1.23
Balearic Islands	7	1.43	2.42
Leon	7	1.43	0.53
Murcia	6	1.23	0.89
Extremadura	5	1.02	0.68
Galicia	4	0.82	0.22
Total for Spain	457		
Europe	10	2.05	
America	21	4.30	
TOTAL	488	100.00	

The leader of the movement, Emric Prat de la Riba, was elected president of the provincial Council of Barcelona in 1907. Seven years later, he became the first president of the Mancomunitat of Catalonia, which brought together the four provincial councils of Barcelona, Tarragona, Lleida, and Girona, and was the first self-governing Catalan body within Spain – though only in the area of administration – since Catalonia had lost its autonomous laws, liberties, and institutions in 1714.

In 1907 the Institut d'Estudis Catalans was established, as a language academy and a leading centre for Catalan science, to which some other scientific associations were soon added. In 1913, a Consell de Pedagogia was established with the aim of studying and adapting modern teaching methods. Eight years later, a body was set up to provide scholarships and grants for study abroad, while from 1915 the Cursos Monogràfics d'Alts Estudis i d'Intercanvi promoted the visits of prestigious European scientists such as Tullio Levi-Civita (1921), Hermann Weyl (1922), and Albert Einstein (1923).[33]

The Mancomunitat also worked to make technical education more effective. In particular, it sought to meet a notorious deficiency in the work-force by encouraging the training of efficient middle-level technicians. The centre established for this purpose, the Escola Industrial,

Escuelas de Ingenieros Industriales during the period 1851–1914.

was opened in 1909, and four years later the Escola del Treball was inaugurated for the preparation of specialized workers and foremen. The Escola del Treball was to achieve a remarkable level of efficiency under the leadership of the industrial engineer Rafael Campalans. Among its teachers were figures of the calibre of the engineer and physicist Esteve Terradas,[34] who introduced the theory of relativity into Spain together with Blas Cabrera. On the other hand, the institution was careful to bridge the cultures by integrating technical and humanistic education. The *Escola* was followed by more schools, too numerous to list here. Mention must be made, however, of the Escoles de Directors d'Indústria, industrial schools that turned out middle-level technicians with a well-balanced theoretical and practical training that was at once suitable for the consolidation of industrialization in the early twentieth century and capable of filling the gap that existed between high-level engineers and foremen. The courses in these schools lasted for four years, culminating in a final examination in which candidates had to carry out an industrially related project in one of three specialities: chemistry, electricity, or

Geographical distribution of the 488 industrial engineers employed in the year 1883. From José Mª Alonso Viguera, *La Ingeniería Industrial Española en el siglo XIX* (Madrid, 1944), pp. 184–5.

Regional distribution of industrial engineers working for the Spanish State in 1883. Adapted from José Mª Alonso Vigera, *La Ingeniería Industrial Española en el siglo XIX* (Madrid, 1944), p. 184–5.

mechanics. Some competence in English and German was also required. It is beyond question that the graduates, the Directors d'Indústria, were highly regarded and sought after by employers.

Backed by a coherent ideology, the Mancomunitat in Catalonia was responsible for seeing through a number of important technical projects: besides advancing the country's electrification, it transformed an almost non-existent telephone network (providing 405 towns with telephones and installing 5,870 km of lines), completed the secondary railway network, and worked for the opening of new roads and the improvement of those already in existence. It had finally understood the need for a good communications network if a market for production was to be created, and it was therefore a tragedy for the region when the promising experiment was curtailed by Primo de Rivera's dictatorship in 1923.

Conclusion: a bourgeoisie in search of profit

It is difficult to say why the process of industrialization in Spain was not carried to completion in the nineteenth century, but I have tried to identify some of the main impediments in this chapter. They include the loss of the colonial empire, and the extreme weakness of the domestic market, aggravated by the country's poor communications network; a bourgeoisie unable to play its full part in history; the existence of two centres – a political one in Madrid and an economic one on the periphery – and of two Spains – the agricultural centre and an industrial Spain along the East–North axis – separated by mutual incomprehension; a strong centralism incompatible with the sense of autonomy of the Catalan and Basque peoples; the bankruptcy which had plagued the State since the beginning of the nineteenth century and which meant that land was sold to a bourgeoisie who did not properly exploit it and that mineral resources fell prey to foreign capital; the blindness of the national government, which missed two golden opportunities of consolidating the move to industrialization – the creation of a railway network and of a modern iron-clad fleet; and the fact that the bourgeois revolution was never fully realized. A final and particularly corrosive impediment was the protectionism imposed in the late nineteenth and early twentieth centuries, which failed to protect national industry when it was needed, though it became damagingly effective when belatedly it was made to work. Finally, with the outbreak of the First World War, Spain failed to take advantage of its neutrality. In fact, the war only fostered the rise of parvenus with no thought for the future and or for any activity other than making money and living in a fool's paradise of idleness and luxury. Only the Basque bourgeoisie was an exception in this respect.

Nevertheless, serious attempts to catch the European train were made. Following the first attempt in the eighteenth century, a second move was made in the mid nineteenth century, in a period of liberal political control: one reflexion of this, as I have shown, was the establishment of the *Escuelas de Ingenieros Industriales*. After the six years of revolution (1868–74), the Restoration was a long and uneven phase that spanned the end of the nineteenth century and part of the present century. In this period, a stage of prosperity known as the period of the 'gold fever' (1875–82) was followed by a crisis and then by recovery at the very end of the century. These fluctuations coincided with the new wave of technological innovation that was spreading rapidly throughout Europe. We know that some of these innovations, especially in electricity, were introduced into Spain very quickly. Despite this, or more precisely because of it, there was a growing conviction that it was necessary to renew the excessively centralized structure of technical education which, far from improving with the passage of time, was aging. Such reformist fervour was evident in the opening of the Escuela de Ingenieros Industriales in Bilbao and, in Catalonia, in the work of the Mancomunitat at the beginning of the twentieth century.

Although the development of technical education paralleled the industrialization process, it is by no means evident that the training received by these professional men was the most appropriate. Initially, it was believed that a thorough scientific training given to the new class of professionals, enabling them to break away from the ordinary routine and to promote rational production methods, would benefit manufacturing most. That events undermined this view is illustrated by the constant litany of complaint from industrialists, who stressed the paucity of practical skills among those who had recently graduated. In Barcelona many employers went so far as to offer their premises for the completion of a training they considered inadequate, although the measure was insufficient. The provision for workshops, laboratories, and research facilities in institutions of higher education was so rudimentary that it had a negative effect on professional training as a whole, while the development of applied research was impeded by a high degree of economic and technological dependence on more advanced nations. Engineers at about the turn of the century were well aware of this. Hence the effect of the bold experiment of the Mancomunitat was limited by political circumstances.

Through all these developments, there ran a recurring disparity between the initial aims in the creation of the discipline of engineering and what the bourgeoisie expected from it. The disparity was widened by the bankruptcy of the Spanish Treasury, the state of economic and technological dependence that already existed when the new professional class of engineers appeared, and the unduly pragmatic anxiety of the bourgeoisie. Conceivably, the disparity was less marked during the second wave of industrialization at the end of the century, since now a scientific training was more in keeping with the increasingly sophisticated demands made on engineers. Nevertheless, it is significant that as this next stage of industrialization unfolded in the more developed countries, technological dependence increased still further. As it did so, the excessively theoretical education of engineers had its effect in Spain, and the gap that seemed to have diminished began to widen again.

The bourgeoisie, for its part, saw professional engineers as intermediaries between itself and the proletariat. The new technical class assumed this role and, with an almost dogmatic faith in science and technology that was very much in tune with the period, it eschewed political engagement and saw to it that the professional associations proclaimed the same apolitical ideology. As a result, the engineer in the nineteenth century was politically neutral and paternalistic towards workers. He was convinced of his own central role in establishing an identity of inter-class interests and thereby in fostering the goal of a contented society. It is hardly necessary to state that this stance failed to achieve its objectives. In the twentieth century, professional groups of engineers were to become increasingly involved in the analysis of social problems that went far beyond their immediately professional concerns.

There remains one question which is difficult to answer but which nevertheless should be posed. Did the bourgeoisie's aspirations towards modernization act as an impediment or an incentive to economic development? In the present state of research, I incline to an analysis that embraces both possibilities. The bourgeoisie understood that it had to modernize itself and believed that, to this end, as in the countries it took as models, it was essential to prepare rationally educated technicians. At the same time, however, because of the conspicuous difference between those other countries and Spain, to say nothing of the marked regional differences within Spain, the bourgeoisie tended to appreciate and even demand a training that could be put to immediate use – despite the impediment of inadequate or, at times, non-existent laboratories, workshops, and facilities for applied research in the teaching institutions. Indeed, it was this repeated action that constituted a major impediment, the more so as the pattern recurred, to a greater or lesser extent, every time a new wave of industrial modernization passed over the peninsula. Needs were always determined by the situation, the right balance was simply never found.

In short, industrialization in Spain was a puzzle, in which the pieces (the economy, modernization, technology, the bourgeoisie, the training of specialist technicians) never seemed to fit together. Against this confused background, Spain, in typical fashion, trailed behind other nations, and modernization was not completed until the 1960s.

Notes

1 It seems that the Escuela de Ingenieros de Caminos y Canales was set up to train the staff of the General Inspectorate of Roads (Inspección General de Caminos), created by Royal Decree on 12 June 1799 with the aim of directing the public works in Spain. It was only subsequently that its courses were fully recognized by the government.

2 Antonio Rumeu de Armas, *Ciencia y tecnología en la España Ilustrada. La Escuela de Caminos y Canales* (Madrid, 1980), p. 298

3 There were three editions of the *Essai*, dated 1808, 1819, and 1840.

4 *Elementos de Cálculo diferencial e integral* by Boucharlat (1830) and *Tratado de mecánica* by Poisson (1845) were both translated by the engineer Jerónimo

del Campo. They were adopted as textbooks in the Escuela de Caminos and other centres set up later.

5 The theme of the contacts between Catalan and French scientists during the Enlightenment is dealt with in Santiago Riera i Tuèbols, *Ciència i tècnica a la Il.lustració: Francesc Salvà i Campillo (1751–1828)* (Barcelona, 1985).

6 On the antecedents of the Escuela de Ingenieros de Minas, see Lluís Solé i Sabarís, 'Raíces de la geología española', in *Mundo Científico*, no. 9 (December 1981), 1,018–32.

7 It is not clear whether he succeeded in obtaining the post or not. Rumeu de Armas maintains that the initiative to involve J. Mª Lanz with the Conservatorio came from the staff of the centre at the beginning of 1832 and that, in spite of this, Lanz remained in Paris until his death; see Rumeu, *Ciencia y tecnología*, p. 405. Another of Lanz's biographers, José A. García-Diego, maintains that the initiative came from Lanz himself who probably obtained the post and spent a number of years in Madrid; see José A. García-Diego, 'Despedida a Betancourt', in García-Diego, *En busca de Betancourt y Lanz* (Madrid, 1985), pp. 29 and 30.

8 The Barcelona Chamber of Commerce (Junta de Comercio de Barcelona) established several technical *Escuelas* offering a modern scientific training for the professional men who were to contribute to the country's modernization. Among the *Escuelas*, special mention should be made of the Nautica (1769), the Gabinete de Maquinaria (1804), the Escuelas de Química (1805), Mecánica (1808), Física (1814), Botánica y Agricultura (1815), and Economía Política (1814).

9 Royal Decree of 4 September 1850, published in *La Gaceta de Madrid* on 8 September 1850. Reproduced in *Colección legislativa referente a los ingenieros industriales* (Barcelona, 1886), introduction.

10 All the *Escuelas* of the Chamber of Commerce, except the Escuela de Nobles Artes, were transferred in 1850 to the Escuela Industrial Barcelonesa (the title adopted by the first Escuela de Ingenieros Industriales).

11 Royal Decree of 4 September 1850, introduction.

12 For further details of the curricula, see Josep Montserrat, 'L'Escola d'Enginyers Industrials de Barcelona: una contribuciò important en el desenvolupament de la industrialització a Catalunya', unpublished doctoral thesis, Universitat Politècnica de Catalunya, 1982.

13 It should be stressed that financially the *Escuelas de Ingenieros Industriales* were mainly supported by municipal and regional authorities, since the proportion represented by the state subsidy (an insubstantial sum that remained constant throughout the century), decreased from roughly 30 per cent to about 20 per cent. See below, the section 'Technical education and the funding of the Escuelas'.

14 Regarding the Asociaciones, especially the one in Barcelona, see Santiago Riera i Tuèbols, *L'Associació i el Col.legi d'Enginyers Industrials de Catalunya, de la Dictadura a la Democràcia (1950–87)* (Barcelona, 1988). On the attempt to develop and enforce their authority, see Santiago Riera i Tuèbols, 'L'évolution de la profession d'ingénieur en Espagne', in André Grelon (ed.), *Les ingénieurs de la crise. Titre et profession entre les deux guerres* (Paris, 1986), pp. 325–42.

15 A few more precise details can be given. Four out of twenty-two works were by Spanish authors (18.2 per cent), fifteen by French authors (68.2 per cent), two by British authors (9 per cent), and one by a German (4.5 per cent). It should be noted, however, that even in the case of the two British works, French versions were recommended. A French translation was also specified for the work by the German Karl R. Fresenius, confirming the strong French influence in Spanish curricula.

16 Joaquín Alfonso, Cipriano S. Montesino, Eduardo Rodriguez, and Julián Bruno de la Peña, all professors at the Real Instituto Industrial de Madrid, had studied at the École Centrale des Arts et Manufactures in Paris. See José Mª Alonso Viguera, *La ingeniería industrial española en el siglo XIX* (Madrid, 1944), pp. 43–9.

17 The *Krausistas*, who enjoyed a high reputation in Spain, were led by Julián Sanz del Rio. On the place of universities in higher education in the nineteenth century, see Santiago Riera i Tuèbols, *Sintesi d'història de la ciència catalana* (Barcelona, 1983), pp. 226–9

18 Alonso Viguera, *La ingeniería industrial*, pp. 64 and 65.

19 The decline of the Andalusian iron and steel industry is evident from the fact that in 1844 it was responsible for 85 per cent of the total production of cast iron in Spain and that this figure fell to 17.6 per cent in 1866 and then to 4.7 per cent by 1868. The first coke-fuelled blast furnace dates from 1865, seventeen years after its introduction in Asturias. At the end of the century, however, the modernity of the Basque steel industry was beyond question. The firm of Altos Hornos built the first steel ingot using the Bessemer process in October 1885, and in 1888–9 the first Martin-Siemens furnace was introduced. On all aspects of Spanish industrialization, see Jordi Nadal, *El fracaso de la revolución industrial en España, 1814–1913* (Barcelona, 1975). An extensive summary on the same subject in Carlo M. Cipolla, *Historia económica de Europa. El nacimiento de las sociedades industriales* (Barcelona, 1982), vol. 4, part 2 pp. 178–272; on the matters discussed here, see pp. 247, 249, and 250.

20 This decision reversed the official policy, which had meant that between 1849 and 1868 Spain imported 305 units (89,000 tons) at a time when Spanish industrial companies were clamouring for such orders. When, in 1883, the tonnage of steamships first exceeded that of sailing ships in Spain, 97 per cent of the tonnage of the former came from abroad. See Santiago Riera i Tuèbols, *Dels velers als vapors* (forthcoming).

21 For an analysis of the different industrial sectors, see Ramón Garrabou, *Enginyers, industrials, modernització econòmica i burgesia a Catalunya (1850-inicis segle XX)* (Barcelona, 1982), especially (on gas) pp. 178 and 179. Also important is Carles Sudrià, 'Notas sobre la implantación y el desarrollo de la industria del gas en España, 1840–1901', *Revista de Historia Económica*, 2 (1983), 97–115.

22 Alonso Viguera, *La ingeniería industrial*, p. 144, says that the first experiments were carried out in 1874 and that those in 1875 resulted in a second, more powerful machine.

23 I am not certain about the year. Alonso Viguera, *La ingeniería industrial*, p. 147, states that the plant was set up in 1879 at 10 Rambla de Canaletas, in Barcelona, a fact that would make the inauguration in 1880 (a date found in

other sources) feasible. The same author also states (though without indicating his source) that the plant consisted of four 50 HP gas engines, built by La Maquinista Terrestre y Marítima, which fuelled Gramme dynamos generating at 200 amps and 200 volts. The production of electricity in the early years was geared towards lighting (factories, street lighting, and domestic supply, in this order), and although initially only the voltaic arc was used, there were already 1,000 incandescent lamps in use by 1884, all of them installed by S.E.E; see Joan Molina, *Narcís Xifra, capdavanter de l'enginyeria electrotècnica a Catalunya* (Barcelona, 1992).

24 Alonso Viguera, *La ingeniería industrial*, pp. 153 and 154. For the specific reference to *l'Electricien*, see J. Mª García de la Infanta, *Primeros pasos de la luz eléctrica en Madrid y otros acontecimientos* (Madrid, 1986), p. 102.

25 The full history of electricity in Spain has still to be written. However, notable studies include F. P. Sintes and F. Vidal, *La industria eléctrica en España* (Barcelona, 1933), and Jordi Maluquer de Motes, 'Cataluña y el País Vasco en la industria eléctrica española, 1901–1935', in Manuel González Portilla *et al.* (eds.), *Industrialización y nacionalismo, Análisis comparativo* (Universitat Autònoma de Barcelona, Bellaterra, 1985), where there is a bibliography on the subject. A study of the production and consumption of electricity in Catalonia is to be published shortly by Jordi Nadal, Albert Carreras, Jordi Maluquer de Motes, and Carles Sudrià.

26 The subject is analysed in detail in Paulino Castells, *Reseña Histórica* (Barcelona, 1942), pp. 30 and 31; Alexandre Galí, *Història de les institucions i del moviment cultural a Catalunya, 1900–1936* (Barcelona, Fundació A.G., 1981), vol. 4, pp. 83–5; and Ramón Garrabou, *Enginyers, industrials, modernitzaciò econòmica i burgesia, a Catalunya*, pp. 53 and 54. I have compared earlier data with the existing, though incomplete, documentation in the archives of the Escuela de Ingenieros Industriales in Barcelona.

27 Josep Serrat i Bonastre, 'La carrera de ingeniero industrial y un plan de estudios', in *Revista Tecnológico Industrial* (June 1905), pp. 125–35.

28 See Carlo G. Lacaita, 'Les ingénieurs et l'organisation des études d'ingénieurs en Italie de l'unification politique à la seconde guerre mondiale', in Grelon, *Les ingénieurs de la crise*, pp. 309–23.

29 On industrial engineers who graduated in Barcelona, the main source is Castells, *Reseña Histórica*, pp. 40 and 41. I am grateful to the staff of the Escuelas de ingenieros de Minas y de Caminos, Canales y Puertos de Madrid for the information they provided.

30 Anuarios de la Asociación de Ingenieros Industriales de Barcelona (years 1888, 1895 and 1912), *Relación de socios numerarios y honorarios constituyendo la Asociación Central de Ingenieros Industriales el 1. de marzo 1885* and *Anuario general de los Ingenieros Industriales de España* (Barcelona, 1931); Garrabou, *Enginyers, industrials, modernitzacio econòmica i burgesia, a Catalunya*, pp. 127–30.

31 Alonso Viguera, *La ingeniería industrial*, p. 184. The data are recorded, corrected, and completed in tables 6.1–6.5 and maps 6.1–6.3. The regional map of Spain in the nineteenth century does not coincide with the present map 'el Estado de las Autonomias'.

32 In drawing up the column for engineers per 10^5 inhabitants, I have used the

1877 census reproduced in Miguel Martinez Cuadrado, 'La burguesía conservadora (1874–1931)', in *Historia de España Alfaguara* (Madrid, 1973), vol. 6 p. 107.

33 The members of the Mancomunitat did not limit themselves to promoting a plan for technical education. They also promoted the cultivation of science and integrated both aspects of their programme in a much wider cultural framework. Thus they established an Escola de Bibliotecaries (1915), a Laboratori de Psicologia Experimental (1922), an Escola d'Agricultura (1914), as well as other institutions. On the other hand, the Escuela de Ingenieros Industriales, which has been the main object of this section, did not wish to escape from the State's protection, even though the state subsidy it received was very small. This led to the withdrawal of the subsidy from the Regional Council, which in turn caused the Escuela some hardship. On the cultural work of the Mancomunitat, the study by Galí, cited in note 26, is indispensable.

34 Terradas planned and directed the construction of the underground railway (Metro Transversal) in Barcelona and was also in charge of the construction of the Catalan Telephone network. His work on the telephone network led to his appointment as director of the Compañía Telefónica Nacional in 1927, where he was responsible for extending the network more widely in Spain, as well as further work on minor railways in Catalonia.

7 Academic qualifications and professional functions in the development of the Italian engineering schools, 1859–1914

Anna Guagnini

On the eve of the First World War, Italy had seven engineering schools. They had different names – Politecnico in Turin, Istituto Tecnico Superiore in Milan, and *scuole di applicazione per ingegneri* elsewhere – but they had the same status: they were all part of the university system, and they awarded the academic as well as the professional title of engineer, following an examination at the end of a five-year course. In all, the schools had a population of 5,291 matriculated students, representing a four-fold increase since the mid-1880s. Although schools of engineering had fewer students than the faculties of law, they had more than the faculties of medicine and they constituted the most rapidly expanding sector of the Italian university system.[1]

One of the main features of this expansion was the shift in the interests of the students. For while civil engineering still accounted for a significant proportion of the enrolments, the growth was especially pronounced in the two institutions that offered degrees in industrial engineering, in Milan and Turin. It was not until shortly before the First World War that the other schools started to expand the range of their teaching in mechanical engineering and manufacturing, and it was only then that their student numbers, which had faltered and declined in the 1890s, began to increase. If we try to relate the development of higher technological education to changes in the Italian economy, the high rate of expansion is remarkable. It is true that, once political unification was complete in 1871, the country entered on a phase of profound economic reorganization, and this process gained renewed strength once the recession of the decade 1887–96 was over. Yet, even if we take account of the resulting demand for technical experts, the growth of the university-level engineering schools still appears exceedingly rapid – far more so than would be expected from any analysis of the transformation of the economy. It was a growth that many industrialists and representatives of the engineering schools' professoriate had come to regard, by 1914, not as a mark of success but rather as the sign of a deep malaise affecting the educational system.

The fact is that the popularity of the *scuole di applicazione* was not the result of a demand for more engineering graduates but rather of pressure from students, for whom an academic degree in engineering was an essential professional qualification. Such a qualification was a condition for appointments not only in the state and regional administration but also in private consultancy and at the highest levels in industry. Hence, it was in the hope of securing access to economically and socially desirable careers, rather than in response to the immediate needs of industry, that young men crammed into engineering courses. The pressure was such that by 1910 there was a clear oversupply of graduates.

The *scuole* were also severely criticized for the content and structure of their curricula. Already in the 1880s, the theoretical character of their teaching, the length of their courses, and their detachment from engineering practice had made them controversial. Thereafter, in the early years of the twentieth century, the pressure for change had grown, but no significant reform was introduced.

It must be said that, at the turn of the century, engineering was not the only branch of university education to experience difficulties. The two other faculties that offered professional qualifications – medicine and law – were subject to precisely the same charges: overcrowding, low standards, and, at least in medicine, inadequate facilities for practical training. As I shall argue, however, the engineering schools faced a special difficulty. They had been created originally as institutions for the education of a relatively small élite of civil engineers going on to careers in the public services or in private practice in the construction industry. It is undeniable that, in the mid-nineteenth century, their graduates played an important role in laying the foundations of the country's economic renewal. In the later nineteenth century, however, the engineering schools strove to adjust to the emergence of new and rapidly growing sectors, such as mechanical and electrical engineering, and to provide a new breed of technical experts for industrial employment. Unfortunately, the result was an institutional hybrid that satisfied neither the advocates of reform nor the more conservative members of the profession.[2]

The legacy of the graduate engineer

The relationship between academic qualification and professional title is one of the most important themes in the history of engineering education in Italy.[3] The relationship was well established before unification stimulated the reform that laid the foundations of the country's present educational system. In fact, in Piedmont (including Liguria) and Lombardy – the two northern regions that became the first constituents of the new state – precise regulations concerning the formal education of engineers had been in existence for some time. Here, before the end of the eighteenth century, would-be engineers were expected to attend courses in mathematics and architecture in a university or a school of architecture before entering a period of apprenticeship with an engineer and finally sitting an examination that allowed them to qualify formally as chartered engineers.

In both Piedmont and Lombardy, strict regulations controlled the use of the term 'engineer' as a professional qualification. The regulations were issued and enforced by different agencies: independent guilds in Lombardy (then subject to the Habsburg empire) and governmental authorities in the Kingdom of Sardinia (of which Piedmont and Liguria were part).[4] Whether they were public or private, these agencies were equally determined to supervise the admission of new members to the profession and to preserve the exclusive hold of chartered engineers on the most prestigious positions. As a result, it was only chartered engineers who had the right to supervise the planning and maintenance of both public and large private buildings, roads, and systems of water supply, and to act as legally recognized land-surveyors or be consulted as experts in legal disputes.

Needless to say, these occupations were not ones that required large numbers of practitioners. And it was precisely with a view to controlling the number of the candidates, while at the same time enhancing the social status of the profession, that the requirement of attendance at an institution of higher education was imposed.[5] This link between the university sector and the engineering profession does not imply, however, that the faculties of mathematics offered special curricula for prospective engineers; in fact, the courses they attended were essentially the same as those for students aspiring to a degree in mathematics.[6]

In other Italian states, the regulations concerning the education of civil servants in technical posts and of free-lance architects and engineers were not so clearly defined. In Florence, the capital of the Grand Duchy of Tuscany, one of the aims of the Accademia delle Belle Arti, from its opening in 1784, was to provide instruction for architects. However, no certificate of attendance at institutions of higher education was required in order to practise engineering and architecture, and apprenticeship was seen as the only relevant qualification.[7] The same was true in the Papal States and in the Bourbon Kingdom of Naples.

It was in the first decade of the nineteenth century, when most of the Italian states came under French control, that the first attempt was made to create special institutions for the education of engineers going on to posts in the civil service. These institutions were expected to feed the engineering corps which the French administration created to supervise its extensive programmes of land drainage and road construction throughout the occupied territories. But the initiative had very limited results. In Milan, in 1808, a plan was approved for the establishment of a Scuola di Acque e Strade, but the school was never opened. Three years later, Joachim Murat, in his capacity as viceroy of Naples, launched a similar scheme in the town which led to the opening of a Scuola di Applicazione per Ingegneri di Ponti, Acque e Strade. But the return of the Bourbons put an end to the experiment, and in 1818 the school was dismantled, along with other vestiges of the French occupation.[8]

In reality, for all their efforts to establish special engineering schools along the lines of the *grandes écoles*, the French administrators did not exclude a role for the universities in the preparation of engineers, especially of those destined for private practice. Indeed, while attempts to establish the equivalents of France's specialized engineering schools foundered, it was the universities that benefited most from the reform of higher education inaugurated during the French occupation. One aim of this reform had been to establish uniform standards in the universities in the various parts of Italy, thereby overcoming the variety of often very loose regulations that affected the relations between education and the professions. As part of this plan, the function of the universities in providing education for engineers was not only confirmed, but also considerably extended, in particular by the decision that a degree (rather than a mere certificate of attendance at university courses) should be required for formal admission to the profession.[9]

The fall of Napoleon and the return of the various old regimes, with their mistrust of free intellectual expression, brought the reform of higher education in the Italian states to an abrupt halt. In the 1820s, however, the restoration gradually relaxed its grip, and the universities began to revive. Throughout this revival, the new educational authorities maintained the guidelines on engineering instruction that had been imposed by the French administration. Hence the faculties of mathematics and physics at the University of Turin in the Kingdom of Sardinia and of the University of Pavia in Lombardy continued to provide for the formal education of engineers. Moreover, similar initiatives were launched even in those countries where, in the past, attendance at university courses had not been required as a condition for practising the profession. Thus in Tuscany, in 1823, Leopoldo II issued a decree that made a university degree a necessary qualification for entry to the civil service. Likewise, in the Papal States, a new Scuola di Applicazione per Ingegneri was opened in Rome by Pope Pius VII in 1817. Based loosely on the French model of the *grandes écoles*, the three-year course at the school was designed to prepare candidates for admission to the élite Corpo del Genio Pontificio.[10] It was a mark of its higher academic standing that it only admitted students who had already completed a course of study in the faculty of mathematics of the universities of Rome or Bologna. Initially, the school stood outside the university system, but in 1826 it became part of the University of Rome, and eventually it was the university that took over the preparation of engineers for private practice as well as for the public services.

From civil engineering to manufacturing: the first phase

While the French reforms succeeded in establishing the principle that higher education was a prerequisite for engineers, it was less successful in effecting significant changes in the curriculum of the faculties of mathematics. It led to no expansion in the range of disciplines, and technical instruction continued to have no place. Left to their own devices, the faculties had no incentive to promote developments in the direction of practice. In fact, their commitment to catering for students of engineering was entirely self-interested. Had it not been for those students, the courses would have had minute attendances: for, as the annual reports indicate, only a small minority of the student body graduated in pure mathematics or physics.

In the 1830s, therefore, the structure and, to a large extent, the content of the courses available to engineering students were virtually the same as at the end of the eighteenth century. The only courses that distinguished their syllabus from that offered to students of mathematics were those in architecture and hydraulics. Of course, such disciplines as hydraulics and geodesy had connections with practical activities, to the extent that the latter raised certain problems which the science professors treated in theoretical terms.[11] But the curricula quite deliberately included no introduction to specific technical practices. Practical training was still left to the period of apprenticeship, which had to be served under a chartered engineer.

It was only in the late 1840s that the problem of renewing the existing curricula began to receive attention. This was prompted by a new concern for the flagging state of the economy throughout the peninsula. In Piedmont, under the Savoyard monarchy, new plans for economic improvement were directed primarily at roads, canals, and, in the 1850s, railways.

Elsewhere, in other states, governments pursued similar plans, albeit on a lesser scale and more cautiously. In addition, the political instability that resulted from the emergence of movements for the unification of Italy led governments to consider measures for the modernization of their various armies and navies. The private sector too began to emerge from a long period of stagnation and to show signs of renewal. The pacemaker, such as it was, was the textile industry, which in the 1830s had made some patchy but significant headway in the mechanization of plants and systems of production. But other sectors, ranging from mechanical engineering to metallurgy, were following, however slowly.[12]

These new activities inevitably highlighted shortcomings both in the number of technical experts and in the quality of their preparation. At the same time, new journals and popular magazines began to appear which took it as a main aim to promote the modernization of agriculture and manufacturing and to spread information concerning the technical advances being made in other European countries.[13] Needless to say, education stood high on their agenda for change, and it is clear that in the 1840s signs of dissatisfaction with the existing provision for technical education and, in particular, for instruction in subjects related to manufacturing were becoming more marked. It was the lack of educational opportunities for foremen and skilled workers which the supporters of modernization cited most frequently among the causes of the difficulties encountered by employees in understanding and incorporating new technologies. For this reason, as early as the 1840s, a number of vocational and trade schools were established in the manufacturing and metropolitan areas of the North and Centre. Some of these schools were organized by the municipalities, but in many cases the initiative came from private patrons and from charities and religious organizations with strong local connections.

Attempts were also made to provide technical instruction at a more advanced level. In Turin, an Istituto Tecnico was opened in 1845 under the aegis of the municipality. Here, professors from the local university offered evening classes in geometry, mechanics, and applied chemistry.[14] A more ambitious initiative was the Istituto Tecnico in Florence. Established in 1850 with the support of Leopoldo II, the Duke of Tuscany, the Istituto was conceived as an institution distinct from the existing Accademia di Belle Arti, where architect-engineers were educated. In reality, it did not begin to function properly until 1857, but once it opened, it was liberally endowed with modern equipment for the teaching of applied chemistry, applied physics, and land-surveying. The aim was to produce not university-level engineers but competent technicians at a level higher than that of the secondary schools.[15] In other regions, it was left for private enterprise to counter the inertia of the educational authorities, at least partially. The outstanding examples were the courses founded in Milan by the Società di Incoraggiamento di Arti e Mestieri. Here, through the initiative of local merchants, intellectuals, and engineers, evening classes in applied chemistry, mechanical engineering, drawing, and textile manufacture were inaugurated in the 1840s.[16]

In contrast, at the highest level of the system, the concern of the educational authorities with the place of education in the improvement of manufacturing practices yielded only limited, and belated, results. Some changes, however, were introduced: in Piedmont, for example, the faculty of mathematics of the University of Turin expanded the teaching of engineering construction. In reality, though, the changes were of a cosmetic nature. Certain other reforms that had begun to be considered were more substantial. In Piedmont and Lombardy, committees were set up in the 1850s to review the state of engineering education and to lay plans for reform. Some of those plans had already been submitted to the educational authorities when they fell victim to the early stirrings of the wars of independence, so that, in the event, very little came of them.[17] Nevertheless, they served to proclaim certain broad principles. Above all, they indicated that any reforms were conceived as being concerned primarily with civil engineering. No attempt was made to open the syllabuses of the mathematical faculties to mechanical engineering and other subjects relevant to manufacturing.

The organization of the *scuole di applicazione*

Following the very uneven results that were achieved before unification, a more systematic plan for the improvement and expansion of technical education was set in train in the immediate aftermath of the first war of independence. In 1859, only a few months after Lombardy was annexed to the Kingdom of Sardinia, a law was passed that reorganized schooling in the two regions at all levels and laid the foundation of the Italian educational system.[18] The reform incorporated a number of the initiatives that had been launched in these regions before the outbreak of the war. One such initiative was the creation of a new tier within the educational system destined to accommodate technical and commercial schools. The original purpose of these institutions, called *scuole tecniche* and *istituti tecnici*, was to constitute a vocational alternative to the traditional secondary schools, the *licei classici*.[19]

With regard to higher technical education, on the other hand, the new

Ministry of Public Instruction acknowledged the importance of establishing special institutions, although it stopped short of creating a complete new range of technical schools. In fact, even those few technical institutions that had been opened in the 1850s to prepare foremen and draughtsmen for industry saw their original function gradually eroded. The case of the Istituto Tecnico of Florence makes the point very clearly. When the laws of Italy were extended to Tuscany, the Istituto, with its explicit commitment to mechanical engineering, did not come under the authority of the Ministry of Public Instruction; it was entrusted instead to the Ministry of Agriculture, Industry, and Commerce and was transformed into a secondary technical school. As a result, the fine workshops for advanced instruction in mechanical and electrical engineering were gradually abandoned, and the laboratories were eventually locked up, with their equipment and instruments inside.[20]

In this way, technical instruction came to be confined to the realm of secondary education. The education of engineers, on the other hand, remained firmly attached to the universities, where the Ministry of Public Instruction decided to reorganize the existing courses for engineering students offered by the faculties of mathematics in such a way as to create a new degree course. It was as a result of this manoeuvre, which was enshrined in the law of 1859, that *scuole di applicazione per ingegneri* were established as a subsection of the university system – more precisely, as schools annexed to faculties of mathematics and physics. But it was only in 1860, when the first *scuola di applicazione* was opened at the University of Turin, that detailed regulations concerning their programmes and internal organization were drawn up. These same regulations were to be adopted by all the other schools that were opened subsequently.[21]

The syllabus of the *scuole*, as laid down by the ministry and adopted by the Scuola di Applicazione of Turin, included the special courses, such as those in hydraulics, architecture, and construction, that were already offered to engineering students in the faculties of mathematics and physics. In addition, new specialities were added, notably applied mechanics, chemistry, and mineralogy, and the hours devoted to geometrical and mechanical drawing were increased, the entire programme lasting three years. Firmly embedded in the Italian tradition of professional higher education, the new regulations confirmed the close relations that existed between academic and professional qualifications. Hence, only the students who attended the full course of instruction and passed the final examination were offered the diploma of *ingegnere laureato*, which was at once an academic degree and a professional diploma.

Officially, the separation of the *scuole di applicazione* from the faculties of mathematics was sanctioned by the decision to make them administratively autonomous, each with a separate board of directors. In other important ways, however, the *scuole* were still crucially dependent on the faculties. First, they admitted only students who had already completed two years of study in the faculties of mathematics.[22] In this respect, the *scuole di applicazione* were conceived as advanced special institutions whose purpose was to build a curriculum in engineering on an existing foundation in science. Secondly, they were expected to rely on the faculties not only for certain teaching facilities, such as laboratories, but also for a number of fundamental courses, in particular in rational mechanics, geodesy, and chemistry.

For all these reasons, the *scuole di applicazione*, as they emerged from the law of 1859, were not simply an extension of the faculties of mathematics; they had also to maintain a close working association with them. And yet the second *scuola* to be founded represented a significant departure from the pattern pioneered in Turin. As I have observed, in Lombardy, before unification, engineers were educated, of necessity, at the University of Pavia, since this was the only institution of higher education in the region, while Milan, the administrative and economic capital of Lombardy and the seat of its most important scientific institutions, had no university. Had the ministry followed the same course as in Turin, the ancient University of Pavia would have been the obvious location for a *scuola di applicazione*. But such a solution would have flown in the face of the long-standing campaign of the Milanese municipal authorities and the Società di Incoraggiamento di Arti e Mestieri for the establishment of an institution of higher scientific and technical education in the Lombard capital.[23] The Milanese lobby was a powerful one, and it duly triumphed in 1862, when an Istituto Tecnico Superiore was founded in Milan, with a *scuola di applicazione* attached to it.[24]

The anomaly of an engineering school existing independently of a university was not repeated. When other parts of Italy were annexed to the new state and their educational systems were reformed along the lines laid down by the law of 1860, *scuole di applicazione* were invariably established within universities that already offered courses for engineering students. This happened in Bologna (1862), Naples (1863), Rome (1873), and Padua (1876), in all cases through the adaptation of existing facilities.[25] It was in this way, by sustaining a state of affairs inherited from the political divisions of the past, that Italy emerged from the process of unification with more university-level engineering schools than England.[26]

In some obvious respects, the situation in Italy resembles that in Germany in the aftermath of unification. But there were also important differences. For in opening the various *scuole*, the Ministry of Public Instruction was not pursuing a plan aimed unequivocally at promoting higher technical education. On the contrary, the reorganization of technical education and, more generally, of the whole university system was seriously constrained. It faced impediments, on the one hand, from the determination of the universities to resist change and avoid restrictions in their activities, and, on the other, from the lack of the resources that were needed to sustain and develop the numerous universities which centuries of political fragmentation had spawned.

Calls for the closure of some of the smaller universities and for an adjustment of the geographical distribution of the faculties were discussed repeatedly in academic circles and in parliament.[27] However, in the towns that were seats of a university, municipal pride weighed heavily in favour of maintaining a local source of professional qualifications. As a result, it was easier for the Ministry of Public Instruction to confirm the status quo than to face the inevitable conflict that would have arisen from any attempt to restrict the number of faculties in each of the existing universities. Political expediency of this kind was at the root of the decision to create a new engineering school at the University of Palermo. A *scuola di applicazione* was duly established there in 1860, a few months after Garibaldi had landed in Sicily, as a mark of the modernizing intentions of the new government and as a way of rectifying, at least in part, the flagrant disparity between the northern, and the central and southern regions. But the provision that was made for launching the *scuole* nationally was inadequate, and it took no account of the particularly poor state of the faculties of mathematics and physics to which certain of these institutions were annexed. This was the case in Palermo, where the Scuola di Applicazione remained inactive for seven years since it could not provide the full range of courses that were required by law.[28]

Political considerations were not the only ones that prevented a serious rethinking of the wisdom of having as many as seven engineering schools. All the universities I have mentioned would have been extremely reluctant to lose their engineering courses, since it was still the case that, without engineering students, enrolments in faculties of science would have dropped dramatically. The case of Pavia is, in this respect, significant. When the Istituto Tecnico of Milan established an internal preparatory school to instruct candidates for entry to its engineering courses in 1870, the University of Pavia protested vigorously. It had good reason to do so. For in 1876, only eleven of a total of seventy-eight students in the faculty of mathematics, physics, and natural sciences were enrolled in the third and fourth years; the others were all engineering students who, at the end of the two-year preparatory course, moved on to *scuole di applicazione*, usually in Milan.

The emergence of industrial engineering

As early as 1859, therefore, Italian engineering schools won the status that German *Technische Hochschulen* only achieved, after a prolonged struggle, about 1890. Yet precious little of the spirit that fired such early initiatives as the evening classes of the Società di Incoraggiamento di Arti e Mestieri in Milan and the *istituti tecnici* in Milan and Turin, was carried over into the educational reforms of the new national government. This was a disappointment to the champions of reform. Their ideal was to create special institutions of higher technical education outside the university, and they viewed the solution that was adopted in 1859 as an unsatisfactory compromise. The fact that engineering students had to share the first two years of their studies with students of mathematics and physics was, in their eyes, a particularly serious defect. For the staple diet in those two years remained exclusively scientific, with calculus and geometry serving as the core of the future engineer's preparation.

Even the additions that were made to the syllabuses of the *scuole di applicazione* had not modified their fundamentally abstract character. The first year remained entirely devoted to rational mechanics and applied geometry, and the applied disciplines of the second and third years were at once limited in number and marked by a distinctive theoretical cast. Still more damaging, in the eyes of the advocates of modern technical instruction, was the fact that the ministry had made no attempt to introduce courses relevant to mechanical engineering and manufacturing practice, so that the syllabuses of the *scuole di applicazione* remained strongly oriented towards civil engineering.[29]

Despite these impediments and the lack of encouragement, attempts to develop industrially oriented curricula within the university setting were not wholly abandoned, and where support was strong, some results were achieved. This was so in the capitals of the economically advanced regions of the North, Piedmont and Lombardy. In Milan, for example, it was a condition for the participation of the Società di Incoraggiamento in the creation of the Istituto Tecnico Superiore that the institution should provide facilities for the instruction of mechanical engineers. The pressure of the members of Società, which represented the interests of local entrepreneurs and manufacturers, bore fruit. For it was clearly through their intense lobbying that the Milanese school possessed, from the beginning, a special section of mechanical engineering, for which the Società even provided the teachers and made available its facilities for the teaching of chemistry.[30] This close partnership was reflected in the goal that the board of directors of the Istituto set for themselves, which was to foster the development of local industry by providing the necessary technical leadership.

In Turin, this explicit regional spirit was less prominent. As the capital of the state that had led the process of unification, Turin initially assumed the role of the capital of Italy, and in this capacity it retained its self-image as the natural source of the nation's political leaders. The institutions of higher education in Turin had traditionally prepared the senior political and military figures of Piedmont, and they continued to see this function as theirs long after the role as capital had been officially transferred to Florence and later, in 1871, to Rome.[31] It is indicative of this self-image that when the problem of the education of mechanical engineers was addressed in Piedmont in the 1860s, the patron that emerged was a governmental agency – the Ministry of Agriculture, Industry, and Commerce. In 1862, at the instigation of Giuseppe De Vincenzi, the secretary of the Italian section at the international exhibition held in that year in London, and with the support of leading Piedmontese politicians, the ministry approved a proposal for the establishment of a Museo Industriale Italiano in Turin.[32] The distinctive aim of the institution was to provide a stimulus for technical renewal that would benefit not only Piedmont but also the country as a whole. Five years later, the Museo began to offer courses in a variety of subjects ranging from mechanical engineering to applied physics, metallurgy, and agricultural chemistry. The hostility of the Scuola di Applicazione of Turin to the strictly technical programme of instruction adopted by the Museo was, and remained, intense.[33] But the expediency of avoiding competition prevailed over protests on pedagogical grounds, and a collaboration was arranged between the two institutions. As a result, in 1879, the courses held by the Museo became the core of mechanical engineering section in the Scuola di Applicazione of Turin.[34]

The new departures in Milan and Turin were carried through with neither the approval nor the financial support of the Ministry of Public Instruction. The ministry accepted the industrial sections created in Milan and Turin as a *fait accompli* but did not seek to modify the regulations concerning the syllabus nor to extend the innovation to other engineering schools. Hence, it was not until 1904 that new sections of mechanical engineering began to be established generally in the other *scuole di applicazione*.

Of course, the palpable indifference of the ministry imposed serious limitations on the development of industrially oriented curricula. One other, even more important, impediment lay in the diversity of views on the programmes and goals of the *scuole* that were held by the professoriate of these institutions. On the need to modernize the curriculum, introduce new disciplines, and increase the applied content of the courses, professorial opinion was unanimous. However, there was considerable disagreement on the extent to which these modifications should be carried out, and, above all, on the desirability of establishing specialized sections. For in the eyes of many teachers, most notably of the influential academic staff of the Scuola di Applicazione of Turin, this trend would have led inevitably to a growing emphasis on narrow technical instruction and to a departure from the traditional ideal of scientific engineering.[35] Moreover, as they argued, the opportunities for employment in the manufacturing sector were limited, so that specialization would indeed have been an obstacle to a graduate's career prospects.

Undoubtedly, one reason for the commitment to general engineering was the desire of the professoriate to keep engineering education, and hence their own academic activities, within the university system. On the other hand, even such staunch advocates of separate sections of industrial engineering as Francesco Brioschi, the first director of the Istituto Tecnico Superiore of Milan, and his successor, Giuseppe Colombo, were unwilling to see their school lose academic standing.[36] Such a downgrading would have been incompatible with their aim of preparing a new generation of technical leaders for industry as well as highly qualified experts for public appointments. According to this élitist conception, the schools had to dispense not only information but also the status that was associated with a university degree.

For all these reasons, the introduction of new technical disciplines in the syllabuses of the industrial sections of the *scuole di applicazione* in Milan and Turin proceeded slowly. In the early 1880s, the first year of the *scuole* was still basically the same for civil and mechanical engineering, with rational mechanics, graphical statics, and descriptive geometry established as firmly as ever as the core disciplines. It was only in the second and third years that technical physics, mechanical engineering, and technical chemistry were tackled. Diversification became more marked from the late 1880s, chiefly through the fragmentation of mechanical engineering into a number of different sub-specialities. Now, more time was devoted to instruction in the design of engines and industrial machinery and to the description of industrial processes. However, the teaching was still confined to the lecture-room, while the facilities for practical demonstrations and laboratory instruction were virtually non-existent.

Academic competition and expansion

There can be no doubt that the inadequacy of financial support for the introduction of new technical disciplines and the equipping of teaching laboratories was a formidable obstacle to the development of modern engineering programmes and in particular of the mechanical sections. However, the Ministry of Public Instruction did not oppose the creation of new courses when these were paid for from other sources. Consequently, any attempt to move in this direction rested entirely on the *scuole*'s capacity to raise special funds. In the case of the Milanese engineering school, local patronage was vital in launching all those initiatives that the Ministry of Public Instruction was unwilling to support. In 1876, a consortium was established involving the municipality, the province, and Milan's learned institutions. The Istituto Tecnico was one of the main beneficiaries of the agreement, as a result of which an internal preparatory school was created and new technical disciplines were added to the syllabus of the *scuola di applicazione*.[37] Moreover, it was thanks to donations from private entrepreneurs, local banks, and of the Chamber of Commerce of Milan, that teaching laboratories for electrical and mechanical engineering began to be opened in the 1890s. Similar initiatives were launched in the Museo Industriale of Turin,[38] where the Ministry of Agriculture, Industry, and Commerce remained the main sponsor of the industrial engineering section. But in addition to the subsidy from this ministry, in 1875 the Museo began to receive generous annual grants from the municipality and the province. These grants were especially earmarked for the purchase of equipment and the introduction of complementary teaching in technical subjects.

By 1890, most universities had established consortia of the kind pioneered in Milan. Usually, the agreement involved both the municipality and the province in which the university was located, as well as a variety of local partners, including on the one side, banks and chambers of commerce and, on the other, academies, observatories, and other scientific institutions. In fact, the desire to improve the provision for science was one of the main incentives for local cooperation, and where engineering schools were part of the university structure, they duly shared in the grants that were bestowed on them and on the faculties of science and medicine. In fact, the potential contribution to the local economy of the engineering schools, allied to accounts of their financial difficulties, was often a powerful argument in the quest for the support of the municipal and provincial authorities.

The grants were not used just for the improvement of the existing provision. There is ample evidence that the very survival of some of the *scuole di applicazione* depended on funds provided by locally based agencies. This was certainly the case at the University of Bologna. In 1877, having failed to maintain the complete programme prescribed by the ministerial regulations for the engineering schools, the university was compelled to close the second and third years of its Scuola di Applicazione. At this point, on a wave of municipal pride, a consortium was created, which provided a grant for the refurbishment of the school, as well as an annual grant to endow all the second- and third-year courses which the ministry required.[39] This injection of funds allowed the school in Bologna to fill the most obvious gaps in its civil engineering programme, and the steady growth of enrolments between 1887 and 1890 was flaunted by the board of directors as a clear indication that the investment had paid handsome dividends, and that more funding was necessary to sustain the momentum.

But 1890 marked a dramatic turning point in the fortunes of the Italian engineering schools. By now, the expansion of the *scuole di applicazione* was being seriously affected by the economic depression of the period 1887–96, in particular by the crisis of the construction sector in the late 1880s. At the same time, the completion of the railway network entailed a rapid contraction in a sector which until then had absorbed a significant number of engineering graduates. The result was a substantial decline in the number of students in virtually all the engineering schools throughout the country – a decline that reached the lowest ebb at the end of the century. The conspicuous exceptions were the schools in Milan and Turin, where numbers continued to rise throughout the 1890s. In fact, though, even here the number of the civil engineers dropped – in Milan more sensibly than in Turin. But the loss of the civil engineers was more than compensated for by the growth of students in the mechanical engineering sections: in the five years from 1895 to 1900, enrolments in the Museo Industriale of Turin doubled from 148 to 292.

By the end of the century, the less buoyant institutions were painfully aware of the advantages possessed by those schools that had mechanical engineering sections. The Scuola di Applicazione of Naples, for example, had sought the Ministry of Public Instruction's permission to open such a section in 1887, but the request had been turned down. Ten years later, a second request had been equally unsuccessful. The obvious reason for the refusal was the ministry's reluctance to contemplate additions to the teaching staff at a time when, on the strength of the decline in the student population, it was far more attracted by the idea of closing institutions. Even within the academic community, there was no general agreement on the wisdom of maintaining so many engineering schools. The division

Table 7.1. *Full-time students of engineering enrolled in the* scuole di applicazione, *1870–1920*

	Turin		Milan		Bologna	Naples		Padua	Rome
	civil	mechanical	civil	mechanical		civil	mechanical		
1865	99		105	21					
1870	174	4	155	50		122			
1875	356	–	132	39	22 (1877)				
1880	297	33	66	55	71	252			
1885	306	102	60	88	119				
1890	266	99	114	112	153	299		154	93
1895	228	148	93	163	111			112	155
1900	187	292	33	202	93	143		75	111
1905	207	381	61	286	113			78	173
1910	202 16*	460	83	353	152 (1909)	105	104	195	297
1914	251 28*	525 (1913)	121	375	288	295	130	327	388 (1913)

The students indicated in this table do not include those enrolled in the sections of architecture. Although virtually all the *scuole di applicazione* had sections of architecture, the number of students that they attracted was insignificant until well after the First World War.

* chemical engineering section.

Sources. Annual reports of the individual *scuole di applicazione*.

of opinion emerged sharply in a parliamentary debate prompted in 1899 by a new appeal of the Scuola di Applicazione of Bologna to the Ministry of Public Instruction. The aim of the appeal was to induce the ministry to take upon itself the financial responsibility for those chairs that had been maintained since 1887 by the local consortium. On that occasion, it was Stanislao Cannizzaro, the *doyen* of Italian chemistry, who warned his colleagues in Bologna and in other universities that, in view of the falling enrolments, governmental grants could be more profitably used for the improvement of a few engineering schools to serve the whole country.[40] He also pointed out archly that, in his view, it would have been more fruitful to devote local contributions to the improvement of the facilities in the science faculties.

In the event, Cannizzaro's criticism went unheeded. The ministry found it difficult to dismiss the plea for help from Italy's oldest university, whereupon the Scuola di Applicazione of Bologna was readmitted to the group of the state-supported engineering schools. However, in this case as in dealing with other engineering schools' requests of funding, the Ministry of Education made no allowance for the improvement of teaching provision. Consequently, other patrons had to be found in order to permit the introduction of new courses of a more explicitly technical character, and the improvement of teaching facilities. Where local authorities, private patronage, or other governmental agencies were less responsive than in Milan and Turin, the results were inevitably modest. Proposals to launch special programmes tailored to suit local interests, such as the opening of a section of hydraulic engineering in the Scuola di Applicazione of Padua, did not trigger sufficient support and faltered. Perhaps the most conspicuous success achieved at the turn of the nineteenth century by the *scuole* in their attempt to add new technical subjects to their civil engineering curricula was the creation of courses of electrical technology. The rapid development of the electric utilities sector in the 1890s encouraged this move, and very often the new courses were privately funded, or sponsored by local authorities. By 1904 electrical technology was part of the engineering schools' third-year programme in Rome, Padua, Bologna, and Naples.[41]

In spite of these difficulties, the efforts to introduce specialization and strengthen mechanical engineering were not abandoned, and eventually they bore fruit. In 1904 separate sections of mechanical and civil engineering were established in Naples; and by 1909 the students of the Scuola di Applicazione of Rome could choose from as many as six specialities in which to graduate: civil engineering, mechanical engineering, electrical technology, railway engineering, hydraulic engineering, and architecture. To what extent these measures were buttressed by the actual expansion of mechanical engineering and by the introduction of new industry-related subjects is a different matter. In the absence of detailed studies on the internal development of these institutions, we have to rely on the information provided by the programmes published in the annual reports, and these do not bear evidence of major shifts until after the First World War.

What is clear is that while at the turn of the twentieth century mechanical engineering was laboriously making progress in Rome, Padua, Bologna, and Naples, a new problem emerged in those *scuole di applicazione* where specialized sections had already been established. In Milan and Turin, the diversification between the programmes of civil and mechanical engineering had been enhanced by the introduction of new industry-related subjects in the syllabuses of the mechanical engineering section. However, the syllabuses were not reorganized, and the expansion occurred simply by the additions of new courses to an already dense programme.[42] At the same time, the modest laboratory facilities that had been set up after much effort in the 1890s were swamped by the dramatic increase in student enrolments in the first decade of the twentieth century. Hence, concern about cramming and overloaded programmes became a recurring theme in the reports of the schools' boards of directors.[43]

Inevitably, the predominantly scientific thrust of the preliminary two-year course offered by the faculties of mathematics and physics, and the absence of technical subjects in the programme of the first year of the *scuole di applicazione* came under renewed criticism. Even the Scuola di Applicazione of Turin, one of the strongholds of the general 'scientific' approach to engineering, acknowledged the need for a reform. And when, in 1904, the plan for the merger between the Museo Industriale and the Scuola di Applicazione of Turin was discussed in parliament, these problems came to the fore in the course of a lengthy debate that also involved representatives of other institutions.

In the debate, a radical reorganization of higher technical education was advocated by Vito Volterra, professor of mathematical physics in the University of Rome and one of Italy's most distinguished scientists. Volterra had been appointed by the Ministry of Public Instruction to carry out a survey of higher technical education in other European countries. As a result of this survey, and on the basis of his experience as a teacher in the Scuola di Applicazione of Turin, he recommended the transformation of the *scuole di applicazione* into self-contained institutions, not connected with the universities.[44] In his view, the programmes in the schools should have been shorter (four years instead of five), and the courses of mathematics, physics, and chemistry should have been so designed as to satisfy the special needs of engineering students. In addition, Volterra strongly recommended the improvement of laboratory facilities and the creation of separate sections for mechanical and chemical engineering.

Volterra's report simply restated what the founders of the Istituto Tecnico of Milan and the Museo Industriale of Turin had advocated in the 1860s, and his proposal met the same muted response. Yet again, the obvious malaise of the *scuole di applicazione* was tackled by piecemeal adjustments that left the main problems unresolved. In 1906, the Politecnico of Turin (the new institution resulting from the merger between the Scuola and the Museo) was authorized by the Ministry to establish an internal two-year preparatory course. Four years later, the Scuola di Applicazione of Padua made similar arrangements, and gradually responsibility for courses of this type was transferred to the various other engineering schools. It was only when the link with the faculties of mathematics and physics was broken that mechanical engineering was introduced in the syllabus of the preparatory courses. But the innovation was not sufficient to counter the theoretical thrust of the two-year course, where scientific disciplines continued to form the core of the syllabus.

The innovations in the organization of the final three years were equally inconclusive and belated. It was not until 1913 that a ministerial decree sanctioned the transfer of rational mechanics and technical physics from the first-year programmes of the *scuole di applicazione* to the second year of the preparatory courses. By then, the effects of overloading in Milan and Turin had been partially alleviated by further specialization. In 1900, the Istituto Tecnico Superiore of Milan opened a subsection of chemical engineering, and six years later the Politecnico of Turin adopted the same measure. At about the same time, in both Milan and Turin, electrical technology became an option within the curriculum for mechanical engineering. But the effects of these measures, which were meant to give a sharper focus to studies, were impaired by the constant proliferation of new complementary courses in a variety of technical subjects.

Conclusion

Clearly, for all their determination to meet the needs of industry, the *scuole di applicazione* were not prepared to abandon the realm of higher education, or to transform themselves into schools of a new type that, in the view of the advocates of reform, would have been better adapted to the growing numbers of students with an interest in mechanical rather than civil engineering. The ministry, for its part, did nothing to promote the development of a separate level of industrially oriented technical schools. And while local authorities, especially in the most active manufacturing areas, encouraged the creation of institutions of a vocational character, they could not meet the cost of advanced technical schools. In this way, as is generally agreed, the educational system failed to support the emergence of a new industrial profession.

There is much justification for the denunciation of the ambiguous policy adopted by the *scuole di applicazione*, and of the unresponsiveness of the ministry. But it is undeniable that obstacles to the development of modern technical schools can also be identified in the nature of the market for graduates. By the turn of the century, a growing number of students had begun to be absorbed in manufacturing – not only as managers and independent entrepreneurs, as was often the case in the 1870s and 1880s, but also as technical experts. However, the career patterns that emerge from surveys published by the Istituto Tecnico Superiore of Milan and the Politecnico of Turin show clearly that a substantial number of students who graduated in the 1890s and in the first decade of the twentieth century, continued to find employment in the civil service and in technical positions in provincial and municipal offices. Here, the development of services such as lighting and public transport offered new opportunities. For those posts, indeed for any post starting from the relatively low position of *tecnico municipale*, a degree in engineering was required.

It is also clear that consultancy still offered the most numerous opportunities for employment, not only for graduates in civil engineering graduates but also for mechanical engineers. Consulting engineers played an important part in preparing plans for new factories and for the introduction of new technologies in existing ones. Moreover, consulting engineers often acted as agents for foreign manufacturing companies. In all these capacities, a degree was a necessary requirement, although fraudulent abuses of engineering qualifications were not uncommon.

In both cases, a university-level degree was a means of legitimizing the right to practice in an area of professional activity which, in both the public and private sectors, enjoyed considerable prestige. So long as the very difficult formal qualification of the engineer appeared to open the way to this kind of career, lesser qualifications had little prospect of success. Such alternatives could only have succeeded in the context of a sustained policy aimed at promoting graduates holding these qualifications, and of a market capable of absorbing and rewarding them.

In the absence of any policy for change, technical education remained, until the First World War, at the mercy of confusing conflicts of responsibility between the Ministry of Public Instruction and local authorities. As a result, no alternative emerged, and the *scuole*, despite some half-hearted moves to become more selective in their procedures for admission, followed a pattern of growth which, far from faltering, accelerated after the disruption of the First World War.

Notes

1 General accounts of the development of secondary and higher technical education include Aldo Tonelli, *L'istruzione tecnica e professionale di stato nelle strutture e nei programmi da Casati ai giorni nostri* (Milan, 1964), and Giacomo C. Lacaita, *Istruzione e sviluppo industriale in Italia, 1859–1914* (Florence, 1973).

2 An analysis of this failure that highlights (with, in my view, some exaggeration) the inhibiting influence of the traditional purist bias of the Italian science faculties, is offered in Roberto Maiocchi, 'Il ruolo delle scienze nello sviluppo industriale italiano', in Gianni Micheli (ed.), *Scienza e tecnica nella cultura e nella società dal Rinascimento ad oggi* [*Storia d'Italia. Annali*, vol. 3] (Turin, 1980), pp. 863–999.

3 This point is discussed in Anna Guagnini, 'Higher education and the engineering profession in Italy: the *Scuole* of Milan and Turin, 1859–1914', *Minerva*, 26 (1988), 512–48.

4 In Milan, the engineering profession was controlled by the Collegio degli Ingegneri. Established as a guild in 1563, the Collegio jealously protected the interests of its members against the competition of unqualified engineers for more than two centuries; see E. De Capitani, 'Il Collegio degli ingegneri ed architetti di Milano', in *Milano tecnica dal 1859 al 1884* (Milan, 1885), pp. xv–xlvii; Paolo Mezzanotte, *Cronache e vicende del Collegio degli Ingegneri di Milano* (Milan, n.d.); and Gino Bozza and Jolanda Bassi, 'La formazione e la posizione dell'ingegnere e dell'architetto nelle varie epoche storiche', in *Il centenario del Politecnico di Milano, 1863–1963* (Milan, 1964), pp. 11–113. On the traditional links between the government and the engineering community in Piedmont, see C. Brayda, L. Coli, and D. Sesia, *Ingegneri e architetti del Sei e Settecento in Piemonte* (Turin, 1963).

5 Education was by no means the only criterion for admission to the profession. The right to practise had to be purchased, and in Milan the fees were particularly high for a candidate whose father was not a member of the guild. Moreover, in both Piedmont and Lombardy, would-be engineers had to prove that their lineage was unsullied by any recent involvement with lower professional occupations.

6 In reality, in 1773 a school of architecture was opened in the Ginnasio di Brera (a Milanese institution whose level was comparable with that of the universities). Here, courses in architecture, hydraulics, mechanics, and geodesy were offered by prestigious teachers, such as Giuseppe Piermarini and Paolo

Frisi, to candidates for admission to the engineering profession. However, the hostility of Pavia to this rival initiative stifled the development of the school. See Angela Piedimonte, 'La formazione degli ingegneri in Lombardia prima dell'Unità', in *Il Politecnico di Milano 1863–1914. Una scuola nella formazione della società industriale* (Milan, 1981), pp. 54–64.

7 Andrea Giuntini, 'La formazione didattica e il ruolo nell'amministrazione granducale dell'ingegnere nella Toscana di Leopoldo II', in *La Toscana dei Lorena. Riforme, territorio, società* (Florence, 1989), pp. 391–417.

8 'La Regia Scuola Superiore Politecnica di Napoli', in *Monografie delle università e degli istituti superiori*, 2 vols. (Rome, 1911–13), vol. 2, pp. 183–223, and Giuseppe Russo (ed.), *La Scuola di Ingegneria di Napoli 1811–1967* (Naples, 1967).

9 It was as part of these centralizing measures that professional guilds, such as the Collegio degli Ingegneri of Milan, were closed (in 1797), whereupon the examinations for the title of engineer began to be conducted jointly by university professors and officers appointed by the government.

10 For a brief account of the facilities for engineering education in the Papal States, see 'La Regia Scuola di Applicazione per Ingegneri di Roma', in *Monografie delle università e degli istituti superiori*, vol. 2, pp. 227–92.

11 In the first half of the nineteenth century, the emphasis on applied mathematics and mechanics was one of the most distinctive features of the teaching offered in the Italian faculties of mathematics and of the research interests of their professoriate. These interests were manifested in the contributions of Italian mathematicians to the meetings of Italian scientists that were held periodically in the 1830s and 1840s. See Pietro Redondi, 'Cultura e scienza dall'Illuminismo al Positivismo', in Micheli, *Scienze e tecnica*, pp. 677–811, and Umberto Bottazzini, 'La matematica e le sue "utili applicazioni" nei congressi degli scienziati italiani, 1839–47', in Giuliano Pancaldi (ed.), *I congressi degli scienziati italiani nell'età del positivismo* (Bologna, 1983), pp. 11–68.

12 The renewal of the Piedmontese economy is examined in detail in Mario Abrate, *Lo sviluppo della siderurgia e della meccanica nel Regno di Sardegna, 1831–1861* (Louvain, 1960), and Guido Quazza, *L'industria laniera e cotoniera in Piemonte* (Turin, 1961). Lombardy's economic and commercial development is discussed in Bruno Caizzi, *L'economia lombarda durante la restaurazione, 1814–58* (Milan, 1972). For the south, see John Davies, *Società e imprenditori nel regno borbonico 1815–1860* (Bari, 1979). A general overview is Luciano Cafagna, *Dualismo e sviluppo nella storia d'Italia* (Padua, 1989).

13 The most influential of these new journals was *Il politecnico*. Founded in 1839 by Carlo Cattaneo, a leading figure in the Lombard movement for cultural and economic reform in the 1830s and 1840s, the journal was for more than three decades the main platform of the champions of modernization. While *Il politecnico* was directed at the intellectual élite, several journals of a more popular character appeared in the main Italian towns. Their objectives were proclaimed by titles such as *Emporio di utili cognizioni* (Turin), *L'ape delle cognizioni utili* (Milan), and *Giornale del commercio, delle arti, delle manifatture, con varietà e avvisi diversi* (Florence).

14 The guiding light was Carlo Ignazio Giulio, professor of mechanics in the University of Turin, who was appointed director of the school. On Giulio's role in the creation of the Istituto, see Mario Abrate, 'Carlo Ignazio Giulio', *Studi Piemontesi*, 2 (1973), 82–8.

15 The leading figure in the organization of technical education in Tuscany was Filippo Corridi, professor of calculus of the University of Pisa. As director of the Istituto Tecnico of Florence, he undertook an extensive survey of the state of technical education in Europe and was personally responsible for the organization of the school's lavishly equipped laboratories. See *L'Istituto Tecnico di Firenze. La sua storia ed i suoi gabinetti* (Florence, 1910), and Riccardo Bacci and Mauro Zampolli, *L'Istituto Tecnico di Firenze* (Florence, 1977).

16 Giacomo C. Lacaita, *L'intelligenza produttiva. Imprenditori, tecnici e operai nella Società d'Incoraggiamento d'Arti e Mestieri di Milano (1838–1988)* (Milan, 1990).

17 Of particular interest for their views on the importance of new technologies in engineering education are the projects submitted to the Austro-Hungarian administration by the Istituto Lombardo and by Antonio Bordoni, director of the University of Pavia. See Ferdinando Lori, *Storia del Politecnico di Milano* (Milan, 1941), and Alessandra Ferraresi, 'La Legge Casati, la Facoltà di Matematica Pavese e le origini del Politecnico di Milano. Alcuni inediti', *Bollettino della Società Pavese di Storia Patria*, 28–9 (1976–7), 297–328.

18 On the organization of the university system in unified Italy, see M. Rossi, *Università società in Italia alla fine dell'Ottocento* (Florence, 1976).

19 In fact, these schools never fulfilled the function that was indicated by their name. Gradually they turned into lower-level general secondary schools for children of working-class and lower-middle-class parents. On the secondary technical schools, see Tonelli, *L'istruzione tecnica e professionale di stato*, and Simonetta Soldani, 'L'istruzione tecnica nell'Italia liberale (1861–1900)', in *Studi storici*, 1 (1981), 79–117.

20 Bacci and Zampolli, *L'Istituto Tecnico di Firenze*.

21 Giovanni Curioni, *Cenni storici statistici sulla Regia Scuola di Applicazione per Ingegneri fondata in Torino nell'anno 1860* (Turin, 1884); Giovanni Pugno, *Storia del Politecnico di Torino. Dalle origini alla vigilia della seconda guerra mondiale* (Turin, 1959); and *La formazione dell'ingegnere nella Torino di Alberto Castigliano. Le scuole di ingegneria nella seconda metà dell'Ottocento* (Genoa, 1984).

22 According to the original plan, students had to attend a faculty of mathematics for three years before being admitted to a *scuola di applicazione*, where the programme was limited to two years. The modification that reduced the preparatory course to two years and extended the programme of the *scuole* to three was introduced in 1876.

23 The keen negotiations that resulted in the opening of the Istituto Tecnico Superiore of Milan are discussed in Ferdinando Lori, *Storia del Politecnico di Milano* (Milan, 1941). See also Aldo Castellano, 'Le relazioni tra il Politecnico e la società del tempo (1863–1914)', in *Il Politecnico di Milano*, pp. 137–65.

24 The institution also included a teacher-training school. However, this section never flourished, and, for all practical purposes, the Istituto Tecnico Superiore became the name of the whole *scuola di applicazione*.

25 Before unification, the universities of Bologna and Padua did not award degrees in engineering, but prepared students of architecture and engineering for examination in other institutions of higher education, namely the Istituto di Belle Arti of Venice and the University of Rome.

26 The number of universities was even more striking. In 1870, Italy had no fewer than seventeen state universities and four private universities.

27 One of the earliest and most authoritative advocates of a reduction in the number of the universities was the physicist Carlo Matteucci, who was Minister of Public Instruction from 1862 to 1864. His views are clearly stated in 'Università, scuole speciali e scuole normali, istituti di perfezionamento', in *Ministero della Pubblica Istruzione. Sulle condizioni della pubblica istruzione nel Regno d'Italia nel 1865* (Rome, 1865), p. 10–145.

28 'La Regia Scuola di Applicazione per Ingegneri di Palermo', in *Monografie delle università e degli istituti superiori*, vol. 1, pp. 229–38.

29 Dissatisfaction with this decision was openly expressed in the report of a committee which the Ministry of Public Instruction set up in 1860 to prepare the plan for an engineering school in Milan. 'Relazione Susani della Commissione presieduta da Quintino Sella, 14 ottobre 1860', in Lori, *Storia del Politecnico di Milano*, pp. 341–7.

30 Lacaita, *L'intelligenza produttiva*, and Castellano, 'Le relazioni tra il Politecnico e la società del tempo'.

31 This national vocation was confirmed by a survey of the geographical origins of the Scuola's graduates that was published in 1910. The survey indicates that, out of the total of 4,938 engineers who graduated in Turin between 1860 and 1910, 1951 came from Piedmont, 1980 from other northern regions, and the rest from central and southern Italy. See Associazione Amichevole tra gli Ex-allievi della Scuola di Applicazione di Torino, *Associazione Amichevole tra gli Ex-allievi della Scuola di Applicazione di Torino. Laureati dal 1862 al 1910* (Turin, 1912), p. xxxii.

32 Giovanni Pugno, *Politecnico di Torino. Dalle origini alla prima guerra mondiale* (Turin, 1959). On the role of Giuseppe De Vincenzi in promoting the creation of the Museo, see Alessandra Ferraresi, 'Le vicende del Museo Industriale Italiano di Torino (1860–1880)', *Bollettino storico-bibliografico subalpino*, 77 (1979), 431–94.

33 This tension is expressed in a chastened but clear way by Giovanni Curioni, deputy director of the Scuola di Applicazione of Turin in the late 1870s, in his account *Cenni storici statistici*.

34 Eventually, in 1906, the two institutions were amalgamated and became the Politecnico of Turin.

35 This 'scientific' approach to engineering was whole-heartedly endorsed by Curioni, *Cenni storici statistici*.

36 Brioschi, who had been one of Italy's most distinguished mathematicians in the mid nineteenth century, before becoming more and more involved in the campaign for the reorganization of engineering education and in political activities, imposed a strict surveillance on the thoroughness of the students'

preparation. The appointment of Giuseppe Colombo, a professor of mechanics as well as a successful consulting engineer and a central figure in the industrial development of Lombardy, furthered the commitment of the Istituo Tecnico to the new areas of mechanical and electrical engineering. But the emphasis on theoretical thoroughness and high standards remained firmly embedded in the school's educational programme. On Brioschi's scientific and political work, see N. Raponi, 'Francesco Brioschi', in *Dizionario biografico degli italiani* (Rome, 1972) vol. 9, pp. 321–4. A detailed biographical survey of Colombo is Carlo G. Lacaita, 'Giuseppe Colombo e le origini dell'Italia industriale', in Carlo G. Lacaita (ed.), *Giuseppe Colombo. Industria e politica nella storia d'Italia. Scritti scelti* (Bari, 1985), pp. 5–86.

37 By the agreement, the province and municipality made available 30,000 lire per annum, 25,000 lire to pay for new courses, the rest for equipment. See *Programma del R. Istituto Tecnico Superiore in Milano, 1875–6* (Milan, 1875), pp. 22–30.

38 In both Milan and Turin the organization of teaching laboratories for electrical technology were presented as a turning point in the modernization of the institutions' facilities and programmes. However, the pace of this transformation was exceedingly slow, and the results were at best patchy. See Anna Guagnini, 'The formation of Italian electrical engineers: the teaching laboratories of the Politecnici of Turin and Milan, 1887–1914', in Fabienne Cardot (ed.), *Un siècle d'électricité dans le monde. Actes du Premier Colloque International sur l'Histoire de l'Électricité* (Paris, 1987), pp. 283–99.

39 R. Scuola di applicazione per Ingegneri in Bologna, *Notizie concernenti la Scuola. Monografie dei gabinetti, delle collezioni, e catalogo delle pubblicazioni* (Bologna, 1888).

40 Abstracts of the debate in the Senate are recorded in *Per la solenne apertura della R. Università di Bologna* (Bologna, 1899), pp. 138–47. For an even more explicit denunciation of the excessive dependence on local patronage, see Ferdinando Martini and Carlo F. Ferraris, *Ordinamento generale degli istituti di istruzione superiore. Studi e proposte* (Milan, 1895).

41 Courses in electrical technology were created in 1899 in Naples, in 1902 in Padua (sponsored by a local bank), and in 1908 in Bologna.

42 See Giuseppe Colombo, *Nel cinquantenario del Politecnico Milanese e del giubileo del Collegio degli Ingegneri e Architetti di Milano* (Milan, 1915); republished in Lacaita, *Giuseppe Colombo. Industria e politica nella storia d'Italia*, pp. 467–720.

43 A summary of the conclusions reached in this debate is Valentino Cerruti's report, 'Senato del Regno. Relazione dell'Ufficio Centrale sul disegno di legge presentato dal Presidente del Consiglio, Ministro dell'Interno, di concerto coi Ministri dell'Istruzione Pubblica e di Agricoltura, Industria e Commercio', in Regio Politecnico di Torino, *Annuario dal 1906 al 1911* (Turin, 1911), pp. 49–72.

44 See Vito Volterra, 'Relazione sul viaggio compiuto dal Professore Vito Volterra per incarico avuto dalla Commissione nominata per il riordinamento del Politecnico di Torino' (1904), *Atti del Senato del Regno. Sessione 1904–9. Legislatura XXII*, vol. 2, no. 144, pp. 19–34.

Part III

The exploitation of knowledge

Introduction

The chapters by Robert Fox and Mari Williams explore aspects of Germany's rise to dominance in science-based industry between the 1880s and the First World War. They focus primarily on the view of this process from within industry in two of the main 'losers' in the race for supremacy: France and Britain. Both chapters confirm how difficult it was for education and research to stimulate industrial activity when the economic contexts for the exploitation of knowledge were unfavourable. In electrical construction and supply, as Fox argues, advanced and middle-level courses in electrical technology proliferated in France, as they did everywhere else in Europe and North America from the 1880s. And, in electricity as somewhat earlier in mechanical engineering, there were determined attempts to forge bonds between the academic world and industry, chiefly through the provision, by universities and advanced technical schools, of laboratory facilities for the testing and precise measurement on which reliability and quality control depended. In these sectors at least, it would be hard to see the educational system as the aloof and unchanging structure that certain critics maintained it was. Indeed, the dependence of the Laboratoire Central d'Electricité and the Ecole Supérieure d'Electricité and other electrical schools on non-governmental funding made overtures to manufacturing interests an essential part of the task of survival.

Whether that forced alliance benefited or hindered the French electrical industry in the longer term is, of course, an open question. But the fact that the rise of the electrical industry from 1880 coincided with a period in the Third Republic when French governments were seeking to reduce the financial burdens imposed by education and to encourage private initiative is essential to an understanding of the way in which the educational and industrial worlds interacted with each other. For reasons that are easily identified in retrospect, the *électriciens* in French academic life who responded to the calls of industry found themselves devoting far more time to the routine, immediate demands of manufacturers than to the more creative and innovative work that we tend to identify with the term 'research'.

The same context is also relevant to the precision instruments industry in France. As Williams shows, the association between instrument-making firms and the educational institutions that shared or sought to share in the training of apprentices was far from remote between the 1890s and 1914. But it was fashioned against a background of governmental indifference and in a sector composed of small firms so preoccupied with reducing expenditure that the fruits of improved education could not be properly absorbed. In Britain, too, the fragmented structure of the industry made it difficult for even the most advanced companies to assimilate formally trained men and to promote the kind of in-house research which those men might have conducted.

Despite the difficulty of the marriage between the academic and industrial worlds before the First World War, lobbies arguing for the importance of education and research for industry grew in strength in both France and Britain. In instrument-making they took as their model Germany, the home of the Carl Zeiss company in Jena and of the Physikalisch-Technische Reichsanstalt at Charlottenberg. Once war came, Germany loomed even larger in a debate that assumed a new intensity, and it was under the stimulus of war and of a reinforced sense of German superiority that the serious attention of the French and British governments was finally secured. Williams's study brings out very clearly how the war served the interests of higher education and research by intensifying the dialogue between industrialists and educationalists and creating a mechanism for the engagement of governmental support.

In other industries as well, the First World War served to bring governmental, industrial, and academic interests into unprecedented harmony. As Williams shows, the BSIRA and, even more obviously, the Institut d'Optique in Paris emerged from this *rapprochement* as important motors for research. But that new status did little to shake the confidence of employers, who continued to regard workshop experience as the most valuable qualification for the employees on whose know-how and manual dexterity profitability was still seen to depend. In this sense, the new departures launched during and immediately after the First World War must be accounted only a qualified success.

8 France in perspective: education, innovation, and performance in the French electrical industry, 1880–1914

Robert Fox

Between the late 1880s and 1914, the weakness of French industry came to be seen as a national scandal. With the outbreak of the First World War, the gathering sense of failure hardened to a consensus. Especially in the booming modern sectors of electrical machinery and supply and organic chemicals, France seemed to have been so palpably outstripped by Germany and the USA that it remained only to analyse the causes and advance the remedies.

The anxiety extended across a broad spectrum. Tariffs and patent laws were a matter of concern in virtually all areas of manufacturing, as was the recurring 'crisis of apprenticeship', which was felt to have left France perilously short of skilled hands. In analyses of the newer science-based industries, however, the thrust of the criticism was different. Here, the emphasis tended to be on the abstract, intellectualist character of higher education and on the neglect of applied research. In 1914, Louis Bruneau was just one of many French observers of the economy who looked enviously across the Rhine to a country blessed by the fertile union of science with industry and adorned with 'des laboratoires qui sont des usines, et des usines qui sont des laboratoires'.[1] France, by contrast, was characterized as a country where practice had been consistently disdained and where educational institutions had remained insensitive to, or had misconstrued, the true interests of the economy.[2]

Plainly, these perceptions could not have been sustained if they had not rested on at least a core of truth. There were indeed *savants* (like Emile Picard) who revelled in the lofty purity of their calling,[3] and there were institutions (like the Ecole Polytechnique) where even courses in engineering were cast as mathematical exercises in canonical principles detached from practical application.[4] But the recent secondary literature has made these other-worldly attitudes appear increasingly atypical.[5] In France, as in other countries, the academic provision for education across the whole range of applied science and technology was so greatly increased between the 1880s and 1914 that it is hard to see how French industry could have suffered from a shortage of men with an advanced technical training or from any general mistrust of applied knowledge. If France failed, the problem, as I prefer to cast it, almost certainly had less to do with the number of men coming through from the educational system than with their appropriateness and with the way in which their knowledge and skills were put to use in industrial careers.

My discussion of the specific case of the electrical industry is informed by these premises and by a conviction that educational systems have been (and still are) invoked too readily as independent causes of industrial success or failure. In attempting to define the peculiarities of the interaction between the academic world and electrical manufacturing and supply in France, I shall treat the state of education and research as something which itself requires explanation. In doing so, I shall come back repeatedly to two points. First, virtually from the start, in the 1880s, France assumed the status of a prey, a country to which new technologies could be quite easily exported rather than a setting for autonomous innovation. Secondly, the new departures in teaching and research in applied electricity that were instituted in France after 1880 had to take root in a structure unfavourable to the kind of large-scale developments that occurred in Germany. Within the established higher technical schools – the *grandes écoles* – electrical technology could never become a dominant discipline, and outside those schools instruction in applied electricity had to make its way in a phase of systematic governmental disengagement from the financing of higher education. The new teaching, as a result, evolved as an uncoordinated and largely private venture. It was constrained by modest levels of funding and forced into an unadventurous preoccupation with the immediate demands of an industrial sector which, because of its overwhelming dependence on foreign technology, had no place for large-scale research and patenting in the German or American style. It seems wrong, in the light of this analysis, to suppose that the provision for education and research in some way 'let down' the French electrical industry, perhaps through lethargy or insensitivity. As I shall argue, academic structures responded accurately enough, in both content and quality, to the calls that were made upon them, and it is therefore to the frequently misapprehended nature of those calls that much of this chapter is devoted.

Education for the electrical age

The age of electricity dawned early and briskly in France. By the mid-1870s, the Belgian Zénobe Gramme and the former Russian army officer Paul Jablochkoff were well established in Paris, enjoying a success that placed them among the most prominent celebrities of the Universal Exhibition of 1878, the first at which electrical devices, in particular the arc lamp for public illumination, made a significant mark. Despite the nationalities of Gramme and Jablochkoff, the sense of French pre-eminence in electricity in the late 1870s was unmissable, and it was both reflected and heightened by three new electrical journals – *L'électricité* (the first specialized journal of its kind, founded in 1876), *La lumière électrique* (1879), and *L'électricien* (1881) – and, in 1881, by the first international exhibition of electricity and the first electrical congress, both held in the magisterial Palais de l'Industrie in the Champs Elysées.[6] The exhibition, with more than 800,000 visitors over a period of fifteen weeks, amply fulfilled the multiple objectives of its main patron, the Minister of Posts and Telegraphs, Adolphe Cochery. It lent authority to Cochery's newly constituted ministry, cemented the association between the modernity of electricity and that of the buoyant young republic, and convinced both inventors and exhibitors, among them Thomas Edison, of the commercial interest of electrical manufacturing. Moreover, it reinforced the status of Paris as the preeminent 'city of light'.

At this stage, the shortcomings of education were not cited as a significant impediment. The possibilities of employment in the electrical industry were few, and invention was predominantly the function of individuals working from personal laboratories or workshops who proceeded to establish a small company for the exploitation of their patents. The disparate nature of the process of innovation is illustrated by the contrasting cases of Gramme, who perfected his dynamos on the shop floor, on the basis of a virtually non-existent training in science, and Jules Jamin, the professor of physics at the Ecole Polytechnique and the Sorbonne, who developed his version of the arc lamp in the calm of his professorial laboratory. Between these extremes in the spectrum of the interaction between science and practice, there lay more typical innovators, who built a new electrical speciality on a general training in mechanical or some other branch of engineering. This was true of Hippolyte Fontaine, a graduate of the *école d'arts et métiers* at Châlons-sur-Marne and a mechanical engineer with a special interest in railway construction, who only turned to electricity in his mid-thirties, when he began his fertile collaboration with Gramme in 1867. The case of the pioneer of electrical transmission, Marcel Deprez, a graduate of the Ecole des Mines, whose interest in electricity dated from 1875, when he too was in his mid-thirties, was similar.

Despite the make-shift character of these first steps, the sense of opportunity that was generated by the sudden emergence of a previously non-existent industry was quite as great in the world of advanced technical education as it was in the world of manufacturing and affairs. The timing could not have been more propitious. By the autumn of 1881, when excitement was at its height, the long campaign of the organic chemist Charles Lauth and others for a new form of instruction that would be at once intellectually demanding and industrial in orientation was beginning to yield fruit in the emerging plans for the Ecole Municipale de Physique et de Chimie Industrielles de la Ville de Paris.[7] It was here, in a municipal school intended to do for science-based industry what the *grandes écoles* did for the various state corps of engineers, that the first systematic instruction in industrial electricity was offered from 1882. The start was unquestionably a modest one. For although pupils could devote the last eighteen months of their three-year course to applied physics (as an alternative to the other speciality, industrial chemistry), electricity had to compete for time and attention with thermodynamics, mechanics, and the physics of solids and gases. Moreover, despite the acknowledged quality of the teaching in the subject which they received from Edmond Hospitalier, students notoriously lacked the practical support in mechanical drawing, applied mechanics, and workshop practice that was essential if they were to be accepted as electrical engineers on a footing with their German peers.[8]

For all their shortcomings, the innovations at the Ecole de Physique et de Chimie Industrielles show that in the education of electrical engineers France was by no means left at the post; she shared as fully as any industrialized nation in the flurry of expansion that occurred in the early 1880s. Over the next decade, however, further developments in France, though not negligible, were conspicuously slow and, by the standards of the more thrusting nations, modest in scale. It is true that less than two years elapsed between the launching of teaching in electrical technology at the Technische Hochschule in Darmstadt and the Eidgenössische Technische Hochschule in Zurich (in 1882) and the Institut Montefiore in Liège (in 1883) and the inauguration of ostensibly similar instruction at the main industrial *grande école*, the Ecole Centrale des Arts et Manufactures, but the commitment to the subject at Centrale was muted. In a single course of only twenty lessons, the applications of light were covered in addition to those of electricity, by a former *centralien*, Démétrius Monnier, who had begun his career as a gas engineer in Marseille and come to electricity in his fifties.[9] By 1900, the number of lectures on electrical technology had increased to forty, and by 1913 it stood at fifty, with another fourteen hours devoted to electrical measurements. But, for many years, the teaching remained overwhelmingly theoretical. It was not until 1894 that a small teaching laboratory was provided for work by final-year pupils on electrical measurements and motors, and only in 1900 that a rather cramped general laboratory was opened for student use.

The case of the Ecole Centrale is symptomatic of the response of most existing institutions. Courses like Monnier's or the twice-weekly lectures that Marcel Deprez gave at the Conservatoire National des Arts et Métiers by 1890, or the elements that found their way into the crowded curricula of the *écoles d'arts et métiers* or (from 1893) the Ecole des Ponts et Chaussées were intended to provide no more than an introduction to applied electricity. There could be no pretence that they offered a full programme of theoretical and practical training comparable with those at Darmstadt, Liège, or even the City and Guilds Central Technical School in London, where a three-year course in electrical engineering was created under the distinguished guidance of William Ayrton in 1885. Essentially, therefore, from the mid-1880s the other industrialized countries of Europe were allowed to edge ahead of France in the provision of advanced training for electrical engineers and then, from the 1890s, to stretch that lead significantly.

It was the somewhat delayed perception that France was being left behind which helped training modelled on that of the best European schools to take root in France from the mid-1890s. The pace was set by the Ecole Supérieure d'Electricité (Supélec), though even here the marks of an enduring lethargy are clear.[10] By the time the school opened, in 1894, in grossly inadequate temporary buildings in Paris, core funding, drawn from the profits of the electrical exhibition of 1881, had been available for over a decade. But the Société Internationale des Electriciens, which had overseen the project from 1883, had had other priorities. It had devoted its main efforts to the funding of the Laboratoire Central d'Electricité, which it opened in 1888 (mainly for testing and standardization), and had limited its involvement in teaching to the admission of occasional students to the laboratory.

The character of the Ecole Supérieure d'Electricité was powerfully shaped by the established values of the *écoles d'application*, such as the Ecole des Ponts et Chaussées and the Ecole des Mines, whose main function was to give specialized training to graduates of the Ecole Polytechnique. Accordingly, the course lasted one year and was conceived as the highly focussed completion of a general training in engineering that had been obtained elsewhere. The commitment to rigorous intellectual standards and to the traditions of the *écoles d'application* was reflected in the practice of admitting graduates of the *grandes écoles* (in particular, former *polytechniciens*) without examination. The remaining entrants were recruited by an entrance examination of extreme severity, chiefly in mathematics (for candidates, such as graduates of the *écoles d'arts et métiers* and other technical schools, who possessed strong practical experience) or in applied mathematics, the structure of materials, and design (for *licenciés-ès-sciences* and others with a predominantly theoretical background).[11] Initially, the corollary of this rigorous selection was a modest level of recruitment. Only twelve pupils were admitted in the first year, but within a decade nearly fifty students a year were receiving the school's *diplôme d'ingénieur-électricien*, after a course that combined lectures by permanent and visiting staff with an aggressively practical initiation in workshop and (so far as the facilities allowed) laboratory techniques, independent projects, and visits to factories and sites.

The expansion of Supélec is a gauge of the demand for advanced instruction in the field. Like the graduates of the *grandes écoles* and other schools who opted for Supélec, younger candidates and (crucially) their parents who paid the annual fees of 1,000 F saw electricity as rich in opportunity. This was no less true of the provinces than of Paris, and it was in fact in the provincial faculties of science that full-scale courses leading to a diploma of a standard barely inferior to that of Supélec took root most easily. Here, the outstanding success-stories were those of the *instituts électrotechniques* that were established in the faculties of science at Nancy and Lille (dating from 1900), Grenoble (1901), and Toulouse (1908).

In all four cases, the institutes emerged on foundations laid, from the 1890s, in laboratory classes and lectures on applied electricity that had been incorporated in existing physics courses or in university extension curricula. The most celebrated of these precedents was set by the special evening lectures that Paul Janet inaugurated at Grenoble in 1892.[12] In perceiving the interest that a short course on electrical technology would arouse and turning from his traditional, highly theoretical formation as a *normalien*, Janet showed himself to be far more prescient than his colleagues in the faculty, who believed that any practical instruction that was offered in the Grenoble faculty should be oriented to the better-trodden paths of applied chemistry. In the event, attendances far surpassed even Janet's expectations, and soon the combined pressure of the Chamber of Commerce and the town council forced the faculty's hand. By the time Janet left for a new appointment at the Sorbonne in 1894, a former laboratory belonging to the department of the Isère had been refurbished for practical work, and instruction in electrical technology was an option in the regular syllabus of the faculty.

Although the success of Janet's teaching owed much to his personal skills as a lecturer and entrepreneur, it is far more significant as an indicator of a taste for vocational instruction in technical subjects that gripped faculties and their publics from the 1890s. The rhetoric of professors everywhere was confident, and such justification as was thought necessary was all-embracing, not to say indiscriminate. In a typical assertion, which reflects the claims to an underlying solidarity between applied science, economic interest, and republican democracy, the annual report of the University of Lille for 1898–9 set its own initiatives in practical teaching in a grandiose wider context:

il existe partout, en France comme à l'étranger, un courant qui entraine vers l'enseignement de la science appliquée. Ce n'est pas un mode ou un caprice, c'est un besoin qui correspond au développement de l'esprit démocratique.[13]

The courses of the *instituts électrotechniques* led, like that of Supélec, to a *diplôme d'ingénieur-électricien*. The essential difference was that, although graduates of the *grandes écoles* and certain other students were admitted, without examination, directly into the final year, most candidates entered immediately after the *baccalauréat* and followed a complete three-year course. As at Supélec, there was great pride in the practical nature of the teaching, and in general the pride was justified. For although the core instruction tended to be the responsibility of teachers who had initially been conventionally trained in physics, lectures by practising engineers, visits, and workshop exercises were part and parcel of every syllabus.

If the all-important quest for status was to be successful, the *instituts électrotechniques* had to set standards that would be recognized as high by the prevailing conventions of the time. Predictably, their models in the matter of entrance requirements were the Ecole Polytechnique and the Ecole Centrale. At Nancy, candidates holding the essential basic qualification of the *baccalauréat-ès-sciences* were advised to attend a preliminary year either in a *classe préparatoire* for candidates aiming for the Ecole Centrale or in a special one-year course in mathematics, physics, and 'sciences techniques' which the faculty of science mounted for the purpose.[14] Thereafter, selection remained rigorous, most notably at Toulouse, where in 1910 only 40 per cent of the candidates for the final examination were successful, and in other years the proportion seldom rose above two-thirds.[15]

The aspiration to a high position in the educational hierarchy paid most of the expected dividends. The demand for places never faltered, and, especially from about 1905, numbers rose fast (see table 8.1). The only exception was the institute at Lille, which remained small and rather poorly housed in disused premises previously used for general physics and applied chemistry.[16] But elsewhere the problem became increasingly that of accommodating students, in particular for the practical classes. Facilities at the Toulouse institute, which at the opening in 1908 had

Table 8.1. *Diplômes d'ingénieur-électricien awarded by the Instituts électrotechniques*

Year	Nancy	Lille	Grenoble	Toulouse	Total
1900 –1	5	–	–	–	5
1901 –2	16	–	–	–	16
1902 –3	13	2	–	–	15
1903 –4	29	3	3	–	35
1904 –5	21	1	7	–	29
1905 –6	33	4	17	–	54
1906 –7	24	12	20	–	56
1907 –8	43	16	44	–	103
1908 –9	32	11	62	17	122
1909 –10	39	12	62	31	144
1910 –11	32	11	84	63	190
1911 –12	38	16	82	59	195
1912 –13	48	15	98	59	220
1913 –14	39	?[a]	121	69	*c*.245

[a] The exact figure for this year is not available but it was almost certainly about 15.
Source: Annual reports of the universities, published by the Ministry of Public Instruction in its series of *Enquêtes et documents* (see note 14). The figures occasionally differ from those in the archives of the faculties concerned, but the discrepancies are small.

seemed lavish, were seen barely a year later to be grossly inadequate.[17] Already, nearly 300 students were enrolled, and here, as at Grenoble, what had begun as an annexe to the faculty of science soon became the dominant partner, contributing almost half of the faculty's total population of students on the eve of the First World War. If the science of the nation's science faculties had once appeared culpably detached from the world of practice and application, that charge (though still voiced) had become totally inapplicable by 1914 or even by 1900. In the provinces at least, it was pure rather than applied science that was hard pressed to survive.

Despite a few dissident voices and an occasional dragging of feet by professors,[18] university authorities tended to crow over this reorientation of the faculties, and even where there was no formally constituted institute, they reinforced the trend by mounting other courses in applied electricity or industrial physics. They also drew a very public satisfaction from the large numbers of foreign students who were attracted to the applied courses. The institutes of applied chemistry were popular enough, but the electrical institutes were even more so. All four of them were inundated with students from Russia and (to a lesser extent) the Balkans, many with an indifferent preparation that undermined the institutes' claims to scientific excellence. The high proportion of failures at Toulouse, to which I have already referred, plainly owed a great deal to the fact that on the eve of the First World War fewer than a quarter of the students in the Institut électrotechnique were French.

Even so, the thirst of French students for instruction in electrical technology between the 1890s and 1914 is beyond question. It is reflected in what was, then as now, one of the most telling accolades for any school: the emergence of preparatory courses to help candidates for the entrance examination. By this criterion, as by others, Supélec was a notable success. Soon after the turn of the century, a new electrical school, the Ecole Sudria, carved for itself a pre-eminent role as the most prestigious 'feeder' to Supélec, while three other electrical schools – the Ecole Pratique d'Electricité Industrielle (commonly known as the Ecole Charliat), the Ecole Breguet, and the Ecole d'Electricité et de Mécanique Industrielle (Ecole Violet) – all of them in Paris like Sudria, combined a minor commitment to the same preparatory function with the complete formation of electrical engineers.[19] In all of them, an optional preparatory course lasting for between one and three years could be followed by a two-year or three-year course leading to a *diplôme d'ingénieur-électricien* at the age of between nineteen and twenty-one. Plainly, the intellectual level could not match that of a diploma from Supélec or an *institut électrotechnique*, but success was reflected in a student population which, despite moderate facilities for practical work, grew steadily until 1914, especially at the Ecole Sudria and Ecole Breguet.[20]

The demand

In a way that is now familiar to historians, the context in which the new teaching developed went far beyond that of a simple response to industrial need. In explaining the growth of the *instituts électrotechniques*, for example, the previous marginality of professors of physics and the evolving aspirations of the academic profession have to be taken into account, as do the existing educational structures and social and academic conventions which helped to fashion the market for potential students and to create the confusing proliferation of engineering courses described by André Grelon elsewhere in this volume. The resulting fuzziness of the interface between the academic and industrial worlds makes it all the more remarkable that the match between supply and demand in the production of engineers was as close as it was. As I shall argue, this closeness is largely explained by the predominantly private character of the schools, which imposed on them an uncommon sensitivity to the market for trained men.

As the courses at the advanced and intermediate levels gained in popularity, any danger of a shortage of trained men receded before the greater threat of an oversupply. In fact, even before the expansion in educational provision had gathered ever more dramatic pace in the decade preceding the First World War, anxiety had been voiced. Most of it stemmed from engineers intent on preserving their scarcity value and from employers who, on the whole, saw little need for the new departures in formal instruction. The early years of the Ecole Breguet, for example, were blighted by the indifference of industrialists whose response to the foundation of the school in 1904 was to warn of the danger of flooding the market with engineers for whom there was no employment.[21] And even then the point was not a new one. As early as 1894, an editorial in *L'étincelle électrique* tempered its good wishes to the newly founded Ecole Supérieure d'Electricité with some dark reflexions on the difficulties that French engineers already encountered in making their way in electrical companies well supplied with foreign staff.[22] In a similar vein seven years later, Eugène Sartiaux accompanied his enthusiastic account of the incipient boom in educational opportunities for electrical engineers with the sobering assertion that it might soon be necessary to limit the numbers of those who obtained the qualification of *ingénieur-électricien*.[23]

With disturbing rapidity, these premonitions proved to have at least some substance. A report published by the Ponts et Chaussées engineer André Blondel in the wake of the Exposition Internationale d'Electricité and the accompanying international congress on the applications of electricity, held at Marseilles in 1908, identified the signs of overproduction in the recent drop in salaries for trained men in the electrical industry.[24] Whereas in America and Russia, a combination of a rapidly growing population and a relatively underdeveloped industrial structure had created a high level of demand and correspondingly high salaries (said by Blondel to be comfortably over 500F per month for a recently qualified engineer in America), such levels were rapidly becoming unattainable in France. Before 1900, most young electrical engineers had advanced quickly to 300F and even to 500 or 700F a month; now, in 1908, a typical starting salary was between 125 and 200F, and salaries above 300–400F were rare. The explanation, for Blondel, was quite simply an overproduction of engineers in the sector, even more marked than that which had also depressed salaries in Germany.

The responsibility of the academic lobby in sustaining the oversupply is beyond question. In the publicity literature and addresses that poured from the universities and engineering schools, the career openings in the electrical industry were portrayed as plentiful and secure enough to justify the lengthy acquisition of qualifications in the educational structures that were being put in place. In the desire to 'sell' the new courses, standards were inevitably at risk. One threat lay in the private or semi-private nature of the institutions, which imposed constraints of the kind I have already mentioned, notably in the emphasis that had to be placed on profitable preparatory teaching as a way of subsidizing the more advanced courses. It is hard to assess the effect of this priority on the tone of the institutions where preparatory courses were offered, but even the commercially successful Ecole Sudria and the Ecole Breguet were vulnerable to the temptation to place the emphasis on the rote learning of theory, which had the advantage of getting pupils through their courses as quickly and cheaply as possible. They also had to add to their attractiveness by providing residential accommodation appropriate to schools which accepted pupils from the age of fourteen, or even earlier, despite the consequent skimping on workshops and laboratories.[25]

In the higher schools, the financial constraints were felt in rather different ways. I have referred already to the readiness of the *instituts électrotechniques* to accept foreign students, many of them of suspect quality. The policy of the institutes was also guided by the quest for patronage and profitability through the courting of regional patrons and a constant vigilance in the task of placing graduates on the local market. Usually, in contrast with many of the lower schools, this implied an emphasis on the inculcation of immediately applicable practical skills. At Toulouse, students devoted as many as sixteen hours a week to practical exercises, and both there and at Grenoble the spectacular growth of hydroelectricity was perceived as an opportunity to be exploited to the full by an appropriate adjustment of the curricula.[26] The goal was an alluring one, and it was regarded as perfectly justifiable to mount courses in which instruction in sophisticated theory and the more refined laboratory procedures tended to be eclipsed by the communication of earthier skills such as soldering and the practical aspects of metallurgy and turbine technology.

The priorities were reflected in a deliberate closeness between the training in electrical engineering and that in mechanical engineering which all the institutes offered. At Nancy, the closeness was given formal recognition in 1905 by the addition to the Institut électrotechnique of a section for mechanical engineering and the adoption of the new title Institut d'électrotechnique et de mécanique appliquée. But even where the institutional bonds were less explicit, the complementarity of the skills of the electrical and the mechanical engineer was recognized and advanced as a strength of the education on offer. At all four of the *instituts électrotechniques*, in fact, there was provision for *ingénieurs-électriciens* to qualify also as *ingénieurs-mécaniciens* through an extra year of study.

The aim of these, as of all curricular measures, was to fashion engineers whose training met the predominantly practical expectations of employers. The inauguration of a new course in electrochemistry and electrometallurgy at Grenoble in 1908 was a typical response to what was seen as a local demand, and it was duly well received.[27] The institute at Grenoble, in fact, was outstandingly successful in its care for the employment prospects of its graduates. At a time when nationally there was at least a danger of an oversupply, the director, Louis Barbillion, resolutely provided local employers with the trouble-shooters and site engineers they sought, rather than the more reflective innovators who might have found a place in, say, the Siemens & Halske research laboratory in Berlin. The emphasis deserves comment. For, as has often been observed, it was the marginality of the process of laboratory-based innovation in French science-based industry between the 1890s and 1914 that marked one of the most fundamental differences between France and at least certain leading firms in the rising powers of Germany and the USA.[28] In the ways I have indicated, the new educational institutions for electrical technology, though numerous and generally prosperous, did almost nothing to remedy what in retrospect might appear a weakness, for example by using laboratory instruction to foster the notion of the engineer as the creator of new ideas. In this, however, they should not be seen as ignoring a flagrant but unmet demand. They were responding to a state of national technological dependence that made France an ideal terrain for exploitation by her more successful rivals. It was a terrain in which the reliability and ingenuity of the engineer were calculated to yield far richer dividends than flair or originality.

Technological dependence

The most obvious indicator of the dependence of electrical manufacturing and installations in France on foreign sources lies in the origins of the equipment that was installed in generating stations, factories, and for domestic and public lighting. A common pattern was for the routine and essentially mechanical parts of an installation to be undertaken by local engineers, but for the more sophisticated electrical equipment to be supplied and controlled from abroad. The Le Bourget works of the Compagnie Electro-Mécanique, for example, made their reputation through the fitting of Brown Boveri alternators imported from Switzerland to locally manufactured turbines.[29] Similarly, in the Alpine region near Grenoble, most of the turbines that existed about the time of the First World War were made by Neyret-Brenier and other local mechanical engineering firms, while the alternators came overwhelmingly from foreign companies or, more commonly, from French companies having intimate associations (sometimes amounting to total financial dependence) with foreign 'giants'.

The invasion of electrical manufacturing in France was achieved in a variety of ways.[30] Before the protective Méline tariffs in 1892, it had been simple enough for foreign manufacturers to export their goods to France. Thereafter, it was far more profitable, and scarcely less easy, for them to establish either manufacturing plants or formally constituted subsidiaries in France, often using at least some French capital, though the financial arrangements that were made were exceedingly varied. Significantly, it seems to have been a more positive lure to French investors to have the name of the parent company made public. This was the case, for example, with the Compagnie Française pour l'Exploitation des Procédés Thomson-Houston (CFTH), the Société Française Sprague, the Société Westinghouse, and the Société Française d'Electricité AEG (set up primarily to exploit the Nernst lamp in France), all of which were established in France within a decade of the Méline legislation. Even the more anonymous public face of the Compagnie Electro-Mécanique was intended in no way to deceive shareholders, who at least in the 1890s were positively attracted by the company's reassuring policy of exploiting the patents of the Swiss company Brown Boveri (the acknowledged leaders in steam turbine technology). Likewise, it was no secret that Schuckert (from 1898 to 1902) and then Siemens were the owners and, increasingly, the managers of the Compagnie Générale d'Electricité de Creil (and its subsidiary manufacturing wing, the Etablissements Daydé et Pillé) or that the Société Alsacienne de Constructions Mécaniques at Belfort was, for all the nationalistic overtones of its name, a device for manufacturing Siemens products on French territory.[31] Schneider et Cie at Le Creusot also had no qualms about basing its production of dynamos on patents leased from the Swiss firm Thury.[32] That said, it was noticeably less open about its association with Siemens, which it concealed by the creation of a subsidiary to handle the collaboration and by dealing with the British firm Siemens Brothers rather than Siemens in Munich.[33]

These bonds endowed France with an electrical industry that was successful (if unspectacularly so) by purely economic criteria, while being technologically derivative. It was a situation in which a general satisfaction with profits and dividends was likely to smother any unease that shareholders and employees may have felt. But, from the later 1890s, the displays of anxiety did become more frequent. At its foundation in 1898, the Compagnie Générale d'Electricité (CGE) presented the intrusion of foreign influence as nothing less than humiliating, and it was duly with a strong dose of chauvinist sentiment that the appeal to prospective shareholders was cast. The sense of scandal was created, in the initial announcement about the company, by a comment on the sheer size of foreign electrical manufacturers.[34] The five biggest firms in the field in Germany (AEG, Siemens & Halske, Schuckert, Union, and Helios) possessed a combined capital of 400mF; the CGE, by contrast, would be launched with a mere 10mF. Nevertheless, the new company would strive to turn the tide of technological subservience, especially through the installation of electricity supply stations and the manufacture of auxiliary electrical equipment. Incandescent lamps, accumulators, carbon rods for arc lamps, and electrolytic copper were all products through which the CGE felt it could respond to the foreign invasion and the tendency for the great majority of firms in France to rely on patents from Germany or Switzerland.

It was a bold call but a vain one. The CGE came quickly to rely on agreements with Brown Boveri and made no significant independent technological contribution until after the First World War, when the first company laboratory was established. The retreat from at least a show of resistance passed virtually unnoticed in a contemporary press all too accustomed to acquiescence in the process of foreign domination. In fact, it was only as national rivalries intensified and the prospect of war with Germany loomed that occasional protests hardened into widespread indignation. The publication of Louis Bruneau's strongly nationalistic examination of the encroachment of German influence in the French economy in 1914[35] was the tip of an iceberg of resentment which had been manifested, two years earlier, in the very public resignation of four of the French directors of the Compagnie Générale d'Electricité de Creil in protest against the filling of senior administrative and technical positions by staff from Siemens-Schuckert.[36] What had begun at Creil as an agreement involving the concession of Schuckert patents had assumed, over an increasingly turbulent decade, the character of a take-over, and gradually French patience had been exhausted.

The smallness of most electrical manufacturers in France, reflected in the examples given in table 8.2, was at once a cause and a consequence of their dependent status. Such companies could export neither to the countries from which they were in varying degrees controlled or from which they derived their technologies nor to any other country where their parent companies had a powerful interest. Hence, there was no incentive to develop the combination of substantial capital and a policy geared to independent innovation and the strategic accumulation of patents on which the success of the leading international concerns depended. It may be that a reluctance among shareholders made some contribution to the disparities in capital that separated electrical companies in France so markedly from the biggest concerns in Germany, Switzerland, and the USA. But my sense is that most French companies secured levels of capital appropriate to the nature of their activities. Certainly, there are no grounds for believing that a policy based on innovation and what would have been seen as risk would have been more attractive to investors. Quite the contrary. It was precisely the caution of the Compagnie Générale d'Electricité, especially in the difficult years of 1901–3, that earned it the support of the financial press and of shareholders more than satisfied with modest but reliable dividends, which they saw as the fruits of providence.[37]

It is instructive, in this context, to look more closely at the one case in table 8.2 that seems, at first sight, to vie for the status of an exception, the CFTH. In fact, this case underlines the limitations to which French electrical companies, and hence activities and careers in the sector, were subject. The growth of the CFTH in the late 1890s, following the economic revival of 1896, was comparable with that of the leading German electrical companies, and profits were moderately attractive.[38] But it was a growth built for and by the securing of a near monopoly in the in-

Table 8.2. *Capital of French and other electrical manufacturers, 1895–1913 (all figures in French francs)*

Company	1895	1900	1905	1910	1913
French					
Breguet	?[a]	4m	4m	4m	4m
CEM	1m	0.5m	1.5m	2m	5m
CFTH	5m	40m	40m	60m	60m
CGE	–	15m	15m	18m	25m
CGE de Creil	–	5m	7.5m	3.8m	?[a]
L'Eclairage Electrique	1.65m	4m	4m	6m	11.625m
S.A.AEG	–	1m	1m	2m	2m(?)[a]
S.A. Westinghouse	–	20m	25m	20m	14m
Société Fr des Electrodes	–	1m	1m	1.2m	2.4
Foreign					
AEG	26.4m	72m	120m	130m	186m
Brown Boveri	–	12.5m	16m	28m	32m

[a] Precise figures not available.

stallation of electric power for domestic and industrial purposes and, most importantly of all, in electric traction. The manufacturing of components, in the factory of the Société des Etablissements Postel-Vinay in Paris (which the CFTH absorbed in 1894), was indispensable to the enterprise, but the core of the CFTH's activity was commercial.[39] Company strategy consisted essentially in securing a dominant interest in municipal and other local tramway companies, mainly in France and her colonies but also in other countries (notably Spain, Portugal, and, for a while, Italy) which the CFTH had been set up to serve. Then from a position of unassailable strength, Thomson-Houston and other technologies under the parent company's control, all of them developed and proven already in the USA, would be imposed, often (as critics were always ready to observe) with little regard for quality or price.[40]

The CFTH illustrates how size and commercial success could be built on a state of technological dependence that made a significant investment in research and development appear not only unnecessary but also foolhardy. In smaller companies, the risk involved in research would have appeared even greater. Here, administrators could not doubt that shareholders were more likely to be reassured by reports of technologies based on the exploitation of well-tried foreign patents than by news of attempts at independent innovation. This was especially so during the renewal of the economic crisis between 1901 and 1903 which had the contingent but, in my view, crucial effect of suppressing the modest readiness for risk-taking that seems to have fired the CGE and several other new companies founded amid the new confidence of the later 1890s.

The research lobby

In the circumstances I have described, it is easy to understand why laboratory scientists engaged in innovative technological research in electricity had such a fragile toe-hold in industrial employment. Such exceptions as there were tended to be found in companies manufacturing a very narrow range of specialized components, many of which managed to retain their independence of foreign interests. The Société de l'Accumulateur Tudor in Lille, specializing in accumulators and miscellaneous equipment concerned with electric traction, is a good example, as are the Société Française Electrolytique (founded in 1907 to exploit the electrolytic production of metals) and the Société Française Radio-Electrique (founded in 1910 as a pioneer in wireless telegraphy). On the eve of the First World War, all three companies maintained laboratories from which a modest flow of technological improvements emerged.[41] By contrast, in the French subsidiaries of the larger, more diversified companies, where foreign technologies ruled supreme, the function of in-house laboratories seldom went beyond a bare minimum of quality control and routine testing.

When this situation is set against what has come to be accepted as the paradigm of the successful innovating company, it can very easily be seen as a mark of failure. But before 1914 even the contemporary critics of the unscientific nature of French industry rarely focussed on the case for laboratories as a vehicle for innovation. The call, in fact, was for diffusion and cooperation rather than secrecy and competition. An early success of Henry Le Chatelier, the most vehement spokesman for the cause of integrating science in industrial practice, is entirely characteristic. It came in 1901, when Le Chatelier put his mark on a programme of patronage for research in industrial science, administered by the Société d'Encouragement pour l'Industrie Nationale.[42] The aim of this programme, which resurrected a rather fragile venture launched nearly a decade before, was to give grants for approved research whose results would be published and made available to any interested manufacturer. The budget was small – it reached a peak of only 12,600F for the year 1904 – but it allowed a number of studies on subjects as varied as ceramics, tanning, and Le Chatelier's own field, metallurgy, to come to fruition.

Le Chatelier's campaign was, in part, a response to the economic realities that made French companies reluctant to devote manpower and investment to laboratory work of an open-ended character. As his close associate and fellow-metallurgist Léon Guillet later observed, and as Le Chatelier would certainly have agreed, a profusion of inadequately funded laboratories in firms that could not have countenanced the risk involved in exploiting untried new ideas would do little for industrial advancement.[43] However, Le Chatelier was also making a principle out of the ideal of cooperative applied research which French industrialists in a number of sectors were beginning to favour, quite independently of his prescriptions. It was typical of this ideal that, in 1909, the national federation of the owners of coal mines, the Comité Central des Houillères, devoted 500,000F and an annual budget of 100,000F to a laboratory at Liévin for the study of safety in mines.[44] And even Lumière frères in Lyons made a practice of publishing a large proportion of the results obtained with the aid of an annual sum of 40,000F which, by 1914, they were devoting to their two laboratories.[45]

The indifference towards research as a source of competitive advantage to individual firms had its unmistakable repercussions in the academic world. One consequence was a purely negative one. Institutions involved in the training of electrical engineers felt no pressure to prepare graduates for the task of innovation: the proposal that engineers emerging from the Institut électrotechnique at Toulouse should have the opportunity of staying on for an additional year to be trained in research was an afterthought and it was never properly implemented. In so far as the products of Supélec or the *instituts électrotechniques* might be expected to pursue laboratory-based careers, the emphasis would certainly be on repetitive testing and control, with some premium on experience of precise measurement. In this respect, the time-consuming but essentially unimaginative laboratory and workshop exercises that formed part of all the courses of advanced training offered a realistic preparation.

The same priorities were reflected in the private research of academic staff, who tended to pursue enhanced certainty and precision rather than the elucidation of new principles or techniques which might be exploited by a company. Indeed, it was precisely because academic laboratories offered a detachment from the mêlée of industrial competition that their services were prized. Situated as they were outside the industrial context, such laboratories could provide authority and hence the independent guarantees of quality and reliability that the purchasers of equipment palpably valued.

No institution encapsulated the French conception of applied research in the academic context more clearly than the Laboratoire Central d'Electricité. From its foundation by the Société Internationale des Electriciens in Paris in 1888, it was devoted almost entirely to the verification of measuring instruments, in particular of supply meters, ammeters, and voltmeters, and to the testing of insulators and other electrical equipment.[46] This range of activities attracted the industrial clients on whose fees the laboratory depended, and it was the consistent appreciation of these clients which made the precariousness of the institution and the poverty of its temporary facilities, fitted out for a mere 30,000F, appear so incongruous. By 1893, a sum of just over 300,000F, made up in roughly equal parts by a share of the capital from the 1881 exhibition, the donations of industrialists, and a grant from the Giffard legacy, allowed a new building to be inaugurated. But even in this more spacious environment, the work remained devoted primarily to the testing of meters and lamps, both in the laboratory and on sites throughout France.

Priorities in the research of the provincial *instituts électrotechniques* were similar. All of them had laboratories for testing and precise measurement, which were used both by staff and by selected students. There, the facilities and practice promoted a conception of research very similar to those which prevailed within industry. The Laboratoire des essais et étalonnages which the Institut électrotechnique in Grenoble established in 1904, evidently in response to local demand, was typical in detaching itself explicitly from commercial rivalries. It was proud to describe its staff as 'non intéressés personnellement aux questions industrielles et financières' and to declare itself to be 'placé en dehors des intérêts de clans'.[47] The emphasis would be placed where it should lie: on the reliability rather than on the novelty of the results.

The sustained flow of commissions from the manufacturers and installers of electrical equipment shows how well the laboratories responded to the expectations of their consumers. Accordingly, as the pace of domestic and industrial installations grew from the late 1890s, the stamp of official approval, in the form of impartial guarantees of reliability and precision, assumed ever greater prominence. The movement also drew strength from the precedent that had been set, in both education and research, by a number of mechanical laboratories with similar objectives, such as the materials testing laboratory of the Ecole des Ponts et Chaussées or the Laboratoire d'essais mécaniques, physiques et chimiques et de machines which the Conservatoire National des Arts et Métiers inaugurated in 1901. That heritage left its mark, for if it made the assimilation of electrical testing laboratories easier, it also transmitted some of the limitations that constrained the work of the mechanical laboratories. Not only was novelty not expected, but also and more crucially the hand-to-mouth dependence on fees, earned for specific tasks, meant that long-term investment in the facilities was hard to justify or afford.

As a result, the laboratory at the CNAM quickly became a symbol of governmental indifference to research,[48] and the Laboratoire Central d'Electricité was soon tarred with the same brush. By the time of the International Electrical Congress in London in 1908, it had come to be regarded as quite unfitted for the status of a national laboratory. Its facilities so paled by comparison with those of the Physikalisch-Technische Reichsanstalt in Berlin, the National Physical Laboratory at Teddington, and the National Bureau of Standards in Washington that France very nearly suffered the humiliation of being excluded from the international network of contributors to the task of establishing electrical units and standards.[49]

Conclusion

It would be hard to conclude that the electrical industry in France was poorly served either by the teaching or by the research offered within the educational system. Secondary education certainly remained bound, as it always had been, to purist values encapsulated in an emphasis on classical and literary studies and, for candidates for entry to the technical *grandes écoles*, a diet of abstract mathematics assimilated in the demanding but intellectually oppressive 'classes préparatoires'; here, quite plainly, there was a running sore calculated to infuriate reformers and leave a trail of prejudice towards utilitarian pursuits in cultivated circles.[50] But, as I have argued, this did not prevent advanced schools and courses in electrical technology from being founded at a pace roughly commensurate with demand. Even the very traditional Ecole des Mines inaugurated a new suite of teaching laboratories for electrical instruction in 1902,[51] at precisely the time when the faculties of science and their associated technical institutes were seizing on the emergence of a new industrial market for trained men and for expert adjudication as a windfall capable of reinforcing the faculties' quest for a serious academic role after decades of marginality. With regard to the content of what was offered, it is clear, once again, that new institutions made a generally fine judgement of the market for skills and knowledge. The function of advanced technical education was seen as the provision of a thorough instruction in practical engineering and in measurement and control, with a judicious nod in the direction of the local profile of industrial demand, whether it was for specialists in coal-fired power stations in the Nord or for hydraulic engineers and electrochemists in the Alps or the Pyrenees.

What else could the educational system in the new electrical sector have offered? Essentially, my answer has been that at the advanced level, with which this chapter has been concerned, very little more could have been done. Education for the electrical age had to make its way as a largely private initiative and hence was bound by immediate, rather than long-term or even medium-term, priorities. Subject to those constraints, it tried to carve out a genuinely new path in French education, seeking (with moderate success) the high status traditionally reserved for the *grandes écoles*, with their tough and strongly theoretical curricula, while responding (with far greater success) to the employers' demands for practitioners. In the process, under recognizable market pressures, the balance of curricula shifted unmistakably to practice, with some marginalization of both theory and the quest for novelty.

It was this orientation which, in a retrospective assessment dating from the First World War, clearly coloured Le Chatelier's analysis of the weaknesses of the French educational system.[52] The system, as he saw it, provided a ready enough flow of employees for routine tasks, even at the highest levels, but it did not fashion the 'officers' of industry on whom renewal was by now recognized to depend: in this respect, for Le Chatelier, the true interests of industry had been misconstrued by the world of higher education. But by the contemporary standards that prevailed before 1914, such a view would be hard to sustain. As I have argued, the academic community before the war had spared no effort to adjust and demonstrate its usefulness to the new industrial order that emerged with the age of electricity. Hence, if it had failed industry, it had done so not by its indifference or a misreading of the economic circumstances but by the very sensitivity of its response, reflected in its zeal to court industrial favour and to respond to immediate needs. In retrospect, of course, we might see those needs as incompatible with the longer-term interests of the economy, and the purpose of this chapter has certainly not been to argue against such a view. It has been simply to adjust for the myopia of hindsight that can so easily detach the strategies of educational and industrial practice from their context, making what were in reality perfectly intelligible and defensible decisions appear as the mainsprings of real or imagined failure.

Notes

1 Louis Bruneau, *L'Allemagne en France. Enquêtes économiques* (Paris, 1914), p. 245.

2 The flavour of a vast literature on this subject is reflected in such statement as those of Joseph Chailley, *La crise économique en France* (Paris, 1885), *passim* but especially pp. 7–9, and André Pelletan, 'La formation des ingénieurs en France et à l'étranger', *La technique moderne. Supplément*, 2, no. 4 (April 1910), pp. i–viii (including the supporting comment of the dean of the Faculty of Science in Paris, Paul Appell).

3 The point is made very strongly in Charles-Emile Picard, 'La science et la recherche scientifique', *Revue scientifique*, 50e année, 2me semestre (1912), 577–81.

4 See Terry Shinn, *Savoir scientifique & pouvoir social. L'Ecole Polytechnique, 1794–1914* (Paris, 1980), especially chapters 4 and 5, and 'Reactionary technologists: the struggle over the Ecole Polytechnique, 1880–1914', *Minerva*, 22 (1984), 329–45, on the conflict between reformers and *intransigeants* on (among many other matters) the syllabus of the Polytechnique between the 1880s and 1914.

5 See, for example, Terry Shinn, 'The French science faculty system, 1808–1914: institutional change and research potential in mathematics and the physical sciences', *Historical Studies in the Physical Sciences*, 10 (1979), 271–332; Harry W. Paul, 'Apollo courts the Vulcans: the applied science institutes in nineteenth-century French science faculties', in Robert Fox and George Weisz (eds.), *The Organization of Science and Technology in France, 1808–1914* (Cambridge and Paris, 1980), pp. 155–81, and *From Knowledge to Power. The Rise of the Science Empire in France, 1860–1939* (Cambridge, 1985), especially chapter 4; George Weisz, *The Emergence of Modern Universities in France, 1863–1914* (Princeton, NJ, 1983), especially chapter 5; Robert Fox, 'Science, the university, and the state in nineteenth-century

France', in Gerald L. Geison (ed.), *Professions and the French State, 1700–1900* (Philadelphia, 1984), pp. 66–145; Charles R. Day, *Education for the Industrial World. The Ecoles d'Arts et Métiers and the Rise of French Industrial Engineering* (Cambridge, Mass., and London, 1987); André Grelon, 'Les universités et la formation des ingénieurs en France (1870–1914)', *Formation-emploi*, nos. 27–8 (July–December 1989), 65–88.

6 Among the numerous studies of the 1881 exhibition, see J. Béthenod, 'L'Exposition internationale d'électricité de 1881. Son influence sur le développement de la science et de la technique', in *Comptes-rendus du Congrès international d'Electricité*, 13 vols. (Paris, 1932), vol. 12, pp. 305–58; Patrice Carré, 'Paris, capitale électrique', *Revue française des télécommunications*, 47 (1983), 65–74, and 48 (1983), 157–80; François Caron and Christine Berthet, 'Réflexions à propos de l'Exposition de Paris de 1881', *Bulletin d'histoire de l'électricité*, 2 (1983), 7–18. On the Congress of 1881, see Christine Blondel, 'Négociations entre savants et administrateurs: les premiers congrès internationaux d'electricité', *Relations internationales*, 62 (1990), 171–82.

7 Terry Shinn, 'Des sciences industrielles aux sciences fondamentales: la mutation de l'Ecole Supérieure de Physique et de Chimie (1882–1970)', *Revue française de sociologie*, 22 (1981), 167–82. For Lauth's own account, see Charles Lauth, *Rapport général sur l'historique et le fonctionnement de l'Ecole Municipale de Physique et de Chimie Industrielles* (Paris, 1900).

8 The reservation was voiced in an editorial, unsigned but probably by Georges Claude (a former pupil of the school), in *L'étincelle électrique*, 1 (1894–5), 25–6.

9 Léon Guillet, *Cent ans de la vie de l'Ecole Centrale des Arts et Manufactures 1829–1929* (Paris, 1929), pp. 122–3.

10 For a contemporary account of the Ecole Supérieure d'Electricité and the associated Laboratoire Central d'Electricité, see 'Le Laboratoire Central et l'Ecole Supérieure d'Electricité', *Bulletin de la Société Internationale des Electriciens*, 2nd ser. 4 (1904), 537–644. See also Paul Janet, 'Nos grandes écoles. L'Ecole Supérieure d'Electricité', *Revue des deux mondes*, 54 (1929), 113–29, and *Soixantenaire de l'Ecole Supérieure d'Electricité: Mai 1954* (Paris, 1954), especially pp. 10–23. A valuable recent study, containing extensive statistical material, is Sarah Singer-Turner, 'La naissance de l'Ecole Supérieure d'Electricité, 1881–1929' (Mémoire de maîtrise, Université de Paris V, Nanterre, November 1984).

11 The performance of graduates of the *écoles d'arts et métiers* in securing entry to Supélec is particularly notable. Day observes that of the 2,804 students who entered Supélec between 1894 and 1925, over a seventh were *gadzarts*; see Day, *Education for the Industrial World*, pp. 103–4.

12 The initiatives at Grenoble between 1892 and 1894 are described by Paul Janet in his *Notes et souvenirs* (Paris, 1933), pp. 125–34.

13 *Compte-rendu . . . Université de Lille* (Lille, 1899), p. 63.

14 *Rapports des conseils des universités . . . 1908–9*, in *Ministère de l'Instruction Publique. Enquêtes et documents relatifs à l'enseignement supérieur*, 100 (1909), 305. In fact, the preliminary year had originally been instituted, in 1908, primarily to cope with the large number of poorly prepared foreign candidates wishing to study electrical technology. See *Université de Nancy (1572–1934)* (Nancy, 1934), pp. 94–8.

15 *Rapports des conseils des universités . . . 1909–10*, in *Enquêtes et documents*, 101 (1911), p. 349, and the reports for subsequent years in vols. 104 (1910–11), 106 (1911–12), and 108 (1912–13).

16 See René Swyngedauw's account of the Institut électrotechnique at Lille, in *Lille et la région du Nord*, 2 vols. (Lille, 1909), vol. 1, pp. 101–13. One of the Lille institute's constant difficulties was the stiff competition it faced from advanced courses in electrical technology offered by the Institut Industriel du Nord de la France and the Catholic Faculty of Science.

17 A building programme continuing up to the First World War did little to counter the sense of inadequacy that was voiced repeatedly in the annual reports of the University. The appeal for help from the city authorities, on p. 349 of the report on the year 1909–10 (see note 15, above), is typical.

18 The reticence of certain professors in the Faculty of Science at Clermont-Ferrand was symptomatic of the more conservative reactions to the changes. See Robert Fox, 'L'attitude des professeurs des facultés des sciences face à l'industrialisation en France entre 1850 et 1914', in Christophe Charle and Régine Ferré (eds.), *Le personnel de l'enseignement supérieur en France aux XIXe et XXe siècles* (Paris, 1985), pp. 135–49 (142–3).

19 André Grelon, 'Les origines et le développement des écoles d'électricité Breguet, Charliat, Sudria, et Violet avant la seconde guerre mondiale', *Bulletin d'histoire de l'électricité*, 11 (1984), 121–43. An informative and often critical report on the Charliat, Violet, and Breguet schools, written in 1921, is in the Archives Nationales: 'Rapport de M. Chaumat sur une mission d'inspection dans trois établissements d'enseignement électrotechnique' (F17bis 7232).

20 On the eve of the First World War, the Ecole Breguet had a student population of 410, roughly half of them in the preparatory classes, and gave about sixty full diplomas a year. See the unsigned 'Note sur l'Ecole Breguet' in Archives Nationales, F17bis 7241.

21 *Ibid.*

22 *L'étincelle électrique*, 1 (1894–5), 25–6.

23 Eugène Sartiaux, 'L'ingénieur-électricien en France', *L'électricien*, 2nd ser. 22 (1901), 9–11.

24 André Blondel, 'Que doit être l'ingénieur-électricien?', in *Congrès International des Applications de l'Electricité. Marseille, 1908. Rapports préliminaires (IIe partie)*, ed. by H. Armagnat (Paris, 1901), pp. 564–92 (588–92). Blondel's comments drew on his experience not only as a practising engineer (specializing in high-voltage transmission lines, traction, and lighthouses) but also as a teacher of applied electrical technology at the Ecole des Mines and the Ecole des Pont et Chaussées and as a prominent member of a committee of the Ministère des Travaux Publics on the distribution of electric power.

25 The strain of providing accommodation for roughly half of the pupils placed a considerable strain on the Ecole Breguet until the First World War, as the 'Note' cited above (note 20) makes clear.

26 Toulouse and Grenoble were by no means unusual in their emphasis on practical exercises, regular visits to factories, and compulsory work experi-

ence in industry during the vacations. The spirit of all the institutes, in fact, was encapsulated in the ideal (borrowed by the Institut électrotechnique in Grenoble) of 'l'étudiant jeune, les études courtes, le savoir pratique et immédiatement utilisable'; see *L'Institut électrotechnique de l'Université de Grenoble* (Grenoble, 1908), p. 5.

27 *Université de Grenoble. Année scolaire 1908–1909. Rapport annuel du Conseil de l'Université (3 novembre 1909)* (Grenoble, 1909), pp. 75–6. Toulouse followed suit in 1911 with its own advanced course in applied electrochemistry.

28 For an excellent study of the traditionally low investment of French firms in research, see Terry Shinn, 'The genesis of French industrial research 1880–1940', *Social sciences information/Information sur les sciences sociales*, 19 (1980), 607–40.

29 The pattern of the company's activity, which extended to agreements with the Parsons Company in Britain and a growing involvement with Brown Boveri (especially from 1901), is described in *La belle histoire de la CEM* (Paris, 1950).

30 These are well analysed in Albert Broder, 'La multinationalisation de l'industrie électrique française, 1880–1931: causes et pratiques d'une dépendance', *Annales ESC*, 39e année (1984), 1,020–43.

31 The bonds I mention emerge clearly from the annual reports and newspaper cuttings in the relevant files in the 65 AQ series in the Archives Nationales: G.207 (Compagnie Générale d'Electricité de Creil), G. 239 (Schuckert), and M.415–416 (Société Alsacienne de Constructions Mécaniques).

32 Thury direct-current dynamoes were unashamedly a centrepiece of the Schneider company's display at the Exposition Universelle of 1900, along with alternators of both the Thury and the Ganz type. See Edmond Hospitalier and Jules-Armand Montpellier, *L'électricité à l'Exposition de 1900*, 2 vols. (Paris, 1900–3), fascicule 3, pp. 32–7 and 58–62.

33 'Les entreprises d'électricité et l'invasion allemande. La Compagnie Générale d'Electricité de Creil', *Journée financière et politique*, 23 April 1914, and a similar article in *La petite côte de la bourse*, 2 April 1914.

34 *Compagnie Générale d'Electricité. Société anonyme en formation. Notice* (Paris, 1908), pp. 3–4.

35 Bruneau, *L'Allemagne en France*.

36 *La vie financière*, 8 March 1912. The article in this issue of *La vie financière* was typical of the many scandalized accounts in the French financial press. Headed 'Le groupe allemand prétendent diriger seul et sans contrôle les affaires sociales. Quatre administrateurs français donnent leur démission', it described the resignation of the Chairman (Bailleux de Marisy) and three other members of the Conseil d'administration in protest against 'les essais de germanisation à outrance' that had afflicted the company since 1902, when the merger between Schuckert and Siemens had disturbed the initially happy relationship with Schuckert.

37 The CGE's policy of providing modest but dependable returns was insisted upon by the founder and 'administrateur-délégué', Pierre Azaria. Financial commentators were unanimous in commending the policy and the prudent dispersion of the CGE's interests in a wide range of manufacturing and supply

companies. The consistent approval of the shareholders is reflected in reports on the annual general meetings through to the First World War; as an example, see the report on the meeting of 21 December 1907 in the supplement to *L'information*, 23 December 1907. A comparison between the CGE and many other electrical manufacturers in France underlines the value of the company's achievement: the Maison Breguet, for example, paid no dividend of any kind between 1901 and 1907.

38 When the capital of the CFTH was raised to 40m F in 1898, the figure was broadly comparable with the corresponding ones for AEG (56m F), Siemens & Halske (42m F), and Schuckert (34m F) in Germany. It was only after 1900 that the capital (constant until it was raised to 60m F in 1909) was outstripped, in particular by that of AEG. The slow growth of the CFTH in this later period was, in part, a result of the waning of 'tramway fever' in France and the consequent weakening of one of its main areas of activity.

39 The policy of the CFTH was expressed clearly in the annual reports and other materials in the Archives Nationales; see 65 AQ. M. 691 (1–5).

40 The CFTH was never popular with the French financial press, which disliked the secrecy that surrounded its financial dealings as well as the technological strategy to which I refer. For an early comment on the securing of 'captive' clients for Thomson–Houston technology, see *Bulletin financier*, 6 September 1896.

41 The laboratory of the Tudor company, at St Nazaire-sur-Loire (Loire-Inférieure), specialized in metallurgical research and materials testing. The establishment of a laboratory for chemical analysis at the main plant of the Société Française Electrolytique in Paris was reported in the company's annual report in 1909; see *La vie financière*, 11 May 1909. In addition to the task of quality control, the laboratory was expected to help to maximize profits by seeking new raw materials and determining the ideal current for the electrolytic production of copper. On the laboratory of the Société Française Radio-Electrique at Surennes, near Paris, which developed techniques of wireless communication that were used by American troops during the First World War, see *Cinquantenaire de la Compagnie Générale de Télégraphie sans Fil* (Montrouge, 1960).

42 The work done under the society's auspices since 1891 is described in Le Chatelier's presidential address, delivered on 23 December 1904, in *Bulletin de la Société d'Encouragement pour l'Industrie Nationale*, 104e année (1905), 12–22 (18–19).

43 Léon Guillet and Jean Durand, *L'industrie française. L'oeuvre d'hier – l'effort de demain* (Paris, 1920), p. 177.

44 Henry Le Chatelier, 'Les encouragements à la recherche scientifique', a paper published in the series 'Mémoires & documents' of *Le musée social* (Paris, 1916), pp. 79–80. I am grateful to Dr Andrew Butrica for drawing this paper to my attention.

45 Chatelier, 'Les encouragements', pp. 85–6.

46 The nature of the work of the Laboratoire Central d'Electricité is conveyed in the series of *Travaux du Laboratoire Central d'Electricité*, of which three volumes appeared between 1910 and 1914, and (more succinctly) in Paul Janet, 'Les travaux et le rôle scientifique international du Laboratoire Central

d'Electricité', *Bulletin de la Société Internationale des Electriciens*, 3rd ser. no. 57, supplement (December 1916).

47 The phrases appear in a publicity brochure, undated but evidently dating from the mid-1920s: *Université de Grenoble. Institut Polytechnique. Département des Recherches et Essais. Laboratoires annexés aux établissements d'enseignement*, pp. 1 and 2.

48 In a review of the work of the CNAM between 1913 and 1919, Henry Couriot took the opportunity of damning the provision not only for the Laboratoire d'essais but also for the institution's other laboratories. See Couriot, 'Conservatoire National des Arts et Métiers (1913–1919). Rapport général du Conseil d'Administration du Conservatoire National des Arts et Métiers sur l'état de cet établissement, le fonctionnement de ses services et les résultats de l'enseignement', *Journal officiel de la République Française*, Annexe (feuille 2), 13 January 1921, pp. 17–28 (19, 22, and 24–6).

49 Henry Le Chatelier, 'Rapport sur les laboratoires nationaux de recherches scientifiques', *Comptes rendus hebdomadaires des séances de l'Académie des Sciences*, 163 (1916), 581–8.

50 The leading rôle of secondary education in perpetuating anti-utilitarian values in the high culture of France, as of many other countries, was fully recognized by reformers from the time of Hippolyte Taine. See, for example, the very critical comments of Chailley and Pelletan in the items cited in note 2. Le Chatelier's concern was specifically with the division that had opened up between the 'modern' and the 'classical' strains in education since the reforms of 1902; see his article 'La réforme de l'enseignement secondaire', *Revue de métallurgie*, 16 (1918), 1–18.

51 H. Roberjot, 'Le laboratoire d'électricité de l'Ecole Nationale Supérieure des Mines', *Annales des mines*, 2nd ser. 'Mémoires', 7 (1905), 527–43.

52 Henry Le Chatelier, Preface to Léon Guillet, *L'enseignement technique supérieur à l'après-guerre* (Paris, 1918), pp. 20–1.

9 Training for specialists: the precision instruments industry in Britain and France, 1890–1925

Mari Williams

Between the late nineteenth century and the inter-war period, the precision instruments industries in Britain and France, in common with other industrial sectors, underwent a number of transformations. These years saw the growth of individual companies, the introduction of structured research and development within several firms, the coming together of representatives from higher education and government, and changes in the market for instruments as other science-based industries were converted to the idea of the continuous monitoring of industrial processes. But in other ways the making of precision instruments in the two countries remained curiously similar over this time. During the 1920s and early 1930s, instrument making was still in many respects a craft; firms, though larger, had not streamlined production: mass production was uncommon; and, particularly in Britain, despite prolonged discussion of the subject, the industry maintained the ambiguous attitude it had long possessed towards the training deemed necessary among its employees. From this combination of changing and unchanging characteristics two will be examined further in this chapter: the development of organized research, and the unresolved problem of training.

Although the instruments industry has never been a significant industrial sector in terms of the percentage GNP generated, it nevertheless makes an instructive case study because of the unusual place it occupies with respect both to scientific research and to industrial development. Because of the market for precision instruments, makers have always had to keep closely in touch with changes in science, technology, and, since the period of this study, industry, and have also striven to bring about such changes. Scientific instruments may be taken as an indicator of scientific, technical, and industrial development, so that beyond being one small-scale example of science-based industry, instrumentation is an industry that interacts closely with the sectors of which it is representative.

During the last quarter of the nineteenth century, the manufacture of precision instruments in Britain and France was undertaken by a large number of firms varying in size from the one-man-band to well established companies like the British-based Elliott Brothers and Duboscq-Soleil in France.[1] While the industry as a whole was growing during these years, this is seen more clearly in the increase in the number of companies involved in the manufacture of instruments than in any particularly dramatic growth in the size of individual firms.[2] But this actual growth of the British and French industries masked a relative decline in world performance; for throughout the final decades of the nineteenth century, the initiative within the precision instruments industry was being taken increasingly by Germany. Firms making a variety of measuring and detecting devices opened across that country at an astonishing rate, so that by the turn of the century, there were at least 100 young companies joining the ranks of such leading establishments as Merz & Mahler and Reichenbach & Ertel.[3]

As case histories have abundantly demonstrated, the Germany of the late nineteenth century forged ahead of her competitors in several science-based industries. What is striking is the apparent ease with which this happened, particularly the absence, in the immediate term, of any counter-challenge from those who had previously led the world. In the case of precision instruments, this meant Britain and France: for throughout the eighteenth century and well into the nineteenth, London and, to a lesser extent, Edinburgh had dominated the manufacture of high-class precision instrumentation; then, during the middle decades of the nineteenth centuries, these cities gave way to Paris, where almost the whole of the French industry was located.[4] But as Germany consolidated her position towards the end of the century, there were few signs of concern in the industries of either of her two predecessors.

Growing awareness of problems

It was the Paris-based industry which was finally jerked into an awareness of the threat it faced from across the Rhine. At the Universal Exhibition of 1900, held in Paris, the makers from Germany staged an impressive, coordinated appearance. German instrument-making as a whole was represented with exhibits categorized by type rather than by individual maker, and with substantial and effective publicity.[5] There can be no doubt that the presence of the Germans at the Paris Exhibition took the makers of the host city by surprise. In the aftermath, the Syndicat des Constructeurs en Instruments d'Optique et de Précision felt the need to respond to the German Exhibition catalogue. An equivalent publication was produced for the French industry, in which the situation in France was assessed and reasons for its relative eclipse suggested.[6]

In this particular case, although the close links between the industry and science education were acknowledged, the educational system was not focussed upon as a primary cause for concern. However, it was around the turn of the nineteenth century, in both Britain and France, that the attention of several commentators on the production of precision instruments turned to the question of the effectiveness of technical education with respect to the performance of the industry. In France in the late 1890s the Syndicat des Ouvriers en Instruments de Précision reported on conditions prevailing in the Paris workshops,[7] exposing problems facing anyone seeking employment within the industry. A formal apprenticeship system was in place, but evidence suggested that it was abused, especially by the smaller firms. As is pointed out in the chapter by Robert Fox, in all areas of manufacturing worries were expressed about a 'crisis of apprenticeship'; the precision instruments industry was one manifestation of the general malaise. In principle, apprenticeship lasted between three and five years, during which time apprentices experienced a combination of workshop training and formal classroom teaching. Courses were provided at one of two professional schools which specialized in precision mechanics: the École Municipale Diderot and the École Congréganiste de Saint-Nicolas. Between them, the two schools could train up to about sixty pupils a year, but as many as 40 per cent of those who qualified were unable to continue with their special craft since they could not find suitable jobs. The problem as diagnosed by the Syndicat des Ouvriers was not one of inappropriate training on the supply side, but one of insufficient demand on the part of instrument making firms.

The difficulty facing newly qualified apprentices was that many firms preferred to engage new apprentices to replace each one who finished the training, using the system to give access to a form of cheap labour. This was especially so in smaller firms which needed to keep costs down. Moreover, they had little difficulty in finding new recruits. Boys were eligible for apprenticeships from the age of thirteen, and on occasion began a year earlier. By the end of the century parents no longer had to pay an employer to take on their sons, but the in-house training provided was sometimes of dubious quality. Often during the first year very little knowledge relevant to the industry was imparted; apprentices were expected to do little more than run errands. Payment for such activity was rare, and even at the larger workshops there was no guarantee that better conditions could be found.[8]

While the regulations governing the hiring and supervision of apprentices gave rise to adverse comment, there were no specific rules about the qualifications needed to fill senior posts. Instrument design was usually in the hands of a very few individuals who either owned the firm or were closely associated with the owners. The educational background of these people was often impressive, although it would not have included specific learning in the art of instrument making or design. For instance, in the electrical instrument sector, such leading figures as Jules Carpentier and Antoine Breguet both studied engineering at the École Polytechnique;[9] and in other branches of the industry similar levels of scientific or technical achievement characterized the senior staff of at least the leading companies.[10]

The pattern of a small number of technically literate designers and owners, with workshop personnel engaged in a combination of on-the-job training and part-time formal classes, was also characteristic of the industry in Britain around the turn of the century. The presence of the German makers at the Paris Exhibition of 1900 had less of an impact on British manufacturers than on the French; but disquiet about the precision instruments industry was building up in Britain for different reasons. At the beginning of the new century, the British army was involved in the Boer War and some of the reports reaching Britain caused grave concern: among other things, the instrumentation available to the army, particularly the optical devices used for taking ranges, performed badly, and this was taken as indicative of wider malaise within the British instruments industry.[11]

The debate generated in Britain over the arming of the forces was seen by some as an opportunity to review the precision instruments industry in terms of the expertise within it and the training available for it. During the last quarter of the nineteenth century, it was not possible for an instrument firm to recruit graduates in instrumentation technology; no such course existed and employers were not worried about this. At senior levels within the firm, as in the French industry, there were in any case few opportunities; firms were small and seldom employed more than one or two individuals on instrument design. Such work was often the province of the founder or owner aided by perhaps one engineer. Nevertheless, within this élite group of instrument designers it is possible to recognize common experience. Some were graduates, often in science, and all, before reaching positions of authority in a company, would have had experience on the technical side of the industry. W. G. Pye, recruited in 1881 as the company's first chief engineer by the Cambridge Scientific Instrument Company, had had extensive on-the-job training in the London workshops, and he was succeeded by Robert Whipple, who had worked as an instrument user at Kew Observatory and as a maker with L. P. Casella.[12] Horace Darwin, co-founder of CSI, was a science graduate from Cambridge, and subsequently spent time gaining work experience at Easton, Anderson & Couldon near the family home in Kent. Similarly, before setting up business as a maker of electrical instruments, R. W. Paul spent some years learning practical aspects of the trade at Elliott Brothers;[13] and at precision engineer and instrument maker R. W. Munro, the founder's son, Alfred James Munro, entered the firm after taking a degree in engineering at Imperial College and gaining practical experience in Belgium.[14]

It is clear, then, that the transition from academic science to instrument making was possible and indeed straightforward for individuals at or near the top of the firm. But, for other employees, the story was different. During the 1880s and 1890s, small but growing companies took on new personnel as and when needed, without specific policies on who should be appointed. However, certain managers worried about the problem of recruiting suitable staff. One man inquiring about employment at CSI listed his very specific qualifications and experience, only to be told that the company preferred less specialist knowledge: general techniques relevant to the making of any instrument rather than understanding of only one or two particular instruments.[15] In another case, the Glasgow company Barr & Stroud was always anxious to take on science graduates, preferably students whom the two founding professors had taught themselves or who had gone through courses known to them.[16] Nor were the problems of finding good recruits limited to the filling of more senior posts. For the more mundane jobs in the workshops, in Britain (unlike Paris) there were few formal apprenticeships in instrument making; before the late 1890s, there were no courses specifically for trainee instrument makers. Nevertheless, at some firms junior employees were encouraged to attend relevant lectures. It was hoped that this, together with supervized, on-the-job training, would provide men with sufficient expertise to carry out the necessary tasks. Attending courses was, of course, easier in some places than in others; in Cambridge and Glasgow, for example, suitable lectures were available, and both CSI and Barr & Stroud persuaded their workers to attend.[17]

It was not until the mid-1890s that courses designed especially for the instruments industry were considered by educationists. Then, in 1896, the Northampton Polytechnic Institute (later City of London University) was founded in Clerkenwell in London. Among the firms to be found in that area were several optical instrument makers,[18] and, as one of the main ambitions of the new institute was to provide suitable training for local industry, in 1898 classes in technical optics were started. They proved successful: by 1903 a separate department for technical optics had been created, and, with the backing of industry representatives, the

Institute had submitted to the Technical Education Board of the London County Council a proposal to establish an imperial school for the subject. Unfortunately for the technical optics lobby, the LCC was reorganizing its education services at the time, and the lobby lost its initiative.

Initiatives in higher education

During the decade before the First World War, the possibility of founding a British technical optics institute resurfaced intermittently. In June 1905, the optical trade organized a convention at the Northampton Institute at which a resolution was passed expressing 'cordial approval of the project of founding an optical technical institute for the training of opticians in the scientific principles of optics and their technical applications which it regard[ed] as a matter of industrial importance to the nation'. In November of the same year, Conrad Beck took the opportunity of stressing that 'there are methods of testing instruments which should be in use in all our large factories which cannot be learnt in any English schools or teaching establishments, and which, so far from being trade secrets, are described in continental schools'. Moreover, 'the fact that they cannot be learnt by any members of the trade who do not belong to existing establishments puts a great bar in the way of progress'.[19]

In 1910, a further conference was held at which a number of people, including the Dublin instrument maker Howard Grubb, Richard Glazebrook of the National Physical Laboratory, Herbert Jackson of King's College, London, and the ever reliable Conrad Beck, all emphasized the need for an optical institute of some description in Britain. Moreover, at this point those arguing in favour invoked the spectre of German superiority, which, it was claimed, resulted from the Physikalisch-Technische Reichsanstalt at Charlottenberg.[20] The case clearly convinced the LCC; in 1911, its Education Committee adopted a detailed report on the need for the new institute, through which all sections of the workforce and management could receive theoretical and practical training appropriate to their stations. But the Committee added a new ingredient. The two basic types of teaching to be offered were to be organized at different institutions: that for the workforce as always intended using and extending facilities at the Northampton Institute, with Imperial College taking on the responsibilities for educating and preparing managers.[21]

It is apparent, therefore, that three years before the First World War the LCC was on the verge of establishing coordinated education in technical optics for instrument makers. Sadly, for reasons of funding, a proposal was all there was to show for it by early 1914.

While negotiations were foundering in Britain, an appreciation of the arguments supporting specialist higher education for precision instrument makers was taking root in France. In contrast with developments in Britain, however, across the Channel two people directly involved in instrument making presented the first strongly argued case for such provision. In the early 1910s, the instrument maker Amédée Jobin, then owner of the influential Maison Duboscq-Soleil, was working with the astronomer and instrument maker Henri Chrétien on new instruments for the service d'astrophysique at the observatory in Nice.[22] It was borne in on the two men during their collaboration that, increasingly, the important reference works on geometrical optics were in German, and that there was virtually no formal education in this discipline at senior levels in France. As a result of an exchange of views between Jobin and Chrétien, the idea emerged of an Institut d'Optique, similar to the British ideas for a national institute for technical optics.[23] The principal roles for such an institution were perceived to be the regaining by France of the academic initiative from Germany, and the provision to French industry of expertise in the forms of relevant technical courses and textbooks in French.

The scope and reasons for the creation of the proposed Institut d'Optique were very similar to those of the British national institute for technical optics. At this point in the debates over the links between higher education and performance within the precision instruments industry, good quality in the former was held to be essential for the latter. But it was not simply a matter of providing suitable theoretical knowledge to individuals who could then apply it in the workshops and designing rooms of instruments firms. In both Britain and France, there was a feeling that their national institutes should be more directly involved with the industry, by supplying expert knowledge derived from research as well as highly trained personnel, and by becoming significant centres for consultation by the trade. The two countries had histories of close collaboration between the makers and users of precision instruments. Until the early twentieth century, many of the trade's most important clients were research scientists and, particularly in France, the great achievements of the precision instruments industry during its heyday were believed to have resulted from the close collaboration between science and instrument making.[24]

The role of research

By the early twentieth century, research as a component of science-based industry was becoming increasingly common. It is well known that the earliest examples of in-house industrial research occurred in the electrical and chemical companies of Germany and the United States during the final quarter of the nineteenth century. By 1900, both Britain and France were beginning to follow suit, and, certainly in Britain, the precision instruments industry had research laboratories before 1914.

Within Britain before the turn of the century, no company contained formal research and development departments; nevertheless, several companies were involved in the development of new products and new designs for established products, with company representatives working closely with the scientists who used them. During the formative years of CSI, for instance, both Horace Darwin and co-founder Albert Dew-Smith spent much of their time in collaboration with Michael Foster, professor of physiology in the university, creating new means of measurement.[25] The site of research in instrumentation was not necessarily company premises: it could be the customer's home or place of work, or the home of the company representative. Links between the makers and the users were sometimes forged and maintained through scientific societies. R. W. Munro was active in the Royal Meteorological Society for many years, and as a result his firm became expert in the production of wind-speed measurers and indicators. Personal contact of the kind, made possible through membership of the RMS, was very important and is apparent in another facet of Munro's work for the firm: his joint development, with John Milne, of the seismograph originally designed by Milne while teaching at the Imperial University in Tokyo.[26]

During the early twentieth century, however, changes started to take place in the ways in which research was undertaken. These changes were most obvious at CSI where the firm itself had changed significantly during the 1890s. In 1895, it became a limited liability company; in the following year, the company moved to new and enlarged premises, and in 1898 an important change was made in the company's management. W. G. Pye left to go into business with his sons and was replaced by Robert Whipple, recently recruited as Horace Darwin's personal assistant. Under the influence of Whipple, several new developments took place: almost immediately, he introduced new accounting techniques and in due course funds began to be allocated to the 'Experimental' department.[27] By 1909 the work carried out in this department was divided into three categories: new instruments and general experimental work; instruments in the company's catalogues which had been redesigned or modified; and experimental work carried out at the customer's expense. Over the following few years, the department regularly had around twenty projects on its books of varying degrees of immediate relevance to the company's instrument making programme.

Other companies were also being exposed, gradually, to the ideas and possibilities of research. At Elliott Brothers during the 1890s the firm advertised facilities to do research leading to patent applications,[28] while in some cases companies became involved in research projects going on elsewhere. R. W. Munro, for example, was one of a number of firms which worked closely with the Admiralty. Munro provided equipment for research on model ships and maintained its links by supplying dynamometers and machines for hull-shaping.[29] Indeed, as an industry, precision instrumentation was more nearly involved in research as an independent activity than any other sector, so it is not surprising that at least the larger of its constituent firms considered having similar facilities of their own. Each already had testing rooms and each had to deal with the problems of instruments returned because of defects or outright failure. In several cases it was to be the First World War that imposed fledgling research departments, but the conflict cannot be seen simply as the cause. Rather the war created an environment within which an industry already quite familiar with the roles of industrial and other research was pushed into organizing research for its own purposes.

Within the French industry, new organizational developments were taking place mainly in electrical instrumentation. Just as it was the leading firms of Carpentier and Breguet which set the pace in the introduction of new, American-style methods of production towards the end of the nineteenth century, so it was the same establishments which imported new forms of company organization. By the 1890s, Carpentier had a reputation for being very up-to-date, with a *bureau d'études*, a *bureau de dessin*, a *bureau de lancement du travail et du planning*, and what was termed a 'laboratoire alternatif'.[30] This transformation of the leading electrical instrument firms coincided with an influx of at least some trained engineers into the profession, and in this respect the same companies were also to the fore. Certain similarities can be seen here with at least one British firm, Elliott Brothers, whose main output during the late nineteenth century was also electrical instrumentation. However, it is not clear that other areas of precision instrument making in France showed any of the tendencies apparent in the electrical sector. As was made evident by the enquiries set in motion in the wake of the Paris Exhibition of 1900, most makers were accused of ignoring new developments, especially those of organization, including research.[31]

Thus in 1914 a curious combination of factors characterized the British and French precision instruments industries. As far as in-house research and the provision of adequate training were concerned, the pattern was uneven, especially when compared with that in Germany. In parts of the industry in Britain and France, organized research was obviously considered important, but most small firms survived without; indeed, in many the possibility of setting up a research laboratory was remote because of the lack both of space and of personnel. The latter lack was not, however, a straightforward failure of higher education to supply suitably trained individuals. There is no clear evidence that the industry could have absorbed many more graduates of any type, even if they had followed courses particularly devised to suit precision instrument making. Links between the industry and the educational system were not close, particularly in Britain, where debates about the need to change were more vehement than those on the other side of the Channel. But in both countries there was an awareness of the difference in Germany: whenever the subject was addressed in either country, the role of Charlottenberg in supplying thousands of trained graduates was emphasized.

The impact of war: higher education in Britain

With the outbreak of war, such debates were intensified, with one very important difference: central government started to take a serious interest. In Britain, within only a few months, the vulnerability and relative inadequacy of parts of British industry were exposed, and many of the well-known arguments and rhetoric about higher scientific education resurfaced.[32] In addition, claims were made that the value of scientific research was insufficiently appreciated by the government. Over-enthusiastic recruitment drives by the armed forces had left university laboratories depleted, and in May 1915 the Royal Society sent a deputation to the Boards of Education and Trade to argue for explicit financial support for scientific research as a specific and necessary part of the war effort.[33]

Later in the year, the particular question of education in technical optics was raised in the House of Commons.[34] In the summer of 1915 Robert Blair, of the LCC's Education Committee, had compiled a document emphasizing the needs of the instruments industry. The industry, he agreed, was a small one, but its products were vital and their manufacture required a wide range of skills.[35] Blair concentrated on the process of production: preliminary operations of cutting, slotting, and rough polishing, followed by the highly skilled optical working of glass, accurate metal working, and careful assembly of parts. But before any of this was possible, the 'brains' of the firm had to be relied upon to design workable instruments, and afterwards experts were needed in the test room to judge and to amend. By common consent, the most difficult aspect of design was lens computation, 'a matter of compromise between conflicting difficulties with limitations imposed by the types of glass available'.[36] It was the kind of work which could take months of effort and in which firms regularly had to rely on buying in results from freelancers.

Blair drew up details of the different courses he believed necessary to meet the requirements of this specialist trade, starting with junior technical courses of six to eight hours a week over two years for fourteen to seventeen year olds, covering elementary science, calculations, drawing, and practical lens grinding. Those workers who successfully completed this would then be able to chose one of two senior technical courses. These were to last three years, with four to six hours weekly devoted to calculations, mechanics, physics, and mechanical drawing, and with optics for those specializing in the mechanical operations of glass grinding and polishing. This would be sufficient to train the workforce; training for the more senior and technically demanding jobs, in designing, draughtsmanship, and testing, required higher basic qualifications. Boys with secondary school education and two years of full-time specialization in mathematics and science at a technical school would be encouraged to attend sandwich courses: six months in the workshop and six in formal education learning optical design, the use of instruments, workshop practices and technical French and German. Beyond this, to qualify as a lens computer would require a university degree in mathematics or physics and a postgraduate qualification in optical theory and manufacturing practice. Moreover, the postgraduate courses would be enhanced with studies of economics and scientific workshop management, of particular importance for the sons of manufacturers, who were anticipated to be the most likely constituency for postgraduate training. As far as the location of these courses was concerned, the junior ones were scheduled for technical institutes near the works; senior courses would be at a suitable centre in north London; and, finally, Imperial College was to host the new high-level course, organized by a group under a new professor of technical optics.

The proposed new department at Imperial College was the cornerstone of Blair's plans for education in precision instrumentation. The department was to provide full- and part-time courses using three laboratories – for physics, mechanics, and optics – two drawing offices, two lecture rooms, a specialist library and workshop, each to house twenty students, and a test room large enough for ten. For the six months of the year during which most students would be working at their sponsoring firms, the department could devote time to research or provide a series of specialist courses for the users of optical instruments, to be given to medical men, scientists, and military personnel. It was also intended that the department should be used as a technical information bureau for the trade. Many firms were too small to support in-house research, but, with individuals outside the business having time and facilities to carry out research, the hope was that free and useful knowledge could be provided without prejudice to those who needed it.

Following consultation with other government departments and the trade,[37] the first major move was the appointment of a professor of technical optics. In April 1917 the position was accepted by the government patent-adviser F. J. Cheshire, who had become involved early in the war in the technical optics lobby.[38] He was determined and set about the creation of his new department with verve. Arrangements were made with Professor Callendar at Imperial College to use rooms in the physics department, and, during the summer, negotiations with the instrument maker W. Watson & Son led to the appointment from there of A. E. Conrady to the newly created chair of optical design.[39] Following this, the main preoccupation of the two professors was the compilation of a satisfactory set of courses.

This proved difficult, since no one had previously thought through the problems of how best to marshal and transfer the knowledge and skills behind the techniques that workers and managers needed to know. The first year of instruction at Imperial College was therefore makeshift, with some confusion over whether courses at the Northampton Polytechnic were competing or complementary.[40] Between the two centres, courses were provided in general optics, designing and computing optical systems, workshop and testing room methods, optical measuring instruments, microscopic optics and techniques, and photographic optics, most including laboratory practice.

A large proportion of the students during the first year were from the London workshops, but as it was still not clear that the courses were meeting the specific needs of the instrument trade, an inquiry into the 'training and education of apprentices in the optical industry' was put in hand. Opinions were sought once again from instrument makers and users as to their precise requirements in terms of training. These did not, however, go far towards ameliorating the difficulties of Cheshire and his colleagues. Each expert had a particular theory about why the industry in Britain failed to meet demands of users and about how improved formal instruction might help; but distilling out a consensus was to be a long process.[41]

During this period of uncertainty, Cheshire attempted to convince central government of the need for a completely new, independent institute for technical optics, echoing ideas then current in France. Cheshire was in favour of luxurious specialist facilities, with the emphasis on research.[42] But following the responses to the inquiry into education, the Technical Optics Committee had to address the teaching question more particularly, and the best solution was still felt to be based on the division between Imperial College and the Northampton Polytechnic.[43] Syllabuses were drawn up for two three-year full-time courses to train two types of student: optical designers and computers, and mechanical and instrument designers. These were to be taught at Imperial College, and are outlined in table 9.1.

On the basis of this structure, Cheshire and his colleagues were to turn out highly trained optical and mechanical instrument designers who would be expected to transform the precision instruments industry by filling senior posts in companies eager to recruit. In the meantime, the

Table 9.1. *Courses proposed for the degree in Technical Optics at Imperial College, London*

	Year 1	Year 2	Year 3
Optical designers and computers		Full course on designing and computing of optical systems	Advanced designing and computing
	Basic courses in:* Mathematics Physics Geometric Optics Chemistry	Advanced courses in:* Mathematics Physics Geometrical Optics	
Mechanical and instrument designers		Short course on designing and computing of optical systems Elements of mechanisms Properties and strengths of materials	Mechanical designing of instruments and apparatus

* Common to both options

Northampton Polytechnic would produce an educated and scientifically literate workforce. There, with its combination of year-long, half-time courses, evening classes, and 'courses for prospective foremen', recruits could learn introductory mathematics, physics, geometrical and mechanical drawing, the scientific basis of glass working, and machine tooling as well as elementary optics and optical instrumentation. Indeed, the proposed syllabus read as a junior version of the first-year course at Imperial College, with some extra emphasis on the mundane tasks of everyday workshop practice.

War research: the influence of the British government

In principle, then, a year after the new department opened at Imperial College, an integrated system of further education in optical and precision instrumentation was in place. However, there were still a number of problems. In the first place, the system was very much London-based, so that the lower-level courses would be of limited availability to the trade. It was certainly of little use to CSI, where the decision was taken to set up a private trade school for junior employees. By this time, the company had a formal, five-year apprenticeship, and to provide back-up for the scheme, a full-time school master was appointed to teach mathematics, chemistry, physics, and mechanical drawing. Apprentices were still encouraged to attend evening classes at local schools, particularly the lectures given by Robert Whipple at the Guildhall. Commonly at the end of the apprenticeship a successful candidate worked in the instrument shop, on the manufacture of the instruments themselves.[44] But arrangements such as these were rare. At other provincial companies junior employees relied on local education facilities which had not changed as they had in London.

For companies outside London, therefore, the advantages of the new educational opportunities would have been in the provision of properly trained senior staff and of research results otherwise unobtainable particularly to the smaller firms. Unfortunately, the organization of advanced courses at Imperial College coincided with the end of the war, which heralded a period of extreme uncertainty for the industry and marked a downturn for recruitment of any kind. Throughout the war the industry was dependent on the government as customer for its products, and, with the coming of peace, all contracts were terminated, leaving the makers to find whatever means they could to survive. Just as the educational system was in a position to supply the specialists deemed so necessary in the early stages of the conflict, so the demand for them dwindled almost to nothing.

Cheshire was well aware of the implications of this, and attempted to protect his young department. In the months just after war, he was successful; a small staff was recruited, and a third professor, of optical engineering and instrument design was appointed.[45] But during the early 1920s the whole idea of the teaching of technical optics came under scrutiny once again, as the trade failed to absorb the graduates emerging from Imperial. Although Cheshire struggled vigorously to defend his department, he was up against severe opposition. The newly created University Grants Committee remained unpersuaded of his case, and the staff of technical optics was absorbed into the physics department, a group devoted to research rather than to teaching.[46]

As a result of this absorption, research became the department's main contribution to the industry in the immediate post-war period. But Imperial College was not the only player in the realm of research. The First World War acted as a catalyst in the development of research facilities at a number of firms. In the optical glass industry, the Ministry of Munitions invested resources in the Birmingham company of Chance Brothers, not only to expand production capabilities but also to investigate the properties and possibilities of new types of glass.[47] Moreover, within the precision instruments industry itself, the Ministry was effective in organizing a variety of research activities: at CSI, Horace Darwin designed height finders and researched methods for locating enemy aircraft; the Munro sons at R. W. Munro were directed into research on aircraft instrumentation; and at C. F. Casella in London, employees were developing photographic devices for aerial reconnaissance work.[48]

In general, this intervention was piecemeal, but as the war continued, a more determined effort was made by central government to coordinate industrial research as a whole. By 1917, the Department of Scientific and Industrial Research had been established, and within it a sub-committee for the standardization of optical instruments and a committee which dealt with precision measurements and radio standards.[49] The DSIR continued to encourage particular pieces of joint work with different firms within the instruments industry, but its most lasting contribution came as a result of its policy on research associations.[50] The intention was for firms in the same industry to contribute financially towards the establishment of a research centre which the individual firms could then use to solve specific technical problems. As an incentive, the DSIR would match pound for pound the amount raised within the industry.[51] Such an idea had obvious appeal for the instruments industry, composed as it was of so many small units each of which found it difficult to support in-house research. Within the industry, it was the optical instrument makers who took the initiative, via the British Optical Instrument Makers Association, an organization formed in April 1916 to promote, deal with, and protect the trade interests of its members. During the second half of 1917, the BOIMA argued with the DSIR over, in particular, the amount the industry was prepared to commit to a joint research initiative.

It was at this point that the idea of the precision instruments industry as a 'key' industry began to surface. This designation was to be of considerable importance to the industry during the 1920s and 1930s, and in the negotiations over the formation of the association it was used to persuade the British government to make special provision for instrument makers. The debate over the DSIR's role in the instruments industry gave commentators an opportunity of reviving the rhetoric about the central involvement of the German government in its industry, and in the event the BOIMA achieved very good terms, with the Treasury agreeing to invest 90 per cent of the initial funds for the research association.[52]

As in the case of the technical optics department, by the time the British Scientific Instrument Research Association came into being, it was well into 1918, and the war, the main motivation for improved research facilities, was almost over. War had certainly focussed the attention of central government on the needs of science-based industry, but, at least as far as precision instrumentation was concerned, by the time any real results had been achieved, hostilities were over and the industry was steeling itself to face very different circumstances. However, the BSIRA was to prove more successful than the department of technical optics in securing continued government support. Unlike other research associations, at its first review, in the early 1920s, the decision was taken to increase the grant to the BSIRA because of the industry's 'key' status. But this was the government's only significant form of support carried over from wartime.[53]

War and the industry in France

Responses to the outbreak of war in France showed some similarities to those in Britain, although initially there was less direct concern about precision instrumentation. Instrument makers had not succeeded in regaining the ground they had lost to their German neighbours, exposed in 1900: in fact, during the first decade of the twentieth century imports of optical instruments from Germany increased by about 50 per cent and stayed at the higher level until the outbreak of war.[54] Unlike Britain, however, France was still a major producer of optical glass and was able to supply most of her own needs in this respect for the duration of the conflict. But, for some specialist glass, France had become dependent on Germany, and this, together with several other gaps in strategically significant areas, caused the French government to turn its attention to its overall capabilities in military-related industries. In this respect, French actions were very similar to those of the British. Steps were taken by the government to transform output from its factories into products with immediate war applications. Munitions factories were created, including sites for the production of optical munitions. A Ministry for Armament and War Manufactures was established and invested with substantial powers. As in Britain, the Ministry was allowed to dictate conditions of work at munitions factories and related production facilities, but it was also given the power to direct technical studies relevant to war materials and munitions.[55]

While central government in France set about re-organizing the manufacture of munitions, other groups were taking stock of the nation's industrial performance. Towards the end of 1915, a number of industrialists created the Association Nationale d'Expansion Economique, which set up a team of inquirers to review particular industries which, it believed, would undertake the changes that were needed to make them internationally competitive.[56] Among these was the optical industry, encompassing the production of optical glass as well as all types of optical and some other precision instruments. In the report on the industry, the first reason suggested for France's comparatively poor performance was the lack of well trained engineers. Once again, as in Britain, the immediate standard for comparison was Germany, in particular the Physikalisch-Technische Reichsanstalt at Charlottenberg. But it was not just that there was no equivalent institution in France; leaders of the precision instruments industry 'ignore[d] preparatory scientific work'.[57] In addition, there was little sign that the apprenticeship system in the French workshops had improved since the end of the nineteenth century, and those who did complete an apprenticeship were often attracted to other specialist engineering professions such as metal working or car building.

In contrast with the story in Britain, the outbreak of war had delayed rather than hastened the creation of the Institut d'Optique. But although war had postponed the realization of plans, it had not stopped the planning itself. Following Chrétien and Jobin's initial discussions, a number of eminent scientists and industrialists pursued the idea of setting up an entirely new specialist school, with the aim of producing suitably trained individuals for all levels within the industry. Those on the Comité de Patronage included de Broglie, Flammarion, and academicians Picard and Sébert, as well as representatives from the Ecole Normale, the Laboratoire Central d'Electricité, and the Bureau International des Poids et Mesures and, from the optical industry, Deloye of Saint-Gobin, Desprez of the Jeumont glassworks, and Doignon, then President of the Syndicat Patronal des Constructeurs d'Optique.[58]

Also among them was Armand de Gramont, whose interest in the optical industry generally and in the provision of military instruments in particular, led to his playing a significant part in the industry during the inter-war years. He was also instrumental in bringing the ideas of the Comité to the attention of the French government. In October 1916, de Gramont dined with Paul Painlevé, Minister of Public Instruction, Clémentel, Minister of Trade, and General Roque and Admiral Lacaze, who had responsibility for the Army and Navy respectively.[59] Following this, Painlevé and Clémentel signed a decree, based on a report prepared by L. Poincaré, director of higher education, and H. Ténot, director of technical education. The report covered the well-known arguments about early French contributions to the subject of optics and the country's subsequent loss of initiative to Germany. The solution offered was simple: 'to give French optics a new vigour, it [was] necessary to create an institute of applied optics'.[60] The proposed institute was to be made up of three sections: the first, the Ecole supérieure, to provide higher general theoretical education; the second, a central testing laboratory for glass and instruments; and, finally, a section for professional training. It was also suggested that a special commission be constituted to work further on the proposal; included on the commission were de Gramont, Jobin, Poincaré, and Ténot.

In the months that followed, negotiations similar to those taking place at much the same time in London started. The commission created sub-groups to consider particular problems, and from then on events in France proceeded more smoothly than in Britain, partly because of the greater commitment apparent on the part of the French government compared with that of Whitehall. By April 1917, the Minister of Trade had approved the proposals put to him by the Commission, retaining the original idea of an institute with three main sections, but including an expanded programme of activities for the institute. It should publish a journal on optical instrumentation as the major outlet for the institute's research work and, on the teaching side, two basic courses were to be taught: one on general optics, the other on optical instrumentation. It was anticipated that students would be recruited from a variety of places, including army and naval officers, graduates from the *grandes écoles*, astronomers, and scientific civil servants, as well as trainee instrument makers. All would spend three years in the professional school, specializing in one of the two fundamental courses; then the best of them would be encouraged to spend further time at the Ecole supérieure. It was also expected that workers and foremen would attend individual courses on a part-time basis. In many respects, this whole system was better-conceived than that in the UK, with all types of training based in the same institute and with the same place destined to become the national focus of research in the subject.[61]

Moreover, possibly because in France the war was an interruption to plans for a new institute rather than, as in Britain, one of the main reasons why such plans came to fruition, the Institut d'Optique fared better in the post-war period than the department of technical optics at Imperial College. Although at the end of the conflict the Institut had not yet materialized, the Armistice did not delay its creation. Indeed, it was in November 1918 that the Chamber of Deputies was first presented with the legislative proposal to make the Institut d'Optique an 'établissement d'utilité publique', clearing the way for its development.

As in London, the first major move was to appoint a suitable director. In February 1919, the post was offered to Charles Fabry, professor of industrial physics at Marseille, and also secretary to the Commission. Initially, however, Fabry was reluctant to move to Paris, so Colonel Dévé, who had previously been organizer of optical and artillery works at Puteaux, was nominated to run the Institut jointly with Fabry, with added assistance from a committee of four.[62] But within two years Fabry was appointed to a chair in the University of Paris, and at the same time became full-time director. By then, the Institut had arranged series of lectures to be given by senior staff of the University of Paris and was preparing to open its doors to its first full intake of students. Those who came attended an introductory course of eleven classes on applied optics given by Fabry; thereafter, the bulk of the basic courses were given by Chrétien, whose lectures were devoted to optical calculations, and Dunoyer, who concentrated on optical instruments. Then students could chose from a variety of short courses on, among other possibilities, optical physiology, the physics and chemistry of glass, spectroscopic apparatus, X-ray spectrography, the uses of different types of instrument, and the design of optical surfaces.[63] Almost all courses involved laboratory experience, and, from the beginning, they were popular. A total of thirty-three people registered for some form of instruction in the autumn of 1921. By the end of that year, the *Revue d'Optique Théorique et Instrumentale* had been launched, a library for the Institut had been started, and its consultative role for the industry was beginning to take shape.

As a centre for technical optics, the Institut made an impressive start and consolidated its position during the 1920s, moving to enlarged and specialized premises in 1927. At the same time, there was evidence that parts of the French precision instruments industry were responding to the calls made during the war for its improvement. In military instrumentation in particular, de Gramont was to play another important role, by establishing a new company, Optique et Précision de Levallois, to supply the French armed forces with rangefinders and other military devices. Within ten years of the end of the war, OPL had succeeded in securing significant orders from the French government and was beginning to make inroads into foreign markets.[64] In addition, during the 1920s several other new companies were established, including Recherches et Etudes d'Optiques et de Sciences Connexes, and the Société d'Optique Appliquée à la Circulation, both of which were founded by two prominent members of the Institut d'Optique: Gaudet and Chrétien.[65]

In the cases of these two firms, an obvious connection existed between the Institut and the instruments industry, but, among new firms, several others also benefited from the Institut. However, it is not clear that the interrelationship was causal; for instance, despite the popularity of the courses at the Institut, only six students in the 1921 intake came from the workshops. The support coming from the Institut, therefore, took the form of research knowledge rather than trained experts.[66] Nevertheless, both the Institut and the trade performed increasingly well as the decade passed. The explanation for this lies partly in the increased commitment of the French government to its precision instruments industry – a commitment demonstrated in the inter-war period in, for example, its readiness to support OPL by buying substantial numbers of rangefinders. This conclusion is further strengthened by a comparison with the situation in Britain. The BSIRA remained in business throughout the early 1920s, despite difficult times for the industry as a whole, because the DSIR continued its large subsidy. On the other hand, the British government was buying very little in the way of precision instruments during this period; for some time, in fact, it compounded the problems of makers by dumping excess supplies of instruments ordered during the war on the open market at prices with which the industry could hardly compete.

Conclusion

I have argued that, between 1890 and the mid-1920s, the precision instruments industries in Britain and France were faced with a number of possibilities for change, only some of which were acted upon. In the case of research, investigations of phenomena relevant to instrumentation remained a feature of leading companies: it paid for makers to keep in touch with the needs of their customers. The most significant developments in this respect were the systematizing in some firms, from around the turn of the century in Britain and from slightly later in France, of procedures for the conduct of research and the involvement of both governments. With the coming of organized R&D, the instruments industries were reflecting similar developments in other industrial sectors and later, and more conspicuously, what had happened in Germany, particularly at the leading firm, Carl Zeiss. Governmental involvement took different forms in the two countries, but in each it was critical. By designating the industry as 'key', the British government was able at least to support the research side, via the BSIRA, and in France cooperation with government ministers certainly hastened the establishment of the Institut d'Optique, which played a central role in the development of French research.

The story of research was therefore fairly successful for the industry in both countries. By contrast, it is not clear that the changes in formal education were nearly as significant. Admittedly, during time of crisis and consequent self analysis on both sides of the Channel, an apparent gap in the educational system was identified, by makers and educationists alike. Moreover, at such times, and particularly during the First World War, people from the industries and from higher education actually talked to one another about the problems. Despite this, especially in Britain, the solution that was reached ultimately failed, and the reality of the gap was never properly established. Furthermore, in France, although the Institut d'Optique was a success, it is not evident that this was because of the courses it offered. What mattered in the end, from the point of view of the makers, was that specialist degree courses seemed irrelevant; nothing could replace actual workshop experience.

Notes

1 T. Woodman and J. Kinnear, 'One hundred and eighty years of instrument making: some historical aspects of Elliott Brothers (London) Ltd., and Fisher Controls Ltd.', *The Radio and Electronic Engineer*, 52 (1982), 164–70; J. Payen, 'Les constructueurs d'instruments scientifiques en France au XIXe siècle', *Archives Internationales d'Histoire des Sciences*, 36 (1986), 84–161 (95–8).

2 W. D. Hackmann, 'The nineteenth-century trade in natural philosophy instruments in Britain', in P. R. de Clercq (ed.), *Nineteenth-century Instruments and Their Makers* (Leiden and Amsterdam, 1985), pp. 53–91; Payen, 'Les constructeurs d'instruments scientifiques'.

3 A. Brachner, 'German nineteenth-century instrument makers', in de Clercq (ed.), *Nineteenth-century Instruments*, pp. 117–58.
4 The dominance of world markets by the Parisian makers is currently being studied by Paolo Brenni at the Centre de Recherche en Histoire des Science et des Techniques, Cité des Sciences et de l'Industrie, Paris.
5 *Catalogue de l'Exposition collective allemande d'instruments d'optique et de mécanique de précision* (Berlin, 1900).
6 Syndicat des Constructeurs en Instruments d'Optique et de Précision, *L'industrie française des instruments de précision* (Paris, 1901–2).
7 P. Delesalle, *Les conditions du travail chez les ouvriers en instruments de précision* (Paris, 1899).
8 *Ibid.*, 9–11.
9 C. Blondel, 'Réponses d'une profession ancienne à de nouveaux besoins: les "ingénieurs-constructeurs" d'instruments électriques à la fin du XIXe siècle', *Bulletin d'histoire de l'électricité*, 11 (1988), 103–20.
10 Biographical details of leading French instrument makers of the period may be found in Payen, 'Les constructeurs d'instruments scientifiques'.
11 R. and K. MacLeod, 'War and economic development: government and the optical industry in Britain, 1914–18', in J. M. Winter (ed.), *War and Economic Development. Essays in Memory of David Joslin* (Cambridge, 1975), pp. 165–203, 168; see also M. Moss and I. Russell, *Range and Vision. The First Hundred Years of Barr & Stroud* (Edinburgh, 1988), pp. 41–2.
12 M. J. G. Cattermole and A. F. Wolfe, *Horace Darwin's Shop. A History of the Cambridge Scientific Instrument Company 1878–1968* (Bristol and Boston, 1987), pp. 6–8, 22; R. S. Whipple, 'Reminiscences of an instrument maker', *Journal of Scientific Instruments*, 19 (1942), 178–82.
13 Cattermole and Wolfe, *Horace Darwin's Shop*, p. 98.
14 R. W. Munro Ltd., *Centenary, 1864–1964* (London, 1964), p. 28.
15 Cattermole and Wolfe, *Horace Darwin's Shop*, p. 23.
16 See Barr's evidence to the Board of Trade Engineering Industries Committee, 20 October 1916, PRO BT 55/23.
17 *Ibid.*; see also R. S. Whipple's evidence, 7 September 1916, PRO BT 55/22.
18 For example, Negretti & Zambra, A. C. Cossor, W. F. Stanley, Gallenkamp, F. Darton, Henry Hughes & Son, J. J. Hicks, and W. Watson & Son.
19 W. Garnett, 'Education Adviser's Report to the LCC Higher Education Sub-committee, Appendix B: Technical Optics', 1 June 1916, PRO DSIR 17/54.
20 See, for example, P. Alter, *The Reluctant Patron. Science and the State in Britain, 1850–1920* (Oxford, Hamburg, and New York, 1987), Introduction; and the chapter by Wolfgang König in this volume.
21 Report of the Education Committee of the LCC, 1 March 1911.
22 F. Le Guet Tully, 'Henri Chrétien, Paris 1879 – Washington 1956', in *Mélanges Paul Gonnet* (Nice, 1989), pp. 217–31.
23 A. Jobin, *Rapport presenté à la Commission Interministérielle d'études d'un Institut d'Optique* (Paris, 1917).
24 See, for example, A. Cornu's Preface to the Syndicat des Constructeurs en Instruments d'Optique et de Précision, *L'industrie française*; A. Picard,

Exposition Universelle Internationale de 1900 à Paris. Le bilan d'un siècle. Tome premier: éducation et enseignement (Paris, 1906), pp. 483–99.

25 Cattermole and Wolfe, *Horace Darwin's Shop*, pp. 8–9, 17.

26 R. W. Munro Ltd, *Centenary*, p. 20.

27 Surviving records of this department are in Box 20 of the CSI archive, University Library, Cambridge.

28 Elliott Brothers, *Catalogue and Price List* (London, 1895).

29 R. W. Munro, *Centenary*, p. 20.

30 Blondel, 'Réponses d'une profession', pp. 115–16.

31 Cornu, Preface.

32 For these arguments, see R. Fox and A. Guagnini, 'Britain in perspective: the European context of industrial training and innovation, 1880–1914', *History and Technology*, 2 (1985) 133–50.

33 M. Sanderson, *The Universities and British Industry, 1850–1950* (London, 1972).

34 Reported in PRO DSIR 17/54.

35 R. Blair, 'Technical optics', 18 June 1915, PRO DSIR 17/54.

36 *Ibid.*

37 See notes on a discussion at the LCC Board of Education, 27 March 1916, in PRO DSIR 17/54; and Imperial College Archives KPT/1/1.

38 See A. H. D. Acland to F. Heath, 4 April 1917, PRO DSIR 17/54.

39 See document dated 20 July 1917, IC Archives, KPT/1/1.

40 First Report of the Technical Optics Committee, July 1918, PRO DSIR 17/54.

41 Some of the answers may be seen at IC Archives KPT/1/2.

42 Technical Optics Committee, 'Comparative scheme of instruction' sub-committee, reports of meetings on 30 October 1918, and 20 February 1919; IC Archives KPT/1/3.

43 Attached to the reports cited above, note 42, see 'Proposed courses of instruction in optical engineering and applied optics at the Imperial College of Science and Technology, South Kensington, and at the Northampton Polytechnic, Clerkenwell'.

44 Cattermole and Wolfe, *Horace Darwin's Shop*, pp. 95–6.

45 'Department of Optical Engineering – Expenditure records', IC Archives, KPT/1/3.

46 IC Archives KPT/1/3–7.

47 *History of the Ministry of Munitions*, 11, part 3, 'Optical munitions and glassware', pp. 10–3.

48 Cattermole and Wolfe, *Horace Darwin's Shop*, chapter 4; C. F. Casella Ltd., '1810–1960: C. F. Casella Ltd.', pamphlet at Hackney Archives, D/B/CAS/66.

49 'Standardisation of optical instruments sub-committee, 1917–1918', PRO DSIR 10/172; 'Richard Deal: panel of standardisation of optical instruments, minutes, 1917–1918', PRO DSIR 10/173; 'Precision measurements and radio standards', PRO DSIR 11/214–35.

50 D. C. Mowery, 'Firm structure, government policy and the organisation of industrial research: Great Britain and the United States, 1900–1950', *Business History Review*, 58 (1984), 505–31.

51 'Government scheme for encouragement and setting up of research associations and revision by industries, 1916– 1922', PRO DSIR 16/1.

52 The suspicion of the makers is, however, clear throughout Beck's correspondence with the DSIR; see PRO DSIR 16/119.
53 See M. E. W. Williams, *The Precision Makers. A History of the Instruments Industry in Britain and France, 1870–1939*, forthcoming (1993).
54 R. Schefer, *La verrerie d'optique* (Paris, 1917), pp. 24–5.
55 As reported to the British Ministry of Munitions, 'Conditions in allied and enemy countries', secret report for week ending 27 January 1917, PRO MUN 4/5328.
56 Association National d'Expansion Economique, *Enquête sur la production française et la concurrence étrangère. Tome 1: Industries diverses* (Paris, 1917).
57 Schefer, *La verrerie*, p. 17.
58 *Ibid.*, 27.
59 C. Fabry, 'L'Institut d'Optique Théorique et Appliquée', *Bulletin de la Société d'Encouragement pour l'Industrie Nationale*, (1922), 636–45.
60 Quoted in *ibid.*, p. 638.
61 A. de Gramont, 'L'Institut d'Optique depuis sa fondation', *Revue d'Optique Théorique et Instrumentale*, 25 (1946), 145–50.
62 Fabry, 'Institut d'Optique', p. 640.
63 *Ibid.*, p. 642; see also H. W. Paul, *From Knowledge to Power. The Rise of the Science Empire in France, 1860–1939* (Cambridge, 1985), pp. 311–12.
64 The archives of OPL are in the Archives Nationales in Paris.
65 G. Yvon, 'Les industries françaises de l'optique', *Revue d'Optique Théorique et Instrumentale*, 25 (1946), 177–94 (193).
66 *Ibid.* See also the chapter by André Grelon in this volume.

Part IV

A transatlantic perspective

Introduction

By 1914, European observers saw in the United States yet another alternative model for higher technical education. Yet, as Arthur Donovan shows, that alternative model had grown from identifiable European roots, not least in the Calvinist tradition inherited from eighteenth-century Scotland, with its emphasis on education as a source of mental discipline, moral probity, and social order. Especially since the Civil War, this and other older traditions had been adjusted by a very explicit confrontation with more recent European models, in particular that of the German universities. Between 1870 and 1910, what Donovan describes as 'the cosy world' of the American ante-bellum college, dedicated to 'godliness, philosophy, and civic virtue' had been overturned, though without being totally destroyed. In the world that succeeded it, universities sought, in different degrees, to unite the old objectives of breadth in education with the very different goal of economic utility and a research ideal almost invariably justified by reference to Germany.

The growth of the land grant colleges, created in the wake of the Morrill Act of 1862, illustrates Donovan's thesis very clearly. Here, an initially dominant commitment to agriculture, engineering, and other practical subjects was diluted, with remarkable speed, by an ennobling emphasis on the disinterested quest for knowledge as well as by an updated version of the old liberal education. The result was a particularly vibrant form of the comprehensive American university of the twentieth century, with its rich diversity of intellectual, social, and utilitarian functions and its corresponding range of internal tensions of the kind identified and pilloried by Veblen.

Like several other contributors to *Education, Technology and Industrial Performance in Europe*, Donovan seeks to dissociate the changes of the last quarter of the nineteenth century from any simple notion of a direct and exclusive interaction between education and the economy. Although he readily concedes that the transformation of the American university system and the rise of the modern industrial corporation were related, parallel developments, he insists that both of them can only be understood in a far broader context in which a multiplicity of forces was at work. In this context, such social and political factors as the emergence of the American conception of the professional man and the spirit of emulation between states and institutions played their part alongside the more obvious economic ones.

An important general conclusion to be drawn from Donovan's account is that the integration of technical and other forms of vocational instruction in the American university reflected local pressures and institutional aspirations that were at once similar in kind to those in Europe and yet distinctively American. This is one reason why the constant references to the desirability of following European models, in particular that of Germany, have to be read with great caution. They were part of a characteristic late-nineteenth-century rhetoric about American higher education, and they contributed to the creation of universities that departed from their European equivalents not only in the variety of the functions that each of them fulfilled but also in the extent of the system and the abundance of the facilities it offered.

10 Education, industry, and the American university

Arthur Donovan

Thematic introduction to a transatlantic perspective

The essays in this volume are united by a shared concern with a common subject and by a rather novel point of view. The common subject is the development in nineteenth-century Europe of institutions designed to provide technical education. Narrative accounts of schools, colleges, and universities constitute a well-known genre of historical writing, but since there are relatively few such studies of institutions that provide technical education, much of the information presented in *Education, Technology, and Industrial Performance in Europe* is fresh and informative. More novel is the way the authors of these essays have sought to explain the development of the institutions they have studied. They have treated as problematic, rather than indisputable, the traditional assumption that new forms of technical education were causally linked, in a functional and utilitarian manner, to the industrial and economic advancement of the nations in which they appeared. By questioning this received idea, the authors have freed themselves to examine less obvious social and cultural factors that shaped the development of technical education in Europe during the age of industrialization. The alternative picture they present is one of considerable complexity and diversity.

The historical significance of an institution inevitably changes over time. At its founding, its place in the world is largely determined by the intentions of those who first gave it shape and substance. As the essays assembled here make clear, few of the European institutions set up to provide technical education were primarily concerned with purveying the kind of training that the industries of the time actually needed. Much more important, especially in the establishment of publicly funded schools, was a recurring anxiety concerning national power. Citing evidence of relative decline proved to be an especially effective way of forcing public investment in novel forms of higher education, however indirect the connexions between the content of that education and economic development might be. Distinct national traditions of education and existing patterns of social order also informed all new departures in technical education, with personal advancement through state service and the perpetuation of professional privileges generally being of much greater concern than service to industry. Thus even at their founding, almost all the new institutions established to provide technical education were shaped by the conservative attitudes of the dominant élites that controlled their operation and funding.

The social and cultural conservatism of these new institutions was generally reinforced as they adapted to the circumstances in which they were obliged to operate. Academic careerism and the hierarchical structure of higher education provided powerful incentives to turn away from practical training towards an emphasis on theory. The struggle for acceptance and funding concentrated institutional competition both in the recruitment of students and in determining which subjects had to be mastered in order to obtain a degree. As a result, a now familiar process of academization emerged, one that transformed avowedly practical schools into centres of theoretical instruction and pure research. Schools that were originally established to serve industry evolved quite rapidly into centres of science and theoretical engineering. Historically, these institutions played a much greater part in the long struggle by which pure science attained parity with the older humanistic culture than in forging links between industry and higher education.

By emphasizing the importance of national élites, educational hierarchies, professional privileges, formalized abstraction, and institutional legitimation, the authors of these essays demonstrate that the great majority of the new technical schools were socially and culturally conservative. Equally important, however, is their emphasis on the ways in which local factors shaped the founding and evolution of specific institutions. Rather than seeing 'technical education' as a homogeneous new genre of higher education evoked by a continent-wide process of industrialization, they point out that the appearance and evolution of new institutions was, like the development of industry itself, largely a local phenomenon that ought to be examined in all its local specificity. In nations which, like Germany, were confederations, educational competition promoted diversification and specialization and made possible localized interactions between industry and higher education. In more highly centralized nations, such as France, local initiatives often linked industry and education in ways that were entirely independent of the national system of education. And in nations such as Great Britain, where the national government exercised relatively little control over higher education, atheoretical traditions of apprenticeship and practice made it especially difficult to form enduring institutional connections between industry and education. By paying close attention to local factors, these essays not only demonstrate the inadequacy of the general assumption that technical education and economic growth were simply different manifestations of a common process, they also show that the various forms that technical education took were far from simple or uniform. The authors' common subject is thus seen to be highly diverse and complex, features that historians welcome as signs of well-informed perception and description.

This more detailed picture of the European experience poses a welcome challenge to received ideas about the evolution of technical education in America during the nineteenth century. Is it enough to say that the United States simply had to choose between the French and the German models and then adapt its choice to circumstances in America? The question seems misguided, once it is realized that the two models were rhetorical artifacts deployed by ambitious educational innovators rather than objective descriptions of the institutional realities that pertained in the two great European nations. Furthermore, we simply do not yet know what effect the development of technical education had on industrial performance in Europe or the United States, although more detailed studies of the careers of those who graduated from technical schools may shed additional light on this question. What we do know is that in the United States, as in Europe, the existing pattern of higher education was seriously challenged by the founding of new institutions ostensibly devoted to technical education. But again as in Europe, the appearance of new institutions and the ways in which they developed were largely governed by existing traditions of education, by emerging opportunities for individual advancement, and by the political concerns of local élites. Yet if the factors that governed the development of technical education in America were basically the same as those in Europe, there were also differences, primarily in the realm of political culture. For when viewed from the perspective of Europe's transatlantic offspring, the development of technical education in Europe appears both highly familiar in its dynamics and yet surprisingly constrained in its consequences.

In the United States as in the industrializing nations of Europe, the existing arrangements for providing higher education were scrutinized and transformed during the years between the middle of the nineteenth century and the beginning of the First World War. The Civil War, which ended in 1865, marks the great divide that separates the early decades of the new nation, in which the United States consolidated its commitment to democracy and national union, from the half-century in which it became an industrial giant and world power. In this latter period, the national economy expanded dramatically as industry and commerce were consolidated into comprehensive corporations, as the vast lands of the American West and other natural resources were incorporated into the economy, as new transportation and communication technologies accelerated social and cultural integration, and as a flood of new immigrants swelled the nation's work force. In the midst of such burgeoning growth and innovation, it was unlikely that the aims and structure of education would escape examination, nor did they. As Noah Porter pointed out in his 1871 inauguration as President of Yale College, higher education in America was already being transformed by revolution.

> It certainly never excited more active controversy, or provoked more various or confident criticism, or was subjected to a greater variety of experiments than with us in these passing years. The remark is not infrequently made that college and university education are not merely agitated by reforms; they are rather convulsed by a revolution.[1]

The revolution in higher education that overturned the cosy world of the American college was still in its early stages in 1871. By 1910, the revolution was over, and the shape and purpose of the modern American university had been largely defined. But what was the relationship between the appearance of new-style universities and the rapid economic growth of the nation? Many prominent educational innovators insisted that the two developments were intimately connected, yet in retrospect such claims appear more accurate as prophecy than as history.[2] The new wealth that flowed from the opening of the American West and the growth of industry undeniably provided the funds used to endow new universities, yet the educational programmes to which these new institutions were committed were not dictated by considerations of national security or the needs of commerce. It was not until the middle decades of the twentieth century that universities in the United States established the near monopoly they currently enjoy in the training of scientists, engineers, and managers for industry and in the organization and conduct of federally and industrially funded research.[3] Since the end of the Second World War, America's universities have played a leading role in the production and diffusion of new scientific and technical knowledge, activities in which America is still a world leader. It is the establishment of this specific form of hegemony that makes the story of the emergence of the American university a topic of central importance in a transatlantic perspective on European innovations in technical education.

From an historical point of view, the influence of European models on the transformation of American higher education appears just as problematic as the influence of industrial and economic development. Leading American educators in the nineteenth century certainly knew a great deal about European educational innovations, but their reactions to what the Europeans were doing were deeply coloured both by their experiences in the United States and by their views on the purpose of higher education in America. While acknowledging that American educational ideas and institutions were European in origin, the founders of modern American universities were committed to creating a culture and society markedly different from those of the Old World. It must also be remembered, as many of the essays in this volume demonstrate, that local and regional interests were profoundly important in shaping European responses to economic and industrial change, and this was certainly true in the United States as well. What is most striking, however, is that in the United States a new national consensus was quite quickly arrived at, one that radically reconceptualized the form and function of higher education.[4] While that consensus incorporated certain European innovations, it was more fundamentally a response to a distinctly American set of concerns. These concerns were articulated in an already venerable American tradition of discourse on the role of education in the political culture of the new nation. Hence to evaluate the role of European models in the reshaping of American technical education, we must focus our attention on this native tradition and its institutional embodiments.

Godliness, philosophy, and civic virtue: the traditional college

The national culture of the United States emerged without rupture from its eighteenth-century colonial antecedents and was especially influenced by the experience of Scotland, another of England's cultural provinces.[5] Many of the colonists in British North America, like their Scottish cousins, were Calvinists of one sort or another and they watched with intense interest as the Scots, who had entered into political union with England in 1707, struggled to preserve key features of their national heritage while strengthening their economic ties with their rapidly modernizing neighbour to the south.

A distinctive pattern of university education was one aspect of their national culture that the Scots succeeded in preserving. By the middle of the eighteenth century, Scotland, and particularly its capital Edinburgh, provided what many regarded as the finest university education in Europe. The modernized Scottish curriculum successfully incorporated the new knowledge pouring forth from the expanding world of science while preserving the doctrinal coherence required by theology and natural philosophy. During the last quarter of the century, several Scottish university professors, most notably Thomas Reid, provided philosophical rationales for Scottish pedagogical practice. The Common Sense school of philosophy, as Reid's distinctive philosophy of mind came to be called, synthesized empirical and idealist theories of knowledge in a way that many nineteenth-century educators considered extremely convincing. Most of the American students studying medicine and theology in Scotland found this school's analysis of mental activity persuasive and congenial, and it was largely through their efforts that the Scottish Philosophy of Common Sense exerted a profound influence on American higher education throughout the nineteenth century.[6]

Instilling mental discipline and a shared sense of social and spiritual order were the foremost tasks of the traditional college in America. In a nation that was politically democratic but socially still quite hierarchical, formal learning was more a sign of personal virtue, family advantage and social station than a certificate of useful training and expertise. Only a relatively small number of young men attended college, and during most of the nineteenth century the number of graduates was, by later standards, tiny.[7] Nor was the traditional college seriously committed to the cultivation of experimental, observational, or practical science. These activities, to the extent that they were pursued at all in the new nation, were undertaken in learned societies and other institutions supported by urban élites.[8] Training in technical subjects and the practical arts was accomplished almost entirely through apprenticeship. The traditional college curriculum was therefore equally irrelevant to the needs of commerce and industry, as Andrew Carnegie insisted as late as 1889:

> While the college student has been learning a little about the barbarous and petty squabbles of a far-distant past, or trying to master languages which are dead, such knowledge as seems adapted for life upon another planet than this as far as business affairs are concerned, the future captain of industry is hotly engaged in the school of experience, obtaining the very knowledge required for his future triumphs . . . College education as it exists is fatal to success in that domain.[9]

As Burton Bledstein has astutely observed, 'the old-time college was not an institution that catered to middle-class ambition and careers'.[10]

Unlike the older European universities, most American colleges avoided becoming completely fixated on classical learning and religious orthodoxy. The Scottish model was influential in this regard, for science occupied a place of great importance in the didactic programme of the Common Sense philosophy. Although the traditional American college was untouched by the research imperative that would transform higher education later in the century, knowledge gained through the empirical investigation of nature was considered relevant to the mental training that constituted its main mission. But this relevance was didactic, not utilitarian, since those who taught in traditional colleges thought of science as natural philosophy rather than as positive knowledge. Alexis de Tocqueville, in his observations on America in the 1830s, asserted that in democracies men do not cultivate science for its own sake, but rather for its practical application.[11] This distinction may have been appropriate for a nation like France, where science and synthetic philosophy parted ways in the Enlightenment. There was, however, a third possibility that de Tocqueville failed to consider, namely that science might be valued as part of a comprehensive natural philosophy, one that informed the entire curriculum for higher education. This older view of science, which probably would have seemed archaic to de Tocqueville, was widely held in America during the nineteenth century. Indeed, the pedagogic commitment to natural philosophy led many American colleges to add new professorships in science long before they felt any pressure to redefine their goals and reconstruct their educational programmes so as to conform to the new university ideals of research and service.[12]

The traditional American college educated an élite charged with providing wise and morally correct governance for the virtuous republic being created in the new world. Viewed in retrospect, the instruction offered by these institutions frequently appears diffuse, antiquated, and smug, and not a few of those who attended the colleges in the first half of the nineteenth century found it so. When the winds of change began to blow, however, the leading colleges demonstrated surprising resilience, and most were reformed rather than abandoned. Furthermore, their traditional commitment to providing moral instruction founded on a comprehensive philosophic understanding of man and nature survived intact. With characteristic American optimism, colleges that were transformed into universities were expected to do everything they had done before, and more. College students, whatever their motivations or specializations, were still to receive a liberal education in a curriculum that included at least a smattering of all the various branches of the arts and sciences. This expectation is a legacy from the earliest years of higher education in America. It was not seriously challenged in the revolution that led to the creation of the modern American university, and it is an expectation that is still honoured, at least in principle, in nearly all institutions of higher education in the United States. In America most programmes of higher technical education were not established as alternatives to the liberal education provided by traditional colleges, they were grafted onto this older and still vital conception of democratic pedagogy.[13]

The challenge of science, pure and applied

Nineteenth-century Americans were not so attached to their nativized tradition of liberal education that they completely ignored technical training and the useful sciences. Indeed, well before the modern American university had evolved into its mature form, several technical schools only marginally indebted to the collegiate tradition were established, and loud calls for practical education in agriculture and mechanics were being heard from the frontier. What is most impressive in retrospect, however, is that once a comprehensive model for the new American university had been articulated, institutions that were initially devoted to practical training and applied science felt compelled to broaden their mandates so as to incorporate the older ideal of liberal education and the newer ideal of pure research. In this way, the earliest American initiatives in higher technical education, many of which were patterned directly on European models, became thoroughly academized according to the new American model of higher education.[14]

During the first half of the nineteenth century, Americans interested in promoting technical education were particularly impressed by French models. As is well known, Thomas Jefferson was especially partial to the French way of doing things, and one expression of his admiration was the founding in 1802 of a Corps of Engineers stationed at West Point in New York, where a Military Academy was established. Jefferson encouraged the Army Engineers to begin instruction in French mathematics so that they could understand the published works of French engineers, but the Academy itself was not originally a degree-granting college. It concentrated instead on the practical training of engineering apprentices, a task in which it was eminently successful. Engineers trained at West Point played a leading role in such major civil engineering undertakings as the canal projects of the 1830s and the building of railroads in the middle decades of the century.

The realization of Jefferson's plan for the Academy at West Point was largely the work of Superintendent Sylvanus Thayer. Thayer had been highly impressed by the educational programme of the Ecole Polytechnique while on a extended tour of European military establishments, and in 1817 he began introducing its methods of instruction at West Point. He appointed Claude Crozet, a graduate of the Polytechnique and a veteran of Napoleon's army, as professor of engineering and Crozet began teaching the subjects and employing the novel methods of instruction, including the use of blackboard and chalk, that were then being introduced in France. New courses in mathematics, physics, chemistry, and engineering were offered, and the Academy soon established itself as the nation's foremost supplier of well-trained engineers.[15]

The Rensselaer School was another Hudson River Valley institution that followed French models of technical education. Founded in 1823 by Amos Eaton, who had studied chemistry with Benjamin Silliman at Yale, and Stephen van Rensselaer, a wealthy landowner and merchant, the School was committed to 'instructing persons in the application of science to the common purposes of life'.[16] Rensselaer introduced an engineering curriculum in the 1830s and was well positioned to benefit from the growing demand for practical education. It was vigorously reformed from 1849 onward under the leadership of Benjamin Franklin Green. Green had made a careful study of technical education in Europe and chose the Ecole Centrale des Arts et Manufactures as his model for Rensselaer. He was persuaded that science and applied science should be linked in a single institution, one that was not a mere adjunct to training through apprenticeship. Green laid out his programme for Rensselaer in an essay titled 'The true idea of a Polytechnic Institute', where he argued that such an Institute should be 'a *series of Special Schools* for the complete training of Architects, Civil Engineers, Mining Engineers, and other Scientific Technists, – all united under a common organization'.[17] It was a conception of technical training that also served as a model for the Massachusetts Institute of Technology, founded in 1862, and for other Institutes of Technology in the United States as well.[18]

The growing demand for courses in engineering and the experimental sciences did not pass unnoticed on the campuses of the well-established older colleges. Just before the mid-century, Eben Horsford, a Rensselaer graduate, persuaded Abbot Lawrence, a wealthy New England mill owner, to give $50,000 to Harvard to found the Lawrence Scientific School. Lawrence was asking that Harvard accept responsibility for training engineers and managers: 'We need a school for young men who intend to enter upon an active life as engineers or chemists or as men of science, applying their attainments to practical purposes . . . Hard hands are ready to work on materials, and where shall sagacious heads be taught to direct those hands?'[19] A few years later Yale was given a gift of $100,000 to endow the Sheffield Scientific School, and in the 1850s engineering programmes were also begun at Union College, Dartmouth, the University of Michigan, and Cornell.

Not all these initiatives in engineering and applied science were welcome or bore fruit. Those who resisted the introduction of courses devoted to practical subjects defended the older curriculum in two ways. One tactic involved exploiting the ambiguity associated with the term 'science'. Lawrence, Sheffield, and their allies clearly thought of science as useful knowledge, not natural philosophy, but once their gifts had been accepted, the choice of what kind of science was to be encouraged remained with the college. At Harvard the eminent geologist and paleontologist Louis Agassiz gained control of the Lawrence Scientific School, and under his leadership it emphasized biological studies rather than engineering.[20] The other tactic was to set up the new scientific and engineering schools as marginal activities within the college by giving them starvation budgets and no access to decision making.[21] This tactic allowed colleges to bring selected studies, such as the mainline sciences, into the fold while keeping less intellectually respectable areas of specialization beyond the pale. Since these struggles were conducted and resolved in different ways in different institutions, the effectiveness of the special school strategy for incorporating technical education in collegiate programmes must be determined on a case-by-case basis.

The Morrill Act of 1862, which provided federal support for state colleges, transformed the struggle for technical education by giving its advocates access to territory that in educational terms had not yet been colonized. This Congressional act authorized grants in the form of transfers of public land to states that established colleges having curricula that included instruction in agriculture and the mechanical arts. While the act applied to all states, it had its most profound effect in those frontier states where there were vast tracts of public land under federal control and where few if any colleges of the traditional sort had been established. The land-grant legislation profoundly altered the long campaign for technical education in America. Whereas Lawrence and Sheffield had tried to convert Harvard and Yale to their way of thinking by endowing new schools, the land-grant programme insisted that new institutions would only be founded, or existing colleges would only be publicly funded, if they taught subjects previously excluded by the traditional colleges. It took time, however, to create these new institutions, and the educational leaders who did so inevitably came not from commerce and industry, but from the traditional colleges themselves. The old tension between received ideals and new mandates therefore surfaced again in the land-grant colleges and universities, although in this instance the institutional mandates were new, while the venerable ideals of education were embedded in the minds of those responsible for their realization.

The Morrill Act was a federal response to a perceived need for greater public investment in practical education, and it was passed while the Civil War was still raging and a decade before Noah Porter spoke of higher education being convulsed by revolution. Today the great land-grant universities founded under the Morrill Act, such as the Universities of Wisconsin and Indiana, are just as representative of the modern American university as are the older colleges that were transformed into modern universities, such as Harvard and the University of Virginia, or the new private research universities founded toward the end of the nineteenth century, such as The Johns Hopkins University, the University of Chicago, and Stanford.[22]

But how were these agricultural and mechanical colleges transformed into comprehensive universities in one generation? It was in fact an astonishing achievement, one that can best be explained by focussing on the intense pride and competition characteristic of relations between the states within American federalism. In those states with prominent land-grant universities, legislators, alumni, and state boosters expected their new public institutions to serve their states in all possible ways. The specific practical concerns of the Morrill Act were not forgotten, but other avenues of development were encouraged as well. As the German model of higher education, and especially its emphasis on pure research, gained increasing favour in America, the presidents of the leading land-grant colleges saw no reason not to incorporate this new conception of higher education into the mission statements of their institutions. State boosterism and a concern with providing the finest possible technical support for local industry loosened state purse strings, enabling land-grant universities to transcend the narrowly practical conception of higher education that had led to their founding. It was emulation between the states, rather than the demonstrable fruitfulness of pure research, that lifted America's public universities into the front rank of modern universities, and the same competitive dynamic is what keeps them there today.[23]

Why were American educators so captivated by the German idea of the university during the last three decades of the nineteenth century? That pure research is an appropriate institutional mission, that a university professor's primary responsibility is to conduct a research seminar or direct a research laboratory, that graduate study consists of participating in such a seminar or working in such a laboratory so as to produce an original piece of scholarship, and that the knowledge which flows from pure research will eventually prove useful – these ideas were not novel in the latter half of the nineteenth century.[24] American educators were familiar with them and the ways they were being put into practice in German universities, and many observers were more impressed by the dangers they posed than by the advantages they promised.[25] Yet from the 1870s, the German university enjoyed an enormous vogue in the United States. To some extent this was a manifestation of what Laurence Veysey has termed a post-Civil War 'Europhilic discontent',[26] a yearning to achieve cultural parity with Europe without abandoning what was distinctively American. One thinks of the novels of Henry James, of prosperous Americans on the Grand Tour, and of the transporting of vast collections of European art and artifacts to America. Another factor was the availability of the great concentrations of wealth created by the expansion and consolidation of American industry and commerce. The distinctive American tradition of philanthropy took shape as newly enriched captains of industry and their heirs sought ways of applying their fortunes to the public good. They soon discovered that founding universities and memorializing themselves by erecting academic-gothic buildings were especially risk-free and gratifying ways of investing their wealth in cultural improvement. A third factor was the perceived need to revitalize existing colleges and reintegrate them into a rapidly changing society and culture. The United States was becoming increasingly secularized and bureaucratized, and the traditional colleges needed to concern themselves with more than forming the character of a genteel social élite. A less deferential and more aggressively competitive nation increasingly looked to higher education for the training of experts and professionals. Such were the needs and opportunities that swept American higher education into the revolutionary era that gave birth to the American university. During this era, new developments in Germany and her universities provided a convenient foil for educational reformers interested in articulating the inadequacies of the received conceptions of higher education and in building for what were perceived to be the needs of the future.

In 1891, the philosopher Josiah Royce, in an essay titled 'Present ideals of American University life', recalled how powerfully the image of the German university had shaped the thinking of his contemporaries. He was, he wrote, part of

> a generation that dreamed of nothing but the German University. England was passed by. It was understood not to be scholarly enough. France, too, was then neglected. German scholarship was our master and our guide . . . The air was full of suggestion . . . One went to Germany still a doubter as to the possibility of the theoretic life; one returned an idealist, devoted for the time to pure learning for learning's sake . . . burning for a chance to help build the American University.[27]

Scholarship, idealism, the theoretic life, and the pursuit of pure learning had nothing to do with technical education, of course. In practice, however, while certain individuals embraced the new Germanic ideal with the unquestioning faith of the converted, American higher education as a whole simply added the new German ideal to the other goals to which it was already committed. Research, graduate study, and the disinterested pursuit of knowledge were included on the list of activities one expected to find supported in a comprehensive university, along with liberal education for undergraduates and practical investigation and training in selected areas of public concern. With the inclusion of the German ideal of research and scholarship, the mission of the modern American university was complete. By the end of the nineteenth century, a national consensus about the nature of higher education and its place in American life was emerging. At its centre stood a new if not entirely coherent conception of the university, a conception that for a century has remained central to what has become a vastly expanded and diversified system of higher education in America.

Captains of erudition

The American university has been a remarkably responsive, adaptive, and accommodating social institution. It has provided a hospitable home for all sorts of programmes of research, training and higher education, and it has made it possible repeatedly to modify those programmes and the facilities that support them as the ideas and methods of the fields they serve have changed over time. But the comprehensive and flexible character of the university has exacted a toll as well, especially in the realm of institutional integrity. The multiplication of departments, colleges, and degree schemes has shattered the sense of community and common purpose that once bound teachers in the college together. Specialization has also reduced talk of a unifying body of common knowledge to a pious remembrance of the texts and doctrines that were once the common property of all educated people. The students, the academic staff, the purposes, and the sources of support for the modern American university have all failed to create the sense of commonality that must exist if we are to speak of an institution rather than an unintegrated collection of disparate activities. And yet this 'identity crisis' did not prove fatal to the growth of the modern university. It was resolved, rather surprisingly, by turning the problem of university identity over to the administrative leaders of these institutions and by assigning to a new set of symbolic activities responsibility for representing the university as a whole.

No one saw this problem more clearly, nor spoke more disparagingly of its administrative resolution, than the unsettled and unsettling social scientist Thorstein Veblen. Historians of technology find Veblen especially interesting. He campaigned vigorously for a more scientific approach to the study of economics and social institutions and his interest ranged widely. In his books on *The Theory of the Leisure Class*, *The Theory of Business Enterprise*, and *The Engineers and the Price System*, all published between 1899 and 1921, Veblen examined many of the institutional consequences of the large technological systems that were emerging at that time. He also formulated analytic concepts, such as 'the instinct for workmanship', which are still useful, and his ideas helped to inspire a generation of enthusiastic scientific managers.[28]

When Veblen turned his attention to the new universities, he saw nothing but compromise and exploitation. His own definition of a university was taken directly from the German ideal: 'A university is a body of mature scholars and scientists, the "faculty", – with whatever plant and other equipment may incidently serve as appliances for their work'.[29] In America, Veblen insisted, the universities had been taken over by administrators who acted like businessmen. These 'captains of erudition' treated knowledge and education as products to be designed for and sold in commercial markets, and they evaluated their own performance by referring to budgets and the acquisition of fixed assets, rather than the advancement of knowledge. It was the administrators, Veblen complained, who promoted intercollegiate athletics and social fraternities, the new symbols of university life, and who used these tribal rituals to curry favour with wealthy philanthropists and men of affairs. As a consequence, he argued, the American university had been thoroughly subverted by forces that would inevitably prove malign.

One need not accept Veblen's single-minded definition of the university or condone his derisive comments on administration to admire the acuity of his perception. His observation that the captains of erudition were emulating the captains of industry is more than an abstract comparison concocted by a theorizing sociologist. What Veblen noticed and deplored was the seizing of university leadership by entrepreneurial administrators. The leaders of the new and transformed universities at the end of the nineteenth century and the beginning of the twentieth century were unquestionably cast in the mould of Carnegie, Rockefeller, and Ford. Gilman of Johns Hopkins, Eliot of Harvard, White of Cornell, Bascom of Wisconsin, and Harper of Chicago – these were the men who created the enduring social institutions that serve the diverse purposes of the many parties with an interest in higher education in America.[30] Like their fellow industrialists, the university presidents created new markets for knowledge and education and new modes of production capable of satisfying them. And however we may respond to the scorn that Veblen heaped on their efforts, it is hard to deny that as institution-builders they were enormously successful.

Given their success and the analogy Veblen seized upon, should we go further and say that, under the captains of erudition, American universities became captive dependencies of industry and commerce? A plausible, if not fully convincing, argument can be made for this conclusion. But I believe it is more fruitful to see the relationship between industry and the university not as one of subordination but as one of parallel development and structural similarity. The transformation of industry and higher education before the First World War can be seen as part of a more comprehensive reorganization of American society into larger, more hierarchically controlled institutions. In commerce and industry this transformation gave rise to the modern corporation, which, as Alfred Chandler has shown, internalized many of the coordinating functions previously left to the market and created the hierarchical administrative structure of modern business.[31] Something similar happened in higher education as well. Major sectors of the system of knowledge production, transmission, and utilization were organized into larger units and brought under central administrative control. But the structural similarities between these two reorganizations does not in itself justify the conclusion that one imposed its will upon the other. Big business certainly has not been shy about making demands on American's universities and in telling them how they should conduct their affairs, but these overtures have not been uniquely important in shaping American higher education. It would be an error to conclude, therefore, that the history of American universities in the early decades of the twentieth century was one of subordination to the hegemony of the newly organized national corporations.

The professionalization of everyone?

Having examined the organizational structure of the American university, we need to look briefly at its functional role in the newly industrialized society of America. Since our central concern is technical education, I shall begin by looking at an essay called 'The ideal engineering education' that William Burr read in 1893 to the newly founded Society for the Promotion of Engineering Education.[32] Burr, a professor in the Columbia University School of Mines, argued that the ideal engineering education should, like a stool, have three legs. The first would be 'a broad, liberal education in philosophy and the arts, precedent to the purely professional training'. The second leg would comprise courses in the science of engineering, including the mathematical and scientific knowledge that constitutes the 'pure theory of engineering operations'. The third leg of the stool would consist of a few 'practical courses, designed to acquaint the student with current practice' and methods.

Burr's 'Ideal engineering education', which describes what an engineering student should study during his four years in college, nicely captures that optimistic eclecticism of the undergraduate professional curricula that has become such a prominent part of the American university in the twentieth century. Time and attention would be equally divided among courses in three areas: the liberal arts, which would give students the broad understanding needed to play a leading role in society; science, which would give students mastery of the modes of knowledge needed to utilize natural resources for human purposes; and practical subjects, which would train students to be immediately employable members of society. The term of study was fixed, as were the types of subjects to be addressed. What was not spelled out were either the principles which justify the tripartite construction and which could be appealed to for its defence, or an account of how these disparate modes of understanding were to be integrated and synthesized into a coherent programme of studies. In other words, Burr had not made explicit the concept of the engineer and his role in society that lay behind his ideal curriculum.

The unstated image of the professional engineer that Burr had in mind was not defined by the experiences or circumstances of engineers alone. It was, rather, a working out within engineering of an image of the role of the professional that was becoming increasingly important at the end of the nineteenth century. The evolution of this image of the professional is a vast subject that is still only partially understood.[33] The point I wish to make here is that in America, the predominant institutional purpose of the modern university was, and still is, to provide an appropriate education for students who want to prepare themselves for professional work in a secular, meritocratic, and technological society.[34] Programmes in technical education were not designed solely to train their students to perform certain industrial tasks, they were designed to educate and train professionals who, as part of their academic preparation, would acquire certain specific types of expertise. By the time Burr presented his ideal educational programme, the struggle between shop-floor apprenticeship and school training as the normal avenue for entry into the engineering profession had been resolved in favour of formal education.[35] Indeed, the professionalization of engineering had proceeded one step further, for Burr, by virtue of his lecture, can be considered a pioneer in the professionalization of engineering education. It was the nature of the professions, and not the technical needs of industry, that led Burr to prescribe a tripartite curriculum for engineering students rather than one that concentrated on practical subjects alone.[36]

Each of the three types of study that Burr stipulated plays a distinctive role in preparing students for the three major aspects of professional life, and each links a major tradition in American higher education to one of the attributes of what it means to be a professional person. The law and medicine, two paradigmatic professions that were well-established long before the advent of industrialization, are both considered 'liberal' professions. To attain the prestige associated with being a professional of this sort, one therefore needed to acquire an adequate command of what is broadly termed liberal education. Just what constitutes adequacy in this regard is, of course, a much debated question, but the underlying expectation has seldom been considered problematic.

A second feature of modern professionalism is the central role played by science. The increasing formalization and academization of professional education, together with the growth of natural science and its application to technology, has promoted the 'scientification' of all forms of knowledge and the creation of ever more delimited and specific disciplines. One consequence is that the research imperative has become coupled to the rapid proliferation of autonomous 'fields', each of which cultivates the modes of knowledge central to a specific profession. The fit between the organization and advancement of knowledge and the allocation of professional jurisdictions has not been perfect, of course, but it has become so close that the professions now play a key role in mediating between theory and practice in modern society. It is engineers and scientists with one foot in industry or government and the other in higher education who set research agendas in the universities of the 1990s.

A concern with practical knowledge is another link connecting contemporary professions and universities. The modern university, unlike the old-time college, takes the solution of social problems as one of its responsibilities. But translating social problems into academic problems involves considerable mediation, and here too the professions have played a key role. From the point of view of the professions, the foremost service provided by universities is the training of those who wish to enter the professions – a key step in professionalization. Here, as in the setting of research agendas, the association of certain types of problems with distinct professions has served as a bridge into the academic world. The linking of formalized programmes of instruction and social service to curricula designed to prepare students for entry into specific professions has been of crucial importance in the expansion and adaptation of the modern American university.

Is there any natural limit to this exfoliating process of academization and professionalization? Can we look forward, as the sociologist Harold Wilensky has suggested, to 'The professionalization of everyone?'[37] The dream is one that has long beguiled progressive-minded Americans.

Their dream is that of a plumber who in 1891 spoke as follows at a meeting of the American Public Health Association:

Plumbing is no longer merely a trade. Its importance and value in relation to health, and its requirements regarding scientific knowledge, have elevated it to a profession. It is clothed with the responsibility of the learned professions and the dignity of the sciences. The high qualities of mechanical skills are combined with the best of the sciences of the most practical utility. It unites skilled labor and high educational qualifications in one. This being the nature of plumbing today, it becomes the duty of the plumber to maintain in every way the dignity of his calling.[38]

Today, of course, those who are experts in certain fields of knowledge and members of self-governing associations can no longer assume that the general public will accede to their being granted special authority or privileges. Yet the desire to transform every occupation into a profession and to democratize all forms of work by according every employee the dignity and compensation normally associated with professional standing has not been completely abandoned. The status and role of the professions in American society is far from settled. So long as these issues are still being contested, the ways in which universities ought to provide technical education and the social consequences of their doing so will remain open questions.

Notes

1 Laurence R. Veysey, *The Emergence of the American University* (Chicago and London, 1965, paperback edition, 1970), p. 1.

2 Louis Galambos, 'The American economy and the reorganization of the sources of knowledge', in Alexandra Oleson and John Voss (eds.), *The Organization of Knowledge in Modern America, 1860–1920* (Baltimore, 1979), pp. 269–82. David Noble, in his *America by Design. Science, Technology, and the Rise of Corporate Capitalism* (New York and Oxford, 1977), argues that from the middle of the nineteenth century university science and engineering in America have been thoroughly subordinated to the concerns of industry. For a case study that concludes, correctly I believe, that Noble's claim is oversimplified and too global, see John W. Servos, 'The industrial relations of science: chemical engineering at MIT, 1900–1939', *Isis*, 71 (1980), 531–49. Wolfgang König, in this volume (p. 81), finds that in Germany, 'the influence of technical education on industrial performance was overestimated by contemporaries and is overestimated by historians today'.

3 See the depiction of the contemporary university provided by Clark Kerr, a former Chancellor of the University of California, in his *The Uses of the University* (Cambridge, Mass., 1963).

4 Edward Shils, 'The order of learning in the United States: the ascendancy of the university', in Oleson and Voss (eds.), *The Organization of Knowledge*,

pp. 19–47; see also the concluding chapter in Veysey, *The American University*, 'The university as an American institution'.

5 John Clive and Bernard Bailyn, 'England's cultural provinces: Scotland and America', *William and Mary Quarterly*, 11 (1954), 200–13; Thomas Bender, *New York Intellect. A History of Intellectual Life in New York City, from 1750 to the Beginnings of Our Own Time* (New York, 1987), p. xiv and *passim*.

6 For a recent survey of the literature on the Scottish Enlightenment and its influence in America, see Richard B. Sher, *Church and University in the Scottish Enlightenment* (Edinburgh, 1985), pp. 373–4. See also George Elder Davie, *The Democratic Intellect. Scotland and Her Universities in the Nineteenth Century* (Edinburgh, 1961); Douglas Sloan, *The Scottish Enlightenment and the American College Ideal* (New York, 1971); Henry F. May, *The Enlightenment in America* (New York, 1976), part VI; and J. David Hoevler, Jr, *James McCosh and the Scottish Intellectual Tradition* (Princeton, 1981).

7 In the decade 1800–9 the average number of students graduating from the thirty-seven leading colleges was 207. This figure did not rise above 1000 until the 1870s; see Burton J. Bledstein, *The Culture of Professionalism. The Middle Class and the Development of Higher Education in America* (New York, 1976), p. 241. For more detailed enrolment and graduation statistics, see Colin B. Burke, 'The expansion of American higher education', in Konrad H. Jarausch (ed.), *The Transformation of Higher Learning 1860–1930. Expansion, Diversification, Social Opening, and Professionalization in England, Germany, Russia, and the United States* (Stuttgart and Chicago, 1983), pp. 108–30.

8 See John C. Greene, *American Science in the Age of Jefferson* (Ames, 1984); George H. Daniels, *American Science in the Age of Jackson* (New York, 1968); Bruce Sinclair, *Philadelphia's Philosopher Mechanics. A History of the Franklin Institute 1824–1865* (Baltimore, 1974). It is notable how little is said about colleges and universities in Alexandra Oleson and Sanford C. Brown (eds.), *The Pursuit of Knowledge in the Early American Republic. American Scientific and Learned Societies from Colonial Times to the Civil War* (Baltimore and London, 1976).

9 Quoted in Veysey, *The American University*, pp. 13–14.

10 Bledstein, *The Culture of Professionalism*, p. 203.

11 Alexis de Tocqueville, *Democracy in America*, trans. Henry Reeve, 2 vols. (New York, 1945), vol. 2, pp. 42–9 (first book, chapter 10).

12 Stanley M. Guralnick, *Science and the Ante-Bellum American College* (Philadelphia, 1975).

13 As is pointed out below, the collegiate pattern of higher education, including technical education, proved to be far more influential in America than either the French alternative of specialized *grandes écoles* or the German alternative of separate *Technische Mittelschulen* and *Technische Hochschulen*. For discussions of these other models for the expansion of technical education, see the contributions to this volume by Robert Fox, Wolfgang König, and Jean Baudet.

14 In America in the nineteenth century there were few attempts to establish non-academic institutes to provide industrial training for skilled workers, though attempts to provide such training in several European nations are

described in the essays by Ahlstrom, König, and Williams. The tension between those who conceive of higher technical education primarily as a way of facilitating individual social mobility and those who conceive of such education primarily as a way of providing trained manpower for specific industrial tasks is evident in the twentieth-century debate over the mission of two-year post-secondary 'Community Colleges' and over proposed para-professional programmes in Engineering Technology. On this latter issue, see the comments of Melvin Kranzberg, reported in Arthur Donovan, 'Engineering in an increasingly complex society: historical perspectives on education, practice, and adaptation in American engineering', in *Engineering in Society* (Washington, D.C., 1985), p. 116; see also *Engineering Technology Education* (Washington, D.C., 1985).

15 A. Hunter Dupree, *Science in the Federal Government* (Cambridge, Mass., 1957), p. 29, and Greene, *Science in the Age of Jefferson*, pp. 131–2, 143–4.

16 Quoted in Noble, *America by Design*, p. 21.

17 Quoted in Bledstein, *The Culture of Professionalism*, p. 194.

18 See Noble, *America by Design*, pp. 22–3. It is important to note that in America new programmes in technical education were initiated by academic innovators who sought to satisfy a growing and diverse market for professional services. This educational market was not directly structured by industry, but rather through negotiation between ambitious young men looking for programmes that would give them the knowledge they needed to pursue successful careers and the academics who constructed and taught the new programmes. The situation in America differed from that in Belgium, where certification as an engineer was regulated by the state, and from that in Italy, where engineering was one of the entrenched liberal professions; see the contributions to this volume by Baudet and Guagnini. See also Anna Guagnini, 'Higher education and the engineering profession in Italy: the *Scuole* of Milan and Turin, 1859–1914', *Minerva*, 26 (1989), 512–48, especially p. 546, where the author concludes that the main objective of new curricula in technical education in Italy 'was to prepare for a professional qualification, rather than for a professional career'. The situation in the United States also differed from that in Germany and other countries in which state service provided the primary market for technically educated young men; on this, see the chapter by König. The market orientation and competitiveness of American higher education had the effect of ensuring that in the United States, as in Germany and France (see this volume, the chapters by König and Fox), there was a relatively close fit between the number of graduates produced by the new programmes of technical education, the skills they acquired, and the markets they supplied.

19 Quoted in Noble, *America by Design*, p. 22.

20 Edward Lurie, *Louis Agassiz. A Life in Science* (Chicago, 1960), pp. 135–40.

21 Veysey, *The American University*, p. 49.

22 The distinction between public (i.e. state) universities and private universities in America is of less importance than is usually supposed; see Veysey, *The American University*, pp. 112–13. During the formative years of the American university, the dominant older institutions in fact functioned as the state universities; this was the case for Harvard in Massachusetts, Yale in Connecti-

cut, Johns Hopkins in Maryland, and Columbia and Cornell in New York, for example. The differences have been further reduced, especially with regard to scientific research, by the rapid growth in federal funding of university-based research since the outbreak of the Second World War.

23 See Veysey, *The American University*, pp. 15, 70–1; see also Charles E. Rosenberg, 'Science, technology, and economic growth: the case of the agricultural experiment station scientist, 1875–1914', in his *No Other Gods. On Science and American Social Thought* (Baltimore, 1976), pp. 153–72.

24 R. Steven Turner, 'The Prussian university and the research imperative, 1806 to 1848', Princeton University PhD thesis, 1972; R. Steven Turner 'The growth of professorial research in Prussia, 1818 to 1848: causes and context', *Historical Studies in the Physical Sciences*, 3 (1971), 137–82. See also Fritz K. Ringer, *The Decline of the German Mandarins. The German Academic Community 1890–1933* (Cambridge, Mass., 1969), and 'The German academic community', in Oleson and Voss (eds.), *The Organization of Knowledge*, pp. 409–29.

25 American college professors teaching in curricula shaped by the Common Sense philosophy were outspoken in opposing the philosophical idealism that informed what Americans understood the German conception of research and education to be; see Veysey, *The American University*, p. 49.

26 Veysey, *The American University*, p. 2.

27 Quoted in Veysey, *The American University*, p. 130.

28 See Dorothy Ross, 'The development of the social sciences', in Oleson and Voss (eds.), *The Organization of Knowledge*, pp. 107–38; Thomas P. Hughes, *American Genesis. A Century of Invention and Technological Enthusiasm 1870–1970* (New York, 1989), pp. 246–8.

29 Thorstein Veblen, *The Higher Learning in America. A Memorandum on the Conduct of Universities by Business Men* (1918; New York, 1957), p. 13. See also Bledstein, *The Culture of Professionalism*, pp. 287–8; Veysey, *The American University*, pp. 346–56.

30 See the 'Chronology of principal university administrators', in Veysey, *The American University*, p. 447, and the appendix containing biographical sketches of leading university administrators in Bledstein, *The Culture of Professionalism*, pp. 335–43.

31 Alfred D. Chandler, Jr, *The Visible Hand. The Managerial Revolution in American Business* (Cambridge, Mass., 1977). For more comprehensive statements of the organizational thesis, see Samuel P. Hays, *The Response to Industrialism, 1885–1914* (Chicago, 1957); Robert H. Weibe, *The Search for Order, 1877–1920* (New York, 1967); and Martin Ricketts, *The Economics of Business Enterprise. New Approaches to the Firm* (Brighton, 1987).

32 Published as the leading article in the first volume (1893) of the *Proceedings of the Society for the Promotion of Engineering Education*.

33 See the historical accounts provided in Gerald L. Geison (ed.), *Professions and Professional Ideologies in America* (Chapel Hill, 1983); Thomas L. Haskell (ed.), *The Authority of Experts* (Bloomington, 1984); Nathan O. Hatch (ed.), *The Professions in American History* (Notre Dame, 1988). For a comparison with England, see Harold J. Perkin, *The Rise of Professional Society. England since 1880* (London, 1989). For a recent theoretical treatment of the

professions, see Andrew Abbot, *The System of Professions. An Essay on the Diversion of Expert Labor* (Chicago, 1988). For a brief introduction to the professionalization of engineering, see Arthur Donovan, 'Engineering education and the professionalization of engineering in the USA', in Melvin Kranzberg (ed.), *Technological Education – Technological Style* (San Francisco, 1986), pp. 85–90.

34 Bledstein, in *The Culture of Professionalism*, explores in great detail the connexions between what he calls the culture of professionalism and the rise of the American university. See also Ahlström's chapter in this volume on the professions in Sweden.

35 For the school versus shop debate in American engineering, see Monte A. Calvert, *The Mechanical Engineer in America 1830–1910. Professional Cultures in Conflict* (Baltimore, 1967), chapters 4 and 5. For Sweden, see Ahlström's chapter in this volume.

36 It should be noted that while by the end of the nineteenth century apprenticeship alone was no longer considered an adequate training for a professional engineer, it continued to be the primary means used for training skilled labour; cf. Veysey, *The American University*, p. 71.

37 H. L. Wilensky, 'The professionalization of everyone?', *American Journal of Sociology*, 70 (1964), 137–58. For an extended critique of Wilensky's analysis, see Abbot, *The System of Professions*, pp. 9–19.

38 Quoted in Bledstein, *The Culture of Professionalism*, p. 35.

Select bibliography

The bibliography contains a selection of mainly recent secondary sources concerning the relations between technical education and industry in the countries treated in the volume. Its coverage corresponds as closely as possible to that of the volume, with an emphasis on advanced technical education for industrial careers between the mid nineteenth century and the 1930s.

COMPARATIVE STUDIES

Ahlström, Göran. *Engineers and Industrial Growth. Higher Technical Education and the Engineering Profession during the Nineteenth and Early Twentieth Centuries: France, Germany, Sweden and England* (London and Canberra: Croom Helm, 1982)

Brock, William, H. 'The Japanese Connexion: Engineering in Tokyo, London, and Glasgow at the End of the Nineteenth Century', *The British Journal for the History of Science*, 14 (1981), 227–43

Broder, Albert. 'Enseignement technique et croissance économique en Allemagne et en France, 1870–1914: quelques éléments d'une analyse approfondie', in Cohen and Manfrass, *Frankreich und Deutschland*, pp. 66–95

Bureau International du Travail. *Les conditions de vie des ingénieurs et des chimistes* (Bureau International du Travail, Etudes et documents, série L [Travailleurs intellectuels], no. 1) (Geneva, 1924)

Caron, François. *Le résistible déclin des société industrielles* (Paris: Librairie Académique Perrin, 1985), chapter 4

Cohen, Yves, and Klaus Manfrass (eds.). *Frankreich und Deutschland. Forschung, Technologie und industrielle Entwicklung im 19. und 20. Jahrhundert* (Munich: C. H. Beck, 1990)

Fox, Robert, and Anna Guagnini. 'Britain in Perspective: The European Context of Industrial Training and Innovation, 1880–1914', *History and Technology*, 2 (1985), 133–50

Frijhoff, Willem. 'Sur l'utilité d'une histoire comparée des systèmes éducatifs nationaux', *Histoire de l'education*, no. 13 (December 1981), 29–44

Grelon, André (ed.). *Les ingénieurs de la crise. Titre et profession entre les deux guerres* (Paris: Editions de l'Ecole des Hautes Etudes en Sciences Sociales, 1986)

Inkster, Ian. *Science and Technology in History. An Approach to Industrial Development* (London: Macmillan Education, 1991), chapter 4.

Jarausch, Konrad H. (ed.) *The Transformation of Higher Learning 1860–1930.*

Expansion, Diversification, Social Opening, and Professionalization in England, Germany, Russia, and the United States (Stuttgart: Klett-Cotta, and Chicago: University of Chicago Press, 1983)

Jarausch, Konrad H. 'Higher Education and Social Change: Some Comparative Perspectives', in Jarausch, *The Transformation of Higher Learning*, pp. 9–35

König, Wolfgang. 'Die technische und wirtschaftliche Stellung der deutschen und britischen Elektroindustrie zwischen 1880 und 1900', *Technikgeschichte*, 53 (1987), 221–9

Kranakis, Eda. 'Social Determinants of Engineering Practice: A Comparative View of France and America in the Nineteenth Century', *Social Studies of Science*, 19 (1985), 5–70

Locke, Robert R. *The End of the Practical Man. Entrepreneurship and Higher Education in Germany, France, and Great Britain 1880–1940* (Greenwich, Conn.: Jay Press, 1984)

Lundgreen, Peter. 'Engineering Education in Europe and the U.S.A., 1750–1830: The Rise to Dominance of School Culture and the Engineering Professions', *Annals of Science*, 47 (1990), 33–75

'The Organization of Science and Technology in France: A German Perspective', Fox and Weisz (eds.), *The Organization of Science and Technology in France*, pp. 311–32

Müller, Detlef K., Fritz K. Ringer, and Brian Simon (eds.). *The Rise of the Modern Educational System. Structural Change and Social Reproduction 1870–1920* (Cambridge: Cambridge University Press, 1987)

Nybom, Thorsten, and Rolf Torstendahl (eds.). *Byråkratisering och maktfördelning* (Lund: Studentlitteratur, 1989)

Ringer, Fritz K. *Education and Society in Modern Europe* (Bloomington, Ind., and London: Indiana University Press, 1979)

Rothblatt, Sheldon, and Björn Wittrock (eds.). *The European and American University since 1800. Historical and Sociological Essays* (Cambridge: Cambridge University Press, 1992)

Torstendahl, Rolf. 'Engineers in Industry, 1850–1910: Professional Men and New Bureaucrats. A Comparative Approach', in Carl Gustaf Bernhard, Elisabeth Crawford, and Per Sorbom (eds.), *Science, Technology and Society in the Time of Alfred Nobel* [Nobel Symposium, no. 52] (Oxford: Pergamon Press, 1982), pp. 253–70; discussion by Svante Lindqvist on pp. 298–303

'Technology in the Development of Society 1850–1980: Four Phases of Industrial Capitalism in Western Europe', *History and Technology*, 1 (1984), 157–74; translated into Swedish in Nybom and Torstendahl, *Byråkratisering och maktfördelning*, pp. 85–101

'Engineers in Sweden and Britain 1820–1914: Professionalisation and Bureaucratisation in a Comparative Perspective', in Werner Conze and Jurgen Kocka (eds.), *Bildungsbürgertum im 19. Jahrhundert. Teil I: Bildungssystem und Professionalisierung in internationalen vergleichen* (Stuttgart: Klett-Cotta, 1985), pp. 543–60

'Career Mobility of Engineers in France and Sweden', in *Technical Education and Social Mobility* [Papers for Section B12 of the Ninth World Congress of Economic History] (Bern, 1986), pp. 32–47

'När ingenjörerna blev professionella och byråkrater: en jämförelse mellan utvecklingen i Sverige och England 1800–1914', in *Kungl. humanistika vetenskapssamfundets i Uppsala Årsbok 1983–84*, pp. 98–113; reprinted in Nybom and Torstendahl, *Byråkratisering och maktfördelning*, p. 325–39

Bureaucratisation in Northwestern Europe, 1880–1985. Domination and Governance (London: Routledge, 1991), especially chapter 10

'Knowledge and Power: Constraints and Expansion of Professional Influence in Western Capitalist Society', in Trow and Nybom, *University and Society*, pp. 35–46

Trow, Martin, and Thorsten Nybom (eds.). *University and Society. Essays on the Social Role of Research and Higher Education* (London: Jessica Kingsley Publishers, 1991)

BELGIUM

Baudet, Jean C. 'Pour une histoire de la formation des ingénieurs à Bruxelles', *Technologia*, 2 (1979), 71–88

'Pour une histoire de la profession d'ingénieur en Belgique', *Technologia*, 7 (1984), 35–62

Les ingénieurs belges (Brussels: Association pour la Promotion des Publications Scientifiques, 1986)

Beckers, L. *L'enseignement supérieur en Belgique. Code annoté des dispositions légales et réglementaires, précédé d'une notice historique sur la matière* (Brussels: Editions Castaigne, 1904)

Brion, René. 'La querelle des ingénieurs en Belgique', in Grelon (ed.), *Les ingénieurs de la crise*, pp. 255–70

Caulier-Mathy, Nicole. 'Le patronat et le progrès technique dans les charbonnages liégeois 1800–1914', in Kurgan-van Hentenryk and Stengers (eds.), *L'innovation technologique*, pp. 41–61

Delaet, Jean-Louis. 'La mécanisation de la verrerie à vitres à Charleroi dans la première moitié du XXe siècle', in Kurgan-van Hentenryk and Stengers (eds.), *L'innovation technologique*, pp. 113–52

Grandmaître, Raoul. *L'ingénieur. Son rôle, sa formation, la protection de son titre et de sa profession* (Paris and Liège: Librairie polytechnique Ch. Béranger, 1937)

Kurgan-van Hentenryk, G., and Jean Stengers (eds.). *L'innovation technologique. Facteur de changement (XIXe–XXe siècles)* (Brussels: Editions de l'Université de Bruxelles, 1986)

FRANCE

Day, C. Rodney. *Education for the Industrial World. The Ecoles d'Arts et Métiers and the Rise of French Industrial Engineering* (Cambridge, Mass., and London: MIT Press, 1987)

'The Making of Mechanical Engineers in France: The Ecoles d'Arts et Métiers, 1803–1914', *French Historical Studies*, 10 (1978), 439–60

Fox, Robert. 'Science, Industry, and the Social Order in Mulhouse, 1798–1871', *The British Journal for the History of Science*, 17 (1984), 127–68

'Science, the University, and the State in Nineteenth-Century France', in Gerald L. Geison (ed.), *Professions and the French State, 1700–1900* (Philadelphia: University of Pennsylvania Press, 1984), pp. 66–145

'L'attitude des professeurs des facultés des sciences face à l'industrialisation en France entre 1850 et 1914', in Christophe Charle and Régine Ferré (eds.), *Le personnel de l'enseignement supérieur en France aux XIXe et XXe siècles. Colloque organisé par l'Institut d'Histoire Moderne et Contemporaine et l'Ecole des Hautes Etudes en Sciences Sociales les 25 et 26 juin 1984* (Paris: Editions du Centre National de la Recherche Scientifique, 1985), pp. 135–49

'Research, Education, and the Industrial Economy in Modern France', in *The Academic Research Enterprise within the Industrialized Nations. Comparative Perspectives* (Washington DC: National Academy of Sciences, 1990), pp. 95–107

Fox, Robert, and George Weisz (eds.). *The Organization of Science and Technology in France 1808–1914* (Cambridge: Cambridge University Press, and Paris: Editions de la Maison des Sciences de l'Homme, 1980)

Grelon, André. 'Les universités et la formation des ingénieurs en France (1870–1914)', *Formation-emploi*, nos. 27–8 (July–December 1989), pp. 65–88

'Formation et développement des élites techniques et commerciales en France, sous la Troisième République', in Cohen and Manfrass (eds.), *Frankreich und Deutschland*, pp. 39–52

'La formation des ingénieurs électriciens' and 'La structuration du réseau de formation des ingénieurs électriciens (1900–1914)', in François Caron and Fabienne Cardot (eds.), *Histoire générale de l'électricité en France. Tome I: Espoirs et conquêtes, 1881–1918* (Paris: Fayard, 1991), pp. 254–93 and 802–48

Nye, Mary Jo. *Science in the Provinces. Scientific Communities and Provincial Leadership in France, 1860–1930* (Berkeley, Los Angeles, and London: Unversity of California Press, 1986)

Paul, Harry W. *From Knowledge to Power. The Rise of the Science Empire in France, 1860–1939* (Cambridge: Cambridge University Press, 1985)

'Apollo Courts the Vulcans: The Applied Science Institutes in Nineteenth-Century French Science Faculties', in Fox and Weisz (eds.), *The Organization of Science and Technology in France*, pp. 155–81

Prost, Antoine. *Histoire de l'enseignement en France 1800–1967* (Paris: Armand Colin, 1968)

Shinn, Terry. *Savoir scientifique & pouvoir social. L'Ecole Polytechnique, 1794–1914* (Paris: Presses de la Fondation Nationale des Sciences Politiques, 1980)

'The French Science Faculty System, 1808–1914: Institutional Change and Research Potential in Mathematics and the Physical Sciences', *Historical Studies in the Physical Sciences*, 10 (1979), 271–332

'From "Corps" to "Profession": The Emergence and Definition of Industrial Engineering in Modern France', in Fox and Weisz (eds.), *The Organization of Science and Technology in France*, pp. 183–208; also published in an earlier, French version, as 'Des corps de l'Etat au secteur industriel: genèse de la profession d'ingénieur, 1750–1920', *Revue française de sociologie*, 19 (1978), 39–71

'Reactionary Technologists: The Struggle over the Ecole Polytechnique, 1880–1914', *Minerva*, 22 (1984), 329–45

Thépot, André. *Les ingénieurs du Corps des Mines en France des origines à 1914* (thèse d'Etat, Université de Paris X, Nanterre, 1991)

Thépot, André (ed.). *L'ingénieur dans la société française* (Paris: Editions Ouvrières, 1985)

Weiss, John H. *The Making of Technological Man. The Social Origin of French Engineering Education* (Cambridge, Mass., and London: MIT Press, 1972)

Weisz, George. *The Emergence of Modern Universities in France, 1863–1914* (Princeton, NJ: Princeton University Press, 1983)

'The French Universities and Education for the New Professions, 1885–1914: An Episode in French University Reform', *Minerva*, 17 (1979), 98–128

GERMANY

Albrecht, Helmuth. *Technische Bildung zwischen Wissenschaft und Praxis. Die Technische Hochschule Braunschweig 1862–1914* [Veröffentlichungen der Technischen Universität Carolo-Wilhelmina zu Braunschweig, Band 1] (Hildesheim: Olms, 1987)

Cassidy, David. 'Recent German Perspectives on German Technical Education', *Historical Studies in the Physical Sciences*, 14 (1983), 187–200

Ferber, Christian von. *Die Entwicklung des Lehrkörpers der deutschen Universitäten und Hochschulen 1864–1954* (Göttingen, 1956)

Gispen, Kees. *New Profession, Old Order. Engineers and German Society, 1815–1914* (Cambridge: Cambridge University Press, 1989)

Klinkenberg, Hans Martin (ed.). *Rheinisch-Westfälische Technische Hochschule Aachen 1870–1970*, 2 vols. (Stuttgart: Deutsche Verlags-Anstalt, 1970)

Kocka, Jürgen. *Die Angestellten in der deutschen Geschichte, 1850–1980* (Göttingen: Vandenhoeck & Ruprecht, 1981)

König, Wolfgang. 'Stand und Aufgaben der Forschung zur Geschichte der deutschen Polytechnischen Schulen und Technischen Hochschulen im 19. Jahrhundert', *Technikgeschichte*, 48 (1981), 47–67

'Technische Hochschule und Industrie – Ein Überblick zur Geschichte des Technologietransfers', in Hermann J. Schuster (ed.), *Handbuch des Wissenschaftstransfers* (Berlin: Springer Verlag, 1990), pp. 29–41

Elektrotechnik. Entstehung einer Industriewissenschaft (Berlin: Akademie-Verlag, 1993)

Ludwig, Karl-Heinz, and Wolfgang König (eds.), *Technik, Ingenieure und Gesellschaft. Geschichte des Vereins Deutscher Ingenieure 1856–1981* (Dusseldorf: VDI-Verlag, 1981)

Lundgreen, Peter. 'Industrialization and the Educational Formation of Manpower in Germany', *Journal of Social History*, 9 (1975–6), 64–80

Techniker in Preussen während der frühen Industrialisierung. Ausbildung und Berufsfeld einer entstehenden sozialen Gruppe [Einzelveröffentlichungen der Historischen Kommission zu Berlin, Band 16. Publikationen zur Geschichte der Industrialisierung] (Berlin: Colloquium, 1975)

'Natur- und Technikwissenschaften an deutschen Hochschulen, 1870–1970: einige quantitative Entwicklungen', in Rürup, *Wissenschaft und Gesellschaft*, vol. 1, pp. 209–30

'Differentiation in German Higher Education', in Jarausch (ed.), *The Transformation of Higher Learning*, pp. 149–79

'Education for the Science-Based Industrial State? The Case for Nineteenth-Century Germany', *History of Education*, 13 (1984), 59–67

Manegold, Karl-Heinz. *Universität, Technische Hochschule und Industrie. Ein Beitrag zur Emanzipation der Technik im 19. Jahrhundert unter besonderer Berücksichtigung der Bestrebungen Felix Kleins* [Schriften zur Wirtschafts- und Sozialgeschichte, 16] (Berlin: Duncker & Humblot, 1970)

Pfetsch, Frank R. *Zur Entwicklung der Wissenschaftspolitik in Deutschland 1750–1914* (Berlin: Duncker & Humblot, 1974)

Rürup, Reinhard (ed.). *Wissenschaft und Gesellschaft. Beiträge zur Geschichte der Technischen Universität Berlin 1879–1979*, 2 vols. (Berlin, Heidelberg, and New York: Springer, 1979)

Schnabel, Franz. 'Die Anfänge des technischen Hochschulwesens', in *Festschrift anlässlich des 100jährigen Bestehens der Technischen Hochschule Fridericiana zu Karlsruhe* (Karlsruhe: C. F. Müller, 1925), pp. 1–44

Scholl, Lars Ulrich. *Ingenieure in der Frühindustrialisierung. Staatliche und private Techniker im Königreich Hannover und an der Ruhr (1815–1873)* (Göttingen: Vandenhoeck & Ruprecht, 1978)

Sodan, Günter (ed.). *Die Technische Fachhochschule Berlin im Spektrum Berliner Bildungsgeschichte* (Berlin: Technische Fachhochschule, 1988)

Sonnemann, Rolf, *et al. Geschichte der Technischen Universität Dresden 1828–1978* (Berlin: VEB Deutscher Verlag der Wissenschaften, 1978)

Zweckbronner, Gerhard. *Ingenieurausbildung im Königreich Württemberg. Vorgeschichte, Einrichtung und Ausbau der Technischen Hochschule Stuttgart und ihrer Ingenieurwissenschaften bis 1900. Eine Verknüpfung von Institutions- und Disziplingeschichte* [Technik + Arbeit. Schriften des Landesmuseums für Technik und Arbeit in Mannheim 2] (Stuttgart: Konrad Theiss, 1987)

GREAT BRITAIN

Alter, Peter. *The Reluctant Patron. Science and the State in Britain, 1850–1920* (Oxford, Hamburg, and New York: Berg, 1987)

Argles, Michael, *South Kensington to Robbins. An Account of English Technical and Scientific Education since 1851* (London, 1964).

Buchanan, R. Angus. *The Engineers. A History of the Engineering Profession in Britain 1750–1914* (London: Jessica Kingsley Publishers, 1989)

'The Rise of Scientific Engineering in Britain', *The British Journal for the History of Science*, 18 (1985), 218–33

Bud, Robert, and Gerrylynn K. Roberts. *Science versus Practice. Chemistry in Victorian Britain* (Manchester: Manchester University Press, 1984)

Cardwell, Donald S. L. *The Organisation of Science in England* (1957; 2nd edn, London: Heinemann, 1972)

Cotgrove, Stephen F. *Technical Education and Social Change* (London: George Allen & Unwin, 1958)

Divall, Colin. 'A Measure of Agreement: Employers and Engineering Studies in the Universities of England and Wales, 1897–1939', *Social Studies of Science*, 20 (1990), 65–112

Donnelly, James. F. 'Representations of Applied Science: Academics and Chemical Industry in Late Nineteenth-Century England', *Social Studies of Science*, 16 (1986), 195–234

'Chemical Engineering in England, 1880–1922', *Annals of Science*, 45 (1988), 555–90

Emmerson, George S. *Engineering Education. A Social History* (David and Charles: Newton Abbot, 1973)

Fox, Robert, and Anna Guagnini. 'The Flexible University: Some Historical Reflexions on the Analysis of Education and the Modern British Economy', *Social Studies of Science*, 16 (1986), 515–27

Gowing, Margaret. 'Science, Technology and Education: England in 1870' [The Wilkins Lecture, 1976], *Notes and Records of the Royal Society of London*, 32 (1977–8), 71–90

Guagnini, Anna. 'The Fashioning of Higher Technical Education in Britain: The Case of Manchester, 1851–1914', in Gospel, Howard F. (ed.), *Industrial Training and Technological Innovation. A Comparative and Historical Study* (London: Routledge, 1991), pp. 69–92

Hilken, Thomas J. N. *Engineering at Cambridge University 1783–1965* (Cambridge: Cambridge University Press, 1967)

Lowe, Roy. 'The Expansion of Higher Education in England', in Jarausch (ed.), *The Transformation of Higher Learning*, pp. 37–56

Marsh, Joseph O. 'The Engineering Institutions and the Public Recognition of British Engineers', *International Journal of Mechanical Engineering Education*, 16 (1987), 119–27

Musgrave, Peter W. *Technical Change, the Labour Force, and Education. A Study of the British and German Iron and Steel Industries 1860–1964* (Oxford: Pergamon Press, 1967)

Pollard, Sidney. *Britain's Prime and Britain's Decline. The British Economy 1870–1914* (London: Edward Arnold, 1989)

Roberts, Gerrylynn K. 'The Establishment of the Royal College of Chemistry: An Investigation of the Social Context of Early-Victorian Chemistry', *Historical Studies in the Physical Sciences*, 7 (1976), 437–75

'The Liberally-Educated Chemist: Chemistry in the Cambridge Natural Sciences Tripos, 1851–1914', *Historical Studies in the Physical Sciences*, 11 (1980), 157–83

Roderick, Gordon W., and Michael D. Stephens. *Scientific and Technical Education in Nineteenth-Century England. A Symposium* (Newton Abbot: David and Charles, 1972)

Education and Industry in the Nineteenth Century. The English Disease? (London and New York: Longman, 1978)

Russell, Colin A., Noel G. Coley, and Gerrylynn K. Roberts. *Chemists by Profession. The Origins and Rise of the Royal Institute of Chemistry* (Milton Keynes: Open University Press, 1977)

Sanderson, Michael. *The Universities and British Industry, 1850–1970* (London: Routledge & Kegan Paul, 1972)

'The University of London and Industrial Progress', *Journal of Contemporary History*, 7 (1972), 243–62

Wiener, Martin J. *English Culture and the Decline of the Industrial Spirit 1850–1980* (Cambridge: Cambridge University Press, 1981)

Wrigley, Julia. 'Technical Education and Industry in the Nineteenth Century', in Bernard Elbaum and William Lazonick (eds.), *The Decline of the British Economy* (Oxford: Clarendon Press, 1986), pp. 162–88

ITALY

Ancarani, Vittorio (ed.). *La scienza accademica nell'Italia post-unitaria. Discipline scientifiche e ricerca universitaria* (Milan: Franco Angeli, 1989)

Giuntini, Andrea. 'La formazione didattica e il ruolo nell'amministrazione granducale dell'ingegnere nella Toscana di Leopoldo II', in *La Toscana dei Lorena. Riforme territorio, società* (Florence: Leo S. Olschki, 1989), pp. 391–417

Guagnini, Anna. 'The Formation of Italian Electrical Engineers: The Teaching Laboratories of the Politecnici of Turin and Milan, 1887–1914', in Fabienne Cardot (ed.), *Un siècle d'électricité dans le monde. 1880–1980. Actes du Premier Colloque International sur l'Histoire de l'Electricité* (Paris: Association pour l'Histoire de l'Électricité en France, 1987), pp. 283–99

'Higher Education and the Engineering Profession in Italy: The *Scuole* of Milan and Turin, 1859–1914', *Minerva*, 26 (1988), 512–48

La formazione dell'ingegnere nella Torino di Alberto Castigliano. Le scuole di ingegneria nella seconda metà dell'ottocento (Genoa: Sagep, 1984)

Lacaita, Giacomo C. *Istruzione e sviluppo industriale in Italia, 1859–1914* (Florence: Giunti Barbera, 1973)

L'intelligenza produttiva. Imprenditori, tecnici e operai nella Società d'Incoraggiamento d'Arti e Mestieri di Milano (1838–1988) (Milan: Electa, 1990)

Maiocchi, Roberto. 'Il ruolo delle scienze nello sviluppo industriale italiano', in *Storia d'Italia. Annali*, vol. 3: Gianni Micheli (ed.), *Scienza e tecnica nella cultura e nella società dal Rinascimento ad oggi* (Turin: Einaudi, 1980), pp. 863–999

Marchis, Vittorio. 'Dalle scuole di ingegneria al Politecnico: un secolo di istituzioni tecniche in Piemonte', in *La formazione dell'ingegnere*, pp. 19–44

Morachiello, Paolo. *Ingegneri e territorio nell'età della Destra (1860–1875). Dal Canale Cavour all'Agro Romano* (Rome: Officina Edizioni, 1976)

[Politecnico di Milano]. *Il Politecnico di Milano, 1863–1914. Una scuola nella formazione della società industriale* (Milan: Electa, 1981)

Il Politecnico di Milano nella storia italiana (1914–1963), 2 vols. (Bari: Laterza, 1988)

Russo, Arturo. 'Science and Industry in Italy between the Two World Wars', *Historical Studies in the Physical and Biological Sciences*, 16 (1986), 281–320

Tonelli, Aldo. *L'istruzione tecnica e professionale di stato nelle strutture e nei programmi da Casati ai giorni nostri* (Milan: Giuffré, 1964)

Zamagni, Vera. 'Istruzione e sviluppo economico in Italia, 1861–1913', in Gianni Toniolo (ed.), *Lo sviluppo economico italiano 1861–1940* (Bari: Laterza, 1973), pp. 187–240

SPAIN

Alonso Viguera, José Maria. *La ingeniería industrial española en el siglo XIX* (Madrid: Blas S.A., 1944)

Castillo A. del y Riu, M. *Historia de la Asociación de Ingenieros Industriales de Barcelona (1863–1963)*, (Barcelona: Asociación de Ingenieros Industriales de Barcelona, 1963)

Coll i Alentorn, Miquel, Joan Vallve i Creus, Santiago Riera i Tuebols, and Enric Freixa i Pedrals. *Quatre enginyers per a la història* (Barcelona: Associació i Col.legi d'Enginyers Industrials de Catalunya and La llar del llibre, 1990)

Garrabou, Ramón. *Enginyers, industrials, modernitzaciò econòmica i burgesia a Catalunya (1850–inicis del segle XX)* (Barcelona: L'Avenç, S.A., 1982)

González Tascón, Ignacio. *Fábricas hidráulicas españolas* (Madrid: Ministerio de Obras Públicas y Urbanismo, 1987)

Nadal, Jordi. *El fracaso de la revolución industrial en España, 1814–1913* (Barcelona: Editorial Ariel, 1975)

Nadal, Jordi, Albert Carrera, and Carles Sudria (eds.). *La economía española en el siglo XX, una perspectiva histórica* (Barcelona: Ariel, 1987)

Pascual, Pere. *Agricultura i industrialització a la Catalunya del segle XIX* (Barcelona: Editorial Critica, 1990)

Riera i Tuèbols, Santiago. 'L'évolution de la profession d'ingénieur en Espagne', in Grelon (ed.), *Les ingénieurs de la crise*, op. cit., pp. 325–42

L'associació i el Col.legi d'Enginyers Industrials de Catalunya, de la Dictadura a la Democràcia (1950–1987) (Barcelona: La Magrana, 1988)

Roca i Rosell, Antoni, and José Manuel Sánchez Ron. *Esteban Terradas (1883–1950). Ciencia y técnica en la España contemporánea* (Madrid: Instituto Nacional de Técnica Aerospacial, and Barcelona: Ediciones del Serbal, 1990)

Rumeu de Armas, Antonio. *Ciencia y tecnología en la España Ilustrada. La Escuela de Caminos y Canales* (Madrid: Colegio de Ingenieros de Caminos, Canales y Puertos and Ediciones Turner, 1980)

[Universitat de Barcelona]. *Historia de la Universitat de Barcelona* (Barcelona: Universitat de Barcelona, 1990)

SWEDEN

Althin, Torsten. *KTH 1912–62. Kungl. Tekniska Högskolan i Stockholm under 50 år* (Stockholm: Kungl. Tekniska Högskolan, 1970)

Anderberg, Rudolf. *Grunddragen av svenska tekniska undervisningsväsendets historia* [Ingeniörsvetenskapsakademien meddelande, no. 5] (Stockholm, 1921)

Bergsman, E. Börje. *Fahlu Bergsskola 1819–1868. Sveriges första civila tekniska högskola* [Dalarnas fornminnes och hembygdsförbunds skrifter, no. 20] (Falun: Dalarnas Museum, 1985)

Berner, Boel. *Teknikens värld. Teknisk förändring och ingenjörsarbete i svensk industri* [Arkiv avhandlingsserie, no. 11] (Lund, 1981); English summary on pp. 249–52

'Engineering identity and economic change: engineers in Swedish society 1850–1990', *Polhem*, 10, no. 2 (1992), 131–60

Björck, Henrik. 'På de tillfälliga uppfinningarnas oroliga haf: tekniska tidskrifter i Sverige, 1800–1870', *Polhem*, 4, no. 2 (1986), 57–126

'Bilder av maskiner och ingenjörskårens bildande: tekniska tidskrifter och introduktion av ny teknik i Sverige, 1800–1870', *Polhem*, 5, no. 4 (1987), 267–310

Chalmers Tekniska Högskola 1829–1954. Minnesskrift utgiven till Högskolans 125-årsjubileum (Gothenburg: Gumperts, 1954)

De Geer, Hans. *Rationaliseringsrörelsen i Sverige. Effektivitetsidéer och socialt ansvar under mellankrigstiden* (Stockholm: Studieförbundet Näringsliv och Samhälle SNS, 1978)

Eriksson, Gunnar. *Kartläggarna. Naturvetenskapens tillväxt och tillämpningar i det industriella genombrottets Sverige 1870–1914* [Acta Universitatis Umensis. Umeå Studies in the Humanities, no. 15] (Umeå: Umeå universitet, 1978); English summary on pp. 205–8

Henriques, Pontus. *Skildringar ur Kungl. Tekniska Högskolans historia* (2 vols., Stockholm: P. A. Norstedts & Sönders, 1917)

Nybom, Thorsten. 'Bernalism och forskningsorganisation: vetenskapsideologi och forskningspolitik i 1930-talets Sverige', *Daedalus 1986* [Yearbook of Tekniska Museet, Stockholm], pp. 82–93

Runeby, Nils. *Teknikerna, vetenskapen och kulturen. Ingenjörsundervisning och ingenjörsorganisationer i 1870-talets Sverige* (Uppsala: Almqvist & Wiksell International, 1976); German summary on pp. 281–95

'Vaganbonden, specialisten och folkens banerförare: På väg mot ett vetenskapsuniversitet kring 1800-talets mitt', in Thorsten Nybom (ed.), *Universitet och samhälle. Om forskningspolitik och vetenskapens samhälleliga roll* (Stockholm: Tidens, 1989); translated in Trow and Nybom (eds.), *University and Society*, pp. 19–34

Sundin, Bosse. *Ingenjörsvetenskapens tidevarv. Ingenjörsvetenskapsakademien, Pappersmassekontoret, Metallografiska institutet och den teknologiska forskningen i början av 1900-talet* [Acta Universitatis Umensis, Umeå Studies in the Humanities, no. 42] (Umeå: Almqvist & Wiksell International, 1981)

I teknikens backspegel. Antologi i teknikhistoria (Stockholm: Carlssons Bokförlag, 1987)

Svensson, Lennart G. *Higher Education and the State in Swedish History* (Stockholm: Almqvist & Wiksell International, 1987)

Torstendahl, Rolf. *Teknologins nytta. Motiveringar för det svenska tekniska utbildningsväsendets framväxt framförda av riksdagsmän och utbildningsadministratörer 1810–1870* (Uppsala: Almqvist & Wiksell International, 1975); English summary on pp. 250–60

Dispersion of Engineers in a Transitional Society. Swedish Technicians 1860–1940 (Uppsala: Almqvist & Wiksell International, 1975)

UNITED STATES

Bledstein, Burton J. *The Culture of Professionalism. The Middle Class and the Development of Higher Education in America* (New York: Norton, 1976)

Cremin, Lawrence A. *American Education. The Metropolitan Experience 1876–1980* (New York: Harper & Row, 1988)

Galambos, Louis. 'The American Economy and the Reorganization of the Sources of Knowledge', in Oleson and Voss (eds.), *The Organization of Knowledge in Modern America*, pp. 269–82

Geiger, Roger L. *The Growth of the American Research Universities 1900–1948* (New York: Oxford University Press, 1986)

Hatch, Nathan O. (ed.). *The Professions in American History* (Notre Dame, Indiana: University of Notre Dame Press, 1988)

Hollinger, David A. 'Inquiry and Uplift: Late Nineteenth-Century American Academics and the Moral Efficacy of Scientific Practice', in Thomas L. Haskell (ed.), *The Authority of Experts. Studies in History and Theory* (Bloomington, Indiana: Indiana University Press, 1984), pp. 142–56

Layton, Edwin T. *The Revolt of the Engineers. Social Responsibility and the American Engineering Profession* (Cleveland, Ohio: Case Western Reserve University Press, 1971)

Noble, David F. *America by Design. Science, Technology, and the Rise of Corporate Capitalism* (New York: Knopf, and Oxford: Oxford University Press, 1977)

Oleson, Alexandra, and Sanborn C. Brown (eds.). *The Pursuit of Knowledge in the Early American Republic. American Scientific and Learned Societies from Colonial Times to the Civil War* (Baltimore and London: Johns Hopkins University Press, 1976)

Oleson, Alexandra, and John Voss (eds.). *The Organization of Knowledge in Modern America, 1860–1920* (Baltimore and London: Johns Hopkins University Press, 1979)

Rae, John. 'The Application of Science to Industry', in Oleson and Voss (eds.), *The Organization of Knowledge in Modern America*, pp. 249–68

Rosenberg, Charles E. *No Other Gods. On Science and American Social Thought* (Baltimore and London: Johns Hopkins University Press, 1976)

Rosenberg, Robert. 'Test Men, Experts, Brother Engineers, and Members of the Fraternity: Whence the Early Electrical Work Force?', *IEEE Transactions on Education*, E-27 (1984), 203–9

'The Origins of EE Education: A Matter of Degree', *IEEE Spectrum*, 21 (1984), 60–9

Veysey, Laurence R. *The Emergence of the American University* (Chicago and London: University of Chicago Press, 1965)

Index